T0214183

Communications in Computer and Information Science 1164

Commenced Publication in 2007
Founding and Former Series Editors:
Phoebe Chen, Alfredo Cuzzocrea, Xiaoyong Du, Orhun Kara, Ting Liu,
Krishna M. Sivalingam, Dominik Ślęzak, Takashi Washio, Xiaokang Yang,
and Junsong Yuan

More information about this series at http://www.springer.com/series/7899

Nelson Zagalo · Ana Isabel Veloso ·
Liliana Costa · Óscar Mealha (Eds.)

Videogame Sciences and Arts

11th International Conference, VJ 2019
Aveiro, Portugal, November 27–29, 2019
Proceedings

Springer

Editors
Nelson Zagalo (iD)
University of Aveiro
Aveiro, Portugal

Ana Isabel Veloso (iD)
University of Aveiro
Aveiro, Portugal

Liliana Costa (iD)
University of Aveiro
Aveiro, Portugal

Óscar Mealha (iD)
University of Aveiro
Aveiro, Portugal

ISSN 1865-0929   ISSN 1865-0937   (electronic)
Communications in Computer and Information Science
ISBN 978-3-030-37982-7   ISBN 978-3-030-37983-4   (eBook)
https://doi.org/10.1007/978-3-030-37983-4

This Springer imprint is published by the registered company Springer Nature Switzerland AG
The registered company address is: Gewerbestrasse 11, 6330 Cham, Switzerland

Preface

The 11th Conference on Videogame Sciences and Arts (Videojogos 2019) was held in Aveiro, Portugal, during November 27–29, 2019. The event was co-organized by the Department of Communication and Art of the University of Aveiro (DeCA), DeCA's DigiMedia Research Center, and the Portuguese Society of Video Games Sciences (SPCV).

The annual conferences of the SPCV promote the scientific gathering of researchers and professionals in the expanded field of videogames and is usually held in Portugal. This year, 10 years after the first conference, SPCV and the co-organizers decided to convert the conference into a full international event, with English as a working language. Indeed, the videogame industry has been challenged over the past years with the need of different knowledge bases – from Gameplay Experience to Artificial Design, Art, Programming, Psychology, Sound Engineering, Marketing, among others. In addition, games have been increasingly adopted as cultural artifacts in a hobbyist and artisan market and, therefore, presenting digitally mediated innovations in this popular but somewhat saturated global market is more and more in demand.

In game design, the symbiosis between player-centric and game-centric approaches seem to be key in bringing fundamental elements to gameplay such as rewarding conditions, a sense of fairness, dilemmas, narrative fantasies, and flow experiences that subsequently may change the way a certain environment or scenario is perceived by a gamer community. In these proceedings, both game theories and the interlink between gameplay, narrative, and fiction are covered. Section 1 "Games and Theories" consists of four papers that discuss the use of gameplay elements and the transcendence in fiction and reality. In "First-Person Refugee Games: Three Design Strategies for Playing the Stories of Refugees and Asylum Seekers," Victor Navarro Remesal and Beatriz Zapata analyze games as a biographical medium and a representation of societal stories. Regina Seiwald advocates games as fiction and an illusory medium in "Games within Games: The Two (or More) Fictional Levels of Video Games." In the same vein, Mateo Torres propose a Mechanics – Performance – Fiction (MPF) framework for the analysis of ludic artifacts. Finally, Su Hyun Nam highlights the importance of rules in videogames and control in Digital Societies.

Section 2 entitled "Table Boards" advances current research on tabletop game-playing and its importance in game design and playtesting. In "Towards a Tabletop Gaming Motivations Inventory (TGMI)", Mehmet Kosa and Pieter Spronck discuss the motivations for tabletop game play and propose a tabletop gaming motivation inventory to assess these motivations. Micael Sousa and Edgar Bernardo recall the origin and characteristics of modern board games, taxonomy, and current trends in "Back in the Game: Modern Board games." Seeram Kongeseri and Christopher Coley describe the process of developing a collaborative tabletop game for social problem-solving and civic engagement. This section ends with the development of a toolkit for game design proposed by Pedro Beça, Rita Santos, Ana Veloso, Gonçalo Gomes, Mariana Pereira, and Mónica Aresta.

eSports and group competition in a multiplayer environment are another topic highlighted in this conference (Section 3). Whereas Cátia Ferreira presents the Portuguese eSports media ecosystem, a literature review on game design decisions and communication theories applied to eSports are identified by Gabriel Canavarro, João Sequeiros, and Farley Fernandes. Furthermore, the negative perspectives on the use of videogames and brands to sponsor eSports are discussed by Bruno Freitas, Ruth Espinosa, and Pedro Correira. Group Dynamics in eSports is then illustrated by Tarcizio Maxedo and Thiago Falcao, who present the (Semi) Professional League of Legends Amazonian Scenario.

A number of papers also discuss innovative uses and methodologies in game design (Section 4). Daryl Marples, Pelham Carter, Duke Gledhill, and Simon Goodson report on "Broad Environmental Change Blindness in Virtual Environments and Video Games." Virtual Reality Arcades and its usage habits and frontiers for exergaming is presented by Tuomas Kari. In "Jizo: A Gamified Digital App for Senior Cyclo-tourism in the miOne Community," Cláudia Ortet, Liliana Costa, and Ana Veloso suggest the use of a co-designed gamified digital app to support Senior Cyclo-tourism. Similarly, Jackeline Farbiarz, Alexandre Farbiarz, Guilherme Xavier, and Cynthia Dias highlight the role of gamification but in this case, for graphic education.

Section 5 delves into Game Criticism. A personalized game review score is in the spotlight with the paper "Personalized Game Reviews" authored by Miguel Ribeiro and Carlos Martinho. Mythogames are introduced by António de la Maza with his paper entitled "The symbolic labyrinth in the mythogame: the axes Minos-Daedalus and Theseus Minotaur in the contemporary video game." A classification of hybrid games is offered by Ryan Javanshir, Beth Carrol, and David Millard in "Classifying Multi-player Hybrid Games to Identify Diverse Player Participation." Finally, Emmanoel Ferreira ends this section with socio-cultural and historical aspects of media archae-ology in a game context.

This book contains a total of 20 papers from academia, research institutes, industry, and other institutions from 7 countries (Brazil, Finland, India, Portugal, Spain, the UK, and the USA) that resulted from a 40% acceptance ratio and a selection of papers in the topics of e-Sports, Game Criticism, Games and Theory, Tabletop Games, and Uses and Methodologies. These contributions address the novel research and development out-comes in the videogame context, gathering in itself several different scientific areas, such as Multimedia, Communication, Technology, Education, Psychology, Arts, among others.

It thereby confirms the decision taken by the conference chairs to take a step forward: out of the national domains, and towards an international platform reflecting global interests and relevance. This move reflects the desire and the will to take on the international challenge by the SPCV of opening up critically, reflecting, and integrating views and ideas, not only nationally but also internationally, towards a wider audience always striving for a holistic perspective, trends, and future directions.

To help the videogame community bridge the gap between industry and academy, two keynotes were invited. Ernest Adams talked about planning and processes for game development, and Diogo Gomes about the use of Artificial Inteligence (AI) in game development, alongside examples on learning practices with AI.

We would like to thank the scientific board for their contribution in guaranteeing and delivering the highest scientific quality, evidenced by the outstanding relevance of this book. We would also like to thank the program chairs (demo, poster, and workshops) and the organization team for all their concerns and efforts with regards to the organization, an extremely important contribution for the overall success of the Videojogos 2019.

Last but not least, we would like to thank the DigiMedia Research Center and SPCV for all the support, and the DeCA for hosting the event and making this conference possible.

November 2019

Nelson Zagalo
Ana Isabel Veloso
Liliana Costa
Óscar Mealha

Organization

Committees

Ana Isabel Veloso (Conference Chair)	University of Aveiro, Portugal
Nelson Zagalo (Scientific Chair)	University of Aveiro, Portugal
José Nunes (Organizing Chair)	University of Aveiro, Portugal

Program Committee

Aaron Rodríguez	Universitat Jaume I, Spain
Abel Gomes	University of Beira Interior, Portugal
Adérito Fernandes Marcos	Open University, Portugal
Alex Mitchell	National University of Singapore, Singapore
Alexis Blanchet	Université Sorbonne Nouvelle, France
Ana Amélia Carvalho	University of Coimbra, Portugal
Ana Torres	University of Aveiro, Portugal
André Neves	Universidade Federal de Pernambuco, Brazil
António Coelho	University of Porto, Portugal
Antonio José Planells	Universitat Pompeu Fabra, Spain
Beatriz Legerén	Universidad de Vigo, Spain
Beatriz Pérez Zapata	Universitat de les Illes Balears, Spain
Carla Ganito	Catholic University, Portugal
Carlos Martinho	University of Lisbon, Portugal
Carlos Santos	University of Aveiro, Portugal
Cátia Ferreira	Catholic University, Portugal
Christian Roth	University of Utrecht, The Netherlands
Ciro Martins	ESTG de Águeda, Portugal
Conceição Costa	Lusófona University, Portugal
Cristiano Max	Universidade Feevale, Brazil
Daniela Karine Ramos	UFSC, Brazil
Diogo Gomes	University of Aveiro, Portugal
Duarte Duque	IPCA, Portugal
Emmanoel Ferreira	Universidade Federal Fluminense, Brazil
Esteban Clua	Universidade Federal Fluminense, Brazil
Eva Oliveira	ESTG IPCA, Portugal
Fanny Barnabé	Université de Liège, Belgium
Filipe Luz	Lusófona University, Portugal
Filipe Penicheiro	University of Coimbra, Portugal
Fotis Liarokapis	Masaryk University, Czech Republic

Frutuoso Silva	University of Beira Interior, Portugal
Ido Iurgel	Hochschule Rhein-Waal, Germany
Joao Jacob	University of Porto, Portugal
João Mattar	PUC São Paulo, Brazil
João Sousa	Lusophone University, Portugal
Jorge Martins Rosa	New University of Lisbon, Portugal
Jorge Palinhos	Escola Superior Artística Porto, Portugal
Jose Zagal	University of Utah, USA
Leonel Morgado	Open University, Portugal
Liliana Costa	University of Aveiro, Portugal
Lynn Alves	UFBA, Brazil
Maite Soto-Sanfiel	University Autonoma Barcelona, Spain
Marçal Mora Cantallops	University of Alcalá, Spain
Mário Vairinhos	University of Aveiro, Portugal
Marta Núñez	Universitat Jaume I, Spain
Micael Sousa	University of Coimbra, Portugal
Miguel Carvalhais	University of Porto, Portugal
Miguel Sicart	IT University of Copenhagen, Denmark
Óscar Mealha	University of Aveiro, Portugal
Patrícia Gouveia	Universidade de Lisboa, Portugal
Paulo Dias	University of Aveiro, Portugal
Pedro A. Santos	University of Lisbon, Portugal
Pedro Amado	University of Porto, Portugal
Pedro Beça	University of Aveiro, Portugal
Pedro Branco	University of Minho, Portugal
Pedro Pinto Neves	Universidade Lusófona, Portugal
Pilar Lacasa	University of Alcalá, Spain
Renira Gambarato	Jönköping University, Sweden
Riccardo Fassone	University of Turin, Italy
Roger Tavares	Federal University of Rio Grande do Norte, Brazil
Rui Prada	University of Lisbon, Portugal
Ruth Contreras	Polytechnic University of Catalonia, Spain
Susana Tosca	IT University of Copenhagen, Denmark
Teresa Piñeiro Otero	Universidade da Coruña, Spain
Thiago Falcao	Universidade Federal do Maranhão, Brazil
Valter Alves	ESTG de Viseu, Portugal
Victor Navarro-Remesal	Universidad Pontificia Comillas, Spain
Wolfgang Mueller	University of Education Weingarten, Germany

Organizing Committee

José Nunes	University of Aveiro, Portugal
Ana Isabel Veloso	University of Aveiro, Portugal
Nelson Zagalo	University of Aveiro, Portugal
Oscar Mealha	University of Aveiro, Portugal
Tânia Ribeiro	University of Aveiro, Portugal

Sofia Ribeiro	University of Aveiro, Portugal
Silvino Almeida	University of Aveiro, Portugal
Liliana Costa	University of Aveiro, Portugal
Mónica Aresta	University of Aveiro, Portugal
Claudia Ortet	University of Aveiro, Portugal
Pedro Beça	University of Aveiro, Portugal
Mário Vairinhos	University of Aveiro, Portugal
Jesse Nery Filho	University of Aveiro, Portugal
Patrícia Oliveira	University of Aveiro, Portugal
Josué Silvério	University of Aveiro, Portugal
Francisco Regalado	University of Aveiro, Portugal
Carolina Abrantes	University of Aveiro, Portugal
Caio Jacobina	University of Aveiro, Portugal

Organizing Institutions

DigiMedia – Digital Media and Interaction
University of Aveiro, Portugal
Sociedade Portuguesa de Ciências dos Videojogos

Support

University of Aveiro, Portugal
American Corners
FCT - Fundação para a Ciência e a Tecnologia, Portugal

universidade de aveiro
theoria poiesis praxis

AMERICAN
CORNERS
PORTUGAL

FCT Fundação
para a Ciência
e a Tecnologia

Contents

Uses and Methodologies

Game Criticism

Games and Theories

First-Person Refugee Games: Ludonarrative Strategies for Playing the Stories of Refugees and Asylum Seekers

Víctor Navarro-Remesal[1] and Beatriz Pérez Zapata[2(✉)]

[1] CESAG-Universidad Pontificia de Comillas, Carrer de Saragossa 16,
07013 Palma, Spain
vnavarro@cesag.org
[2] University of the Balearic Islands, Cra/Valldemossa km 7, 5,
07122 Palma, Spain
beatriz.perez@uib.es

Abstract. This paper aims to offer a critical analysis of recent games by and/or about refugees, with a strong focus on the narration and reconstruction of personal experiences and biographies. We have selected three European (French and German) productions and a global one (created by UNHCR), describing the journeys refugees fleeing their country: *Finding Home* (UNHCR, 2017), *Bury Me, My Love* (Playdius Entertainment, 2017), and *Path Out* (Causa Creations, 2017). We also consider a fourth game: *North* (Outlands, 2016), an experimental cyberpunk indie game that presents well-known bureaucratic and systemic obstacles for refugees. This paper contextualizes the media representations of refugees and studies these selected games first by describing their conditions of production and communicative aims, including their intended effect on players and their calls to action (if any) beyond the act of playing. Secondly, we consider the narrative design choices they employ, in particular, their narrators and focalizers, paying attention to if and how they give voice to actual refugees. Lastly, we study the genres, goal structure, and mechanics of interaction they use, separating them in three main ludonarrative strategies: interface-based newsgames, reality-inspired interface games, lost phone newsgames, autobiographical JRPG-like, and experimental cyberpunk first person adventure. In this, we observe how these works apply the language of videogames to bridge their ludofictions to the real world stories behind them.

Keywords: Refugees · Persuasive games · Compassionate play

1 Introduction

Postcolonial studies have, for many decades now, provided us with tools to analyze and question relationships of power in an increasingly globalized world. Literature and film have been the focus of many scholarly analysis in postcolonial studies and, of late, the study of postcolonial games and videogames has come to the fore. Recently, Souvik Mukherjee and Emil Lundedal Hammar [1] have called for the critical exploration of colonial discourses in games, which persist up to date under many neocolonial guises.

© Springer Nature Switzerland AG 2019
N. Zagalo et al. (Eds.): VJ 2019, CCIS 1164, pp. 3–17, 2019.
https://doi.org/10.1007/978-3-030-37983-4_1

Both mass-produced games and independent, serious, and activist games have addressed postcolonial concerns to varying degrees and have sought to contest discourses and means of production and consumption. These narrative forms aim to give voice to the subaltern, those whose voices have been systematically silenced. In contemporary times, mass displacement has oftentimes turned refugees into subaltern subjects, their voices silenced or highly mediated. Not in vain does David Farrier [2] label them the "new subaltern". Thus, as Stephen Morton [3] argues, we need "narratives of postcolonial refugees" that can "take account of the histories of dispossession and abandonment associated with the global expansion of capitalism". And games are one of the ways in which refugees' experiences can be expressed.

The purpose and ethics of "refugee games" raise many questions. This paper focuses on two central ones: first, how do games portray refugees' lives? And second, what do games do to change both the refugees' realities and the way in which Western audiences and host countries relate to these experiences? In order to answer these questions, we will first contextualise the representation of refugees in the media to then analyze the narration and/or reconstruction of personal experiences in four games: *Bury Me, My Love* (The Pixel Hunt, 2017), *Finding Home* (UNHCR & Grey Malaysia, 2017), *Path Out* (Causa Creations, 2017), and *North* (Outlands, 2016). The first two use a "reality-inspired" approach to try and mimic the way Syrian and Rohingya refugees use technology to communicate with their loved ones. The third one uses gaming tropes to present his protagonist, an actual Syrian refugee, as a gamer youngster, not different from its intended audience. The fourth one, *North,* eschews referencing the current "refugee crisis" to present a science-fiction tale about a refugee living in an alien city.

We argue that some of the most relevant strategies these games use to portray the refugees' experiences are the representation of suffering and the appeal to emotions, more particularly, compassion. Therefore, the analysis of these games will focus on narrative devices such as focalization and strong characterization, as well as on the different genres and interfaces. This paper will also draw attention to the creators, intended audiences, and the calls to action the games propose. Thus, we will study a selection of relevant "refugee games" through the lenses of postcolonial theory, emotion in media, and ludonarrative (that is, the combination of fictional, narrative, and gameful elements) analysis. Furthermore, using the concept of the "implied player" [4], we explore the affective responses these games seek to create in order to contest current misrepresentations of refugees, allow the player to recognise their suffering, and bridge the gap between the mere act of witnessing and action.

2 Suffering and Media Representations of Refugees

When refugees are portrayed as victims in humanitarian texts, their defining trait is often suffering, and especially their capacity to endure continued suffering. Mustapha Marrouchi [5] explains that "It is the subaltern's resilience that defines his or her literary representation". Refugees, as well as other types of dispossessed, are recurrently shown as devoid of agency or personality, means to an editorial end: "He or she is often the interface between the reader and the text's scheme of values, which is regularly undercut by the subaltern's canny presence, still winking at the reader" [5]. The stories in the different games this paper analyzes, make it clear that those voices have to be heard, that we need to be open and exposed to their truths. As we shall see, the use of first-person narrative strategies closely entangles players with histories that could, at one point, seem too foreign. These games remind us that, as Lyndsey Stonebridge [6] affirms, "far from being a 'crisis' affecting just the poor unfortunates of the world, the history of placelessness is everybody's history".

Media representations of refugees often paint a collective picture rather than focusing on individual stories. Against these biased and/or incomplete representations, there are numerous literary, cinematic, and ludofictional representations of refugees' lives that try to imbue their narratives with the humanity that they have lost in the processes of displacement and placelessness, and which try to communicate their suffering without falling into a "regime of pity" [7]. The suffering of refugees is often framed within histories of drowning, impossible escapes, and traumatic histories, so much so that some can only think of refugees as "suffering people" [8]. These images and preconceived ideas are part of what Chouliaraki [7] describes as "the spectacle of suffering", which raises ethical questions about our relationship with "distant sufferers" and our subsequent engagements with their suffering. Although this research is very much necessary in order to understand responses towards suffering, it is still very much focused on the reactions towards suffering rather than in the articulation of others' suffering.

Recent studies have nevertheless analyzed how refugees' voices are raised and mediated. Wright [8] and Sigona [10], for example, denounce how the media do not allow refugees to speak for themselves, turning them into "anonymous passive victims" and draw attention to the political agency of refugees telling their stories. However, Pantti and Ojala [11] see these increasing first-person accounts as embedded in "a pervasive 'culture of disbelief'", which arises from seeing refugees as suspicious and the assessment of truth in processes of Refugee Status Determination. Smets, Mazzochetti, Gertmans, and Mostmas [12] interviewed refugees and found that, while "they want their suffering to be represented", they reject current "suspicious" and "*miserabilist*" portrayals and favour more realistic representations that show "the ugly truth" (italics in original). Smets et al. further argue that "making suffering visible becomes a gateway for our participants to express frustration, or at least disappointment, with the fact that there is a lack of realistic media representations about their histories of individual trajectories". Thus, we need individual accounts of refugees' experiences that lay bare the whole truth and show suffering in an honest way to challenge current discourses.

3   Emotions, Suffering in Games, and Compassionate Play

There seems to be some overlapping in the definitions of certain emotions in the existing literature that calls for an explanation that establishes clear differences between empathy, compassion, and pity. *Empathy* is currently understood as "a feeling of emotional resonance between people" [13]. *Compassion*, on the other hand, refers to our concern for "the well-being of others", closely connected to "justice", and has been traditionally seen as "a central bridge between the individual and the community" [14].

Lastly, Watt Smith [13] defines pity as "more of a spectator sport". *Pity* is moreover connected to power and establishes a clear barrier between safety and suffering [6] and, "releash[es] us from the discomfort of responsibility" [13].

Compassion is the emotion that could potentially bring about change. For Nussbaum [14], it is a matter of education as well as of institutional concern, and we should aim at becoming "compassionate spectators", those who are "always attempting to compare what [they] sees with [their] own evolving conception of the good" and "keenly aware of hidden impediments to flourishing in the lives [they] encounter". Nussbaum [14] concludes, referring to the classical origins of compassion, that "without being tragic spectators, we will not have the insight required if we are to make life somewhat less tragic for those who […] are hungry, and oppressed, and in pain". We are all spectators, which may not be negative *per se*. However, if our role in society in only limited to that of spectator, the potential for compassionate connections and, ultimately, a more just world, may be lost.

Chouliaraki [7] argues that "the ethics of public life insists that suffering invites compassion, it must be acted on and on the spot if it is to be an effective response to the urgency of human pain". It is true that nowadays, as she argues, it may seem impossible to act and re-act compassionately towards the images and stories of suffering. In our globalized times, we are all witnesses to the suffering of others. Most of the time we can only observe, acknowledge, and communicate a limited version of what is being witnessed. Sontag [15] argued that if we are unable to do anything about what we witness we become "just voyeurs". Nowadays, the spectacles of suffering have multiplied exponentially, which may result in "compassion fatigue", defined by Chouliaraki [7] as "the audience's indifference towards distant suffering". Indeed, some players may detach themselves from the realities of the refugees and concentrate on the ludic aspects of the games. However, the ludonarrative strategies of the games analyzed here, put the focus on fiction, on setting and character, in what can be related to the "non-ludus" design templates discussed by Craveirinha and Roque [16]: complex choices, tragedy, and theatre. By placing the players as protagonists and/or in very short proximity to the refugees' experiences, these games aim to bring to the fore more reflective forms of compassion that go beyond both that acting "on the spot" and bearing witness, by questioning the rules within and outside their ludofictional worlds. They are based on a procedural rhetoric of suffering.

How can games portray this suffering? Navarro-Remesal and Bergillos [17] distinguish between "ludic suffering", that caused by the challenge, the controls, the skills the game demands from us, and the desire for a better state, and fictional suffering or "suffer-believe", expressed by player and non-player characters (NPCs) via character animations, voice acting, text messages, and other narrative strategies. This form of vicarious suffering could lead to the recognition of a character's suffering (a sort of "recognise-believe") and could effectively prompt an ethical response. Rentschler [18] warns that, when confronted with images of others' suffering, "people may simply not know how to act or what to do with their vicarious experience of others' suffering, because they have not been taught how to transform feeling into action". It is our contention that the videogames here analyzed promote transformation and that compassion can extend beyond the act of playing.

In our approach to games and play, we follow Fernández-Vara [19], who views play as a performance and the player as both a spectator and a performer. She explains that "The role of the player [...] is just one element that straddles between the role of the audience and the interactor", and thus, "the performance of the player is a negotiation between scripted behaviours and improvisation based on the system". This hybrid, dual role offers players multiple modes of affective identification, as Isbister [20] argues: the "parasocial interaction" of non-interactive media, in which "over time, some viewers/readers form powerful attachments to characters", but also a projection of themselves into their avatars, as well as interactions with NPCs that move beyond parasocial feelings into "consequential social experiences with accompanying social emotions and behaviours".

Elsewhere [21] we define compassionate play as "the acknowledgement of one's own suffering as a player as well as the suffering of others (human or fictional agents), and the interconnectedness between them", with "interconnectedness" being a key concept. We argue that this way of playing is thus a "critical reflection where the player can see clearly who is suffering, how and why, what impact it has on the ludofictional world, and what she can (or cannot) do about it", as well as establish parallelism with the real world and use the game as a basis for ethical reflection. For this conceptualisation, we understand "ludofictional worlds", following Planells [22], as "a system of concatenated possible worlds that generates a play space determined by a fictional content and rules closely related. Meaning is then generated through the combination of the fictional elements (characters, locations, actions) and the rules that govern them.

Ludofictional worlds can serve as commentaries on the real world. Several creators have referred to the possibilities for change that games offer. Alter [23], from Subaltern Games, states that "Video games can't change the world any more than books or movies can. But they can change how someone perceives the world". Similarly, Karam [24], the Syrian refugee whose experience is told in *Path Out*, claims that "I believe games and interactive media are a great way to learn and change perspectives. In my opinion as long as its [sic] being used to show the truth + neutrality". By confronting players with first-person refugee stories, these games put players in the refugees' shoes and allow them to experience the anxiety of waiting, the struggle to escape, and the difficulties in narrating their stories of suffering. These games encourage a heightened awareness of the refugees' experiences and urge players to act accordingly, which will be later analyzed.

4   Games for Compassion? The Makers and Audiences of "Refugee Games"

Except for *Finding Home,* conceived and built by Grey Malaysia (the local branch of an advertising company established in New York), all of these games were created by small teams. *Bury Me, My Love* (from now on, *BMML*) was conceptualized by Florent Maurin, a former journalist and founder of the French independent studio The Pixel Hunt in 2009. *Path Out* was made by Causa Creations, a two-person team founded in 2014 by Tilmann Hars and George Hobmeier, which had previously produced activist games such as *Burn the Boards* (2015), on which they denounce the human cost of e-waste recycling in developing countries. Finally, *North* was created by Outlands, a team of two French artists living in Berlin, Gabriel Helfenstein and Tristan Neu. *BMML, Path Out* and *North* are thus European games with a primary intended audience of European (or, at least, Western) players. They are all (*Finding Home* included) in English, and *BMML* has also been translated to Spanish, French, Italian, and German.

BMML, Finding Home, and *Path Out* are well researched and have been inspired by real cases: *BMML* (described as a "reality-inspired interactive fiction" [25]) by the assistance of Dana, a Syrian refugee, and of Lucie Soullier, a French journalist who wrote an article entitled "*Le Voyage d'une migrante Syrienne à travers son fil Whatsapp*" for Le Monde; *Finding Home* by interviewing young refugees in Malaysia; and *Path Out* by re-telling the autobiographical escape of Abdullah Karam, a Syrian refugee, who actively participated in the making of the game. Although the voices of the refugees are inevitably mediated, these games have worked closely with refugees and do not present them as voiceless, passive victims, but rather as political agents.

North is the outlier in "refugee games" since it is a first-person cyberpunk adventure game based on a fictional, science-fiction city inhabited by aliens. It deals with the topic of refugees in an oblique and abstract manner, but its connection to the real-world refugee crisis is made clear through paratextual strategies. At the time of release (sold on Steam and Switch for a bit over 1 euro and on Itch.io with "name your own price"), the game soundtrack could be bought separately and half of the proceeds went to NGOs Refugees on Rails and Refugee Open Ware. Helfenstein [26] claims that the game's design was inspired by their work on a web documentary about European migration policies: "We also worked in refugee centers and saw all these people getting lost in endless paperwork and absurd procedures. So we had all this background knowledge and personal attachment to the refugee situation that we wanted to come across in the game". Therefore, *North* reflects on the consequences of forced displacement and, more particularly, on the bureaucratic barriers/borders that host countries have established.

These games have a more or less overt persuasive purpose and could thus be considered "persuasive games" [27], meaning games that build an argumentation through procedural rhetorics, dialectical user responses, and simulations. However, they differ in their approaches. *Finding Home* is a free smartphone app commissioned by the UNHCR (United Nations Commissioner for Refugees), with a clear persuasive message addressing the player at the end: "Kathijah and Ishak found each other, but they are far from secure. [...]. There are over 150,000 refugees registered with the UNHCR, UN Refugee Agency in Malaysia, who work hard every day for existence on the fringes of society. [...] The refugee situation is the biggest humanitarian crisis of our time, one which demands action from all of us". The app concludes with a call to action offering links for several ways to help: making a donation to refugee projects, volunteering the player's time, and raising awareness on social networks. *Path Out* is also free on Steam (and under a "name your own price" model on Itch.io), but on its official website the developers reject taking a purely educational stand: "Despite politicizing a genre that is mostly known for fantasy and horror themes, the game doesn't want to appear moralistic or educational, but create a radically different way to tell the story of a young Syrian refugee from his very own perspective" [28]. Thus, although the calls to action are relevant, these games highlight the persuasive power of narratives to change minds. An evaluation of such change would require a larger audience study, which escapes the scope of this paper, but these games work towards that possibility.

Telling a personal story, fictional or more (auto)biographical, and inviting players to think about it seems to be a priority for all these games: the official website for *BMML* [29] states that "This story is about those [migrants] who achieve that goal [getting to Europe]", "It is about those who don't. It is about those who die trying. It is about the world around us. Something which we hope will lead you to keep pondering on after it is over". Their off-game goal is to promote understanding. As mentioned before, these games have "compassionate play" in mind, which is achieved by making us play as or walking alongside refugee characters. And, although their focus is on individual stories, they also direct players to question the world through the rules of their ludofictional worlds.

5   First-Person Stories: Focalization, Strong Characterization, Narrators

The main strategies shared by all these refugee games are the focus on a single story together with the use of a single-character focalization. As such, all of them include voices written in the first person. Personal communication is also central in these narratives: they resort to letters, instant messaging, and Twitch/YouTube-like feeds. These games put forward individual stories and highlight the need to create a conversation, both as a survival strategy in their escape journeys and re-settlement and as a way to connect with wider audiences. In what follows, we describe each game in detail and pay attention to their respective strategies, pointing to further commonalities and their differences.

The main character in *BMML* is Nour, a Syrian woman who flees her country aiming to reach Germany. However, we play as (and from the perspective of) Majd, her husband, who had to stay behind in Syria and is in constant communication with her through his smartphone. As Majd, we receive messages from Nour telling us about her situation and progress (or lack thereof) in her journey. She often asks us for advice, and this is where player agency comes in, although in a very limited and controlled manner. Our capacity to influence the game state is quite minimal. In a talk for the GDC (Game Developers Conference) of 2018 entitled "Exploring helplessness in games with *Bury Me, My Love*", Maurin [30] explained that their goal was to make Nour "feel like a real person", and thus she is consistent, hesitates, and may lie to Majd. They wanted to avoid being "too player-centric" and make players feel they are "not on the ground", "not in control", and that "life is not fair". *Finding Home* uses a very similar narrative design, with the player taking on the role of Kathijah, a 16-year-old Rohingya forced to flee her home with her brother Ishak. When the game starts, she has reached Malaysia and lost Ishak on the way, and they communicate through their phones. The main difference with *BMML* is that the roles are somehow reversed: as Kathijah we can and must communicate with more people, especially with Rohingya people already settled in Malaysia, in order to try and survive there while waiting for Ishak.

Autobiographical videogames are not very common, with *Dis4ia* (Anna Anthropy, 2012), *Cibele* (Nina Freeman, 2015) or *Memoir En Code: Reissue* (Alex Camilleri, 2016) being rare examples. Having the author speak or appear on-screen, as a sort of developer's commentary integrated in the game, is even rarer, with meta-narrative exercises such as *The Beginner's Guide* (Davey Wreden, Everything Unlimited, 2015) exploring this less travelled path. *Path Out* combines both by having the player control Syrian youth Abdullah Karam as he tries to escape his country, while having him interrupt the game to comment on its events and act as a narrator in recorded videos. The game starts in 2014 in a forest in northern Syria and forces the player into an ambush by a soldier. It is then that the action is interrupted for the first time and a video feed of Karam is shown on the top left corner: "You just killed me, man. In reality I wasn't as clumsy as you. Yeah, you don't get it, right? You're playing me in the game. You see that little guy with the yellow shirt? That's me, trying to escape Syria and stuff. But the adventure started a few years ago. Let's take you there, shall we?". During the first episode (the only one released at the time of writing)[1], he, the player avatar, needs to talk to his family and friends in order to progress, while he, the real person, talks directly to the player in a one-to-one manner. Moreover, videogames are used as a shared cultural space that reinforces identification, as well as a communication channel: "I used to be an average kid – going to school, listening to music, and playing video games... Lots of video games", writes Karam in the game's Steam page. *Path Out* plays with scenes of the quotidian and direct addresses to players, which makes them confront the loss of home and the quick disruption of everyday life that refugees face.

As a first-person adventure game, *North* does not show the body of its main character, nor do we ever know exactly how different he is from the aliens living in his new host city. However, we are granted access to his subjectivity in three ways: first, we are made to inhabit his daily life, including working, sleeping, and doing paperwork. Second, there are sections that take place within his dreams, using an internal focalization. Lastly, and more importantly, in order to progress we have to send letters to the protagonist's sister, who still lives in the South. These letters are written in the first person by the protagonist and include vital clues and instructions for the player, while giving us access to the protagonist's thoughts. The first one we send reads "Dear sister, yesterday I arrived in the city. [...] I applied for asylum today. The people here speak strangely so I don't really understand what I have to do". Language and its barriers are thus a key element for the narrative. Unlike *BMML* and *Finding Home,* where we can communicate with the protagonists' loved ones, the sister in *North* never writes back. These two ludonarrative choices, together with themes of vigilance and opaque bureaucracy, enhance the sense of alienation and loneliness. *North*, in fact, portrays the lack of communication as almost a kind of prison (coincidentally, the Spanish language uses the same word for "lack of communication" and "solitary confinement": *incomunicación*).

---

[1] We contacted Abdullah Karam and Georg Hobmeier and they explained that although "many publishers still shy away from the refugee theme", they are negotiating with a publisher to expand *Path Out* to a proper game.

All these four games, thus, share a focus on dialogue and one-to-one communication, the use of a first person voice, and limiting the player's access to one half of the story, and they do so to tell personal stories about escape journeys and/or survival in the host countries. However, they differ in their narrative design strategies, offering three different approaches which we analyze in the next three sections.

6 Reality-Inspired Interface Games: *Bury Me, My Love* and *Finding Home*

In his GDC Talk, Maurin described *BMML* as a "reality-inspired game", a kind of "newsgame" that is made by respecting reality, gathering documentation, and listening to people [30]. In this particular game, they wanted to "mimic the way migrants use messaging apps", and this affects the whole formal construction of the game. *BMML* takes on the appearance of an Instant Messaging (IM) app, not unlike WhatsApp, and limits its ludofictional world to that very narrow window. Nour writes to us and sends us pictures, including selfies, but we never see the action directly from her point of view. Our role as Majd, accordingly, is only inferred from the answer options we are offered and the pictures we send.

Although it can be argued that all gameworlds are "interfaces to the game system" [31], *BMML* belongs in a category of literal "interface games", together with *Sara Is Missing* (Kaigan Games, 2016), *Her Story* (Sam Barlow, 2015), or *Emily Is Away* (Kyle Seeley, 2015). In these works, we are presented with a fake computer or smartphone interface in which the whole game takes place. There is no *mise en abyme*, unlike in *Stories Untold,* nor a reverse-shot of the character using the interface and as whom we are supposed to be playing. The interface of *BMML* is the IM app and as such it is clear that the game was designed with smartphones as their main platform. "We imagined its core mechanics with two main references in mind: *WhatsApp* and *Lifeline"*, reads the official site [26]. Not only does the game's interface look like a real IM app, but its very existence on that platform, as inspired by *Lifeline* (3 Minute Games, 2015), also allows the use of a synchronic time, which Jayemanne [32] has labelled "ethical temporality", and a game structure based on very short playing sessions. Playing *BMML* requires a lot of waiting times, and Nour's answers can arrive at any time via push notifications. Her status changes from online to busy or offline following pre-set times, regardless of whether the player opens the game or not. This creates a naturalistic integration of the game structure in the player's real time, with a blurred magic circle, if any.

Finding Home could be considered an "interface game", although it is formally closer to *Sara Is Missing* (*SIM*) or *A Normal Lost Phone* (Accidental Queens, 2017) than to *BMML.* This means that we have access not only to an IM app, but also to the whole operating system of someone else's smartphone. On its store page, *Finding Home* is described as a "revolutionary new mobile experience [that] creates a simulated OS that literally takes over your phone" [33]. As in the aforementioned "lost phone" games, our very phone is playfully turned into an element of the ludofictional world. However, in *SIM* and *A Normal Lost Phone* we are supposed to play as ourselves, whereas in *Finding Home* we take on the role of Kathija and use her phone roleplaying as her. If *SIM* and *A Normal Lost Phone* frame their fiction as a sort of interactive version of "found footage" films, where the player is supposed to have found a lost phone and must unravel a mystery to which the actual phone is the key, *Finding Home* asks us to imagine we inhabit a wholly different ludofictional world that extends beyond the screen. The game still uses access to everything in a phone as a setup for mystery: on the store page, they encourage us to "view the image gallery to uncover Kat's past and find clues to help her". We can and must check her emails, chats, photos, videos, and even voice and video calls (which we cannot answer) to learn more about her and Ishak. The phone's date and time are used as a narrative device and its battery allows the designers to create tension. In addition to this pseudo-mystery, the apps' educational purposes are always evident: a UNHCR app is presented at all times in the phone's desktop, allowing the player to get more information and bridge the fiction they are playing with the realities of Rohingya refugees in Malaysia.

BMML and *Finding Home* present similar stories and interfaces, but they take radically different approaches to game structure. Decisions made as Majd can and will change the path taken by Nour and the game's ending. There are 19 different outcomes and 39 different end states. According to Maurin, they designed different types of choices and consequences: direct decisions, "blind" decisions, and cumulative effects [30]. The game uses four system variables: Nour's morale, the couple's relationship status, Nour's budget, and her inventory; but these variables are never displayed. "Contrary to lots of other interactive fictions", the game's site says, "your choices in *Bury Me, My Love* really have an impact on the story" [29]. In this regard, *BMML* posits itself as a narrative challenge that demands attention and effort from the player. *Finding Home,* as a free educational app, is less intended for traditional videogame players and more for a general audience: not only is it highly accessible and self-explanatory, but there are also limited branching choices and none of them truly change the critical path of the story. The game reaches the same ending, no matter what, in which the two brothers are reunited. It is very telling that it is normally described as an "app" and not as a "game", though we consider the ontological limits of the two products to be fuzzy enough to consider them part of a similar trend. Moreover, *Finding Home* asks us to roleplay and fits within broad notions of "interactive narrative". Thus, it could be argued that they use videogame elements to present two versions of the same idea, with *BMML* being more gameful and *Finding Home* offering a narrower performance space and restoration of behaviours.

7   Autobiographical JPRG-Like Game with YouTube Aesthetics: *Path Out*

If *BMML* uses a more traditional gaming approach and is sold in core markets and platforms of "gaming culture" (Switch, Steam), *Path Out* goes one step beyond and uses well-established gaming genres and conventions. Not only does Karam presents himself as a gamer, but the game's store description also describes it as "camouflaged as a Japanese RPG". "The game is deliberately designed in the style of classic role playing games", it continues, "a graphical language which stands in sharp contrast with the portrayed sujet [sic] and the dramatic events of the game" [34]. The game aspires to be familiar to gamers, especially to players of RPGs and JRPGs. This is reinforced by the choice of engine: the game is made with RPG Maker (called RPG Tsukûru in Japan), a popular tool among amateur (and sometimes professional) creators. Visually, the game looks like an RPG Maker product, which in itself calls back to the JPRG games of the 16-bit era. However, one key element of the genre is missing in *Path Out*: combat. Posting in the RPG Maker fora, Hobmeier [35] explained: "We did try out some combat, but it simply didn't fit. Basically violence doesn't suit the character and a traditional RPG battle system would be ridiculous considering the depiction of an actual war. So it really is more of an adventure with tons of story, quests and some stealth action".

The second distinctive ludonarrative element of *Path Out* is its integration of Abdullah Karam himself as a commentator and narrator. As explained above, Karam appears on screen at certain pre-scripted moments and addresses the player directly. This "ongoing presence of Abdullah as a youtuber style video commentator in the game itself" [34], is meant to let him tell his story from his own perspective, while at the same time acknowledging the impossibility to simply reproduce reality by having him "scolding the player for getting "himself" killed or making snide remark on oriental design elements that might be too stereotypical" [28]. With this metanarrative exercise, the relationship between the real Karam and with his pixel-art version (or "the-player-as-Karam") is meant to be kept "ambiguous on purpose": "While the journey is clearly based on Abdullah's personal path, the player character will also experience stories by friends and relatives. Again, this narrative freedom will be commented on via video" [28].

Narrative freedom, as suggested in *BMML*'s promotional material, is very important to traditional players. By highlighting it and using a "paradoxical humour" reminiscent of key works such as *The Stanley Parable* (Galactic Cafe, 2013), *Path Outh* winks at its implied players, using a knowing "gamer's game" style to present Karam as a regular teenager, one gaming and social media savvy. He is not different, *Path Out* says, from its implied players, from us.

8   Surreal Cyberpunk First-Person Adventure: *North*

Unlike the other games in this paper, *North* makes no claim to represent a specific reality. With a highly stylized cyberpunk and surreal aesthetics, it starts when the protagonist arrives in a new city after a journey through the desert. Then, he has to solicit asylum and work to meet the requirements for it. While he waits for a resolution, he uses writing as a way to communicate with his sister, who has stayed in the South, and also as an attempt to better understand the new surroundings. *North* presents an alien city which is purposely difficult to navigate. It is poorly lit (the game seems to take place in a perennial night), labyrinthine, full of buzzing hums, almost uninhabited. The dark world in which the player must survive is one of harsh working and living conditions, making it clear that even though the protagonist has escaped, he is nevertheless trapped. This feeling is heightened by the pervasiveness of security cameras that constantly surveil you and the fact that the way to work is mined with crosses signalling graves.

To achieve his goal, the player has to complete a series of disorienting tasks: work in the mines (under a very strict time limit that can result in the only death state of the game), find every camera and be seen, convert to a local religion, pass some medical and police tests, and visit the immigration office with all the documents (from work, the doctors, and the police). With little action and a focus on exploration and observation, *North* could be considered a "walking simulator" game, a recent subgenre whose name started as a derogatory term meant to criticize the lack of traditional gaming challenges, and later became a common classification label (for example, in Steam). In fact, a review for Switch Player stated: "North is a brave entry into the Walking Simulator pantheon [36]. These works are, according to Grabarczyk [34], "the result of subtractive design practices" that often defy traditional definitions of games, and have even been conceptualized as a "new literary genre" [37]. However, the opaque and disorienting qualities of its level design and goal hierarchy make *North* hard to navigate, retaining some gameful qualities. Moreover, the mines level requires trial and error, speed, and reflexes, mirroring the high-risk nature of the job.

It is implied that the protagonist had to flee to the North because of his homosexuality. To do so, the player needs to pick the right choice in a dream that is being watched by the doctors. Persecution for same-sex relationship is still enforced in 70 countries from the United Nations. And the process whereby asylum seekers have to justify their sexual orientation to asylum officers can be excruciating. The doctors' test can feel invading and depowering, taking place within psychedelic nightmares in which rectangular forms that seem to emulate city landscapes quickly follow one another. Everything in *North* is clinical, cold, trippy, and alien, as removed from affect as possible, and proving one's affective orientation in this environment becomes a matter of harsh paperwork. *North* replicates the limbo that many refugees face, in that the player is caught in a seemingly endless waiting in the hope that their status is recognised and asylum granted. "We wanted to make a game that highlighted the Kafkaesque absurdity of a refugee's situation", said Helfenstein to Vice.com [26]. He added that "Our main goal was to confront the player with feelings like confusion, boredom and frustration without putting her in an outside or observer position. It was an interesting challenge to make an unpleasant game that is still engaging". The strange physicality of the city's aliens and their indecipherable language creates a wall of uncanniness between the player and the gameworld. To add to the general unpleasantness, *North* can only be played in one session, with no save points. The last level takes place in a highly surreal location, where the player has to leave his documents, stained with blood, in a machine. It is an ambiguous ending that makes the game all the more impenetrable for general audiences. Even if *North* is the least accessible game and, seemingly, the one further removed from the realities of refugees, it is certainly the one that probably best reflects the sense of dislocation and frustration since its opaque and confusing game design is meant to capture the hardships of the refugees' experience.

9 Conclusions

Although these games, as narratives, tell fictional stories, they have all been inspired by and/or made with the help of refugees, which, as has been shown, brings to the fore more truthful representations that recreate their anxieties, fears, and placelessness within the asylum circuits and leave behind simplistic humanitarian approaches. Moreover, and despite their difficult circumstances, the refugees in these game show limited, but real, agency. In this manner, these games move away from the representation of refugees as extremely resilient people or as seen through the lens of pity. Even the option to give blind advice allows players to act, and when nothing else can be done there is always joking, small talk, or comforting their loved ones. Narrative uncertainty, even in lineal experiences like *Finding Home* or *North*, is often combined with long, frustrating waits without rendering the characters voiceless.

The struggles of refugees are presented in a realistic way by paying minute attention to details: getting ready to leave, communicating in real time, filling up paperwork, being unable to charge their phones... There is an emphasis on daily life aspects and process minutiae that takes refugee narratives beyond iconic images. The use of synchronic time adds an ethical dimension in how it reinforces communication, social dynamics, and mutual support. The main unifying element in these games is that of connection, as well as the severing of ties. As Maurin [30] says in his GDC presentation, "What we learned listening to migrants? [...] Being connected with your loved ones is nice - it is also very hard [and] helplessness is the most difficult thing to deal with". The use of branching paths and multiple outcomes, when present, make some of these games include every conceivable variation of a single story, showing the player how easy it is for things to go awry. The stories of Nour, Kathija, or Karam portray refugees' hardships without reducing it to a single experience or making them be "the" refugee, a single archetype with no characterization.

How do games portray refugees' lives? Not in a single way, not always through recreating our world and time as a ludofictional world. What do games do to change both the refugees' realities and the way in which we relate to those experiences? Although practical calls to action are often included, the general focus is on *performing the refugee,* living from their perspective for a brief time, and blurring the barriers between their world and ours. Our phones become their phones. They talk to us via (fake) streaming. We make choices as them. We are lost in alien cities and alien bureaucracy as them. This paper has shown that by means of different strategies of identification and communication, these games encourage compassionate play, that is, they transmit the suffering of refugees to players as audience and performers. They create an interconnectedness that leads to reflection. We are interconnected to these fictional refugees as players, to their loved ones in a parasocial interaction and a (simulated) social relationship, and to the real refugees serving as inspiration as engaged users.

Since these games promote ethical, compassionate players, they could also expand the conversation about ethics to pressing political questions that surround the refugee question, such as rescuing (even when forbidden by governments) or the inhuman treatment of asylum seekers in camps, detention centres, and precarious temporary accommodations. Not only do they put players in the *others'* shoes, they also raise awareness and broaden the possibilities to engage in political questions in smaller and larger scales. Of course, public perception of such broad issues and the impact of small initiatives such as these games are hard to measure, and they fall outside the scope of a paper like this one, focused instead on game analysis. Moreover, the claim that games promote instant empathy should make us wary. But, at the same time, we cannot deny these four games constitute a burgeoning trend that show clearly defined implied players and reframe the media representation of refugees under a nuanced, personal light, hopefully countering other hostile or simplistic discourses.

References

1. Souvik, M., Hammar, E.L.: Introduction to the special issue on postcolonial perspectives in game studies. Open Libr. Hum. **4**(2), 33 (2018). https://doi.org/10.16995/olh.309
2. Farrier, D.: Postcolonial Asylum: Seeking Sanctuary before the Law. Liverpool University Press, Liverpool (2011)
3. Morton, S.: Postcolonial refugees, displacement, dispossession and economies of abandonment in the capitalist world system. In: Ramone, J. (ed.) The Bloomsbury Introduction to Postcolonial Writing: New Contexts, New Narratives, New Debates, pp. 215–236. Bloomsbury, London (2018)
4. Aarseth, E.: I fought the law breaking. Situated play. In: Proceedings of DIGRA (2007)
5. Marrouchi, M.: Edward Said at the Limits. Sunny Press, New York (2004)
6. Stonebridge, L.: Placeless People: Writing, Rights, and Refugees. Oxford University Press, Oxford (2018)
7. Chouliaraki, L.: The Spectatorship of Suffering. Sage Publishing, London (2006)
8. Volkan, V.D.: Immigrants and Refugees: Trauma, Perennial Mourning, Prejudice, and Border Psychology, vol. xiii. Karnac, London (2017)
9. Wright, T.: The media and representations of refugees and other forced migrants. In: Fiddian-Qasmiyeh, E., Loescher, G., Long, K., Sigona, N. (eds.) The Oxford Handbook of Refugee and Forced Migration Studies, pp. 460–470. Oxford University Press, Oxford
10. Sigona, N.: The politics of refugee voices: representation, narratives, and memories. In: Fiddian-Qasmiyeh, E., Loescher, G., Long, K., Sigona, N. (eds.) The Oxford Handbook of Refugee and Forced Migration Studies, pp. 369–382. Oxford University Press, Oxford
11. Pantti, M., Ojala, M.: Caught between sympathy and suspicion: journalistic perceptions and practices of telling asylum seekers' personal stories. J. Media Cult. Soc. (2018). https://doi.org/10.1177/0163443718756177
12. Smets, K., Mazzocchetti, J., Gerstmans, L., Mostmans, L.: Beyond victimhood: reflecting on Migrant-Victim representations with Afghan, Iraqi, and Syrian Asylum Seekers and Refugees in Belgium. In: d'Haenens, L., Joris, W. (eds.) Images of Immigrants and Refugees in Western Europe: Media Representations, Public Opinion, and Refugees' Experiences, pp. 177–198. Leuven University Press, Leuven (2019)
13. Watt Smith, T.: The Book of Emotions: An Encyclopedia of Feeling from Anger to Wanderlust. Welcome Collection, London (2016)
14. Nussbaum, M.: Compassion: the basic social emotion. Soc. Philos. Policy **13**(1), 27 (1996). https://doi.org/10.1017/s0265052500001515
15. Sontag, S.: Regarding the Pain of Others. Picador, New York (2003)

16. Craveirinha, R., Gomes Roque, L.: Looking for the heart of interactive media: reflections on video games' emotional expression. In: Proceedings of Fun and Games, Third International Conference (2010)
17. Navarro-Remesal, V., Bergillos, I.: Press X to recognize the other's suffering: compassion and recognition in games. In: Videogame Cultures - 8th Global Meeting (2016)
18. Renstschler, C.: Witnessing US citizenship and the vicarious experience of suffering. Media Cult. Soc. **26**(2), 296–304 (2004)
19. Fernández-Vara, C.: Play's the thing: a framework to study videogames as performance. In: Breaking New Ground: Innovation in Games, Play, Practice, Theory. Proceedings of DIGRA (2009)
20. Isbister, K.: How Games Move Us: Emotion by Design. MIT Press, Cambridge (2016)
21. Navarro-Remesal, V., Pérez Zapata, B.: Who made your phone?: Compassion and the voice of the oppressed in phone story and burn the boards. Open Libr. Hum. 4(1). https://doi.org/10.16995/olh.209
22. Planells, A.: Videojuegos y Mundos de Ficción: de Super Mario a Portal. Cátedra, Madrid (2015)
23. Alter, S., Ramone, J.: Postcolonial gaming: an interview with Seth Alter, creator of neocolonialism: ruin everything. In: Ramone, J. (ed.) The Bloomsbury Introduction to Postcolonial Writing: New Contexts, New Narratives, New Debates, pp. 205–212. Bloomsbury, London (2018)
24. Karam, A.: https://twitter.com/Deohvi/status/999223404371808256
25. https://www.gamasutra.com/blogs/FlorentMaurin/20161118/285793/What_realityinspired_games_are.php
26. https://www.vice.com/en_us/article/jpgmwy/north-is-a-dark-surreal-game-about-being-a-refugee
27. Bogost, I.: Persuasive Games: The Expressive Power of Videogames. MIT Press, Cambridge (2007)
28. https://causacreations.net/portfolio/path-out/
29. http://burymemylove.arte.tv/
30. https://twvideo01.ubm-us.net/o1/vault/gdc2018/presentations/Maurin_Florent_ExploringHelplessnessIn.pdf
31. Jörgensen, K.: Gameworld Interfaces. MIT Press, Cambridge (2013)
32. Jayemanne, D.: Ethical temporality: reconfiguring time as political speech in 13 minutes and bury me, my love. In: Philosophy of Computer Games Conference (2018)
33. https://apps.apple.com/us/app/finding-home-a-refugees-journey/id1234931023
34. https://store.steampowered.com/app/725980/Path_Out/
35. https://forums.rpgmakerweb.com/index.php?threads/path-out-demo-available.80008/
36. http://switchplayer.net/2018/03/22/north-review/
37. Grabarczyk, P.: "It's like a walk in the park": on why are walking simulators so controversial. Transformacje **3**(4) (2016)

Games Within Games

The Two (or More) Fictional Levels of Video Games

Regina Seiwald[(✉)]

Faculty of Arts, Design, and Media (ADM), Birmingham City University,
Birmingham B4 7XG, UK
Regina.Seiwald@bcu.ac.uk

Abstract. Video games that incorporate other games in their game-world create interlacing fictional levels. These can be used to engage with concepts of "gameness" from within the game itself without abandoning the aesthetic illusion created by the macrogame, in which the minigame is embedded. In my paper, I delve into the question why we are willing to immerse ourselves in video game worlds even if they contain elements that overtly emphasise the fictionality of these games. I explore concepts of illusion as well as interlacing fictional levels from a theoretical perspective before I research various modes of games within games with or without an impact on the gameplay of the macrogame as well as their relationship to illusion. The outcome of my paper will be a comprehensive study of the critical potential of minigames, which is accomplished by discussing a large corpus of different video games.

Keywords: Minigames · Narrative video games · Illusion · Make-believe · *Mise-en-abyme* · Chinese-box structures

1 Introduction

(Video) games differ from reality because we[1] engage with them in an attitude of make-believe. This means that we, while playing a game, immerse ourselves in the fictive world[2] in which we move. We control the avatar, through which we use the weapon, explore, fight, and engage with others. In the process of immersion in this fictive world, the knowledge that the game-world differs from reality is suppressed in order to allow for the acceptance of its illusion. Immersion is thus important for how we approach games since it marks the difference between lie and invention. However, it is not equivalent to naïveté, meaning that the player actually believes in the game-world or

---

[1] In the context of my paper, "we" is used to denote players of video games.

[2] Following Grant Tavinor [1], narrative video games are regarded as fiction and defined as a work 'in which the characters, places, events, objects, and actions referred to are fictional rather than real. A strong fictive thesis might claim that videogames are *essentially* fictions in that they necessarily depict fictional characters, places, objects, events, and actions' [1]. The world created in (narrative) video games consequently differs from reality due to its status of being fictional, yet might be referred to by other terms than fiction, such as Roger Caillois's description of them as 'a second reality or [...] a free unreality' [2].

© Springer Nature Switzerland AG 2019
N. Zagalo et al. (Eds.): VJ 2019, CCIS 1164, pp. 18–31, 2019.
https://doi.org/10.1007/978-3-030-37983-4_2

confuses it with reality; rather, the concept denotes a sense of accepting the illusion of the game-world and the rules governing therein as valid. The existence of the game-world might even have validity for us beyond the game, namely when we exchange our experience with other gamers on platforms or discussions. Despite this immersion, however, play is a fundamentally reflective, conscious, controlled, and distanced mode.

What happens, however, if these game-worlds, which create self-contained illusions, comprise elements that are ludic, yet different from the game-world we move in? In the sections that follow, I want to explore the effects games within games have on our perception of the game-world and games in general as well as on the concept of make-believe. Analogous to the minigames[3] that are contained in other games, I will term games containing other games "macrogames". By drawing attention to ludic elements, such games need not necessarily disturb the illusion when reflecting on "gameness"[4] and games from a critical perspective.

In order to engage with various forms of self-reflexive modes employed in games within games, my paper will set out with a theoretical discussion of games and their relationship to illusion[5] in order to determine why we are willing to play games as well as how we engage with the worlds created by them. This is followed by a discussion of the interlacing fictional levels constructed by games within games. I will distinguish between two kinds, namely Chinese-box structures, meaning that a game contains a game that is separate from the main game, and *mise-en-abyme* structures, which is a term denoting the mirroring of characteristics of the embedding game. These two sections form the theoretical foundation for the analysis of various games within games, comprising the third part of the present paper. I will further distinguish between minigames that are not needed to progress in the macrogame, and minigames that are an inherent part of the macrogame. This analysis is guided by the questions how the incorporation of minigames affects our perception of the game-world of the macrogame as well as how they can be used to critically engage with "gameness" from within games (without abandoning the illusion of the main game). The outcome of this paper will be a comprehensive analysis of minigames and their relationship to the concept of illusion, which is accomplished by drawing on various exemplary video games.

---

[3] The defining characteristic of minigames is that they are embedded in another game, wherefore they differ from independent minigames as, for example, defined by Clark Aldrich [3].

[4] My understanding of "gameness" is based on Sébastien Genvo's argument that 'gaming-oriented devices must convince the recipient of their playfulness through pragmatic markers that meet certain cultural representations of the activity and incite to consider this object as a game' [4]. In other words, the game must contain elements that suggest to the player that it is a game. These characteristics are further defined and discussed by Genvo, particularly with regard to the concept of "ludic ethos", which 'invites us to understand how individuals are guided in their play activity by some "pragmatic markers", and how structures build a universe of specific values to be accepted as a game' [4].

[5] Following Werner Wolf [5], illusion is not to be understood as a deceptive mode but as the aesthetic process of creating a world that differs from reality. While the immersion of the recipient in this illusion created by the medium is desired, an awareness of its difference from reality and, thus, a reflective, conscious, and critical stance counterbalances a potential delusion.

2 Our Willingness to Play Games

Games are frequently associated with a mode of distraction, as something superfluous to real life. However, if the history of games is considered, their vital contribution to the formation of culture soon becomes evident. Johan Huizinga determines the characteristics of play, which can be seen as the activity of the object game, as follows:

> [P]lay is a voluntary activity or occupation executed within certain fixed limits of time and place, according to rules freely accepted but absolutely binding, having its aim in itself and accompanied by a feeling of tension, joy and the consciousness that it is "different" from "ordinary life." [6]

Huizinga does not make a hierarchical distinction between games and reality, but states that play is different from life. This definition allows for a degree of freedom with regard to the inclusion of what is considered as play or game. Roger Caillois links to Huizinga's definition, yet adds aspects and presents them in form of six characteristics of play: free (not obligatory), separate (exists in its own time and space), uncertain (not fixed despite some rules), unproductive (situation at the end is the same as at the beginning), governed by rules, and make-believe [2]. The last feature is particularly important in the context of my paper, and Caillois says of make-believe in reference to play that it is 'accompanied by a special awareness of a second reality or of a free unreality, as against real life' [2]. These definitional qualities are similar to Clara Fernández-Vara's definition of video games as performance, proposing five basic features:[6] 'a special ordering of *time*, a special value attached to *objects*, *non-productivity* in terms of goods, *rules*, and *performance spaces*' [7]. That games are essential parts of culture is not only true of "traditional" games as identified by Huizinga and Caillois but, I would argue, also of video games: they are, after all, simulations of aspects of reality, such as social relationships, negotiating skills, or economic strategies. Seen in this light, the reason for the willingness why people play games soon becomes intelligible: they resemble reality, but they are different from it. However, particularly the notion of the "magic circle" assigned to games by Huizinga, Caillois, and Fernández-Vara has been criticised in recent years because, as argued by Mia Consalvo [8], outside knowledge about games and gameplay as well as the players' personal life experience is always brought along when a new game is played. That is to say, despite games being assigned specific locales (e.g. the boxing ring or the console), they are not entirely separate from other places.

In order to invest oneself in a game, it is necessary to let oneself in for the illusion created in the game-world and to accept the rules being in effect in the game as valid. Games create illusions of a world that might be close to or utterly different from the world we perceive as real.[7] This illusion is not a negatively connoted deception, but an aesthetic

---

[6] These five features are shared by play, games, sports, theatre, and rituals [7]. As Fernández-Vara notes, there are exceptions to this definition, such as, for example, online poker, which includes monetary gain and, hence, productivity.

[7] The similarity between the real and the game-world depends on the game's deviation from reality. Games can depart from reality to a large extent while they are still being perceived as believable; this, however, is only the case if they follow their own inner logic, regardless of how much they differ from reality.

process. While non-aesthetic illusion is mainly interpreted in negative terms and concerned with uncovering deceptive modes, fictional or aesthetic illusion wants to intensify the ability to create a world that differs from reality outside the game [5]. Yet, a game can never be congruent with a subjectively perceived reality. It always creates illusion. For literature, Wolf analyses the relationship between text (game) and reader (player) on the basis of this illusion. He proposes the two terms *Distanz* (distance) and *Partizipation* (participation) to outline the reader's (player's) cognition of the illusion [5].[8]

Distance denotes the idea that users of media with fictional content are aware of the difference between illusion and reality. Patricia Waugh argues the following for literature: 'Of course we *know* that what we are reading is not "real", but we suppress the knowledge in order to increase our enjoyment' [13]. Distance is created, for example, through our awareness that we enter a video game world via a screen or a console or that it is perfectly logical that zombies exist in one game-world, while they do not make any sense in another. This difference can be approached with recourse to a question posed by Erving Goffman: '*Under what circumstances do we think things as real?* The important thing about reality […] is our sense of its realness in contrast to our feeling that some things lack this quality. One can then ask under what condition such a feeling is generated […]' [14]. During the process of immersing oneself in the fictional medium, distance fades into the background and the player participates in the illusion. Goffman defines participation as 'a psychobiological process in which the subject becomes at least partly unaware of the direction of his feelings and his cognitive attention' [14]. Thus, distance and participation are both related to illusion, within which they initially follow an order since distance is replaced by participation. This process is not linear but alternating because the recipient can change from distance to participation and back to distance in an endless regress (e.g. when pausing or reloading a game), or simply move from distance to participation (e.g. when finishing a game in one playthrough). If no progression is made, the recipient does not participate in the illusion.

Video games in general demand from the player to acknowledge the "as if" nature of the game-world and the readiness to take part in the make-believe. Only then it is possible that they immerse themselves in the illusion created by the game. An example that illustrates this argument is the ending of *BioShock* [15], when it is revealed that Jack has been used by Atlas and manipulated with the phrase 'Would you kindly' to fulfill the orders he is given. In this sense, the game admits that the avatar is moved by another entity – by Atlas within the story-world, yet also by the player outside of it. Despite this bold admission, *BioShock* nevertheless creates an image of characters and of a coherent game-world. Although the concept of agency is made explicit, the illusion constructed in the game still persists.

---

[8] Similar concepts are Samuel Taylor Coleridge's "willing suspension of disbelief" [9], Kendall L. Walton's "make-believe" [10], Peter Lamarque's "Thought Theory" [11], and, yet more extensive, Wayne C. Booth's "fictional pact" [12]. These theories were developed to describe the relationship between a fictional text and the reader, yet for video games, the situation is entirely different, mainly due to the agency of the player in the creation of the story. In order to avoid terminological ambiguities, Wolf's concepts of distance and participation are therefore more beneficial to a description of the potential interaction with illusion.

One of the questions of the present paper is how this preparedness to accept the fictional illusion of the game is affected if a game occurs within this game. The consideration is that the game's illusion and its difference from the real world are emphasised if a system of a similar or even the same structure is presented within it. It appears, however, that players are still willing to accept the game-world despite the fact that it is marked as invention. In order to explore this argument, I will be looking at video games of a specific type. The games I am considering are narrative video games,[9] i.e. games that create a linear or branching story either through language or through aspects of world-creation. These games are considered because they can potentially generate a strong fictional illusion while simultaneously possessing various modes how to call this illusion into question by inserting games within their own fictive worlds. Additionally, the narrative presented in the game-world needs to be doubled based on an insertion of another game in the story-world, either one that resembles the nature of the embedding game or one that is different from it. If these two criteria are fulfilled, it is possible to explore the various functions games within games can have. Games that are not considered, on the other hand, are those that are collections of games, such as *Mario Party* [17], which is a compilation of minigames. Before the analysis of interlacing fictional levels in exemplary video games can be conducted, however, it is necessary to define fictional levels as well as what effect they have on our perception of illusion.

3   The Interlacing of Fictional Levels

Any artefact that contains more than one fictional level unavoidably signposts its own fictionality. Although this might initially suggest that the fictional illusion and the recipient's willingness to participate in it run the risk of being denied, it actually has the effect that a critical discourse about the nature of the artefact and fictionality can be initiated in the artefact itself. This process is termed "self-reflexivity", yet in literary studies, which has, to date, most comprehensively researched this tendency, it is referred to as "metafiction". Since the interest of the present paper lies with the interlacing of fictional levels in video games, it is appropriate to use these two terms synonymously and, hence, metafiction is discussed in more detail in order to determine what is meant by self-reflexive games. In her seminal work *Metafiction*, Patricia Waugh has proposed that

> *Metafiction* is a term given to fictional writing which self-consciously and systematically draws attention to its status as an artefact in order to pose questions about the relationship between fiction and reality. In providing a critique of their own methods of construction, such writings not only examine the fundamental structures of narrative fiction, they also explore the possible fictionality of the world outside the literary fictional text. [13]

---

[9] Although I focus on narrative video games, illusion is also possible in non-narrative games. In *Tetris* [16], for example, players are still willing to accept that the purpose of the world they enter is to put blocks of various shapes atop each other. However, no (complex) narrative is told.

In the context of my paper, several points of this definition will be relevant, yet some need to be modified in order to be appropriate for video games. Firstly, the notion "fictional writing" can be extended to "fictional artefact" because metafiction (as a term and as a concept) can be realised in other media besides literature; the only characteristic that needs to be given is that their subject matter is fictional (as is the case with video games). Secondly, this process of self-reflexivity must not be accidental, but intended by the programmer or the author of the narrative level in the game. Thirdly, it is not obligatory that the relationship between fiction and reality is explicitly thematised as Waugh would suggest; rather, through critically engaging with world-creating processes of the illusion and how they are perceived, questions about the creation and perception of reality are implied. This argument links to the fourth point, namely that this suggests that our perceived reality is not objective and might even be fictionalised in the process of perception.

These preliminary considerations therefore suggest that any engagement with the fictionality of the game in the video game itself draws attention to its illusion (in contrast to reality). One mode to achieve this is through the device of multiplying the fictional levels of the video game. In other words, as soon as a game occurs in a game, the "gameness" of the macrogame is emphasised. In the following section, I will define, from a theoretical perspective, two modes how these games can be embedded in the main game, namely Chinese-box structures[10] and the *mise-en-abyme*. Again, I will draw on literary studies to lay the foundation for the focus of my paper, namely the exploration how video games can multiply their fictional levels and what effects this has on the perception of the main game.

Games within games constitute one or more gaming level(s) separate from the main game to establish an analogy to the embedding game.[11] They can be potent metafictional devices that render the act of gaming by making it a central part of the game itself. The represented world-creating process of a game has the effect that the artefactuality of the game it appears in can be commented on without necessarily having to state that it is a game; the illusion of the game-world can still be maintained. With regard to literature, Dorrit Cohn states that such multi-layered narratives constitute an 'interior [...] metalepsis that occurs between two levels of the same story' [20]. For video games, this means that the avatar can play the game in the game (sometimes even by playing another avatar), thus moving from one fictional plane to another, while the player still plays the avatar.

---

[10] Brian McHale describes narrative structures of 'forking paths' as 'nesting or embedding, as in a set of Chinese boxes or Russian *babushka* dolls' [18]. Wolf [5] also speaks of "Chinese-box structure". This metaphor is adopted here since it depicts the relationship between the individual fictional levels and their interdependence.

[11] These added levels can but need not be hypodiegetic. Games within games are hypodiegetic if they possess their own narrative elements, i.e. if they fulfill all elements of narrative as defined by Gerald Prince: 'The representation (as product and process, object and act, structure and structuration) of one or more real or fictive events communicated by one, two, or several (more or less overt) narrators to one, two, or several (more or less overt) narratees' [19]. The inclusion of *Maniac Mansion* in *Day of the Tentacle* generates a hypodiegetic narrative structure due to the minigame's fulfilment of Prince's definitional aspects, while the game of connecting pipes in *BioShock* does not.

Analogous to literature, two forms of games within games can be distinguished: the Chinese-box structure, where the embedded game only possesses a weak link to the structure of the embedding game, and the *mise-en-abyme*, where the second game level strongly resembles the first; both metafictionally signpost the "gameness" and fictionality of the embedding game. Games within games are used for 'foregrounding the ontological dimension of recursive structures' [18]. An embedded game explicitly alludes to its own and implicitly to the fictionality and "gameness" of the embedding game, hence an analogy to the latter's relationship to reality can be drawn, namely that it is absorbed in fiction and ludic structures.

The function of including a game within a game can be linked to Michel Foucault's emphasis on the importance of mirrors in art.[12] He argues that they 'play a duplicating role: they repeated the original contents of the picture, only inside an unreal, modified, contracted, concave space' [23]. Mirrors distort reality because of the spectator's awareness that they present a reflection, that they do not show the actual world, but only a representation of it. The same holds true for games: a game within a game is a reflection of the procession of the game as such, hence also of the embedding game. What McHale states for the *mise-en-abyme* is also true of Chinese-box structures: 'mise-en-abyme is another form of short-circuit, another disruption of the logic of narrative hierarchy, every bit as disquieting as a character stepping across the ontological threshold to a different narrative level' [18].

How this ludic underpinning is foregrounded through incorporating games within games is the focus of the next section, explained in recourse to exemplary video games possessing the characteristics defined above.

4   Games Within Games

Based on the discussion of fictional illusion and the theory of games within games, I will now discuss various modes of embedded games, their functions, and their effects in recourse to exemplary games. I will work on a spectrum, meaning that on the one side we find embedded games that do not have an impact on the gameplay of the macrogame, while on the other side we can locate embedded games that are inherent (or maybe even necessary) elements of the game they appear in. On both ends of the spectrum, the games can either be realised as Chinese-box structures (frequent) or as *mises-en-abyme* (infrequent). The first section of the analysis below is therefore concerned with games within games that do not add anything to the macrogames but they are a nice addition to the embedding game. The second section focuses on minigames that benefit or are even necessary for the macrogame, for example through obtaining bonuses or upgrades, having to be played in order to achieve 100% completion, or even through being an essential aspect of the macrogame.

---

[12] The metaphor of the mirror is later also utilised by Lucien Dällenbach: 'the *mise en abyme* is any internal mirror reflecting the narrative as a whole by simple, repeated or specious duplication' [21]. Mieke Bal suggests to abandon the term *mise-en-abyme* as it does not depict 'the totality of an image, but only a part of the text, or a certain aspect. […] I suggest we use the term "mirror-text" for *mise en abyme*' [22].

4.1 Games Within Games Without an Impact on the Gameplay of the Macrogame

The first category of minigames that is analysed are those that do not have to be played in order for the macrogame to progress. Nevertheless, since they constitute a second fictional level in the embedding game, they indirectly emphasise the "gameness" of the macrogame. The reason for this is that these minigames often follow very simple structures or resemble games we know as games (such as hide and seek); we approach them in an attitude of a game, while the embedding game might nevertheless be perceived as different from it. In order to develop, research, and exemplify this argument further, various minigames occurring in macrogames are analysed by exploring the relationship between the two (or more) fictional levels they constitute.

The first examples to be considered are games appearing in a classical video game series: *Grand Theft Auto*.[13] Of the series, the games *GTA Vice City* [24],[14] *GTA San Andreas* [25], *GTA IV* [26], *GTA V* [27], and *GTA Online* [28] contain arcade-style video games that are found in various places, such as bars, restaurants, clothes shops, 24/7s, etc. These minigames are based on real video games, wherefore they immediately evoke a point of reference and an association with "gameness". An example is the game *Let's Get Ready to Bumble* found in *GTA San Andreas*, in which the player assumes the role of a bee that has to collect flowers. This 2-D platform game is based on Tehkan's classic arcade game *Bomb Jack* [29], where the aim is to collect red bombs. This strong intertextual link to a game that exists in the player's reality has the effect that the "gameness" of the game within the game is strongly emphasised; at the same time, however, the illusion created by the macrogame is not abandoned. Rather, it is supported because the player is confronted with the fictional nature of the minigame, which stands in contrast to the macrogame, and the latter is perceived as a framework of reality in which the embedded game exists.

Another example from *GTA IV*, which also occurs in the two add-ons *GTA IV: The Lost and Damned* [30] and *GTA IV: The Ballad of Gay Tony* [31], is *QUB^{3}D*.[15] The aim of the game is to match up four or more blocks of the same colour before the screen fills up. This game is inspired by *Puyo Puyo* [32] and partly also by *Tetris* [16]. Both games can be seen as iconic and are associated with the early days of an emerging gaming culture. These two minigames as well as the others found in the games of the *GTA* series share some features with classic arcade games, such as straightforward objectives, simple (2-D) graphics, a retro style, and lists with high scores.[16] Furthermore, the games do not add anything to the advancement of the macrogame, but are simply a pastime. Still, the illusion of the embedding game remains intact (i.e. it is not overtly presented as a game) and it is situated on a different plane from the embedded game.

---

[13] Abbreviated to *GTA* hereafter.

[14] The minigames in *GTA Vice City* are unplayable.

[15] The game also occurs in *GTA V*, yet it is not playable.

[16] The high scores can be seen and are saved on every machine of the same type. This would not happen in reality unless the machines are connected.

Fallout 4 [33] contains a game called *Red Menace*, which has similar effects on our perception of fictional levels as do the games in *GTA*, partly due to its intertextuality. The game is highly allusive of *Donkey Kong* [34] but instead of a gorilla it features an alien. It is played on a terminal or a Pip-Boy and the player collects the cartridge in Vault 111. Similar to the arcade games in *GTA*, this game is physically separate from the macrogame, meaning that it has to be accessed through a device. This has the effect that its "gameness" is immediately exposed, thus requiring an attitude of gaming. A special case of this kind of games within games is presented in LucasArts's *Day of the Tentacle* [35], in which one of the computers contains Lucasfilm Games's *Maniac Mansion* [36]. The game is fully playable for free. The inclusion of this game within the game can be understood as homage to the original title, but also as a self-reflexive comment on the status of games. It is a clear example of metafiction and can be seen as a commentary on the industry, using real-world agents and reframing the first game as precisely that, a game.

Other prominent kinds of games within games are those resembling a puzzle-structure. In *Batman: Arkham City* [37], deciphering plays a prominent role. When using the radio scanner, three unregistered stations can be found, which play rows of numbers. By using cyphers, messages can be decoded, such as "Fear will tear Gotham to shreds" uttered by Scarecrow. This message foreshadows the role he will play in *Batman: Arkham Knight* [38], yet it does not add anything to the embedding macro-game. Similar to this puzzle-game, forms of gambling are frequently incorporated in macrogames. *Red Dead Redemption* [39] contains many different gambling games, such as poker and horseshoe throwing. A prominent example is *Liar's Dice*; the player gets five dice, which s/he needs to shake in a cup, put them on a table, secretly look at, and say how many of a certain number they have. In order to beat the others, they need to bluff and lie. If you get caught, you lose. This game can be played for as long as the player wants, yet it is not necessary for the progression of the macrogame. While they do not directly contribute to the main game, such puzzle and gambling games have the effect that the player's analytical skills are trained, which, in turn, can be useful in the macrogame.

Sometimes, games appear within games that are not playable, wherefore it can be argued that they are not minigames in the strictest sense of the term. However, since they certainly foreground "gameness" by evoking a sense in the player that they are different from the game-world they appear in, they are worth further consideration in the context of the present paper. *Uncharted 4: A Thief's End* [40] features a narrative sequence where Elena Fisher introduces Nathan Drake to the original *Crash Bandicoot* [41]. It is unplayable for the player but since we are aware that it is a game, we nevertheless approach it in a game-like attitude. By including this game in the macrogame, it is possible to present a critical analysis of the gaming culture from within the game itself, particularly when Drake declares 'I don't know why people get into video games' [40]. This ironic, self-reflexive comment on the attitude towards games as a pastime stays within the fictional illusion of *Uncharted*'s game-world, wherefore players are not encouraged to move from participation to distance.

Minigames without an impact on the gameplay of the macrogame are additions that allow for a critical engagement with the status of games and gaming from within a game. They can therefore be seen as a mode of theorisation through practice because they can be used as testing grounds for ludic elements of the game itself, while simultaneously allowing the player to observe the act of playing from a position external to it. In this sense, such games within games are elements that emphasise the illusion created by games without abandoning it.

4.2 Games Within Games with an Impact on the Gameplay of the Macrogame

Unlike the minigames discussed above, the minigames in this section are an inherent part of their macrogame, while the game they are embedded in still consists of a coherent story, thereby being different from "Party Games" such as *Mario Party* [3]. Since they are marked by such a tight connection to the game they appear in, they differently emphasise the existence of fictional levels in a game in contrast to minigames without an impact on the gameplay of the macrogame. The examples below all support the argument that the illusion created by a game-world need not be abandoned only because the "gameness" of the macrogame is laid bare by emphasising the "gameness" of the minigames. How various manifestations of games within games can do so shall now be discussed in detail.

Games of *The Legend of Zelda*[17] [42] series contain many minigames of different shape and form. They all share that they are inherent parts of the game they appear in; they thus resemble the structure of their macrogames because one of the core characteristics of the *Zelda* series is their puzzle structure. That is to say, *Zelda* consists of a series of compulsory minigames (mainly located in dungeons and shrines) that are framed by an overarching narrative (Link has to help Princess Zelda to fight Ganon (dorf) and free Hyrule). Furthermore, these minigames reward the player either with Pieces of Heart or with upgrades. Generally, the minigames can be grouped into three major categories: (1) simulations of real-life activities, such as fishing or shooting galleries,[18] (2) games resembling "classic" analog games, such as hide and seek, and (3) games of gambling and luck, such as lottery or the treasure chest game.

A minor category of more complex games can be added, which often share features of the three major categories. An example is the *STAR Game* in *Twilight Princess* [43]. The aim is to collect light orbs, which are suspended in the air, in order to be rewarded with Quiver upgrades. The game comes in three levels, which have to be completed consecutively and this can only be accomplished if Link possesses a Clawshot and a Double Clawshot[19] because otherwise light orbs that are out of reach cannot be collected. In the third stage of the game, Link has to beat his personal best time. The game thus comes with a number of premises and features: Link needs to be in possession of two items, which already need skill to be collected; the game is a combination of the three categories of games described above because it is a blend of luck and skill as well

---

[17] Abbreviated to *Zelda* hereafter.

[18] It is important to note that for Link, these activities are real-life practices, wherefore they are termed "simulations" and not "games".

[19] A Clawshot is a latching device with which Link can hang off suspended objects such as trees or walls. A Double Clawshot allows him to shoot a second latch once hanging on the first.

as classical game features and real-life simulations. The *STAR Game* is not imperative for the successful completion of *Twilight Princess*, but the reward in form of a Giant Quiver allows Link to hold up to one hundred arrows, making it easier to defeat more difficult enemies.

Another popular example, in which one particular minigame plays a central role since it massively contributes to the success of the macrogame, is *Final Fantasy VIII* [44]. *Triple Triad* is a card game that forms a sidequest. It is played on a 3x3 board and the aim is to capture the other player's cards by putting one of a higher rank next to theirs. These cards can then be refined into items through Quezacotl's[20] card mod ability, making it easier to obtain rare items; the game therefore has an impact on the gameplay of the macrogame. This minigame has become so popular that it has been transformed into an independent game that is playable outside *Final Fantasy VIII* (and other games of the series containing the game). This postulates a very rare case of a minigame because besides constituting an additional fictional plane within the macrogame, it also establishes a separate fictive world, thus becoming its own main game, while it is still strongly associated with its original *Final Fantasy* game-world.

Minigames can serve the purpose of a training ground for skills needed in the macrogame. The puzzle-platform game *Catherine* [45], which focuses on the protagonist Vincent Brooks, is played in two modes – a daytime sequence following social simulations and a nighttime sequence consisting of nightmares. The daytime sequence takes place in the Stray Sheep bar, where Vincent can play the *Rapunzel* minigame, which simulates the gameplay of the nighttime sequence. By including the structure of one aspect of the game in another part of the very game, a *mise-en-abyme* is created, which emphasises the act of playing from a meta-perspective. A similar situation can be observed in *Far Cry 3* [46]. Comparable to the gambling games in *Red Dead Redemption* discussed above, *Far Cry 3* incorporates poker, yet this time with an immediate effect on the game itself. It contains tutorials where you can learn how to play poker in a very realistic setting created by a tense atmosphere in a saloon. The newly learned skill is not initially needed to succeed in the game, but poker is also contained in the ending, making it easier for the player who has practiced. The secondary game level created by the embedded game hence has an impact on the primary game level of *Far Cry 3*, yet not to the effect that the illusion of either of them is running the risk of being abandoned. Rather, the tight embeddedness of the minigame has the effect that it is not immediately perceived as separate from the main game, but as an integral element of it.

The final category of games within games that shall be of interest here are those following a puzzle structure. In *BioShock* [15], some vending machines allow for the player to play a minigame where they have to connect pipes to form a continuous steam outlet. The reward takes the form of discounts on weapons and ammunition. The faster the steam moves, the harder it gets to connect the pipes in time, but also the higher the discounts are. Although the minigame is not vital for the progression of the macrogame, it nevertheless has positive impacts on it, such as the possibility to gain cheaper access to better weapons. A puzzle-structure minigame is also found in *LEGO Star*

---

[20] In *Final Fantasy VIII*, Quezacotl is a winged Guardian Force.

Wars [47], yet with a different status regarding its relationship to the macrogame. One of the doors in the hallway on Kamino leads to a room where a puzzle has to be solved. If successful, the floor becomes a disco, playing a disco version of the *Star Wars* theme song. Although this Easter Egg[21] does not immediately impact the macrogame, it is needed to achieve 100% completion. These two examples of puzzle-structure mini-games share that they follow a constitution that differs from that of the main game. Furthermore, they are very obviously presented as games, drawing particular attention to their characteristics of "gameness". They therefore have the effect that the illusion of the fictive world presented by the game is strengthened, inviting the player to partic-ipate in the make-believe.

5 Conclusion

As the analysis of the two categories of minigames has shown, games within games emphasise their "gameness" in a much stronger mode than the macrogames do. One possible explanation is that macrogames actually want to disguise the fact that they are games by creating an illusion that masks their unreality. It is also notable that minigames do not have the effect that the illusion of the macrogame is laid bare or even destroyed. Rather, characteristics of games can be presented up close without risking that the players abandon their willingness to take part in the illusion. This is true for both categories of games within games analysed above, namely games that do not add anything to the progression or achievements in the macrogame and those games that do.

What, then, can we learn about the fictional levels of video games through looking at minigames and their relationships to the macrogames they appear in? Firstly, that video games generally create illusions (similar to literature or film) that players are willing to immerse themselves in, at least for the time of playing. Secondly, by pre-senting a game within a game, the concept of "gameness" can be evaluated from an interior perspective, thus allowing for a critical engagement with characteristics of games. And thirdly, despite inserting a second fictional game layer within a game, the illusion created by the macrogame is still intact. As a final note it can therefore be stated that minigames constitute a practical approach to the formation of a games theory.

References

1. Tavinor, G.: Videogames and fictionalism. In: Sageng, J.R., Fossheim, H., Larsen, T.M. (eds.) The Philosophy of Computer Games, vol. 7, pp. 185–199. Springer, Dordrecht (2012). https://doi.org/10.1007/978-94-007-4249-9_13

---

[21] Easter Eggs – "treasures" hidden within games – need not be games *per se*. They can be, for example, extra money as in *The Legend of Zelda: A Link to the Past* [48], where a hidden room, "The Chris Houlihan Room" [49], contains extra Rupees. While Easter Eggs need not be games, their discovery follows game-like structures because they are hidden and not actually part of the main game. Their detection is akin to a treasure hunt and very often treasures are awaiting the inquisitive player.

2. Caillois, R.: Man, Play and Games. University of Illinois Press, Urbana (2001). Translated by Barash, M.
3. Aldrich, C.: The Complete Guide to Simulations & Serious Games: How the Most Valuable Content Will Be Created in the Age Beyond Gutenberg to Google. Pfeiffer, San Francisco (2009)
4. Genvo, S.: Defining and Designing Expressive Games: The Case of Keys of a Gamespace, pp. 90–106. Kinephanos (2016)
5. Wolf, W.: Ästhetische Illusion und Illusionsdurchbrechung in der Erzählkunst: Theorie und Geschichte mit Schwerpunkt auf englischem illusionsstörenden Erzählen. Niemeyer, Tübingen (1993)
6. Huizinga, J.: Homo Ludens: A Study of the Play-Element in Culture. Angelico Press, Kettering (2016)
7. Fernández-Vara, C.: Play's the thing: a framework to study videogames as performance. In: Proceedings of DiGRA 2009, Breaking New Ground: Innovation in Games, Play, Practice and Theory, vol. 5. Brunel University, London (2009). http://www.digra.org/digital-library/publications/plays-the-thing-a-framework-to-study-videogames-as-performance/
8. Consalvo, M.: There is no magic circle. Games Cult. **4**(4), 408–417 (2009). https://doi.org/10.1177/1555412009343575
9. Coleridge, S.T.: Biographia Literaria, vol. 2. Claredon Press, Oxford (1907)
10. Walton, K.L.: Mimesis as Make-Believe: On the Foundations of the Representational Arts. Harvard University Press, Harvard (1990)
11. Lamarque, P.: The Philosophy of Literature. Blackwell, Oxford (2009)
12. Booth, W.C.: The Rhetoric of Fiction. University of Chicago Press, Chicago (1961)
13. Waugh, P.: Metafiction: The Theory and Practice of Self-Conscious Fiction. Methuen, London (1984)
14. Goffman, E.: Frame Analysis: An Essay on the Organization of Experience. Penguin, Harmondsworth (1974)
15. 2K Games: BioShock (2007)
16. Infogrames, et al.: Tetris (1984)
17. Nintendo: Mario Party (1998–2018)
18. McHale, B.: Postmodernist Fiction. Routledge, London (1987)
19. Prince, G.: A Dictionary of Narratology, Rev edn. University of Nebraska Press, Lincoln (2003)
20. Cohn, D.: Metalepsis and Mise En Abyme. Narrative **20**(1), 105–114 (2012). Translated by Gleich, L.S.
21. Dällenbach, L.: The Mirror in the Text. University of Chicago Press, Chicago (1989). Translated by Whiteley, J., Hughes, E.
22. Bal, M.: Narratology: Introduction to the Theory of Narrative. University of Toronto Press, Toronto (2009)
23. Foucault, M.: The Order of Things: An Archeology of the Human Sciences. Routledge, London (2005)
24. Rockstar Games: Grand Theft Auto: Vice City (2002)
25. Rockstar Games: Grand Theft Auto: San Andreas (2004)
26. Rockstar Games: Grand Theft Auto IV (2008)
27. Rockstar Games: Grand Theft Auto V (2013)
28. Rockstar Games: Grand Theft Auto Online (2013)
29. Tehkan: Bomb Jack (1984)
30. Rockstar Games: Grand Theft Auto IV: The Lost and Damned (2009)
31. Rockstar Games: Grand Theft Auto IV: The Ballad of Gay Tony (2009)
32. Compile, Sega: Puyo Puyo (1991)

33. Bethesda Softworks: Fallout 4 (2015)
34. Nintendo: Donkey Kong (1981–2018)
35. LucasArts: Day of the Tentacle (1993)
36. Lucasfilm Games: Maniac Mansion (1987)
37. Warner Bros. Interactive Entertainment: Batman: Arkham City (2011)
38. Warner Bros. Interactive Entertainment: Batman: Arkham Knight (2015)
39. Rockstar Games: Red Dead Redemption (2010)
40. Sony Computer Entertainment: Uncharted 4: A Thief's End (2016)
41. Sony Computer Entertainment, Vivendi Games, Activision: Crash Bandicoot (1996)
42. Nintendo: The Legend of Zelda (1986–2017)
43. Nintendo: The Legend of Zelda: Twilight Princess (2006)
44. Square: Final Fantasy VIII (1999)
45. Atlus: Catherine (2011)
46. Ubisoft: Far Cry 3 (2012)
47. Eidos Interactive, Giant Interactive Entertainment, Aspyr: LEGO Star Wars (2005)
48. Nintendo: The Legend of Zelda: A Link to the Past (1991)
49. Fandom: Top Secret Room. https://zelda.fandom.com/wiki/Top_Secret_Room

MPF Framework: An Aesthetic and Phenomenological Approach to Ludic Difficulty in Video Games

Mateo Terrasa Torres[(⊠)]

Universitat de les Illes Balears, 07122 Palma, Illes Balears, Spain
mateoterrasatorres@gmail.com

Abstract. Challenge is an intrinsic part of play. From the academy it is presented as one of the basic elements of its language, as a set of obstacles that oppose the player's advancement and, at the same time, as a motivator to achieve personal triumph. In this sense, the domination of the ludic system is related to the set of rules that make it up and the mechanics that give agency to the player. But challenge can also be shown differently, as an hermeneutic obstacle or ethical decisions, such as narrative puzzles, disempowerment fantasies or the feeling of vertigo. All these elements are fundamental pieces of the challenge in a broad sense and constitute the ludic difficulty aesthetics. This phenomenological study of video game addresses the question of ludic difficulty from personal perception and experience, that is, of every significant element for the construction of the game aesthetics. From this perspective, the ludic difficulty aesthetics consists of the rules system, the player's performance, and the fictional elements that contextualize the gameplay. As a result, we present the aesthetic and phenomenological MPF framework for the analysis of ludic difficulty and challenge, which is divided into three different and interconnected patterns: mechanics, performance and fiction.

Keywords: Challenge · Difficulty · Experience · Mechanics · Performance · Fiction

1 Introduction

Challenge is often presented in academia as an intrinsic part of the language of games, of its aesthetics. It is the opposing force in the face of the player's advancement through the ludic text, a set of obstacles set to make him fail [1], but at the same time exert a motivating impetus to achieve personal triumph or *fiero* [2], an Italian word used by Niccole Lazzaro to talk about triumph over adversity and an important part of her theory about the emotions in play. To arouse the player's interest, the challenge requires some effort to be overcome, to achieve the domination of the ludic object. This setup of challenge, failure, effort, and triumph is one of the game's sources of fun [3]. But first, fun should not be the only relevant emotion in the ludic experience; and second, challenges in games should not be reduced to the *win/lose* binary model [4], given that this reductionism denies some of the aesthetic power of ludic language, such as its hermeneutic possibilities, political potential or feeling *vertigo* [5], abandoning

© Springer Nature Switzerland AG 2019
N. Zagalo et al. (Eds.): VJ 2019, CCIS 1164, pp. 32–45, 2019.
https://doi.org/10.1007/978-3-030-37983-4_3

oneself to sensations and enjoyment. Any challenge means much more than the pursuit of personal triumph and domination. It can entail, for instance, a disempowerment fantasy in games where the player has many impediments to his advancement or can get away from fun-related emotions, with works seeking greater emotional complexity through sadness, pain or boredom.

This paper seeks to deepen these ideas and nuance them, in order to widen the concept of ludic difficulty and the video game itself. This is a phenomenological study of video games, since these are mediated experiences in which a multitude of internal and external elements come together, they do "not solely rely on what we feel, see, and interpret" [6].

This study proposes a framework for ludic difficulty aesthetics based on three ludic patterns that encompass the same significant fields of ludic experience: the rules of the game, the player's performance, and the fictional world. From these three elements, referred to as *Mechanics*, *Performance* and *Fiction* or *MPF*, an analysis framework is built open to all kinds of video game creations, whether considered traditionally difficult or not. In this tripartite model, its elements are not closed, nor are they built around impassable walls, but rather they are imbricated with each other. Thus, this paper aims to nuance the meaning of ludic challenge and difficulty and expand its scope, locating the tropes and ludic motifs that allow to create a language around this particular element of ludic aesthetics.

2 Background

As already mentioned, challenge is considered one of the axes of play. Salen and Zimmerman [7] explain that "A game is a system in which the player engages in an artificial conflict, defined by the rules and with a quantifiable result". Suits [8] states that the rules give the least efficient means in order to reach a specific state. And Avedon and Sutton-Smith [9] talk about opposition between forces and unbalanced results, that is, a conflict between game and player, where the former proposes a series of rules and systems that the latter accepts with a lusory attitude. This conception of challenge is closely linked to the concept of the obstacle, since they are a central system element that stands between the player and his desirable states and propose a skill or cognitive challenge. From this perspective, the aesthetic experience of video games is understood mainly from its ludic characteristics: the mechanics, dynamics and design. This kind of classic challenge can be seen in video games like *Cuphead* [10], which recovers retro mechanics where the player's ability and accuracy are essential, and mistakes are severely punished, but renew the art and visuals, bringing games closer to contemporaneity.

But a multitude of elements participate in the ludic experience. When the academic Anable [11] talks about video game aesthetics she does not refer to a particular aspect of games, but a method to identify the affective relationships created between and through the video game image, sound, mechanics, hardware, algorithms and players. To understand its potential, the representation and computing, or the display and the code, should not be separated. The imbrication between image and mechanics, between symbol and action, is the central axis of the video game, its expressive capacity.

Therefore, accepting that all these elements are part of the gaming experience means they also affect the challenge as a source of ludic difficulty. The obstacles are governed by the rules and the ludofictional world, that is, they have guidelines configured based on the rules, but also by fiction, which envelops the rules and gives a context to the player. Challenges should then include those understood as artificial conflict and opposing force to advance to a desired state, any fictional or hermeneutic element that fulfils that function. In this sense, a desired state can be discovering how the plot develops and the relationship between the protagonists of *The Last of Us* [12] evolves, more than overcome the combats with a bunch of enemies. In a narrative-driven game like *Life is Strange* [13], for example, the player advances through the game exploring the spaces and resolving simple puzzles, normally involving the time travel ability of the protagonist. But the main characteristic of *Life is Strange* is the dialogues with the NPC's, and the forking-path narrative constructed by the actions of the player. So, most obstacles are based on dialogue trees. Selecting the most convenient option depending on the player's role and interests is a narrative and interpretative challenge and, therefore, an obstacle. This makes us think that challenges can also be conceived as a narrative and hermeneutic aspect, of emotional involvement, of understanding the plot and of the implicit meanings. Therefore, these fictional and narrative elements represent an important part of the ludic difficulty aesthetics.

The other axis of the ludic experience is the player. Salen and Zimerman [14] explains that "the experience of play is not something that a game designer directly creates (...) The game designer creates a set of rules, which the player inhabits, explore and manipulate (...) the game designer only indirectly designs the player experience by directly designing the rules". The ludic experience belongs to the subjective and personal field of the player. Navarro-Remesal [15] similarly speaks of "mental processes", which make the experience "intangible and difficult to describe". Klastrup [16] writes that the ludic experience "deals with aspects of design, of gameplay, of aesthetics, as well as with the social and cultural framing of the player that takes place within a given gameworld". Returning to Navarro-Remesal, he says that "Each player has a different profile, preferences and context; combining these with the ludic system creates a unique and personal experience". Then, the difficulty of a game is a personal experience, more complex than a designed challenge with a specific result. The player, then, understands the challenge based on her previous experiences and expectations, and interpret the experience itself from her subjective framework.

One of the main features of ludic difficulty aesthetics is ludic suffering and other negative emotions. The survival/strategy game *This War of Mine* [17] places the player as civilians who must survive in the middle of war. The player must spend the last days of war protecting his refuge, maintaining both physical and mental health of the survivors and looting resources and food, which can become a conflict with other survivors, not necessarily violent but moral. This game moves away from the power fantasies that war games usually evoke, taking away almost all the destructive power and making all our decisions have consequences in our community and those around us. This game evokes feelings like sadness, pain, and hopelessness, and the decisions we are forced to make place us on a moral grey scale rarely seen in other war games. As Sicart [18] "play is not necessarily fun. It is pleasurable, but the pleasures it creates are not always submissive to enjoyment, happiness, or positive traits. Play can be pleasurable when it hurts, offends, challenges us and teases us, and even when we are not playing". And the source if that kind of pleasure maybe due to a high-difficult challenge, from complex narratives or situations of doubtful morality. In fact, Sicart itself or Ruberg [19] advocate the expansion, complication and variety of emotions linked to video games. Sicart says that "Let's not talk about play as fun but as pleasurable, opening us to the immense variations of pleasure in this world".

The ludic suffering is one of these negative emotions that video games evokes. Navarro-Remesal [20] argues that video games "make us want the game state to be other than what it is. They also demand some effort from us. These are the bases of our ludic suffering, and from them we can suffer with the character (a vicarious experience), as the character (a ludonarrative experience), and as players (a ludic experience)". The player, says Navarro-Remesal, can suffer, provoke suffering, or alleviate it, and this suffering can arise from any game element. In Fumito Ueda's game *Shadow of the Colossus* [21], one of the elements of difficulty is how the death of the colossi affect the player. The player turns into a murderer who generates suffering in the peaceful colossi that inhabit the world and the world itself. And the world responds by generating suffering in the player herself, with audiovisual resources, like the melancholic music or the after-death animation of the colossi, where the soul of the beast becomes part of the player, transforming his physical state.

In this sense, Bown [22] introduces the Lacanian concept of *Jouissance* to the studio of video games to talk about the emotions that border on pleasure and pain. These types of negative emotions arise both from the rules of the game, like obstacles, puzzles or enemies, as well as from the performance of the player, executing agent of the actions that advance the ludic text, and the fictional elements, like the construction of an emotional bond from dramatic construction. *Bloodborne* [23] is a video game known for its high difficulty and punitive design. It's a difficult game in a traditional way, since it demands the players effort and skill and harshly punishes failure through repetition dynamics and tortuous paths, searching a save point or a new shortcut that facilitates the navigation through the world. But it's not only difficult because its punitive design, but also because its sad and fatalistic atmosphere, the obscure narration and the desolation and abandonment of the player by a system that she does not understand. *Bloodborne*'s challenge is connected to both skill and hermeneutics, creating an almost masochistic relationship between the game, or designer, and the player, thus oscillating between power and disempowerment, between pain and pleasure, and becoming, rather, a pleasurable pain.

Bown [24] talks about "sadomasochistic oscillation" to refer to that feeling between the active and the passive, the pleasure that arises between having power and losing it, between controlling a situation and getting carried away with it. Bown refers to the survival horror genre, like *Silent Hill* [25] or *Dead Space* [26], to reflect on this dynamic, since "the player is usually weaponless and passive, unable to do anything except run and hide, reversing the traditionally active pleasure of gaming". This can relate to Roger Caillois conception of the feeling of *vertigo*, of abandoning oneself to the sensations and ludic pleasures, which do not have to be positive, leaving aside the obsession with control and domination. With these words, Bown refers to one aesthetical principle of the ludic difficulty: the *disempowerment fantasy*. In this aesthetic configuration, the player controls a vulnerable character, with a few resources for defence and attack, has a labyrinthine structure, in addition to dealing with a dark and nightmarish atmosphere, and treats sad and painful issues.

3 MPF Framework

The MPF is a phenomenological framework for the critical analysis of ludic difficulty in games that allows the understanding of this element from a broader and more inclusive perspective. The MPF framework moves away from those approaches centred on the classic challenge and difficulty centred on the player's skill. This phenomenological model allows the introduction of the figure of the player as an agent that brings with it a series of knowledge, habits and skills that modify the understanding and execution of the ludic text into the scheme of classic difficulty. It is a framework that highlights the uniqueness of the player. It also introduces the fictional factors that contextualize mechanics and rules, offers a narrative and affects that modulate and direct, to a greater or lesser extent, the ludic experience.

The MPF framework is a tripartite framework like the MDA [27]. These two frameworks share one of its components, the *mechanics*, and take the role of the player as essential in the construction of the ludic experience. In addition, both dynamics and aesthetics are intrinsic part of the MPF framework, but not as defined components. The main difference between these two frameworks is that MPF departs from the purely formal approach of the MDA to build a phenomenological framework.

In addition, the approach to video games of the MPF framework, due to its experiential condition, configures a direct relationship between its different components instead of linear one like MDA. In the MDA framework, the mechanics are embedded in the dynamics, which are "the run-time behaviour of the mechanics acting on player inputs and each other's outputs over time". While these directly relate to the aesthetics, "the desirable emotional responses evoked in the player, when she interacts with the game system". The relationship in this model is linear or bidirectional, depending on the perspective, the designer, "the mechanics give rise to dynamic system behaviour, which in turn leads to particular aesthetic experiences"; and the player, "aesthetics set the tone, which is born out in observable dynamics and eventually, operable mechanics".

In the MPF framework, the relationship of each of its elements is connected straightforward to the rest. These mechanics, then, depend on the fiction that gives them an artistic and narrative context, and on the player's performance, while the player executes them, she launches the text and uses his agency depending on his context and past experiences. Fiction needs mechanics to be able to navigate its fictional universe and player performance to be interpreted and take a role within the fiction. The player integrates into and remains within a ludic universe based on the interest aroused by the game design and its fictional framework. It is a tripartite model of imbricated and interdependent elements that highlights the relevance of all the pieces that build the ludic experience, that is, its aesthetics.

The MPF framework, as already mentioned, is divided, into three defining elements of the ludic experience, the mechanics, the performance, and the fiction. These three elements are, in turn, divided into a group of patterns that describe the relation with the difficulty aesthetics in depth. The next section will describe each of the aesthetics elements and their respective patters.

3.1 Mechanics

The MPF framework conceives Mechanics in the same terms as the MDA. Thus, the mechanics "describes the particular components of the game, at the level of the data representation and algorithms", that is, the system and rules of the ludic object, which defines the aesthetic experience of the game based on its ludic character, it's essential and defining characteristic. This is the interaction with the states of the ludic text and its modification through the player's agency. Hunicke et al. explains that "Mechanics are the various actions, behaviours and control mechanisms afforded to the player within a game context. Together with the game's content (levels, assets and so on) the mechanics support overall gameplay dynamics" Similarly, Fernandez-Vara [28], states that mechanics in videogames "become incarnated in the code, which is the system that enforces the rules (...) we will extend the concept of mechanics to all the formal aspects that are needed to play the game, from the rules themselves, which tell the player what she can or cannot do, to the objects needed to play the game and the space". Therefore, applying this theory to the elements that constitute the ludic difficulty, the obstacles and configurations that hinder the advance of the player in pursuit of reaching a desirable state, I propose a list of nine mechanical patterns that constitute the ludic difficulty experience:

- *vulnerability*, understood as those factors that constitute players' mortality, like the avatars life and resistance and the games over dynamic;
- the *structure*, the arrangement of those elements that make up the game world, the player's navigation through these and how the tension and rhythm of the game is built in the progress in order to achieve a desired state or objective;
- *information*, such as the elements of communication between game and player, the tools they use, like the HUD, and its opacity or clarity;
- *temporality*, including the temporary construction of its world, its temporary structures, conditions, and limitations;
- *randomness*, seen as the degree of uncertainty [29] and variability within a given structure, mainly used in game with procedural generation, and also in the degree of chance in role-playing and strategy games;
- *resources*, such as objects, power-ups and statistics usable by the player to advance in the structure of the game and through the obstacles;
- *obstacles*, such as any element of the system that stands between the player and his objectives, like puzzles, bosses or ethical decisions;
- *control*, perceived as the player's direct communication system with the ludic system through the input device, its mapping and its mechanical complexity;
- *difficulty level*, or the modification of certain elements of the system that increase or decrease the difficulty, either by the player or the system itself.

These nine mechanical patterns can then build a conceptual map of the elements that dictate the experience of ludic difficulty from regulations.

3.2 Performance

The player is at the centre of the ludic experience. Bearing this in mind, and considering design, Cook [30] explains that "Games are not mathematical systems. They are systems that always have a human being, full of desires, excitement and immense cleverness, sitting smack dab in the centre". According to Navarro-Remesal [31], the player, "at the very moment he starts playing, becomes the driving force of the system, located in a specific environment and combining the elements of the central system (…) Previous experiences are part of the player's profile and environment, so the video game's super-system is built as a feedback cycle". The player and his experiences are part of the game and make it unique. Upton [32] thinks of games as a system of constraints, a game element that "emphasizes the deliberate nature of the boundaries of play space". Not only are they imposed from the rules, the player's performance also involves a series of constraints. Any line of action that is privileged over another implies a limitation (constraint), so our own role as players within the game world, our own experience or social situation also assume, Upton argues [33], a limitation. Our knowledge, both about the environment and our personal experiences, represent limits, translatable in generic expectations or conventions, which Upton calls pre-existing constraints.

The player's context is other essential element for the gaming experience, since this influences the player and, therefore, the game. Crawford and Muriel [34] explain that "everything was happening inside a determined space, a social one, where the experience could be altered at any moment". The elements surrounding the player modify the ludic experience, revealing "the complexities behind the articulation of a gaming experience; making explicit the socially and physically embedded reality that it is", as Muriel and Crawford claim.

The figure of the player within the ludic difficulty aesthetics is called performance since it encompasses a whole academic tradition very useful to describe who, how and where she acts and modifies a ludic text. As Fernández-Vara [35] states: "Performance studies devotes itself to the study of how human action takes place and in what context. In semiotic terms, the field deals with performance as a process of making meaning on the part of the originators of the activity and their audience". Fernández-Vara adds that "the performance space is represented on the screen and does not exist in the real world. However, the videogame space must also extend beyond the screen (…) Videogame players are thus both performers and spectators (…) Thus, there is a multiplicity of aspects that define the space involved in videogames as performance, from the represented space on the screen, to the physical space the player is occupying (…). The transitions and negotiations between these aspects are part of the process of 'making meaning' that takes place during the performance". The players' agency in the world is one of the keys of meaning-making videogames. Moreover, for Fernández-Vara, "The player is on the side of the aesthetics, since she is the one who experiences the game. (…) The look-and-feel of the game and specific triggered events are also part of the experience of the player as spectator of her own interaction". The player operates both as spectator and agent, and this specific nature of video game language should be integrated into the performance patterns.

By applying this argument to the elements that constitute the ludic difficulty from the player's perspective, I propose another list that reflects those performance patterns that constitute and modify the difficulty ludic aesthetics:

- the player's *knowledge*, both internal and external to the game world, which may be relevant in the future of the playthrough;
- *preferences* or personal taste, since they define what the player plays and how she plays, favourite genres and themes, his ideas and emotions, his involvement and dedication or the focus (agenda) of the game;
- the player's *analytical* ability is relevant in both intellectual challenge and action games;
- *skill* at the controls, in a language so focused on action and challenge, is essential and therefore seems to be the only relevant thing. Although I have considered this for the present study, I have put it in context with other issues that concern the player within the game;
- the player's *perception* within the context in which the game occurs which should be considered, since the game is never given within a vacuum of optimal conditions. This would also influence the context of creating a work;
- understanding of the work in a *hermeneutic* sense, that is, the discursive capacity of a work and the meanings that a player, given his background, can extract from that work;
- the *identity* of the player within the game universe, both in the sense of restoring behaviours when it comes to taking a pre-set role, and playing a role decided by the player herself.

These seven performance patterns can define how a player is and how his background, context and skills influence the experience of ludic difficulty.

3.3   Fiction

The last element that shapes the aesthetics of video-ludic difficulty is fiction, which surrounds and frames the design and mechanics and offers a context to the player, building the game world. Considering fictional elements as a source of ludic difficulty, the concept of *non-mechanical difficulty* is introduced into this study to refer to the moments of difficulty whose source is not in the mechanics, but rather in other elements such as narrative, ethics or hermeneutics. Non-mechanical aspects in the game affect the ludic experience and are therefore part of the perception of difficulty. The non-mechanical aspects of difficulty are not the same as the "passive interactivity" describe by Zagalo, Torres and Branco [36], though it shares with it a focus on the design of difficult ludic emotions.

In video games it is preferable to talk about fiction, since "(n)or all video games tell stories or do in traditional modes" [37]. But, like Navarro-Remesal argues "Even if it doesn't try to tell a story, every video game contains fictional elements: a world with its own rules, objects and/or subjects that inhabit it, a time of its own". So, in this framework we talk about fiction in the same terms that Antonio J. Planells uses the concept *fictional world* [38] or Linderoth [39] uses *guise*, that's it, the whole of the game-world, the narrative and the characters built on the system. That is, the concept of fiction refers to everything that surrounds the game system, which gives a narrative and artistic context, offering a reference framework to the player beyond the system itself, regulations and ludic patterns. Fiction, as considered in this article, is the representational aspect of the designer's ideas, which builds the universe in which the player acts, gives a reason to be to mechanics, regulation and level design and builds much of the emotional framework of the player. Fiction in the game is built on artistic finish, narrative, thematic and atmosphere. From this set of elements and its relationship with the regulations, the player's universe of action is built, the margins in which she can move and where she will build his ludic experience.

The fictional world, then, is essential when talking about the ludic difficulty aesthetics. In this case, four fictional patterns have been detected that can influence the experience of the difficulty, which could be defined as non-mechanical difficulty. With this in mind, I have configured four fictional patterns that constitute the fictional way for the ludic difficulty aesthetics:

- the *narrative*, how the game counts its ideas and how it transmits them to the player, what tools and narrative spaces, the camera positions in the world and the *mise-en-scéne* it uses and how it all relates to mechanics and design;
- the *art*, such as the representational apparatus of the game, its audio-visual elements, the art direction and technology used to contextualize the rules and attract the player through the senses;
- the *theme,* what the game describes, the content beyond its genre, the approach to the ideas it supports, the narrative tropes it uses and what motifs it addresses;
- the *atmosphere*, the game's tone and the emotional frame, the environment which in his world unfolds, its textures and the sensations and affects it conveys.

Although it could be modified in future studies, from these four fictional patterns a map of significant elements is configured in the construction of the ludic difficulty aesthetics and how these interrelate with the mechanics and the player.

4 Case Study

This framework, despite dealing with the aesthetics of ludic difficulty, is not only applicable to difficult games, given that difficulty, as an experience, is subjective and cannot be assumed in specific games. As shown, there are many elements that conform the ludic difficulty aesthetics, therefore, any video game can have elements of difficulty, even if it is not a challenge in the traditional way. Thus, the MPF is applicable to games considered as difficult as *Darkest Dungeon* [40] or narrative games such as the walking simulator *What Remains of Edith Finch* [41]. This selection of video games is made with the wide application of the framework in mind.

In the first example, *Darkest Dungeons*, it is a turn-based SRPG that combines resource management phases and exploration and combat phases, with bleak atmosphere and dark visual aesthetics. First, we will apply the *mechanics* patterns of this game. In *Darkest Dungeons*, the *vulnerability* is designed to deal with the mortality of the characters, a bunch of mercenaries with different characteristics and backgrounds. Players face a game with very vulnerable characters, both physically and mentally, in a permadeath design. This permadeath design "is the permanent loss of a character with no option to respawn or retrieve the character in any way" [42]. The loss of the characters becomes significant since it is definitive and hire the services of more mercenaries is expensive. The loss of the characters cannot only come from death in combat, something very common since their resistance is minimal, but they can be affected by mental illnesses that make them useless resources. As in other SRPG with permadeath, the characters are considered as *resources*, which in this case must be paid with a salary. Then, the main resources are money and mercenaries, in addition with the buildings that we must upgrade in the resource management phase. In this sense, the *structure* of the game splits in two phases: the aforementioned resource management, in which mercenaries are hired and healed, and the village where they reside is managed; and the exploration and combat phase, where mercenaries are sent to a series of randomly generated dungeons. This *randomness* gives the game uncertainty and variability -and also establishes it in the roguelike genre, characterised by the randomness, among others aspects- which combined with the *obstacles*, which take the form of enemies and traps, along with final bosses in the bigger dungeons, configure the main challenge source. The enemies and traps cause a lot of damage and getting an acceptable amount of resources demands a lot of effort and sacrifice. The player must deal with a lot of features and has a minimum *information* to deal with it. Like other turn-based games, don't demand a lot of skill, but the *control* changes a lot depending on the input device, be it the controller, keyboard and mouse or the touch screen. In any case, it does not mean a great difficulty level change. The game has a *difficulty* selector with three levels that affects the objectives and the duration of the campaign. These three levels affect the *temporary* construction of the world, whit a harder objectives in less time in the third level, which means greater temporary pressure. All of these *mechanical* patterns build a disempowering phantasy, among a *sadomasochistic oscillation* in the Alfie Bown terms.

The *performance* patterns will be the following that we apply. The player's *knowledge* constitutes the first obstacle, since depending on this, the player has more tools to face the difficulties. If the player has knowledge in genres like SRPG, RPG or strategy games, such as roguelike, it has a great advantage over the player who lacks it. The *preferences* in these genres defines the player's approach to the game. The *analytical* ability is more relevant in Darkest Dungeon than the *skills* at the control. In this sense, the most cautious and strategic player has an advantage over the others. And the focus on exploration or management can make the playthrough a bigger challenge. The player needs to focus at many parameters and statistics, so his *perception* of the game universe must be in the data above the world itself, although this is also relevant since the design of the enemies offers a lot of information. In an *hermeneutic* sense, the game has a lot to offer at the players who enjoy dark fantasy, an the discourses about death, futility and corruption of the world. The last pattern have to do with *identity*, which affects the role of the player in the world and how he approaches the challenge, given that there is no role that directs the course of the game or conditions the player's performance like in a character-driven game.

Finally, we will analyse the *fictional* and *non-mechanical* patterns of *Darkest Dungeon*. The *narrative* elements are opaque, reduced to a few brief descriptions, the narrator's gloomy narration and the diary that describes the events of the town. The lateral camera perspective in the dungeons approaches the characters when they attack and are attacked, showing their painful faces when they are affected by some evil. This lateral perspective approaches the bodies of the mercenary group, creating an oppressive environment with a few resources. The *art* of the game reinforces this idea with the dark aesthetics reminiscent of the comic book artist Mike Mignola. All these aspects built a gloomy and sad *atmosphere*, conveying the fatality and hopelessness of the world, that maybe it shouldn't be saved. The *themes* that *Darkest Dungeon* deals with support these fictional aspects, since we could detect their themes in death, disease, madness, the demonic and the human fragility when faces the unknown. All these elements, regardless of all the factors, makes the aesthetic ludic difficulty of this game. The disempower fantasy shown from the mechanics is intertwined with fictional factors that reinforce the desolation of the world, the suffering and effort that demands both player and characters, and the almost masochistic relationship between player and game.

The second example, *What Remains of Edith Finch*, is a narrative driven game encompassed within the walking simulator genre. It is a video game that traces the history of a family marked by fatality and death. The conceptual map that *mechanical* patterns built in this game differs from the previous, since the difficulty elements come from its plot's complexity, which transforms a family home into its sad history. In *What Remains of Edith Finch* the player cannot die in the sense of the death and resurrection loop. The character is not *vulnerable* in mechanical sense. The game world *structure* is linear despite the complex architecture of the family home, that reflects the complexities of the family. The home space can be explored with a simple *control* scheme, but depending on the room, belonging to a deceased family member, the game modifies its mechanics. This is a metagame in which each story modifies its mechanics, and these have a meaning with the told story. These mechanical changes are the few *obstacles* that the player can find, since the game communicates to the player all the necessary *information*, lacks *randomness*, *resources* and *difficulty level*, and *temporality* don't affect in a mechanical sense.

On the *performance* level, the game demands to the player a lot of ludic background and *knowledge* to understand the complexity of its discourse and its relations with mechanics. The game demands also a *preference* for narrative video games, with a marked literary character and slow gaming [43], devoid of challenge in a classic sense. Given this lack of challenge and the simple control scheme, the game only demands a basic *skill* level. It does not happen the same at an *hermeneutic* and *analytical* level, since this is where there is the major complexities of the game, in the interweaving between mechanics and meanings, its 'alterbiography' [44]. In this sense, the game demands the player's *perception* to look at the space details that evoke the family's story. At last, since the game poses a very personal history, although the gaze of several family members throughout its history, the player takes this multiple *identity*. As in a history-driven game, the player express herself through the restoration of behaviour. The relation between game and player is, in this case, more emotional and empathy based with the character and the remnants that still inhabit the family home.

As a narrative-driven game, the fictional patterns of *What Remains of Edith Finch* has a great relevance. The main *narrative* tools that the game uses, in addition to a voice-over narrator and the text that integrate in the space, is the game space and the vicarious experiences it evokes. In these memories, the character remembers the last moments of the life of his relatives and change the mechanics, modifying the meanings and the narrative itself. Even the *art* is modified in these memories, moving away from realism and entering the realm of dreams, of the evocative. The atmosphere is *melancholic*, and the *themes* are the death and destiny, home and family, memories and dreams. These fictional patterns reflect the narrative complexity of the game, the narrative layers that build its speech and the interweaving between mechanics and meaning. Then, the difficulty of the game comes from its hermeneutic complexity and emotional involvement with a character who cannot escape his fateful destiny.

These two examples show how the MPF framework is applied to two opposite ludic proposals. Both show how the skill challenges are not essential for the difficulty aesthetics, being able to be shown as interpretative, analytical or hermeneutical challenges. They also show how the fictional elements, such as the atmosphere and the themes, are essential for the ludic experience and the perception of difficulty.

5 Conclusions

The analysis of these two case studies has shown the relevance of the three elements that built the MPF framework. They also reveal some motifs present throughout these games as well as in the games mentioned in the 'Background' section. Thus, *death* is one of the main motifs of ludic difficulty aesthetics, as the examples in the present study show to different degrees: either as the destiny that runs the *Finch* family history or the *permadeath* of the mercenaries in *Darkest Dungeon*. In the same way, *suffering* or *mental illness* and *physical* and *emotional pain* are examples of fictional motifs in most of the given games. In *Darkest Dungeon* the *mental illness* and *physical* and *emotional pain* are also presented as mechanical through altered states that affect the vulnerability of the characters. The *terrifying* and *nightmarish* atmospheres could also be considered fictional and mechanical motifs in games like *Darkest Dungeon* or *Silent Hill* and *Dead Space*, since the representation of the enemies and game spaces affect the design of challenge.

One main motif, found in both *Darkest Dungeon* and *What Remains of Edith Finch* or the rest of the spoken games, is the vulnerable condition of the player through the game world, that is, the *disempowering fantasy*. In the first example, as in *Bloodborne* or the terror games, the player has a lot of power, but the world is so aggressive and punishing that it remains insufficient. In the second example and *Life is Strange*, the powerlessness comes from the mundanity of the characters and situations, away from the powerful characters so common in video games. Even when the main character of *Life is Strange* has the power to travel in time, the situations she faces do not differ from those shown in any teenager fiction.

Other motifs of ludic difficulty aesthetics are *guilt* and *moral decisions*, as proven by *Shadow of the Colossus* and *This War of Mine*, or the *narrative complexity* of *What Remains of Edith Finch*, where the narrative and mechanical layers are intertwined, demanding from the player analytical and hermeneutic abilities to deploy and understand their meanings. The ludic text *implication* becomes another motif seen, mainly but not exclusively, in narrative and character-driven games. This implication with the text depends on the way that the player faces the ludic text, although the affects that it evokes also depend on its fictional and mechanical design. A player can face *This War of Mine* as a management game regardless of morals, while others will maintain a balance between morals and survival. The last motif is shown in the player's relation with the ludic text. The *sadomasochistic oscillation* establishes a significant dynamic between power and disempowerment for the understanding of the ludic difficulty aesthetics.

This paper has outlined the MPF framework for the aesthetic and hermeneutical analysis of ludic difficulty through its theoretical basis with descriptions of the tripartite framework and its patterns. Through this analytic framework, this paper provides a tool that can highlight the multiplicity of the ludic experience and its challenges, moving away from the focus on rules, mechanics and players' skills. The MPF framework has a focus on non-mechanical and fictional elements. These motifs, together with the ludic system and the active participation of the player, create a complex ludic experience that is greater than traditional understandings of just challenge-based difficulty.

References

1. Juul, J.: The Art of Failure: An Essay on the Pain of Playing Video Games. The MIT Press, Massachusetts (2013)
2. Lazzaro, N.: Why We Play Games: Four Keys to More Emotion Without Story, p. 3 (2004)
3. Juul, J.: Without a goal: on open and expressive games. In: Krzywinska, T., Atkins, B. (eds.) Videogame/Player/Text. Manchester University Press, Manchester (2007)
4. Costikyan, G.: Uncertainty in Games, p. 11. The MIT Press, Massachusetts (2013)
5. Caillois, R.: Los juegos y los hombres: la máscara y el vértigo. Fondo de Cultura Económica, México D.F (1986)
6. Muriel, D., Crawford, G.: Video Games as Culture. Considering the Role and Importance of Video Games in Contemporary Society. Taylor and Francis, New York, p. 109 (2018)
7. Salen, K., Zimmerman, E.: Rules of Play: Game Design Fundamentals, p. 96. The MIT Press, Cambridge (2004)
8. Suits, B.: The Grasshopper: Games, Life and Utopia, p. 34. Scottish Academic Press (1978)
9. Avedon, E.M., Sutton-Smith, B.: The Study of Games, p. 7. Wiley, New York (1981)
10. Moldenhauer, J.: Cuphead. Studio MDHR (2017)
11. Anable, A.: Playing with Feelings: Video Games and Affect, p. 122. University of Minnesota Press, Minnesota (2018)
12. Druckmann, N.: The Last of Us. Naughty Dog (2013)
13. Life is Strange. Dontnod Entertainment (2015)
14. Salen, K., Zimmerman, E.: Rules of Play: Game Design Fundamentals, p. 316. The MIT Press, Cambridge (2004)
15. Navarro-Remesal, V.: Libertad dirigida. Una gramática del análisis y diseño de videojuegos. Asociación Shangrila Textos Aparte, Santander, pp. 167–168 (2016)
16. Klastrup, L.: Why dead matters: understanding gameworld experience. J. Virtual Reality Broadcast. **4**(3), 2 (2007)
17. Wlosek, R.: This War of Mine. 11-bit studios (2014)
18. Sicart, M.: Play Matters, p. 3. The MIT Press, Massachusetts (2014)
19. Ruberg, B.: No fun: the queer potential of video games that annoy, anger, disappoint, sadden, and hurt. QED: J. GLBTQ Worldmaking **2**(2), 108–124 (2015)

20. Navarro-Remesal, V.: Regarding the (game) pain of others: suffering and compassion in videogames. In: Concerns About Video Games and The Video Games of Concern Conference, 20–22 January 2016, ITU Copenhagen (2016)
21. Ueda, F.: Shadow of the Colossus. Team ICO (2005)
22. Bown, A.: Enjoying it: Candy Crush and Capitalism, pp. 45–46. Zero Books, Hants (2015)
23. Miyazaki, H.: Bloodborne. From Software (2015)
24. Bown, A.: Playstation Dreamworld, pp. 111–112. Polity Press, Cambridge (2018)
25. Toyama, K.: Silent Hill. Team Silent (1999)
26. Robbins, B.: Dead Space. EA Redwood Shores (2008)
27. Hunicke, R., LeBlanc, M., Zubek, R.: MDA: a formal approach to game design and game research (2004)
28. Fernandez-Vara, C.: Play's the thing: a framework to study videogames as performance. In: Breaking New Ground: Innovation in Games, Play, Practice and Theory, Proceedings of DiGRA, p. 5 (2009)
29. Costikyan, G.: Uncertainty in Games. The MIT Press, Massachusetts (2013)
30. Cook, D.: The Chemistry of Game Design. Gamasutra (2007). https://www.gamasutra.com/view/feature/129948/the_chemistry_of_game_design.php?page=2. Accessed 30 July 2019
31. Navarro-Remesal, V.: Libertad dirigida. Una gramática del análisis y diseño de videojuegos. Asociación Shangrila Textos Aparte, Santander, p. 32 (2016)
32. Upton, B.: The Aesthetic of Play, p. 16. The MIT Press, Massachusetts (2015)
33. Upton, B.: Situational Game Design, pp. 14–21. Taylor & Francis Group, Boca Raton (2018)
34. Muriel, D., Crawford, G.: Video Games as Culture. Considering the Role and Importance of Video Games in Contemporary Society. Taylor and Francis, New York, p. 108 (2018)
35. Fernandez-Vara, C. Play's the thing: a framework to study videogames as performance. In: Breaking New Ground: Innovation in Games, Play, Practice and Theory. Proceedings of DiGRA, pp. 1–6 (2009)
36. Zagalo, N., Torres, A., Branco, V.: Passive interactivity, an answer to interactive emotion. In: Harper, R., Rauterberg, M., Combetto, M. (eds.) ICEC 2006. LNCS, vol. 4161, pp. 43–52. Springer, Heidelberg (2006). https://doi.org/10.1007/11872320_6
37. Navarro-Remesal, V.: Libertad dirigida. Una gramática del análisis y diseño de videojuegos. Asociación Shangrila Textos Aparte, Santander, pp. 25–26 (2016)
38. Planells, A.: Videojuegos y mundos de ficción: De Super Mario a Portal. Ediciones Cátedra, Madrid (2015)
39. Linderoth, J.: Making sense of computer games: learning with new artefacts. In: International Conference on Toys, Games and Media, London University, Institute of Education (2002)
40. Sigman, T.: Darkest Dungeon. Red Hook Studios (2016)
41. Bell, C.: What Remains of Edith Finch. Giant Sparrow (2017)
42. Copcic, A., McKenzie, S., Hobbs, M.: Permadeath: a review of literature. In: 2013 IEEE International Games Innovation Conference (IGIC) (2013)
43. Navarro-Remesal, V.: Slow gaming, notas para un juego de la contemplación. O magazine (2017). https://abcdefghijklmn-pqrstuvwxyz.com/es/slow-gaming-notas-juego-la-contemplacion/. Accessed 04 Oct 2019
44. Calleja, G.: In-Game: From Immersion to Incorporation. The MIT Press, Massachusetts (2011)

Rules of Videogames and Controls
in Digital Societies

Su Hyun Nam[(⊠)]

Syracuse University, Syracuse, NY 13210, USA
snam03@syr.edu

Abstract. Rules in games are one of the most significant aspects to characterize games, and they allow players to temporarily live in a virtual world, which is separated from the real world. The author questions how the implication of rules in games has been altered based on the transformation of their forms from analog to digital. Furthermore, this paper analyzes rules and controls in contemporary technological societies by focusing on how video games are constructed as well as how contemporary game players experience them in the digital space.

Keywords: Rules · Magic circle · Videogames · Digital societies · Controls

1 Introduction

Playing games is an inherently social activity, as participants interact with each other by following rules, getting rewarded and making free choices. The rules of games define what is allowed and disallowed, set limitations and order, and differentiate between the inside world of the game and the outside world. Game play temporarily separates participants from ordinary life, forming a boundary, which is called the "magic circle".[1] Despite the apparent boundaries between the inside and outside world of a game, play still exists within - or even has engendered – the larger framework of society, which in many ways resembles game play.[2] In digital societies, game worlds and ordinary life are almost indistinguishable because of the integration not merely of virtual and real space like Augmented Reality on the technical level, but also of game elements and everyday activities on the socio-economic level. These activities range

---

[1] Dutch historian Johan Huizinga coined the term the "magic circle" in Homo Ludens: A Study of the Play-Element in Culture (1938). He wrote: "All play moves and has its being within a play-ground marked off beforehand either materially or ideally, deliberately or as a matter of course.... The arena, the card-table, the magic circle, the temple, the stage, the screen, the tennis court, the court of justice, etc., are all in form and function play-grounds, i.e., forbidden spots, isolated, hedged round, hallowed, within which special rules obtain. All are temporary worlds within the ordinary world, dedicated to the performance of an act apart".

[2] "He (Huizinga) argues for a direct connection to be made between play and culture, that play is not simply something that exists within culture, but on the contrary that culture arises in and through play" Galloway (2010), p. 20.

© Springer Nature Switzerland AG 2019
N. Zagalo et al. (Eds.): VJ 2019, CCIS 1164, pp. 46–56, 2019.
https://doi.org/10.1007/978-3-030-37983-4_4

from credit card transactions for game items to gamified applications, including challenges in activity tracker applications.

Mutually agreed game rules are increasingly codified in digital media as algorithms, and the digitization of games brought about transformations in the gaming experience. As pre-digital games are often recreated in digital media, games become portable and networked. Video games engender diverse forms of interaction and expand game play into much more complex systems, networks and simulations, which operate as autonomous part of the games. Furthermore, digital games allow players to get into the magic circle without physical restrictions, and they also enlarge – or blur the boundaries of - the magic circle in the ordinary world.

Digital video games carry over characteristics from pre-digital games, such as rule-based operations and regulated player's activities, to computer-based media and they also entrain players in temporary artificial systems. Code and algorithms in video games are subsumed under digital societies, in which computer-based, networked control systems liberate and simultaneously regulate cultural systems. Individuals become sampled "dividuals", as Deleuze noted, in highly networked and technological societies regulated through protocological control.[3] Individuals also become more evidently codified and parameterized (as dividuals)[4] in video games - for example, a player becomes a rectangle in *Thomas is Not Alone*, or one gets to create a game character from a set of selections in Role Playing Games (RPGs) such as *World of Warcraft*. Although the magic circle still separates the world inside of a video game from the real world, underlying control systems from both inside and outside of the game are built upon the same technological, computable functions and codes.

This paper identifies controls in contemporary technological societies by focusing on how video games are constructed as well as how contemporary game players experience them in the digital space. Both game rules and digital media code are voluntary regulations mutually agreed on by participants, and they are complementary and interdependent in creating a video game. Video game rules should be simultaneously understood both from traditional cultural perspectives and from programmable code in the context of technological society. I begin the discussion by clarifying the definition of terms that have seemingly close meanings – play and game. Both of the terms are more complicated than they seem and need to be more carefully interpreted. In this paper, by highlighting the distinction between play and game based on the presence of rules, I investigate the significance and function of rules in pre-digital games. As many cultural media have become digitized since the advent of personal computers, games are also increasingly developed in computer-based media, and the operation and play of video games have been transformed from that of the conventional pre-digital games. It is important to acknowledge what changes have occurred in the process of digitalizing games, in which game rules are programmed and managed by

---

[3] Galloway (2001), p. 12.

[4] Robert W. Williams explains, ""'dividual"—a physically embodied human subject that is endlessly divisible and reducible to data representations via the modern technologies of control, like computer-based systems." Williams, R. W. (2005). Politics and Self in the Age of Digital Re (pro)ducibility. Retrieved from http://www.uta.edu/huma/agger/fastcapitalism/1_1/williams.html Issue 1.1.

digital media rules. Programmed rules in video games have changed their functions and meanings from those of traditional games. I examine how codified rules in video games mimic controls of modern digital societies, and how similar control mechanisms permeate digital game play and regulate players' actions.

In control societies, as code and protocols are distributed to manage digital spaces without a central control - in sharp contrast to confinement as a means to discipline in the eighteenth and nineteenth centuries - all digital media we consume is digitized, codified and programmed behind their recognizable representation on screens. Digital media uses code and protocol to maintain control over populations, and game play is one expression of control. This paper investigates contemporary technological societies through video games, which are separated from the real world yet mirror the networked digital culture in artificial systems for play.

2 Game and Play

A game is meaningful only once it is played. Unlike mass media such as literature, film or television are read and watched, video games are experienced through actions[5], and those gaming actions are play. Gaming and playing are often regarded as similar forms of activities, both of which we voluntarily engage to seek for pure entertainment and enjoyment. However, game theorists distinguish ontological, epistemological and experiential differences between game and play, and such clarification on those abstract concepts will help guide which aspects of games I focus on in this paper.

The relationship between these two words, play and game, is complex and unsettled. Play can be a subset of games when it represents one aspect of games like gameplay, however, games can be also a subset of play when play describes a distinct form of activities, including free play and rule-based games.[6] In both cases, play seems as a more open and abstract concept than game, while game clearly refers to restricted and rule-based systems designed to achieve goals. Johann Huizinga provided the definition of play in his book Homo Ludens, published as early as 1938, as "a free activity standing quite consciously outside "ordinary" life as being "not serious," but at the same time absorbing the player intensely and utterly." Although his popular concept the "magic circle," in which normal rules of reality and ordinary life are suspended when one participates in games (or rituals), remains still influential in game studies and theories, his definition does not distinguish between game and play. While his work is widely employed as a theoretical foundation, game theorists have attempted to elaborate on those words of play and game and their distinction. The distinction is not meant to separate them, but to fundamentally confirm the cultural legitimacy of games as one of the most influential media in contemporary societies by understanding their roles and examining the impacts of game and play.

---

[5] Galloway notes, "If photographs are images, and films are moving images, then video games are actions." Galloway (2010), p. 2.

[6] Salen and Zimmerman discuss the relationship of game and play in Rules of games (2010).

The most notable elements to distinguish games from play are the rules of games. David Parlett discusses two different kinds of games, informal and formal. Formal games have "ends" to achieve an objective and means – an agreed set of equipment and of procedural "rules".[7] While play has always been essential to societies, as it has been increasingly integrated with a cultural medium, its formal structure and rules, which are the foundation to forming the gamic structure, became more critical than pure entertainment in the definition of games and play. By extensively examining definitions provided by philosophers and theorists, Salen and Zimmerman suggest their own definition of a game as "a system in which players engage in an artificial conflict, defined by rules, that results in a quantifiable outcome." Rules are fundamental properties of formal games beyond the pure pursuit of enjoyment, as they lead participants to act and play in a determined manner while playing games.

3 Rules in Games

Rules are the key factors to differentiate games from other kinds of play, because they impose limits to keep players inside the artificial world.[8] What are the game rules that separate us temporarily from ordinary life? Different sets of rules in games form unique identities between various types of games.[9] Therefore, while game rules share some fundamental traits, they have divergent forms in different games. As games themselves are imagined and artificial worlds, what they can be is unlimited, and it is difficult to define the scope and standard of game rules in general. In this discussion, Salen and Zimmerman's list of characteristics of rules in games provide a concrete framework – *Rules limit player action, and rules are explicit and unambiguous, shared by all players, fixed, binding, and repeatable.*[10] By focusing on commonly shared characteristics of conventional game rules – despite the fact that they cannot always be true to all games – based on Salen and Zimmerman's list and extending their discussion, I identify the significant roles of rules in games and examine how they distinguish artificial systems of gaming from the real world.

The primary role of game rules is to limit player action. Unlike free play without rules, games have a set of instructions that clarify what is allowed and disallowed, deciding who will be the winner and loser in the fictitious world, and stipulating when the world ends. As player action is temporarily controlled by the freely accepted rules, social norms and cultural customs in the reality are disregarded, and new formal systems, orders, and player relationships emerge in a game and vanish after the game – without affecting the real world. Rules also provide a different meaning and purpose to objects, signs and colors, which normally have different meanings (or no meaning) in ordinary life – for example, a 'Joker' card in *Uno* gives the player the power to change

---

[7] Davis (2013), p. 62.

[8] Marc Prensky's Digital Game-Based Learning, quoted in Salen and Zimmerman (2010), Chapter 11, p. 4.

[9] Parlett (1999), "'Every game has its rules,' says Huizinga in Homo Ludens. But we may go further, and say, 'Every game is its rules,' for they are what define it."

[10] Salen and Zimmerman (2010), Chapter 11, pp. 4–5.

the current color, players trade real estate with play money in *Monopoly*, signs like 'X' and 'O' represent each player in *Tic-tac-toe*, and 'love' means 'zero' in tennis. Players who voluntarily participate and submit to the fictional game world limit their action based on rules accepted by all participants. Rules in games might seem senseless in the real world, but they are the essential elements that enclose the artificial environment as a sacred playground.[11]

The set of rules properly functions as the formal structure of games when the rules are transparent, explicit and univocal, while many forms of rules in the real world are often hermeneutic in different contexts. Game worlds are regulated in limited spaces with a certain number of participants, and therefore situations occurring in games are relatively simpler and easier to manage than ones that occur in daily experiences, such as laws and legal cases. To avoid ambiguity, methods and props like a game token, board and score system are utilized in games, and players take turns in a very clear order – turns alternating between two players or going a certain direction in a circle. In *Halli Galli*, the bell in the center of the table helps the clarification of rules – a player has to ring the bell first to win the game, noticing that there are five of the same fruits on the table. This situation stands in contrast to everyday situations. For example, at a 4-way stop intersection, it is often difficult to tell precisely which vehicle reached this point first, therefore this rule has to largely rely on drivers' judgment. The magic circle of games is too fragile to afford arguments on unclear and questionable rules, which would collapse the whole game system.

On the other hand, the limited and controlled environment of game worlds makes rules flexible and transformative. It might sound contradictory to the binding, explicit and unambiguous characteristic of game rules, but as long as it is agreed and shared clearly by all players, game rules can be amended and transformed while still functioning as a rigid structure. Salen and Zimmerman note rule variants built on largely consistent rule sets in the excerpt discussing how "Rules are repeatable," giving Monopoly as an example for its different version of "Free Parking" spaces. Rules could also be adjusted to keep the game challenging or to make it playable in a certain situation, such as kids racing with adults or an odd number of players playing basketball in two teams.[12] Flexible and transformative rules are possible because the magic circle (a game world) exists only temporarily among participants who submit to the game for entertainment. The changes of rules in games do affect neither players' ordinary life nor the real world. While in pre-digital games, rules limit player action, are transparent so as to be transferrable, and are flexible enough to accommodate different situations. In video games, there is a shift to a more immutable practice of rule-making that changes the dynamic of control.

---

[11] Huizinga quoted by Salen and Zimmerman (2010), Chapter 9, p. 3.

[12] Salen and Zimmerman (2010) discuss Transformative play, Chapter 22, p. 5. Additionally, see Walter (2003).

4   Videogames

Digital and electronic games have emerged from the initial popularity of arcade games and have evolved into various formats including console games, computer games and mobile games. Videogames commonly refer to a wide range of digital games that require both programmed hardware and software, which limit the scope of the players' movement (for example, they are required to look into a digital screen during the entire play time). The introduction of computable media in games facilitated divergent formats of game play, including Role Playing Games (RPGs), Real-Time Strategy (RTS) and simulation games, and it accordingly changed the gaming experience and its landscape. Video games still absorb and separate the artificial gaming world from ordinary life with a set of rules. However, as programmed computers – both hardware (circuits) and software (code) – are indispensable in videogames, rules are no longer only shared by human players but also machines. The machine becomes another active participant in the game – which makes a single player game possible. I will explore the relationship between traditional game rules and those written in computer code. While the basic principles of game rules remain valid in video games, digital media augmented a layer of complexities in games and play. This new layer of complexity changes the player's gaming experience with codified rules as well as discloses control systems in contemporary societies.

5   Codified Game Rules

While video game rules still limit players' gaming actions, players' physical actions are more limited and reduced than in pre-digital games. As game rules are codified in video games, playing digital games is akin to playing algorithms. Explicitly defined game rules are interpreted into machine languages, which become even more regimented and univocal rules. As machine languages are mathematical and logical, a player's action becomes eventually a set of numerical data, and computer interfaces and game controllers mediate between the player's action and computable media. Programmed inputs require players to act in a certain way and control their actions without discipline. While videogame players are already transfixed in front of computer screens, their physical actions are further limited to an interface - game rules are enacted only when a player sends a digital signal through the interface, through a button pressed or a keystroke made. Furthermore, players are required to learn how to operate the programmed game system by controlling buttons with a precise timing.[13] Therefore, video game player's actions are limited by not only the game rules in the virtual space but also the programmed interface in the physical space. However, digital game players often do not realize such limitations because their minimal physical actions are amplified in digital spaces. With one button press, the game character can jump, teleport, attack enemies and do much more, and such amplified actions in video games

---

[13] For example, the list of moves in Street Fighter II shows button combinations for different actions. http://streetfighter.wikia.com/wiki/List_of_moves_in_Street_Fighter_II.

generate plausible narratives. Lev Manovich calls this "user amplification."[14] In video games, player's actions are required to move only within both game rules and algorithms, which is an apparently limiting space (Fig. 1). However, the restrained actions prevalent in the physical world can become augmented and liberated in digital spaces.

Fig. 1. The image from an eSports competition shows their limited physical movements while playing video games.

While traditional game rules should be unambiguous and transparent, rules in digital games are not always apparent to all players. In addition to the programmability, digital media is capable of storing and manipulating information. As digital media becomes the platform of games and rules become codified, it is not anymore necessary for human players to "master" rules before they fully engage in the game. Furthermore, such ambiguity of game rules is used purposefully, and exploring the hidden rules is often the primary aspect of game mechanics. Those characteristics of digital media – data storage and manipulation - engendered a unique genre such as Real-Time Strategy (RTS) games and puzzle games. Puzzle games have ambiguous rules, as their primary game play is to solve problems, recognize patterns and identify game rules. Braid, developed by Jonathan Blow in 2008, incorporates complex game mechanics that manipulate time and space, and the puzzling game rules in each level are the key features of the game play. Jenova Chen's flOw adjusts the difficulty level based on the player's ability in real time, making them realize the flow experience during the game play. Therefore, players cannot have the exact same experience of playing flOw, as the game adjusts the game mechanics based on real time data of players' capabilities. In such games, the rules' operation remains obscure in a way that allows players to focus on their experience in the game, rather than confounding them.

---

[14] Chun (2013).

Automated systems through data storage and manipulation enable complex procedures in computer games, and they make digital game rules too complicated and extensive for players to fully assimilate. Video games are preprogrammed in hardware and software leaving no space for the player to redesign the complicated game rules. While non-digital games allow a possibility to alter game rules among participants - to make it more challenging or interesting for them - computer games do not reveal their internal algorithm, which is called a "black box".[15] Video games have an advantage with their capacity to effectively hide information from players, especially in simulating war games, and such ambiguous mechanics make game play more difficult and complex. Although the complex algorithms in video games keep game rules from being altered by participants, computer game players often hack the system and cheat in game play. This new gaming culture is opposed to what Huizing and Caillois claimed that cheaters, or "spoil-sports", threaten play[16] and break the fragile "magic circle".

In online gaming communities, cheat sheets are widely shared and obtaining useful cheating data becomes a part of game play. For example, in Starcraft, fog of war – which reveals only the terrain features and hiding enemy units until the player's reconnaissance finds out - works as the game's main feature, but the commonly used cheating command "black sheep wall" uncovers the entire map. Cheating became easier in digital games, especially online games, because players play video games in physically separated spaces, connected through networked computers. Furthermore, as video games are another digital media, which is easy to duplicate and manipulate, computer-savvy players are able to hack or modify a part of the video game (mods) without understanding the entire system of a game. All variations of games, including cheating, hacking and modification, occur only on the personal level of game play, merely affecting player's personal experiences. Such alterations are normally not approved of by all participants in the game. Therefore it is different from the mutually shared and agreed transformation of rules among participants around the same table in non-digital games.

6 Video Games in Modern Digital Societies

Video games are a virtual world that exists only temporarily outside of ordinary life, but they often simulate social mechanisms and human experiences in the real world in which we reside. Although the magic circle separates the gaming world from real life, both contemporary societies of technology and video games are largely operated through computable media and digital information - digital code. As computer code becomes the basis of control in both the virtual and real world, we often find that codified rules in video games mimic control mechanisms in technological societies.

While control societies seemingly liberate people from the enclosed systems of discipline, highly networked and technological societies regulate actions and behaviors of people without confining them. Deleuze notes that freeways exemplify controls in

---

[15] Dunnigan (2010), p. xii.

[16] Galloway (2010), p. 21.

technological societies because driving on freeways seems to infinitely extend mobility, yet simultaneously the freeways perfectly control the flow of movement.[17] The interconnected digital spaces and heterogeneous systems are regulated by such a means of control, especially computer protocols in digital spaces. Drawing on the analogy of the highway system, Galloway points out how protocols became the primary means for voluntarily regulation of technologies and users in highly networked digital societies. He also notices the potency of code in digital control and notes that "these regulations always operate at the level of coding—they encode packets of information so they may be transported; they code documents so they may be effectively parsed; they code communication so local devices may effectively communicate with foreign devices."[18] Codified information and rules are distributed management systems that consistently regulate heterogeneous languages, patterns and practices without a central or decentralized control agency.

Protocols and code are already similar to game rules in terms of the participants' voluntarily regulation of their own behaviors to participate in the controlled system, and their controls in digital spaces become a fundamental foundation to video game systems. In the same way as the Internet protocols, video games, which are operated on digital computers, govern the implementation of play through various gadgets. Console games require gamers to acquire hardware as well as to understand the system to run software to play. Ian Bogost compares it to "the sex shop", because in the Play Station Network and Xbox Live console stores, "a special, committed knowledge is required even to make sense of these services. They involve special, dedicated hardware and software installation, intricate, custom-created interface grammars, and idiosyncratic interaction models".[19] The game console becomes a platform to manage the operation of the game contents. To publish a game, (qualified or registered) developers should buy the expensive game development kit (GDK), a distributed system that governs the game design process and software, and in turn it controls gamers and players through codified rules and programmed hardware. Both developers and players are required to learn protocols and rules based on code and algorithm to participate in game design and play. As a citizen of control societies, we are constantly asked to learn automated computer systems – such as self-checkout systems in a grocery store, ATM machines in a bank, and a new iOS version every year – to be part of the society. Unlike a society of discipline, people living in digital cultures are not forced to adopt themselves to a regime, yet they voluntarily engage in the regulated system.

While technology has advanced exponentially for the last few decades, human interaction with technology has been transformed dramatically since the first introduction of personal computers, and technological interaction became more natural to human experiences. Video games quickly adopt advanced and efficient processors, and video game technology leads the development of human-computer interaction. In modern video game play, players do not necessarily operate traditional computer interfaces like buttons, joysticks and keyboards. While interfaces and software

---

[17] Galloway (2010), pp. 87–88.

[18] Galloway (2001), p. 7.

[19] Bogost (2015), p. 184.

obfuscate source and machine code[20], natural user interfaces (NUI) hide even such communication devices from users. In the natural interaction with machines, we may say that we are no longer asked to act in a certain way on programmed buttons, however, natural user interfaces take an enormous amount of data and scrutinize it to render it as useable inputs for the computer system. While players are liberated from physical constrains, the minutia of their behaviors are under surveillance.

Since 2009, game console companies released action-based controllers, for examples, Kinect of Xbox 360, Motion Navigation controller of Play Station 3, and Wii remote of Nintendo. The controllers often contain different sensors including a gyroscope, accelerometer and Infra-Red sensor to read players' gestures more precisely, and Xbox Kinect even tracks the positions of players' body joints in real-time. Modern video game play could be physically more liberated at the expense of our rights to privacy, and this phenomenon mirrors our society's interaction with networked technology. A GPS system on our advanced mobile devices tracks where we go, and intelligent software analyzes patterns of our mobility. It also recognizes who we know and where we are supposed to be by reading our emails.

As interfaces hid source code in the early era of technology, in advanced technological societies natural game controllers and mobile devices – both of which become an extension of our bodies - now hide interfaces and obscure how far intelligent machines penetrate into our personal life and how collected data is used. Analyzing patterns of users' behavior, intelligent software suggests what the user might like at a certain moment and affects their decision. An intelligent surveillance system is rampant in our life including in gaming activities, and this is how we are controlled in modern digital societies.

7 Conclusion

Games are a virtual culture, in which participants voluntarily regulate the system and conform to game rules to collectively maintain the "magic circle." Although game worlds are still fictitious and temporal in video games, the existence of the magic circle's boundaries become vague as the virtual and real worlds often merge together in technological society. Streams of data unceasingly flow around us, and human activities in the real world are scrutinized at every moment in digital spaces. As video games are susceptible to changes in current digital technology, virtual game spaces manifest how citizens in modern digital societies are controlled and regulated to fit into the basis of technological culture – as parts of computable digital systems. People naturally interact with digital computers and technologies more than ever, yet intelligent machines and software further obscure their intricate mechanical operations. In the same way, simulation games are realistic not because of the high-end graphics but because of the complexities of game mechanics.[21]

---

[20] Chun (2013).

[21] Galloway (2010), Chapter 3 - Social realism.

In modern technological culture, game rules are no longer unambiguous, temporary nor limited to the game table, but are rather concurrent with the advancement of technology and transformation of controls of societies. Video games' rules - traditionally transparent and shared among all players - become puzzling and intricate, and the boundaries of game worlds become indistinguishable as video games employ control mechanisms that regulate and operate technological societies. It is critical to acknowledge that video game play is now an extension – or a part - of contemporary societies, rather than merely childish and mindless play in a temporary virtual space for pure entertainment. Digital societies are operated through a set of rules (protocols and code) that humans voluntarily established for communication with machines. As we submit ourselves to control systems in modern technological societies, we agree to participate and actively engage in this game of coevolution with digital technology.

References

Galloway, A.R.: Gaming: Essays on Algorithmic Culture. University of Minnesota Press, Minneapolis (2010)

Galloway, A.R.: Protocol, or, How Control Exists after Decentralization. The MIT Press, Cambridge (2001)

Salen, K., Zimmerman, E.: Rules of Play: Game Design Fundamentals. The MIT Press, Cambridge (2010)

Davis, M.D., Morgenstern, O.: Game Theory: A Nontechnical Introduction. Dover, Mineola (2013)

Parlett, D.: The Oxford History of Board Games. Oxford University Press, Oxford (1999)

Bogost, I.: How to Talk about Videogames. University of Minnesota Press, Minneapolis (2015)

Chun, W.H.: Programmed Visions: Software and Memory. MIT Press, Cambridge (2013)

Walther, B.K.: Playing and Gaming. Game Studies, vol. 3 (2003). http://www.gamestudies.org/0301/walther/

Dunnigan, J.F.: Wargames Handbook: How to Play and Design Commercial and Professional Wargames. Writers Club, San Jose (2010)

Table Boards

Towards a Tabletop Gaming Motivations Inventory (TGMI)

Mehmet Kosa$^{(\boxtimes)}$ ⓘ and Pieter Spronck ⓘ

Tilburg University, 5037 AB Tilburg, The Netherlands
{m.kosa,p.Spronck}@tilburguniversity.edu

Abstract. Tabletop gaming is currently experiencing a golden age. The size of the tabletop gaming industry and the number of people engaged with the hobby are at a peak, and are still increasing. However, what motivates people to engage with tabletop games is not well studied. This study aims to understand the motivations for tabletop game play; it does so by introducing a questionnaire, called the tabletop gaming motivation inventory (TGMI), to measure these motivations. The inventory is based on literature, in particular literature which deals with similar inventories used to investigate video gaming motivations. We carried out a survey with tabletop game players (N = 867). Our inventory is validated using factor analyses, which lead to a final questionnaire consisting of 11 factors based on 39 items. Moreover, we investigated how these motivations vary with respect to prior experience of players, their frequency of play and geographical locations.

Keywords: Tabletop gaming · Player motivations · Player experience · Questionnaire building

1 Introduction

The term "tabletop game" is an umbrella term which encapsulates traditional games, mass-market games and hobby games [1]. "Traditional games" refer to the games that have no authorship and are passed down from generation to generation, such as Chess and Go. "Mass-market games" refer to the games that are developed to be sold in large numbers for a prolonged time for years, such as Monopoly [2] and Pictionary [3]. "Hobby games" (sometimes called "designer board games") refer to the commercial games that are developed for a specialized group of hobby gamers, such as Settlers of Catan [4] and Puerto Rico [5]. Embracing these categories, we define tabletop games, or "board games", broadly as games that require a tabletop, are played on a tabletop, and feature physical components that are made of cardboard, plastic, wood, and similar materials.

Modern tabletop gaming is a billion-dollar industry and is growing steadily [6, 7], though it should be noted that a relatively small selection of games is responsible for the majority of the sales. The popularity of tabletop games can be found in multiple factors, such as (1) they support face to face interaction between players, (2) they come in a large variety of types and genres that feed players' need for novelty, (3) they help players to distance themselves from technology, and (4) they provide an opportunity

N. Zagalo et al. (Eds.): VJ 2019, CCIS 1164, pp. 59–71, 2019.
https://doi.org/10.1007/978-3-030-37983-4_5

for players to spend time with their families. The mobile market, on which digital versions of many tabletop games are available, expand the audience for these games and drive their growth in digital sector as well [8]. Tabletop games are also featured heavily in YouTube channels which review games; popular examples of such channels are "Rahdo Runs Through", "The Dice Tower", and "Shut Up & Sit Down". In addition to their social aspects, some tabletop games also allow for solo gaming, which appeals to players who prefer playing alone or cannot find playing partners [9].

The research on tabletop gaming has not kept up with the rising popularity of tabletop games. Recently the area started to attract more researchers, who wish to gain an understanding of the engagement of players with these games. The motivations for tabletop gaming are as yet unexplored in research, and no dedicated measurement tool exists to evaluate or survey the motivations of tabletop game players. Therefore, this study aims to provide a perspective on the factors which contribute to motivations for playing of tabletop games. It also aims to develop and psychometrically validate a tabletop gaming motivation questionnaire, which may be beneficial to researchers who are interested in studying tabletop games and their players.

2 Background

2.1 The Questionnaire

Research into tabletop gaming has been performed in the past. Most of this research is from the perspective of making computers play these games, but sporadically research investigates the history and culture of tabletop games. "A History of Board Games Other Than Chess" [10] and "The Oxford History of Board Games" [11] are two of the key texts in the area which inspect the history of tabletop games. The "Board Game Studies Colloquium" is a notable conference being held since 2014 and "Analog Game Studies" is an open-access journal that publishes work on tabletop game analyses and encourages analog game study theory.

Recently, research on modern tabletop gaming gained momentum. Literature can be found on multiple aspects of tabletop gaming, such as prototyping with tabletop games [12], understanding the tabletop play/design to improve digital design [13, 14], understanding the collaboration in tabletop play to inform future collaborative game design [15], reporting the development processes of tabletop games [16, 17], educational aspects of tabletop games [18–21], paratextuality in modern board games [22], translating board games [23], and how opportunities are created for play in the hobby when tabletop gaming is constrained by parenting [24]. Although research on tabletop gaming became more diverse in the last two decades, there are few studies that address the measuring of tabletop gaming motivations/experiences. Some studies use digital game inventories such as the Game Experience Questionnaire (GEQ; [25]) to measure player experiences in tabletop gaming [26]. The GEQ was attempted to be validated as a tabletop game experience measurer. However, it is very high level and covers only a few aspects of tabletop gaming [27].

Since there is no questionnaire that specifically addresses tabletop motivations, we attempted to close that gap in the literature. To design a questionnaire which measures tabletop gaming motivations, we took a deductive approach and initially based our tabletop gaming motivation model on the literature of video gaming motivations. There are several major studies that attempted to delineate the factors contributing to video gaming motivations. One of them found that the main motivations for playing MMORPGs are achievement, social and immersion factors [28]. Another one proposed a more detailed taxonomy of video gaming motivations, and introduced the factors completion, escapism, story, customization, autonomy-exploration, loss aversion and social interaction [29]. Yet another study, utilizing Uses and Gratifications Theory [30], distinguish competition, challenge, fantasy, arousal, diversion and social interaction as the driving factors influencing players for video gaming [31]. Integrating these findings, a study attempted to come up with a unified model of gaming motivations [32]. As a result, it was stated that there are 13 dimensions to video gaming motivation: Customization, Escapism, Relationships, Completion, Story, Socializing, Loss Aversion, Fantasy, Competition, Arousal, Autonomy-Exploration, Challenge and Teamwork [32, 33].

Because of its all-encompassing nature, we decided to use this study as a starting point for our investigation of tabletop gaming motivations. However, in addition to these dimensions, we added the dimension of "Aesthetics" which was previously found as a motivating factor for tabletop gaming [34]. We also changed "Challenge" to "Mastery" to better fit the tabletop gaming terminology. Therefore, our final model and questionnaire consists of 14 dimensions. Where needed, we adapted the formulation of items from the literature to the tabletop gaming context, and added three items in the aesthetics scale. This then formed our questionnaire (Appendix A).

2.2 Motivations and Their Associations

Motivations can be affected by player- based variables such as demographics or player characteristics. For instance, it was shown for digital games that prior experience of players can affect their competence in a game [35], their frequency of play might affect their engagement levels [36] and their geographical locations may influence their motivations [37]. We though similar associations might hold true in tabletop gaming domain and therefore, we also investigated whether prior experience, frequency of play and geographical locations were associated with player motivations to play tabletop games.

3 Method

3.1 Procedure and Participants

We prepared and implemented the questionnaire, which we called the Tabletop Gaming Motivation Inventory (TGMI), in Qualtrics, which is a browser-based environment used for collecting participant data. We announced our study at the two most prolific websites for discussing tabletop gaming, namely boardgamegeek.com and shutupandsitdown.com. A link to the questionnaire was provided in the announcement. Data collection progressed from the 13th of February 2018 to the 17th of March 2018.

In total, 1038 players participated in the study. 171 of the participants were unengaged (agreed to participate in the first page of the questionnaire and then aborted without answering any item) and we therefore discarded their entries. We were left with 867 participants, which were all included in the analyses. Among 867 participants, 708 were male and 149 were female (10 chose "other" or "prefer not to say"). Average age was 39.12 (SD = 11.19). More than half of the participants had a college degree (459, 52.9%) and most of the participants were employed full time (617, 71.2%). 647 of the participants stated that they had at least middle class income.

On average, participants were playing tabletop games for 3.16 years (SD = 1.70) and they were playing 1.82 days per week (SD = 0.79) (Tables 1 and 2).

Table 1. Years of tabletop game playing

Years playing	# of participants	Percentage
1–5	227	26.2
6–10	157	18.1
11–15	84	9.7
16–20	47	5.4
More than 20	351	40.6
Total	867	100.0

Table 2. Tabletop gaming frequency

# of days per week	# of participants	Percentage
0–1	322	37.1
2–3	414	47.8
4–5	95	11.0
6–7	36	4.2
Total	867	100.0

More than half of the participants (52.7%) resided in the United States, followed by the United Kingdom (10.8%), Canada (9.1%), Netherlands (5.5%), Australia (3.7%) and Germany (2.5%). In total, participants came from 49 different countries.

3.2 Measures

We had an initial pool of 42 items, where there were 14 subscales each having 3 items. We adopted a seven-point Likert scale, with responses ranging from "Strongly Disagree" (1) to "Strongly Agree" (7). Each factor contributing to the overall motivation had its own score whereas the accumulated score of all the items represented the global score for overall tabletop motivation.

We also collected participant's demographic information. The prior experience of the players were measured by the single question of "For how many years have you been playing board games?". Players' frequency of play was measured similarly by a single question: "How many days on average per week do you play board games?". We also asked participants to state their country of residence.

4 Results

Initially, we carried out a Confirmatory Factor Analysis (CFA) to see if our developed motivational model fits well without any modification, using SPSS 22. A model fit is advised to be good depending on the values of the fit indices: TLI > .90, CFI > .90, RMSEA < .08 and SRMR < .09 [38, 39]. In our case, the result of the CFA did not show a good fit (TLI = .86, CFI = .88, RMSEA = .05, %90 CI [0.050, 0.055], SRMR = 0.07) and there were low loading items (such as Teamwork2 = 0.25 and Customization1 = 0.28). Therefore, we carried out an Exploratory Factor Analysis (EFA) to let the items load freely in their factors. The KMO (0.81), the communalities (>0.20) and the Bartlett test [$\chi 2$ (741) = 14127.91, p < 0.001] verified the adequacy of the 42 items included in the EFA [40]. We extracted 11 factors with the total explained variance of 67% (Appendix B). There were no correlations between factors greater than 0.7 (Table 4), indicating good discriminant validity. Also, on average, every factor loaded more that 0.5 on its own factor indicating good convergent validity.

To be able to achieve the desired validities, we discarded items that cross-loaded or loaded poorly (i.e. Completion1: "I like to complete all the scenarios that the game offers", Mastery3: "I enjoy finding new and creative ways to play board games" and Teamwork2: "It is important to me that I do not need support from other players to do well"). For poor loadings we used the cut-off point of 0.45 [41] and we accepted an item as a problematic cross-loading item if it loaded at least 0.32 on two or more factors [40]. We also checked if a cross-loading item was loading at least at 0.2 difference between factors [42, 43].

Most of the reliabilities values (Cronbach's alphas) of the resulting sub-scales were above 0.70, indicating good reliabilities [44] and some of them were between .60 and .70, meaning that they were in acceptable limits [45] (Table 3). The Spearman-Brown reliability is a better reliability estimate for two item scales [46] and the values of Spearman-Brown coefficients of Customization ($\alpha = 0.90$) and Socializing ($\alpha = 0.74$) were acceptable. The reliability of the overall scale was good as well ($\alpha = 0.85$).

We further analyzed the inventory to certify its reliability, convergent and discriminant validities: All of the composite reliabilities (CR) were above the threshold level of 0.7, ensuring reliability and all of the average variance extracted (AVE) values were above the threshold value of 0.50, ensuring convergent validity [47]. The square root of each construct's AVE value should be more than its correlation values with other constructs to ensure divergent validity [48] and this criterion was met as well (Tables 3 and 4).

With the modified and new version of the model, we have checked the factor structure of the remaining 39 item utilizing CFA. The result indicated a good fit (TLI = .90, CFI = .91, RMSEA = .05, %90 CI [0.044, 0.049], SRMR = 0.05).

Finally, we have investigated how motivations of the players differ in terms of their prior experience, their frequency of plays and geographical locations. Prior experience of players was negatively correlated with Customization and Arousal whereas frequency of play was negatively correlated with Socializing and Teamwork (Table 4). For geographical locations, we have aggregated the scores of the players in the same continent according to their respective country of residence. Welch's t-test analyses, which is used when sample sizes/variances are unequal [49], showed that players in North America are significantly more motivated by Mastery and Story-Fantasy when compared to players in Europe (t (544) = 2.82, p < 0.01 and t (605) = 2.23, p = 0.03, respectively). Although players in North America were more motivated by Autonomy-Exploration than players in Oceania (t (41) = 2.20, p = 0.03), they were less motivated than players in Europe (t (542) = −2.39, p = 0.02). Player in Oceania were significantly more motivated in terms of Teamwork but less motivated in terms of Autonomy-Exploration compared to players in Europe (t (7) = −2.42, p = 0.05 and t (48) = 3.22, p < 0.01, respectively). We did not analyze South America, Asia and Africa continents which had less than 30 participants [50]. Other pairwise comparisons -including total motivation scores- did not yield significant results (Table 5).

Table 3. Cronbach's alpha, composite reliabilities and average variance extracted values of the measures

	Cronbach's α	CR	AVE	Sqrt (AVE)
Customization	.90	.87	.77	.88
Escapism	.92	.95	.87	.93
Relationship	.81	.85	.66	.81
Mastery	.71	.82	.53	.73
Fantasy-Story	.83	.83	.70	.84
Socializing	.74	.82	.70	.84
Competition	.81	.87	.53	.73
Arousal	.69	.85	.65	.81
Autonomy	.60	.78	.55	.74
Teamwork	.67	.81	.58	.76
Aesthetics	.84	.82	.60	.77

Table 4. Factor correlations

	1	2	3	4	5	6	7	8	9	10	11	12	13
1. Customization	1												
2. Escapism	$.16^{**}$	1											
3. Relationship	$.13^{**}$	$.13^{**}$	1										
4. Mastery	$.08^{*}$	.02	$.19^{**}$	1									
5. Fantasy-Story	$.26^{**}$	$.33^{**}$	$.20^{**}$	$.11^{**}$	1								
6. Socializing	.06	−.01	$.41^{**}$	$.19^{**}$	$.19^{**}$	1							
7. Competition	.01	$.13^{**}$	−.02	$.17^{**}$	.003	$-.11^{**}$	1						
8. Arousal	$.13^{**}$	$.17^{**}$	$.22^{**}$	$.38^{**}$	$.20^{**}$	$.21^{**}$	$.07^{*}$	1					
9. Autonomy	$.09^{**}$	$.13^{**}$	$.11^{**}$	$.13^{**}$	$.20^{**}$	$.09^{**}$	$.07^{*}$	$.12^{**}$	1				
10. Teamwork	$.16^{**}$	$.12^{**}$	$.27^{**}$	$.15^{**}$	$.37^{**}$	$.32^{**}$	$-.13^{**}$	$.22^{**}$	$.14^{**}$	1			
11. Aesthetics	$.46^{**}$	$.09^{**}$	$.14^{**}$	$.18^{**}$	$.28^{**}$	$.12^{**}$	$.07^{*}$	$.23^{**}$	.05	$.24^{**}$	1		
12. Years Playing	$-.07^{*}$	−.03	.05	−.05	.01	.05	.002	$-.13^{**}$	−.002	−.01	−.06	1	
13. # of Days per Week	.02	−.02	−.06	.06	−.01	$-.09^{**}$	−.06	.01	.01	$-.08^{*}$	−.03	.02	1

* p < .05, ** p < .01

Table 5. Breakdown of means and standard deviations of continents in terms of motivations

	S. America (N = 14)		N. America (N = 511)		Europe (N = 289)		Asia (N = 12)		Africa (N = 5)		Oceania (N = 36)	
	Mean	SD	Mean	SD	Mean	SD	Mean	SD	Mean	SD	Mean	SD
Customization	4.57	1.48	4.34	1.52	4.30	1.51	3.71	1.70	4.30	1.20	4.21	1.56
Escapism	3.67	1.93	3.92	1.60	3.71	1.57	4.03	1.78	4.80	0.65	4.06	1.65
Relationship	4.07	1.74	4.56	1.31	4.53	1.25	4.19	1.38	4.53	1.15	4.41	1.33
Mastery	5.68	0.96	5.68	0.75	5.51	0.84	5.52	0.93	5.60	0.52	5.50	0.87
Story-Fantasy	5.13	1.28	4.81	1.02	4.65	1.00	4.61	0.89	5.43	0.90	4.83	0.86
Socializing	5.18	1.50	5.59	1.01	5.46	1.03	5.08	1.00	5.70	0.91	5.33	1.04
Competition	2.10	1.03	2.55	0.96	2.43	0.93	2.78	1.11	2.10	0.78	2.46	0.97
Arousal	5.45	1.04	5.18	0.92	5.23	0.85	5.28	0.69	6.07	0.55	5.19	0.75
Autonomy	4.36	1.36	4.72	0.83	4.88	0.94	4.53	0.76	4.60	0.43	4.43	0.78
Teamwork	4.79	1.01	4.87	0.98	4.77	1.01	4.53	0.81	5.67	0.91	5.19	0.90
Aesthetics	5.86	0.85	5.57	0.93	5.53	0.99	4.97	1.16	5.67	1.58	5.44	0.89

5 Discussion

This study aimed to examine the motivations to play tabletop games and develop a reliable and valid questionnaire to measure them. We started from the video gaming literature and built on the pillars of major studies on motivations for gaming.

5.1 TGMI - The Questionnaire

The results were partially in line with our initial starting point. Some of the factors remained unchanged where corresponding items loaded well in their own respective factors. Escapism, Aesthetics, Relationship, Arousal and Autonomy-Exploration emerged as motivating factors as expected. Therefore it can be inferred that players may choose to play tabletop games because they like to escape real life issues, they like the look and feel of the game, they can form/continue relationships, they find the tabletop playing activity exciting, and they think tabletop gaming provides them with an environment in which they can be free to explore without external controlling. Since the items of Autonomy-Exploration did not specifically mentioned the exploration aspect of board games, we renamed this factor as "Autonomy".

Besides the five aforementioned factors, Customization and Socializing were the two factors that were preserved as well, though for each one of their items had to be moved to different factors. The existence of these factors entail that players like to take care of their games, making them nicer and more eye pleasing, and that tabletop games create social affordances for players to interact with other players.

Some of the factors merged together. The Loss Aversion and Competition items loaded together and formed a single factor. This suggests that tabletop players who feel strongly about wanting to avoid losing are also motivated by a desire to compete with other players. We simply named this factor as "Competition". Moreover, Completion items were correlated with Mastery items and formed a factor together as well. This might imply that, in the context of tabletop game playing, "completing a game" refers to acquiring the full mastery of that game in the mind of a player. We named this factor as "Mastery".

The items of Story, Fantasy and one item from Customization loaded together and created a factor. Our tentative explanation for this is that it is not common for tabletop games to have a full-fledged story, and the ones that have a story mostly include fantasy elements such as out-of-world creatures, fables, tales or time travel [51]. Therefore, it is probable that tabletop players associate the story items with fantasy items. One item that we initially put under Customization ("I like to personalize my character if the game allows it") also loaded in this factor; we assume that this is because this item refers to the role-playing aspect of gaming, and roleplaying frequently takes play in fantasy settings such as in D&D [52] or Call of Cthulhu [53].

Lastly, an item which we initially placed in the Socializing factor ("I enjoy helping other players") loaded together with Teamwork items. We assume that this item was registered close to Teamwork by the participants because of its wording. It proved to be valid in the Teamwork factor, and also loaded much better than one other Teamwork item ("It is important to me that I do not need support from other players to do well"), which we ultimately discarded.

Looking at the factor correlation matrix, it can be seen that there are moderately and positively correlated factors ($r > .30$; [54]). For instance, Aesthetics and Customization were associated, which implies that players who would like to make their games prettier were also motivated to play more aesthetically pleasing games. Socializing and Relationship were moderately correlated as well, suggesting that players who like to chat and interact with other players also like to share their more personal issues with them. Socializing was moderately associated with Teamwork, suggesting that players who likes to chat, also like to cooperate. In terms of Arousal and Mastery, we speculate that players find it arousing to gain mastery of games, in general. Teamwork and Fantasy-Story were associated, suggesting that players like to cooperate in fantasy settings or story driven games. This might also be due to the fact that many cooperative games in the market are in a fantasy setting or are story driven such as Pandemic Legacy [55], Eldritch Horror [56] or Mice and Mystics [57]. Fantasy-Story was found to be moderately associated with Escapism. This is in line with the literature, since fantasy and escapism are stated as the sub constructs of the imaginal experiences [58]. This might suggest that players who play tabletop games to escape reality might be more inclined to prefer games that have a fantasy aspect to it.

Some factors were negatively associated, albeit with low correlations ($r < 0.30$; [54]). Teamwork had a negative relationship with Competition, which was as we expected, as they are polar opposites. A negative relationship was observed between Socializing and Competition, which suggests that players who like to chat with and know other players do not like to compete with them. We wish to point out that this study does not claim any causation of factors since their relationships are entirely correlational.

5.2   Motivation - Prior Experience, Frequency of Play and Geography Associations

We investigated how prior experience and frequency of playing were associated with the motivations (Table 4). Years of playing tabletop games, indicating how experienced a player is, was negatively associated with Arousal and Customization, suggesting that aged players may not feel aroused by tabletop play after a while and start to care less about the customization aspect of tabletop games. Also, the number of tabletop gaming days per week was negatively associated with Teamwork and Socializing suggesting that players who play more frequently may prefer games that are more competitive and they socialize less often during the game. However, it should be noted that these associations were zero-order and extremely weak ($r = \sim .1$).

We also investigated how the geographic location of the players affected their motivations. We found that, in general, Aesthetics in tabletop games was mostly appreciated by players in South America. Players in Africa were more motivated by Escapism, Arousal and Teamwork whereas players in Europe scored higher on Autonomy compared to other continents. Although this might give a general idea about how the geographic locations relate to tabletop gaming motivations, more targeted research is needed in order to get more definitive results. While some differences found were significant, the overall picture that one gets when examining Table 5 is that motivations for playing games are rather similar in all aspects between the continents.

5.3   Limitations and Future Studies

There are some noticeable limitations and threats to validity in the study. Although we have developed the questionnaire with a broad definition of tabletop games in mind, it can further be segregated for traditional or mass market games. In addition, the subdivision of tabletop games (e.g. War Games, Abstract Games, Party Games or Strategy Games) might reveal different kind of motivations for each category and provide a more nuanced approach. To be able to better capture the motivations to play different kinds of tabletop games, more specific inventories might be required. Moreover, some of the significant correlations found can be due to the offers on the market and might not be reflecting the actual player motivations. For instance, players might be rating cooperation and story similarly (both as high or low) since cooperative games in the market mostly incorporate story elements in their design. Future studies can explicitly investigate the differences between such motivations. Also, cross-cultural validation is required to ensure the generalizability of this measurement. The questionnaire was distributed in English but filled in by participants from a wide variety of non-native-English-speaking countries. Future studies should take this into account and possibly translate the questionnaire.

Moreover, the participant pool that we used was likely to consist of a majority of enthusiastic players of tabletop games, so we may have missed the more casual game players. We can see this in the reported experience of the participants, of which 40% claimed to have over 20 years of experience with tabletop gaming, while only 26% reported 1-5 years of experience. To be able to capture better results, future studies should aim for a more normally distributed participant pool in terms of experience.

We also wish to point out that after the validation process, some of our subscales consisted of only two items. Although in some cases two item scales can be acceptable [59], three item scales are usually more robust [60].

Although we reported how motivations vary in terms of the continent players are from, one should be extremely cautious interpreting these results. The sample sizes of South America, Asia and Africa were radically small and future studies might aim for a more homogenous sample selection.

Lastly, this study had a deductive approach. Future studies may want to take an inductive approach to reveal tabletop gaming motivations, and investigate whether the results corroborate with the findings presented here.

As a next step we will be adding new items to the smaller number of item subscales, eliminating lower loading items from the higher number of item subscales, and consequently making the questionnaire a more homogenous scale by equalizing the number of items of the subscales.

6 Conclusion

This study was carried out to serve as a base for future studies on tabletop gaming motivations. The instrument described here is in ongoing development, and will be tested with other studies utilizing this instrument. We aim for it to open up some perspectives for researchers who will study tabletop game motivations and enjoyment of tabletop gaming. This study also took an initial step into revealing how tabletop gaming motivations are associated with prior experience, frequency of play and geographical locations. In the future, experimental studies that attempts to tie the motivations presented here to the game mechanics or genres might give better insights into player-tabletop game interaction. Practically, that may also serve as a tool for a board game recommendation system. Lastly, future studies might also investigate whether and how these newly discovered motivating factors are associated to tabletop purchase intentions.

Note: Appendix A (item pool) and B (factor loadings) can be found in: https://drive.google.com/open?id=1GlOs5Y916DiriiOHbf1xHH4xdDaSvCqf

References

1. Woods, S.: Eurogames: The Design, Culture and Play of Modern European Board Games. McFarland, North Carolina, USA (2012)
2. Maggie, L., Darrow, C.: Monopoly. Hasbro, Rhode Island, USA (1935)
3. Angel, R.: Pictionary. Angel Games, Seattle (1985)
4. Teuber, K.: Settlers of Catan. Kosmos, Germany (1995)
5. Seyfarth, A.: Puerto Rico. Ravensburger, Germany (2002)
6. Martin, T.: How board games became a billion-dollar business. https://www.newstatesman.com/culture/games/2017/01/how-board-games-became-billion-dollar-business. Accessed 23 May 2019

7. Birkner, C.: From Monopoly to Exploding Kittens, Board Games Are Making a Comeback. https://www.adweek.com/brand-marketing/from-monopoly-to-exploding-kittens-board-games-are-making-a-comeback/. Accessed 23 May 2019

8. Taylor, H.: Tabletop games are bigger than ever, and its driving growth in the digital sector. https://www.gamesindustry.biz/articles/2018-10-25-asmodee-digital. Accessed 23 May 2019

9. Leorke, D.: Solo board gaming: an analysis of player motivations. Analog Game Stud. 5(4) (2018). http://analoggamestudies.org/2018/12/solo-board-gaming-an-analysis-of-player-motivations/

10. Murray, H.J.R.: A history of Board-Games Other Than Chess. Clarendon Press, UK (1952)

11. Parlett, D.: The Oxford History of Board Games, vol. 5. Oxford University Press, Oxford (1999)

12. Jones, C.E., Liapis, A., Lykourentzou, I., Guido, D.: Board game prototyping to co-design a better location-based digital game. In: Proceedings of the 2017 Computer Human Interaction Conference Extended Abstracts on Human Factors in Computing Systems, pp. 1055–1064. ACM, New York (2017)

13. Xu, Y., Barba, E., Radu, I., Gandy, M., MacIntyre, B.: Chores are fun: understanding social play in board games for digital tabletop game design. In: Digital Games Research Association Conference (2011)

14. Whalen, T.: Playing well with others: applying board game design to tabletop display interfaces. In: ACM Symposium on User Interface Software and Technology, vol. 5. ACM Press, New York (2003)

15. Zagal, J.P., Rick, J., Hsi, I.: Collaborative games: lessons learned from board games. Simul. Gaming 37(1), 24–40 (2006)

16. Kosa, M., Yilmaz, M.: The design process of a board game for exploring the territories of the United States. Press Start 4(1), 36–52 (2017)

17. Eisenack, K.: A climate change board game for interdisciplinary communication and education. Simul. Gaming 44(2–3), 328–348 (2013)

18. Weisz, J.D., Ashoori, M., Ashktorab, Z.: Entanglion: a board game for teaching the principles of quantum computing. In: Proceedings of the 2018 Annual Symposium on Computer-Human Interaction in Play, pp. 523–534. ACM, New York (2018)

19. Peppler, K., Danish, J.A., Phelps, D.: Collaborative gaming: teaching children about complex systems and collective behavior. Simul. Gaming 44(5), 683–705 (2013)

20. Berland, M., Lee, V.R.: Collaborative strategic board games as a site for distributed computational thinking. Int. J. Game-Based Learn. (IJGBL) 1(2), 65–81 (2011)

21. Triboni, E., Weber, G.: MOL: developing a European-style board game to teach organic chemistry. J. Chem. Educ. 95(5), 791–803 (2018)

22. Booth, P.: Game Play: Paratextuality in Contemporary Board Games. Bloomsbury Publishing, London (2015)

23. Evans, J.: Translating board games: multimodality and play. J. Spec. Transl. 20, 15–32 (2013)

24. Rogerson, M.J., Gibbs, M.: Finding time for tabletop: board game play and parenting. Games Cult. 13(3), 280–300 (2018)

25. IJsselsteijn, W., Poels, K., De Kort, Y.A.: The game experience questionnaire: development of a self-report measure to assess player experiences of digital games. TU Eindhoven, Eindhoven (2008)

26. Al Mahmud, A., Mubin, O., Shahid, S., Martens, J.B.: Designing and evaluating the tabletop game experience for senior citizens. In: Proceedings of the 5th Nordic Conference on Human-Computer Interaction: Building Bridges, pp. 403–406. ACM, New York (2008)

27. Barbara, J.: Measuring user experience in multiplayer board games. Games Cult. 12(7–8), 623–649 (2017)

28. Yee, N.: The demographics, motivations, and derived experiences of users of massively multi-user online graphical environments. Presence: Teleoperators Virtual Environ. **15**(3), 309–329 (2006)
29. Hilgard, J., Engelhardt, C.R., Bartholow, B.D.: Individual differences in motives, preferences, and pathology in video games: the gaming attitudes, motives, and experiences scales (GAMES). Front. Psychol. **4**, 608 (2013)
30. Rubin, A.M.: Media uses and effects: a uses-and-gratifications perspective. In: Bryant, J., Zillmann, D. (eds.) Media Effects: Advances in Theory and Research, pp. 417–436. Lawrence Erlbaum Associates, Hillsdale (1994)
31. Sherry, J.L., Lucas, K., Greenberg, B.S., Lachlan, K.: Video game uses and gratifications as predictors of use and game preference. Int. J. Sport. Mark. Spons. **24**(1), 213–224 (2006)
32. Tekofsky, S., Miller, P., Spronck, P., Slavin, K.: The effect of gender, native English speaking, and age on game genre preference and gaming motivations. In: Poppe, R., Meyer, J.-J., Veltkamp, R., Dastani, M. (eds.) INTETAIN 2016 2016. LNICST, vol. 178, pp. 178–183. Springer, Cham (2017). https://doi.org/10.1007/978-3-319-49616-0_17
33. Tekofsky, S.: You are who you play you are. Ph.D. thesis, Tilburg University, Tilburg (2017)
34. Rogerson, M.J., Gibbs, M., Smith, W.: I love all the bits: the materiality of boardgames. In: Proceedings of the 2016 CHI Conference on Human Factors in Computing Systems, pp. 3956–3969. ACM, New York (2016)
35. Birk, M.V., Mandryk, R.L., Atkins, C.: The motivational push of games: the interplay of intrinsic motivation and external rewards in games for training. In: Proceedings of the 2016 Annual Symposium on Computer-Human Interaction in Play, pp. 291–303. ACM, New York (2016)
36. Hoffman, B., Nadelson, L.: Motivational engagement and video gaming: a mixed methods study. Educ. Technol. Res. Dev. **58**(3), 245–270 (2010)
37. Yee, N.: Chinese Gamers are More Competitive and Completionist, More Homogeneous in Gaming Motivations Than US Gamers. https://quanticfoundry.com/2018/11/27/gamers-china-us/. Accessed 32 May 2019
38. Hu, L.T., Bentler, P.M.: Cutoff criteria for fit indexes in covariance structure analysis: conventional criteria versus new alternatives. Struct. Equ. Model.: Multidiscip. J. **6**(1), 1–55 (1999)
39. MacCallum, R.C., Browne, M.W., Sugawara, H.M.: Power analysis and determination of sample size for covariance structure modeling. Psychol. Methods **1**(2), 130 (1996)
40. Tabachnick, B.G., Fidell, L.S.: Using Multivariate Statistics. Allyn & Bacon/Pearson Education, Boston (2007)
41. Comrey, A., Lee, H.: A First Course in Factor Analysis. Psychology Press, New York (1992)
42. Hinkin, T.R.: A brief tutorial on the development of measures for use in survey questionnaires. Organ. Res. Methods **1**(1), 104–121 (1998)
43. Ferguson, E., Cox, T.: Exploratory factor analysis: a users' guide. Int. J. Sel. Assess. **1**(2), 84–94 (1993)
44. Nunnally, J.C.: Psychometric Theory, 2nd edn. McGraw-Hill, New York (1978)
45. Hinton, P.R., McMurray, I., Brownlow, C.: SPSS Explained. Routledge, UK (2004)
46. Eisinga, R., Te Grotenhuis, M., Pelzer, B.: The reliability of a two-item scale: Pearson, Cronbach, or Spearman-Brown? Int. J. Public Health **58**(4), 637–642 (2013)
47. Fornell, C., Larcker, D.F.: Structural equation models with unobservable variables and measurement error: algebra and statistics. J. Mark. Res. **18**(3), 382–388 (1981)
48. Hair Jr., J., Sarstedt, M., Hopkins, L., Kuppelwieser, G.V.: Partial least squares structural equation modeling (PLS-SEM) an emerging tool in business research. Eur. Bus. Rev. **26**(2), 106–121 (2014)

49. Kohr, R.L., Games, P.A.: Robustness of the analysis of variance, the Welch procedure and a box procedure to heterogeneous variances. J. Exp. Educ. **43**(1), 61–69 (1974)
50. Hogg, R.V., Tanis, E.A., Zimmerman, D.L.: Probability and Statistical Inference, vol. 993. Macmillan, New York (1977)
51. The Dice Tower: Top 10 Story Driven Games - with Tom Vasel. YouTube. www.youtube.com/watch?v=VRI7cyxJEfE. Accessed 23 May 2019
52. Wizards of the Coast: Dungeons and Dragons Role Playing Game, 5th edn. Wizards of the Coast, Washington (2014)
53. Chaosium: Call of Cthulu Role Playing Game. 7 edn. Chaosium, Michigan (2014)
54. Cohen, J.: Statistical Power Analysis for the Behavioral Sciences. L. Lawrence Earlbaum Associates, Hillsdale (1988)
55. Daviau, R., Leacock, M.: Pandemic Legacy. Z-Man Games, New York (2015)
56. Konieczka, C. Valens, N.: Eldritch Horror. Fantasy Flight Games, Minnesota (2013)
57. Hawthorne, J.: Mice & Mystics. Plaid Hat Games, USA (2012)
58. Wu, J., Holsapple, C.: Imaginal and emotional experiences in pleasure-oriented IT usage: a hedonic consumption perspective. Inf. Manag. **51**(1), 80–92 (2014)
59. Lewis, J.R., Utesch, B.S., Maher, D.E.: UMUX-LITE: when there's no time for the SUS. In: Proceedings of the SIGCHI Conference on Human Factors in Computing Systems, pp. 2099–2102. ACM, New York (2013)
60. Hair, J.F., Black, W.C., Babin, B.J., Anderson, R.E.: Multivariate Data Analysis, 7th edn. Prentice Hall, Upper Saddle River (2010)

Back in the Game

Modern Board Games

Micael Sousa[1(✉)] and Edgar Bernardo[2]

[1] Universidade de Coimbra (CITTA), Coimbra, Portugal
micaelssousa@gmail.com
[2] Universidade de Trás-os-Montes e Alto Douro (CETRAD),
Vila Real, Portugal
edgarbernardoutad@gmail.com

Abstract. This research intends to contribute to extent the understanding of the renewed interest in analog games phenomenon. We expose the origin and characteristics of modern board games, taxonomy and timeline and demonstrate the growing interest in the subject by presenting current trends, main contributions, themes and some potential research gaps for future researchers, all via a bibliometric survey in the Scopus and Web of Science Databases.

Keywords: Analog games · Board games · Phenomenon

1 Board Game Market Trends

Growing groups of people are playing boardgames. By board games we mean all analog games played on a table. In the last 40 years these games have been developed mainly by enthusiasts who turned them into a hobby even before they became mainstream consumer trends selling millions of copies. These games include role-playing games, collectible card games, wargames and eurogames.

Board games sales have grown sharply since 2013. According to NPD Group Tracker they grew 9% in 2014 and 12% in 2015 [1], and Aritzon's [2] market study for 2017-2023 suggests an annual growth rate of more than 9%, reaching $12 billion. TechNavio [3] expects that the growth of board games should even reach 17% growth in 2023. These values show that there is a growing interest in analogue games, despite the multiple trends for digitalization in the contemporary entertainment industry. That's probably why Paul Booth [4] and Marco Arnaudo [5] point out that we're in an era of board game revival. What is especially curious because they have been developed simultaneously with digital games over the last 40 years [6, 7].

These new games have gained worldwide notoriety through the great success achieved by *Settlers of Catan* [8]. Although the game was created in 1995 and has won the prestigious *Spiel des Jahres*, it was only in the 21st century that the game gained worldwide fame, when it became a social trend in the college student's community. Especially in the tech startups centers like in Silicon Valley [1]. Since then *Catan*, as it is known today, has contributed to open pathways to new players who have joined this international phenomenon and hobby.

N. Zagalo et al. (Eds.): VJ 2019, CCIS 1164, pp. 72–85, 2019.
https://doi.org/10.1007/978-3-030-37983-4_6

Today, online platforms have contributed to generate considerable collective funding of millions of analog gaming projects, and to connect hobby communities online. On the *Kickstarter* (https://www.kickstarter.com/) platform in 2018 board games outperformed digital games in collected funding. Board games collected $165 million, 19.8% more than in 2017, while digital games on this platform accounted for $15.8 million in 2018 [9]. This does not mean that digital games are losing ground to board games, but it does highlight the community's mobilization and ability to invest in new board game projects. *Boardgamegeek* website (www.boardgamegeek.com) as a major importance, with its extensive database, evaluation and characterization methods for games based on votes and contributions from users, that has been online since 2000. In December 2018 there were 19.8 million visits, and, in February 2019, the 2 million registered users mark was reached [10]. The new media, social networks, video production and streaming by enthusiasts and professionals have contributed strongly to the globalization of the phenomenon, which is based on a strong community [11].

Shops, conventions, fairs and other events were very important for the emergence of groups of players, and also competition for international prizes like *Spiel des Jahres*, since 1979, that aim to award prizes for the best games produced and published annually in Germany. We also highlight *Essen Spiel* (see https://www.spiel-messe.com/de/), the world's largest specialty fair that registered 192 thousand participants last year. Every year hobby players, designers, publishers and content creators came to the Essen Spiel in October from all over the world. There they find the latest games, vendors publishers and the opportunity to talk to the designers and test games. But what are modern board games?

2   When Games Started to Become Modern

Defining modern board games presents a challenge. Initially what differentiated traditional and modern games, was that the latter was considered as *"the manufactured commodity, designed and published at a particular time in history, and produced for a particular market and for essentially commercial reasons"* [7] a definition that emphasizes the commercial side of games. Board game players that adopt board gaming as a hobby also use the term "modern" to differentiate the games they play [12] as some academic and mainstream publications.

Parlett [13] refers to historical games as *"largely positional and abstract, and folk or traditional in the sense of being anonymously composed and in the public domains"*, he also states that *"The point of interest about modern board games is their gradual shift of emphasis away from the board and into the circle of players"* in relation to the multiple components involved in the new games, giving *Monopoly* as one such example [13]. Crossing these two definitions we can infer that modern board games (MBG) refers to those that are created for commercial purposes and that have an identifiable author, but are they all the same?

Woods [7] consider 3 different types of board games: classic board games *"those non-proprietary games that have been passed down from antiquity and whose authorship is presumed to emerge from multiple iterative changes over time"*; mass-market games *"refers to those commercial titles that are produced and sold in large numbers year after year, and which constitute the common perception of commercial board games*"; hobby games "*that are differentiated from other forms by their appeal to a particular segment of the population over the last half-century*".

Hobby games are further subdivided into different types: wargames, role-play games, collectible card games, eurogames [7], and American games or Ameritrash [14].

Similarly, Parlett [13] classified board games according to production type, namely: classics, including traditional games and mass market games (i.e. *Monopoly* and *Scrabble*); specialized, traditional or proprietary-products related to skills and strategy, appealing to more specific audiences; family, market games for all ages with role and move play, and educational games; Pulp games, consumption trend games or other cultural products like movies, books and tv shows, with little or no innovation in game mechanics.

On the other hand, Nicholson [15] and Mayer and Harris [16] consider that games like Monopoly and Risk are not modern board games. To them only those that fit the description of eurogames and games influenced by them (i.e. designer games) can be classified as such. Duarte and Battaiola [17] also used this definition to choose modern board games for their research, as did Rogerson and Gibbs [12] to study the role of new designer games. To reinforce that lack of consensus on the definition of MBG Arnaudo [5] considers modern games those that were created over the last 40 years.

Although it appears to be some general acceptance of what conceptually MBG are, confusion persist. One that is aggravated when other terms as 'eurogames' is commonly used in books and articles as a synonym of MBG. Are eurogames and MBG the same? It becomes clear that we need to conceptually define MBG in order to undoubtedly state our position and understanding of the definition and continue to explore the phenomenon. So first we must characterize MBG and then follow through with a concept proposition.

Donovan [18] argues that we are in the age of connectivity and eurogames are to be valued differently from previous mass games, especially considering today's enormous online communities. Woods [7] points out that the board game players' community differentiates between MBG and the other types of games, pointing out the design elements of the games produced in Germany from the early 1980s onwards as the landmark moment that differentiate them from previous designs.

Shapiro [19] argues that a new type of games emerged in the 1960s, considered a second generation of games. Sid Sackson's *Acquire*, a game published by 3M in 1962, was a main influencer of new designs, combining strategy and themes for adults, that latter inspired German and eurogames. Shapiro also argues that the *Cosmic Encounter*, a game published in 1977, would also revolutionize American games, combining fantasy and strategy. The American interpretation is commonly called Ameritrash, a rather offensive name [5] that over-emphasize the dice component or luck and randomness elements of many mass-produced games produced in the United States [14]. In fact, the term ameritrash is used mostly by eurogamers that see their games as being of superior design, but recent years have shown there has been trends towards rapprochement between both markets in terms of design. It is common to see hybrids between American and eurogames nowadays (i.e. Scythe [20]), eurogames that include storytelling, make them closer to Role-Playing Games (i.e. Dixit [21]).

Wargames have their own history; these were inspired military games to practice tactics and strategy simulation. The first wargame was *kriegsspiel*, design by a Prussian official and developed by Prussian army as a simulation for their commanders during the XIX century [1]. In *kriegsspiel* and other games inspired by it, two miniature armies battled in a board, usually made with hexagon tiles, that simulate real terrain. There were specific rules for each terrain, type of unit, weather, etc. making it as real as possible. This design originated very complex systems of rules and long and unpredictable games were luck was also a factor. War games were rediscovered after the World War II, when hobby players started to adapt them and create their own games (Fig. 1). Today Wargames are an important board game type with new games being released regularly even though they are not as popular as the other hobby game types.

In the Role-Play subtype there is one game that cannot be ignored, Dungeons & Dragons (D&D), published in 1974, was a game changer. It was inspired by wargames design and used dices to determine the outcomes and pencil and paper to register information referring the changes in the game and player status, and a game master (player) to push the story. It simplified the rules used in wargames and created a whole new fantasy universe were the narratives would dominate the game play, making it all about the story and the possibilities of the players choices to alter it [1]. Since then the Role-Play boardgames evolved, with a lot of new games, and physical upgrades that contributed to create deeper narrative experiences, in multiples universes [5]. Today D&D popularity is rising, as we can see it in popular TV shows like "*The Big Bang Theory*" [22].

Eurogames are introduced as a brand-new way of playing, associating and cooperating. This means eurogames are a type of modern board games with specific characteristics. Woods [7] states that eurogames tend to be accessible games that privilege role of mechanics over theme, choice over chance, control of conflict, and quality components and presentation over price and design simplicity. He also spotlights the importance of graphic design and the recognition of the game authors, both game designers and illustrators, i.e. the game boxes display the authors name right next to the game title, which promotes the author's status.

In eurogames the number of choices is conditioned for player interest and their complexity scalable, from family-friendly complexity to greater complexity, but never reaching the complexity and volume of choices of a *chess* game. These choices occur through interconnected carefully developed mechanics that activate systems and sets of subsystems. This allows for a smaller and gradual learning curve and reduced game time, while still playing a considerable deep strategic game in 1 to 2 h. These choices work towards the game theme, models and intended simulation, with rare broad abstract creations.

Some eurogames are described as multiplayer solitaires, although they are a group activity [7]. This relates to the design elements that lead players to implement optimization systems without confrontation or direct attack. They become competitive, but with no player elimination or domination. This is achieved through option locking systems and victory points accumulating throughout the game, hiding the victor before the game is over. This characteristic is related to the origin of these games, has in post-World War II Germany the actions of conquest, domination, attack, exclusion and elimination were avoided in social and cultural activities [1, 7].

Eurogames tend to be played in individual turns and sequentially, allowing to implement short, medium- and long-term strategies. Information tends to be imperfect, but discernible enough for simple statistical intuitive player analyzes. One of the main characteristics of eurogames consists of removing the chance factor or at least the deterministic effect of the randomness chance in the player's decision-making process. Finally, eurogames are multiplayer games, usually designed to be played by between 2 to 6 players. This forces social interaction between players which makes them a type of social experience and maybe that's what makes them so attractive.

Magic: The Gathering (MGT) was the first Collectible Card Game, published in 1993, by *Wizards of the Coast* and designed by Richard Garfield. It has still a very active community all over the world and many other Collectible Card Games have been released since. Today there are still more than 38 million players of worldwide and the revenues in 2018 were more than 500 million dollars [23].

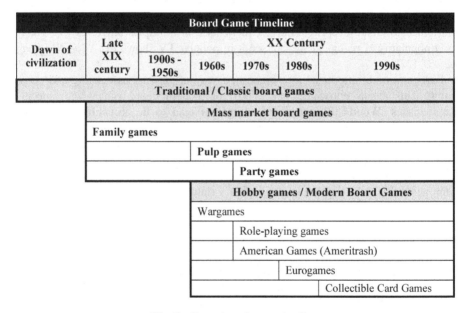

Fig. 1. Game board types timeline

The following Table 1 shows a description of the each of the type of board games identified in our literature review, highlighting its mean features and characteristics.

Table 1. Game board settings and features, own source based on [7, 14].

Board game type and subtype	Main characteristics
Traditional and classical	**No attributed author and no commercial rights**
Mass-market	**Properties of companies and distributors of mass production games with no particular attention given to the authors or the innovation of its designs**
Family games	For the general mass market, with mechanics and rules that tend to be similar among various products, and with considerable luck mechanics
Pulp games	Inspired by licensed films, series, books or other creative author products, have game systems that tend to be copies from other mass games with a recognizable theme
Party games	Simple games for large groups, focused on social interaction and entertainment
Hobby games	**Owned by companies or individual owners, in which the author and originality of the design is recognized and emphasized**
Wargames (1960s)	Deep military simulations, usually for 2 players, with dice or other random system, and use maps that try to recreate the realistic environments, and a tendency to include miniatures
Role-play games	Usually cooperative, games using thumbnails and various registration elements to support a narrative story that is built by the players' choices, with a mediator that controls rules and narratives
Collectible card	Games in which players can buy or trade cards to create decks of unique cards with which they play against other players in multiple formats
American games/Ameritrash	USA and UK inspired games that combine elements of wargames and role-play games, focusing on the theme rather than in the mechanics
Eurogames	Games that avoid randomness in mechanics with simplified themes simulations, relatively simple rule systems, for groups and with limited durations, multiple paths to victory. Known for their game mechanics and originality, as well as the quality of the components

Considering these distinctive characteristics, we argue that MBG can be defined as commercial products, created in the last five decades, with an identifiable author or authors, with original mechanics design and theme, with high quality components, created for a specific public. We can consider MBG to be the same as Hobby board games, although the new games being created can have more than one subcategory of hobby games influence. Figure 2 consist in a taxonomy based on the literature review and linked to proposed definition, monthly focused in the relation and distinction of hobby games.

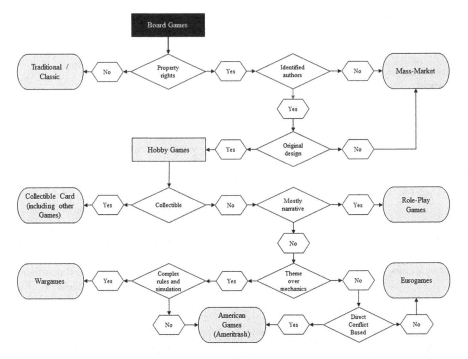

Fig. 2. Board game archetypes and proposed taxonomy, own source.

3   Modern Board Games Publishing

In the first inaugural article of the blog *Analog Game Studies* (http://analoggame studies.org/), which later came to be edited as a book, the authors argue to the need to create a regular publication in the field of game studies directed to analog games. They felt that the new designs and board games could no longer be ignored by the scientific community. Every year, since then, there has been an annual book publication with multiple articles on analogue games, following a scientific criterion [24–26].

There are, however, a few published books on contemporary board games. As early as 2010, Mayer and Harris [16] published "*Libraries got game: Aligned Learning through Modern Board Games*" a short guide recommending the use of modern board games for educational library activities that would be the staple for many other field articles. In the following year, "*Tabletop: Analog Game Design*", a compilation of articles by various authors and experts on contemporary games by Costikyan and Davidson [6] was published, referring to the designs and culture associated with MBG's trend, and in 2012 Steward Woods' doctoral thesis was also published in book format with the name "*Eurogames: The design, culture and play of modern European board games*" [7], contributing towards concept systematization and the establishment of these new games as modern board games. We must mention Paul Booth [4] book "*Game Play: Paratextuality in contemporary Board Games*" focusing on contemporary board games media studies, specifically the more complex designs we consider modern, and Likewise Tristan Donovan's [1] mainstream book on the history of board games "*It's all a games: from monopoly to settlers of catan*".

We can also find other books, almost all written by players and amateurs, without any academic or scientific systematization, based on their passions and subjective experiences. Following his Dice Tower segment, Engelstein [27] released his book on board games Mathematics and Science called "*Gametek: The Math and Science of Gaming*", and Erway [28] made a passionate account of his two decades long family experiences playing MBG in "*Loving Eurogames: A Quest For The Well Played Game*". Thrower's [29] book "*Tabletop gaming manual*" gives a summary introduction to the spectrum of contemporary games, similarly to Dee [30] "*Ticket to Carcassonne: 21st Century Tabletop Games*" and Duffy's [31] book "*The Board Game Book: volume I*". We also found books sharing experiences and interviews with designers in "*Designing Modern Strategy Games*" [32], Barrett [33] "*Board Game Design Advice: From the Best in the World*" and Dean's [34] "*For the love of boardgames*". We can also identify books with empirical, instructional-related approaches and game-building guides, such as Slinker *et al.* [35] "*The Kobold guide to board game design*" and Slack [36] "*The Board Game Designer's Guide: The Easy 4 Step Process to Create Amazing Games That People Can't Stop Playing*". Finally, in 2018 we highlight Arnaduro's [5] book dedicated MBG narratives "*Storytelling in modern board games*".

With regard to scientific publications on MBG, we decided to look for recent trends in research, namely those that relate directly or influenced by eurogames, because they are the most innovative and influencing games design in this hobby in the last years [1, 7]. Of the database research on articles and scientific conferences in *Web of Science* (WOS) and *Scopus*, we initially used as research keywords: modern board game, tabletop, contemporary board games, eurogames, and German games. However, the results were marginal and so we decided to use the broad keywords "Board Games" as the search criteria. This yielded a considerable number of occurrences specifically 1151 (WOS) plus 1721 (Scopus). We then narrow the search for article dating from 2004, the year when the first article directly related to the modern board games was published.

Of the 43 journal articles and conferences we identified only 18 described games as modern, 13 as eurogames, 6 as hobby games, 3 as German games, and 2 as contemporary games. This meant that more than half did not make any reference other than being board games or table games, which makes it difficult to distinguish between modern board games from other board games. However, after close analysis we found that all the games were Eurogames, in fact some of them were really known and popular like *Catan* [8], *Dominion* [37], *Pandemic* [38], etc. The 43 articles found on MBG could be divided according to research area: 6 articles related to social sciences; 9 related to science education; 8 on games as a product and game studies; 8 articles related to media and communication; 12 in computer science and technologies (see Table 2).

Articles on player behavior and the social dynamics of MBG hobby emerge on social and human sciences articles, i.e. articles on the cooperative aspects of modern board games [39], on formal and informal social rules [40] on cultural values [41], on family and affectionateness hobby players dynamics [12] and on the online player community impact and development [11].

As for the education sciences articles, they related to environmental education [42–44] to discourse and mathematics [45], chemistry contents [46], to digital applications development [47] library activities [48] and to urbanism [49].

As for media and communication articles most focus on the game narrative dimension [50–52], speech typology during games [53]; and iconography and components [54], their aesthetics [55], language used in game rules [56], and games multimodal linguistic aspects [57].

In the case of game studies research, they tackle their effects, like socialization through material components [58], the elements and characteristics of board games that make them more collaborative [59], motivation for consumption [60], board games comparing methodologies [52], and focus on the differentiating effects of game materiality on group play enjoyment [58] or on how best to teach game rules [61] and identifying game design elements [17].

Finally, in the area of technology and computer science, most research is related to the use of MBG as a testing ground for artificial intelligence [62–66] and articles board games use for automation and inclusive use of digital devices [67, 68].

Table 2. Published articles and their authors and research areas since 2015

Research areas	No.	Authors
Social and human sciences	6	[11, 12, 39–41, 69]
Educational sciences	9	[42–49, 70]
Media and communication	8	[50, 51, 53–57, 71]
Game studies	8	[17, 18, 52, 58–61, 72]
Technology and computer science	12	[62, 63, 65–68, 73–77]

We must emphasize the fact that the game *Catan* [8] was the most used in some of these researches, demonstrating the importance that it had in the dissemination of the modern board games. Six articles use *Catan*, mostly in the technology and computing sciences field, as an information, negotiation and strategy game [62, 74–77]. A game of great importance for modern board games studies, which reinforces even more the fact of being used as a reference for the development and establishing of MBG. Some suggest that we could consider *Catan* to be the game that changed eurogames perception, because of its rapid world spread beyond the board game hobby community and culture.

Several articles in institutional and specialty journals linked with the use of MBG in educational activities in libraries are clearly present [15, 78–82], just as well as Steward Woods [7] influence overall, as mentioned in Rogerson, Gibbs and Smith [11, 12].

Although research on the subject of MBG is still in its infancy, comparing with the volume of work on board games in general and on digital games, we have to agree with Trammell *et al.* [24] that the scientific community has not given this topic the appropriate attention. This is a phenomenon that deserves to be discussed giving the sector's economic and social growth [2, 3] that might even be acknowledged as a kind of golden era of board games, where modern designs play an important role [51].

4   Conclusion

Board Game's recent market trend suggests an increasing interest in analog games. All over the globe board games are increasing their market shares in game sales. A particular type of modern board games are establishing themselves as staples of contemporary gaming, being eurogames one of them. These MBG differ from other games due to their high-end components, focus on design, and the designer, and refreshing mechanics, namely reduced randomness, and stress on cooperation and non-aggressive competition among players.

Modern board gamers seem to see themselves as hobbyist players [7, 12] that seek for one another, form communities and organize regular events, and participate in the development of board game culture. This demonstrates a sense of community and passion for MBG, a statement made by hobbyists in several board game books.

However, our findings open the door for other future researches with new questions on this subject. For instance, on consumption habits, communication and networking or social behavior, to mention a few examples. Further understanding consumption helps companies (publishers and shops) to better position themselves in the market and increase market shares, and designers to produce more successful games, hence it is important to ask where do players buy their games, what type of games to they prefer; are themes, components, mechanics, authors important for purchase motivation, etc. In relation to this, it is important to better understand if players are playing both digital and modern board games or are they replacing digital games, or even if digital games will adapt and capture this growing niche market game characteristics.

From a scientific standpoint, it seems that few researches on the field of board games are being published. The conceptualization still need further clarification and new taxonomies must be created to classify new games. It was our goal to create a simple and clear concept of what are modern board games and what characterized each different type, which we did, but our scientific literature review focused only on eurogames. Further researches, more border, are needed.

Future research should consider different hobby game, but also different approaches to MBG, focusing on the players, the community, designer and design, themes and mechanics, market and marketing trends.

Acknowledgements. The authors would like to thank "Fundação para a Ciência e a Tecnologia" (FCT), the Portuguese funding agency, that supported this research, under the grant PD/BD/146491/2019 and the research project "FlavourGame – Participate and Change, Playing with textures and flavours" (POCI-01-0145-FEDER-031024).

References

1. Donovan, T.: It's All a Game: The History of Board Games from Monopoly to Settlers of Catan. Macmillan (2017)
2. Arizton: Board Games Market - Global Outlook and Forecast 2018–2023 (2018). https://www.researchandmarkets.com/reports/4602850/board-games-market-global-outlook-and-forecast

3. TechNavio: Global Board Games Market 2019–2023 (2019). https://www.researchandm arkets.com/reports/4768320/global-board-games-market-2019-2023

4. Booth, P.: Game Play: Paratextuality in Contemporary Board Games. Bloomsbury (2015)

5. Arnaudo, M.: Storytelling in the Modern Board Game. McFarland (2018)

6. Costikyan, G., Davidson, D.: Tabletop: Analog Game Design. ETC Press (2011)

7. Woods, S.: Eurogames: The Design, Culture and Play of Modern European Board Games. McFarland (2012)

8. Teuber, K.: Settlers of Catan. Kosmos (1995)

9. Hall, C.: Tabletop games dominated Kickstarter in 2018, while video games declined. Polygon (2019). https://www.polygon.com/2019/1/15/18184108/kickstarter-2018-stats-table top-video-games

10. BGG: 2,000,000 Users! (2019). https://boardgamegeek.com/thread/2147066/2000000-users

11. Rogerson, M.J., Gibbs, M, Smith, W.: Exploring the Digital Hinterland: Internet practices surrounding the pursuit of "offline" hobbies. Paper presented at AoIR 2017: The 18th Annual Conference of the Association of Internet Researchers, Tartu, Estonia (2017a)

12. Rogerson, M.J., Gibbs, M.: Finding time for tabletop: board game play and parenting. Games Cult. **13**(3), 280–300 (2018)

13. Parlett, D.: Parlett's History of Board Games. Echo Point Books & Media (2018)

14. Costikyan, G.: Board game aesthetics. In: Tabletop: Analog Game Design. ETC Press (2011/2015)

15. Nicholson, S.: Modern board games: it's not a Monopoly any more. Libr. Technol. Rep. **44**(3). 8–10, 38–39 (2008)

16. Mayer, B. Harris, C.: Libraries Got Game: Aligned Learning Through Modern Board Games. ALA Editions (2010)

17. Duarte, L.C.S., Battaiola, A.L.: Distinctive features and game design. Entertain. Comput. **21**, 83–93 (2017)

18. Donovan, T.: The four board game eras: making sense of board gaming's past. Catalan J. Commun. Cult. Stud. **10**(2), 265–270 (2018)

19. Shapiro, D.: To boldly go. Games J. (2003). http://www.thegamesjournal.com/articles/ToBoldlyGo.shtml

20. Stegmaier, J.: Scythe. Stonemaier games (2016)

21. Roubira, J.-L.: Dixit. Libellud (2008)

22. Souza, P.A.C., dos Santos, A.T., Brito Neto, S.J., Moreira, H.S.: 9. A influência do product placement na série The Big Bang Theory. Revista Científica UMC **1**(1), 1–13 (2016)

23. Rogers, A.: The Story Universe of Magic: The Gathering is Expanding. The Wired (2019). https://www.wired.com/story/comic-con-2019-magic-the-gathering/

24. Trammell, A., Torner, E., Waldron, E.: Analog Game Studies, vol. I. Lulu.com (2016)

25. Trammell, A., Torner, E., Waldron, E.: Analog Game Studies, vol. II. Lulu.com (2017)

26. Trammell, A., Torner, E., Waldron, E.: Analog Game Studies, vol. III. Lulu.com (2018)

27. Engelstein, G.: Gametek: The Math and Science of Gaming. BookBaby (2018)

28. Erway, S.: Loving Eurogames A Quest for the Well Played Game. Griffin Creek Press (2018)

29. Trower, M.: Tabletop gaming manual. Hayness (2018)

30. Dee, S.: Ticket to Carcassonne: 21st Century Tabletop Games (2019)

31. Duffy, O.: The Board Game Book, vol. I. Clyde & Cart Press. (2019)

32. Philies, G., Vasel, T.: Designing Modern Strategy Games. Studies in Game Design Book 1, 2nd edn (2017)

33. Barret, G.: Board Game Design Advice: From the Best in the World. CreateSpace Independent Publishing Platform (2018)

34. Dean, E.: For the Love of Boardgames. BookBaby (2019)

35. Selinker, M., Ernest, J., Garfield, R., Jackson, S.: The Kobold Guide to Board Game Design. Open Design (2011)
36. Slack, J.: The Board Game Designer's Guide: The Easy 4 Step Process to Create Amazing Games That People Can't Stop Playing. Crazy Like a Box (2017)
37. Vaccarino, D.: Dominion. Rio Grande Games (2008)
38. Leacock, M.: Pandemic. Z-Man Games (2008)
39. Zhang, T., Liu, J., Shi, Y.: Enhancing collaboration in tabletop board game. In: Proceedings of the 10th Asia Pacific Conference on Computer Human Interaction, pp. 7–10. ACM (2012)
40. Bergström, K.: The implicit rules of board games: on the particulars of the lusory agreement. In: Proceedings of the 14th International Academic MindTrek Conference: Envisioning Future Media Environments, pp. 86–93. ACM (2010)
41. Borit, C., Borit, M., Olsen, P.: Representations of colonialism in three popular, modern board games: Puerto Rico, struggle of empires, and archipelago. Open Library of Humanities, 4(1), p. 17, pp. 1–40 (2018)
42. Eisenack, K.: A climate change board game for interdisciplinary communication and education. Simul. Gaming 44(2–3), 328–348 (2013)
43. Castronova, E., Knowles, I.: Modding board games into serious games: the case of Climate Policy. Int. J. Serious Games 2(3), 41–62 (2015)
44. Chappin, E.J., Bijvoet, X., Oei, A.: Teaching sustainability to a broad audience through an entertainment game–the effect of Catan: Oil Springs. J. Clean. Prod. 156, 556–568 (2017)
45. Thompson, D.: Teaching validity and soundness of arguments using the board game: the resistance. PRIMUS 25(6), 542–552 (2015)
46. Triboni, E., Weber, G.: MOL: developing a European-style board game to teach organic chemistry. J. Chem. Educ. 95(5), 791–803 (2018)
47. Andrews, J.H.: Killer app: a eurogame about software quality. In: 2013 26th International Conference on Software Engineering Education and Training (CSEE&T), pp. 319–323. IEEE (2013)
48. Copeland, T., Henderson, B., Mayer, B., Nicholson, S.: Three different paths for tabletop gaming in school libraries. Libr. Trends 61(4), 825–835 (2013)
49. Stephens, R.: Urban planning games and simulations: from board games to artificial environments. In: Kaneda, T., Kanegae, H., Toyoda, Y., Rizzi, P. (eds.) Simulation and Gaming in the Network Society. TSS, vol. 9, pp. 253–273. Springer, Singapore (2016). https://doi.org/10.1007/978-981-10-0575-6_19
50. Brown, A.G., Waterhouse-Watson, D.S.: Reconfiguring narrative in contemporary board games: story-making across the competitive cooperative spectrum, Intensities: J. Cult Media (7), 5–19 (2014)
51. Booth, P.: Board, game, and media: Interactive board games as multimedia convergence. Convergence 22(6), 647–660 (2016)
52. Chircop, D.: An experiential comparative tool for board games. Replay Pol. J. Game Stud. 3, 11–28 (2016)
53. Kato, T., Sugiura, J., Iida, M., Arakawa, C.: A typology of speeches within board game players for analyzing the process of games. In: DiGRA Conference (2007)
54. Bakker, S., Vorstenbosch, D., van den Hoven, E., Hollemans, G., Bergman, T.: Tangible interaction in tabletop games: studying iconic and symbolic play pieces. In: Proceedings of the International Conference on Advances in Computer Entertainment Technology, pp. 163–170. ACM (2007)
55. Rogerson, M.J., Gibbs, M.R., Smith, W.: What can we learn from eye tracking boardgame play? In: Extended Abstracts Publication of the Annual Symposium on Computer-Human Interaction in Play, pp. 519–526. ACM (2017b)

56. Masuda, R., de Haan, J.: Language in game rules and game play: a study of emergence in pandemic. Int. J. Engl. Linguist. **5**(6), 1 (2015)
57. Evans, J.: Translating board games: multimodality and play. J. Spec. Transl. **20**, 15–32 (2013)
58. Rogerson, M.J., Gibbs, M., Smith, W.: I love all the bits: the materiality of boardgames. In: Proceedings of the 2016 CHI Conference on Human Factors in Computing Systems, pp. 3956–3969. ACM (2016)
59. Zagal, J.P., Rick, J., Hsi, I.: Collaborative games: lessons learned from board games. Simul. Gaming **37**(1), 24–40 (2006)
60. d'Astous, A., Gagnon, K.: An inquiry into the factors that impact on consumer appreciation of a board game. J. Consum. Mark. **24**(2), 80–89 (2007)
61. Sato, A., de Haan, J.: Applying an experiential learning model to the teaching of gateway strategy board games. Int. J. Instr. **9**(1), 3–16 (2016)
62. Pfeiffer, M.: Reinforcement learning of strategies for Settlers of Catan. In: Proceedings of the International Conference on Computer Games: Artificial Intelligence, Design and Education (2004)
63. Mahlmann, T., Togelius, J., Yannakakis, G.N.: Evolving card sets towards balancing dominion. In: 2012 IEEE Congress on Evolutionary Computation, pp. 1–8. IEEE (2012)
64. de Mesentier Silva, F., Lee, S., Togelius, J., Nealen, A.: AI-based playtesting of contemporary board games. In: Proceedings of the 12th International Conference on the Foundations of Digital Games, p. 13. ACM (2017)
65. Woolford, M., Watson, I.: SCOUT: a case-based reasoning agent for playing race for the galaxy. In: Aha, D.W., Lieber, J. (eds.) ICCBR 2017. LNCS (LNAI), vol. 10339, pp. 390–402. Springer, Cham (2017). https://doi.org/10.1007/978-3-319-61030-6_27
66. Boda, M.A.: Avoiding revenge using optimal opponent ranking strategy in the board game Catan. Int. J. Gaming Comput.-Mediat. Simul. (IJGCMS) **10**(2), 47–70 (2019)
67. Hartelius, U., Fröhlander, J., Björk, S.: Tisch digital tools supporting board games. In: Proceedings of the International Conference on the Foundations of Digital Games, pp. 196–203. ACM (2012)
68. Wallace, J.R., et al.: Exploring automation in digital tabletop board game. In: Proceedings of the ACM 2012 Conference on Computer Supported Cooperative Work Companion, pp. 231–234. ACM (2012)
69. Rogerson, M.J., Gibbs, M.R., Smith, W.: Cooperating to compete: the mutuality of cooperation and competition in boardgame play. In: Proceedings of the 2018 CHI Conference on Human Factors in Computing Systems, p. 193. ACM (2018)
70. Robson, D., Phillips, J., Guerrero, S.: Don't just roll the dice: simple solutions for circulating tabletop game collections effectively in your library. Libr. Resour. Tech. Serv. **62**(2), 80 (2018)
71. Rogerson, M.J., Gibbs, M., Smith, W.: Digitizing boardgames: issues and tensions. In: Proceedings of DiGRA (2015)
72. Xu, Y., Barba, E., Radu, I., Gandy, M., MacIntyre, B.: Chores are fun: understanding social play in board games for digital tabletop game design. In: DiGRA Conference (2011)
73. Berland, M., Lee, V.R.: Collaborative strategic board games as a site for distributed computational thinking. Int. J. Game-Based Learn. **1**(2), 65–81 (2011)
74. Guhe, M., Lascarides, A.: Trading in a multiplayer board game: towards an analysis of non-cooperative dialogue. In: Proceedings of the Annual Meeting of the Cognitive Science Society, vol. 34, no. 34 (2012)
75. Guhe, M., Lascarides, A.: Game strategies for the Settlers of Catan. In: 2014 IEEE Conference on Computational Intelligence and Games, pp. 1–8. IEEE (2014a)

76. Guhe, M., Lascarides, A.: The effectiveness of persuasion in the Settlers of Catan. In: 2014 IEEE Conference on Computational Intelligence and Games, pp. 1–8. IEEE (2014b)
77. Roelofs, G.: Monte Carlo tree search in a modern board game framework. Research paper available at umimaas. nl (2012)
78. Nicholson, S.: Go back to start: gathering baseline data about gaming in libraries. Libr. Rev. **58**(3), 203–214 (2009)
79. Nicholson, S.: Making gameplay matter: designing modern educational tabletop games. Knowl. Quest **40**(1), 60 (2011)
80. Mayer, B.: Games and the 21st-century standards an ideal partnership. Knowl. Quest **40**(1), 46 (2011)
81. Crews, A.: Getting teachers on "board". Knowl. Quest **40**(1), 10 (2011)
82. Alvarez, V.: Engaging students in the library through tabletop gaming. Knowl. Quest **45**(4), 40–49 (2017)

Design of a Collaborative Tabletop Game for Civic Engagement: Serious Games in Rural India

Sreeram Kongeseri$^{(\boxtimes)}$ ⓘ and Christopher Coley ⓘ

Amrita Vishwa Vidyapeetham, Amritapuri 690525, Kerala, India
{sreeram.kongeseri, chris.coley}@ammachilabs.org

Abstract. This paper presents research on a tabletop game design for enhancing focused discussion strategy creation, engagement motivation, planning and resource allocation, and service leadership through collaborative gameplay. Background: Although the field of serious games has developed over the last three decades, the potential of games to be used as civic engagement and educational tools still lay unrealized. People in rural communities in India experience a range of barriers for constructive engagement. Serious games have been used to address the issue of civic engagement effectively. In this paper, we present a case study of *Aadarsh Gaon, build your ideal village*, a tabletop game where participants work together to discuss strategies to solve social issues in their community, in order to win the game. The paper discusses the concepts in the game, evolution of the game during playtesting and aspects of collaborative gameplay. Results: Three phases of playtesting with diverse participants suggest that the game could trigger focused discussions on strategy creation to solve social problems, but do not indicate significant progress in attitude towards service leadership, and planning and resource allocation. We conclude that serious games with purposeful game design elements could lead to constructive civic engagement.

Keywords: Serious games · Collaborative games · Civic engagement · Tabletop games · Social problem

1 Introduction

The potential for games as a learning and engagement tool has been a recurring theme over the last three decades [1–3]. Various types of games from physical board games to virtual reality and "Exergames" are being studied for purposes other than entertainment including education, training, and emotional well-being. Gaming habits have also changed significantly during the past decades, from classic board games, to computer games, to mobile phone gaming and other types of games involving pervasive computing "gaming" has been incorporated into a vast field of activities and platforms [4]. Despite this proliferation, the act of playing a game still has a unique effect on players, providing a more natural setting for group cohesion, team work, goal setting, and other positive experiences [2]. It is these positive, social elements of games that are leveraged

© Springer Nature Switzerland AG 2019
N. Zagalo et al. (Eds.): VJ 2019, CCIS 1164, pp. 86–98, 2019.
https://doi.org/10.1007/978-3-030-37983-4_7

in applications for education and training. These social skills are also critical for development work and supporting poverty-alleviation programs. This paper will present a game designed specifically for assisting development programs among the rural poor in India, demonstrating its effectiveness as a kick-starter for discussions, and eventual actions around community mobilization to solve social problems.

The game discussed in this paper, called Aadarsh Gaon in Hindi, or "Ideal Village" was designed to target the slow-acting dangers of poor civic engagement around social issues, such as failure to invest in sanitation infrastructure, education, disaster planning, and other issues that impact well-being in communities already challenged by poverty. Such social problems are complex and interwoven with multiple other problems. In addition, it is well researched that populations at or below the poverty line often a lack the basic education, capabilities [5], and agency [6] needed to recognize, understand, and eventually solve social problems. However, any intervention must accurately reflect the local needs, sensitive to the local beliefs and behaviours, and otherwise contextually relevant in order to be embraced by the target population. This point was made at the 2015 UN Academic Impact meeting where humanitarian leader and Amrita University's chancellor, Sri Mata Amritanandamayi [7] stated: "When we try to love or serve without understanding those whom we are serving, we often end up harming society and ourselves. In order for service to be beneficial, it needs to go hand in hand with discernment. This is the essence of sustainable development." It is in this context that Aadarsh Gaon board game was created. The game is meant to engage the target population with complex social issues in a safe, controlled environment in order for them to better understand the problems and role that they can have in solving them. Aadarsh Gaon was created to support existing development programs managed by the authors' university research labs. It is our thesis that by designing collaborative tabletop games, barriers to engagement on community social problems, which are often obstructed by social factors, will decrease and motivation to engage will increase.

This paper is organized as follows: First, the game design and the concepts covered in the game is described. Second, the game set up and the development process through the playtesting phase is discussed. Three phases of playtesting were conducted to investigate the impact of the game design on focused discussions on four measures of interest: enhancing collaborative strategy planning creation, engagement motivation, planning and resource allocation, and service leadership. Third, the results of the play testing are discussed. Finally, we conclude the paper with limitations of the study and recommendations for future research.

2 Related Work

2.1 Serious Games

The application of a serious games approach has been shown to improve achievements in a variety of domains including education, well-being, advertising, cultural heritage, interpersonal communication, and health care [8]. One of the main challenges of a serious game designer is to balance the entertainment aspect with learning or other beneficial life skills. In successful serious games, one cannot be sacrificed for the other [10]. Studies indicate that serious games are linked to a diverse set of impacts and outcomes from a range of perceptual, cognitive, behavioural, affective and motivational measures. Not all serious games, however, have proven as effective as anticipated. Certain domains such as formal school education have witnessed more success than other fields [11–14]. Its application in a field like sustainable development requires more study. Further research is also required to connect the specific learning outcomes to game design elements, but the potential of serious games remains of active interest to academicians and industry alike [15].

2.2   Games for Civic Engagement

Gordan [16] argues that, "Civic engagement represents the ability of people to acquire and process information, voice and debate opinions and beliefs, and take action" Games for civic engagement are seen as legitimate ways to constructively engage citizens in policy discussions, solve community issues, increase volunteer motivation and citizen science [17]. Serious games for enhancing the civic engagement processes is an active area of interest in the communities of research and practice. One example of this is the scientific community's application of games to engage the public around climate change through raising awareness [18]. Various video games and tabletop games have been used as a part of the consultation process in urban planning [19, 20]. The benefits of large-scale deployment of such initiatives can create real-life change in people's lives [21–23]. However, it is a challenge to meet the minimum requirements to use digital tools in rural India due to the presence of social, economic and technological barriers [5]. Therefore, tabletop games could be an alternative medium for designing games for civic engagement.

2.3   Four Measures of Interest for Civic Engagement

The cycle of poverty in India is complex and multi-dimensional, and often singular approaches are ineffective in producing sustainable development [24–26]. Limited educational opportunities and lack of monetary resources or financial support, as well as societal barriers associated with the caste system, limit the ability of the rural poor from participating in community decision-making. Research has shown that empowering people with the knowledge and skills to make informed life decisions, along with economic resources, is the most effective ways of reducing poverty within entire communities [27]. One of the more subtle barriers to upward mobility in India is the lingering social stigmas associated with the caste-system and caste-specific occupations. These stigmas span multiple generations, often representing psychological as well as economic barriers that can impede the development of a positive sense of self-worth [26]. Individuals, especially rural groups in the "lower" castes as they experience far more difficulties participating in community decision making, often need training and support in general life skills including civic responsibility, human rights, civic engagement and support, critical thinking and decision making skills, money management and communication skills to overcome all of the barriers that prevent reaching a higher quality of life [26].

The effects of general perceptions of low self-worth can manifest as feelings of exclusion or unwillingness to engage with other groups. This, in turn, leads to under participation in community decision making or mobilization around solving social problems [28, 29]. Taking stock of the existing literature on serious games and development, four measures were selected: (1) collaborative strategy creation, (2) engagement motivation, (3) planning and resource allocation, and (4) service leadership. Based on aforementioned factors, a serious game was developed to supplement the ongoing development work by the authors' university and parent NGO—programs that include women's empowerment, vocational training, life skills training, and infrastructure improvements. The measures could potentially address challenges concerning strategies to improve overall development work in rural India.

3 Game Design and Testing Method

3.1 Game Design and Development

In this section we describe the game concept, followed by the design challenges in developing the game, and finally a discussion of the implementation and potential impact of Aadarsh Gaon. Researchers, from the study conducted on another competitive game, Abhi Ya Kabhi [30] reflected on game design elements that contributed or hindered the engagement levels. Serious game design goal of this game were to trigger discussion around collaborative strategy creation, engagement motivation, planning & resource allocation, and service leadership.

The motivation behind the game Aadarsh Gaon was to encourage collaborative engagement in discussions about social problems plaguing one's community, and address the same as a group. This game is part of our research labs' goal of creating effective solutions for Technical Vocational Education and Training (TVET), life skills, and women's empowerment. This collaborative game requires the participants to form teams and solve three social problems to win the game. In order to solve a social problem, the participants will need to use their trust and skill tokens, issued at the start of the game and earned during play, and exchange them for resource and volunteer tokens that are used to advance. A team goal card is given which specifies the number of tokens and combinations required to solve the three social problems selected by the teams. At the start of the game, each player chooses a role from among Role Cards and starts from the space specified in their role card. Other game pieces include Insurance, purchased at the start of a turn that minimizes the effects of a disaster, and 18 Scenario cards. The participants will only get 18 rounds to solve their social problems. Figure 1 shows the options available to players during each round.

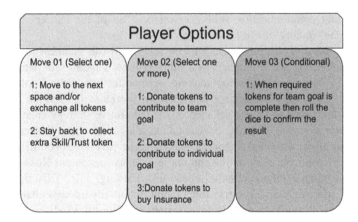

Fig. 1. Player options

3.2 Playtesting Method

Participants (N = 44) belonged to various classes of socioeconomic status, culture, languages and geography. Staggering the play testing across several weeks, as show in Table 1, was essential to process the feedback, modify the game, and prepare for the next phase. Field notes were collected from observation, informal and unstructured interviewing during and after each playtesting session. Observations included changes in focus of the group (individual goals versus team goals), preference between playing individually or with a team, strategy creation and risk taking/aversion. Main focus of the field notes were to document discussions around collaborative strategy creation, planning and resource allocation. A time log provided the average time per round taken by the group.

The focus of the first phase was to facilitate collaborative strategy creation and discussions concerning service leadership. Multiple test plays in the host university with members of the research lab. Phase 01 set-up included core elements of the game including different team and individual goals, and scenario cards for 18 rounds. The focus of the phase 02 was to increase engagement motivation and discussions around planning and resource allocation. Phase 02 play testing was conducted in a rural village called Kanti in Haryana, north India. The participants belonged to the lower socioeconomic community within the village. The focus of the phase 03 was to modify the game mechanics for better game experience viz. level of challenges and opportunities provided in the game.

Table 1. Details of three playtesting phases

No.	Design focus and game mechanics	Sample
Phase 01 (Jan 12–17, 2018)	• Collaborative strategy creation and Service leadership discussion • Team and Individual goals • Donate resources and volunteer to solve social problems • Scenario cards to provide more context	4 groups (16 participants) Staff from AMMACHI Labs, Kerala
Phase 02 (Feb 12–16, 2018)	Increase engagement motivation and Facilitate planning and resource allocation discussion • Customize game board before start of the play • Select goals/social problems of relevance • Select role of their preference • Constraints on movement, exchange and donation of participants	3 groups (25 participants) Villagers from Kanti, Haryana
Phase 03 (Mar 12–16, 2018)	Enhance balance of the game • Role of village chief (Sarpanch) • Disaster events and Insurance options • Increase in outcome event possibilities • Selection of dice based on individual goal achievement	4 groups (16 participants) Students and Faculty members from Amrita University

4 Results

Time logs, as show in Table 2, from the play testing revealed that there significant differences were only seen in phase 02. Differences in time logs were due to the extra set of translations that were required to conduct the playtesting in Kanti, Haryana. The participants do not speak English there so the content had to be translated to Hindi with the help of local translator (Fig. 2).

Table 2. Time log

Phase	Average time/game (in minutes)	Average time/round (in minutes)	Remarks
1	40–50	2–4	1–4 rounds were longer
2	50–90	3–5	1–5 rounds were longer
3	40–50	2–4	1–3 rounds were longer

On an average, game rulebook reading did not last more than 20 min, and participants claimed to understand the instructions. Duration of rulebook reading was not added to the time log. Clarifying questions on the rules were regularly asked during initial rounds, but rarely after round 4. Participants from the three phases differed on number of insurance secured, selection of social problems to solve and numbers of dice

Fig. 2. Students and faculty members from Amrita University, Phase 03 playtesting.

roll attempted. Response to Scenarios cards from groups in three phases were different and this was observed in the amount of changes groups made once they drew the Scenarios card. The role of the Sarpanch or Village chief was significant in the phase 01 design, but it was later modified to be the role of "gatekeeper of the community" in order to reflect the administrative role a chief plays in a village community.

4.1   Collaborative Strategy Creation

In general, the participants reported that they found the game challenging, entertaining, and worth their time. The game set-up process triggered participants to have discussions even before the game started on social problems they wanted to address and player roles. Scenario cards, adverse and favourable ones, made participants change their to acquire tokens for solving social problems. Alternate strategies were discussed due to constraints placed via. Individual goals and changing scenarios. However, it was noted that the presence of a dominant personality in a group may derail the opportunity for nuanced strategy creation. This was evident in the two groups in phase 02, Haryana. None of the participants that the authors interviewed preferred the same game in a single player mode. The authors propose that having an individual goal and team goal provided a balance to the competition versus collaborative narrative. This was more evident in the play testing in phase 02 where participants reported that they felt like 'fighting the system' as a group and individually, matching their description of the problems with the local government in the community. Thematically, the game may have been successful in nudging people to discuss about specific plans to solve social problems, but it requires modifications to balance the game play experience viz-à-viz getting the combination of resources and volunteer tokens achievable during the course of 18 rounds of play. A few issues were reported in phase 01 individual goals and team goals since the number of rounds in the game (18) were limited.

"This is too tough. I can't, no team can reach the target in 18 rounds. You have to increase the number of rounds or do something about it." Group 1, Phase 01.
"It was fun playing this game together. Normally we play against each other, now we create plans to win together. I like it" Participant from Group 4, Phase 01 (Fig. 3).

Fig. 3. Group 2 from AMMACHI Labs Research Institution - Phase 01 playtesting.

4.2   Engagement Motivation

Field notes indicate that almost all of them spoke during 18 rounds of game and voiced their opinion on the strategy to solve. Participants from phase 01 and phase occasionally checked their mobile phones and engaged in conversations not relating to the game. Participants from phase 02 were engaged in more activities not related to the game compared to other phases. However, the phase 02 was conducted in front of the participant's house and non-participants from the rural village would often strike a conversation with the participants.

"We are in this together, like in real life. Playing together is fun. I would like to play this again and discuss issues that concern my village".
Participant from Group 1, Phase 2

"I want my friends to play this game so that we can discuss these issues".

Participant from Group 2, Phase 2

The authors postulate that the engagement motivation could be triggered by the relevance of the game content and narrative, and the perceived control participants felt during the game play may be attributed to multiple game elements. Player options, as illustrated in Fig. 1, provided a chance for the players to anticipate and prepare for adverse events. For instance, a disaster event could be triggered by the result of a dice roll, and it impacts the game in two ways: cutting off access to a community space or losing tokens. Participants can choose when to roll the dice, so most groups planned ahead counter measures including securing Insurance (Fig. 4).

Fig. 4. Group 1 from Kanti Village, Haryana.

4.3   Planning and Resource Allocation

It was noted that significant amount of time was spent in discussion over specific strategies to solve social problems to win the game. Most groups did not go beyond planning for the immediate set of rounds, only a few teams were planning beyond three or four rounds. Lack of synchronicity between planning, resource allocation and long term strategy were observed in the discussions around the play in few of the groups. Group 2 and group 3 in phase 02 were mostly concerned about collecting resources or volunteer tokens rather than specific combinations of them to solve a particular social problem. This phenomenon was present in phase 01 and phase 03. When participants were probed on their progress, majority of them were comfortable whatever position their groups were in, during the game.

> *"I think we can win this game. We just need to plan better for the next round and then we solve two problems"* Participant from Group 03, Phase 03.

4.4   Service Leadership

Volunteering tokens and the game mechanic to donate tokens were introduced to reinforce the concept of service leadership. There are six types of volunteering token and each symbolised an act of service. Team goals required a specific combination of volunteering tokens and resource tokens to solve a social problems. Beyond targeting the tokens, no specific discussions were observed around service leadership or significance and meaning of the volunteering or donating tokens.

5   Discussion

Results from this case study are consistent with findings and recommendations from the seminal paper on collaborative games, Zagal [31]. Four lessons and 3 pitfalls reported in Zagal's paper is used as a framework to review the results of playtesting (Table 3).

Table 3. Adapted review framework from Zagal [31]

No	Lessons (to follow)	Pitfalls (to avoid)
1	Conflicting individual utility and team utility	Weak narrative for collaboration
2	Autonomy in decision making in collaborative gameplay	Diminutive outcomes
3	Ability to trace long-term rewards	Non evolving game challenges and experience
4	Different roles and abilities	

Results from this case study are consistent with findings and recommendations from the seminal paper on collaborative games, Zagal [31]. Four lessons and 3 pitfalls reported in Zagal's paper is used as a framework to review the results of playtesting.

Lesson 1: Setting a constraint of 18 rounds created a tension between achieving individual and team goals to win the game. This game element may have provided a balance to the game, thereby having a positive effect on the perceived experience of the game.

Lesson 2: Opportunity to select different roles to the participants gave them a chance to contribute to the team goals in unique ways that other players may not be able to. However, the game design was not able to completely avoid pitfall 01, which was to avoid one person take over the playmaking. A few groups had dominant personalities who may have dictated the collective strategy, which may not be conducive for Engagement Motivation, Planning and Resource allocation, and overall experience. If the discussions around the four measures of interest were limited due to the this phenomenon then revisions to the game design is required.

Lesson 3: Discussions around strategy to secure tokens and solve social problems stretched to more than 2 or 3 rounds in the future. This may be an indicator of the connections perceived by the participants between moves in the game and progress that could be made to win the game.

Lesson 4: Roles provided in the game also the participants to start the game from different positions on the board and collect different combinations of tokens, yet contribute to the same team goals. Discussions around planning and resource allocation revolved around possibilities of different players making certain moves and acquiring different tokens.

Pitfall 1: The narrative that most participants identified with, were the nature of the challenges presented in the game. Scenario cards contained common events, both adverse and positive, reported in rural communities in India. This game element added to the narrative, as evident in the discussions in creating strategy.

Pitfall 2: The challenge of solving a social problem, as reported by the participants, was an identifiable and relevant goal. The presence of Scenarios cards, Sarpanch (village chief) controlled by game AI, and individual goals may also have helped to create motivating risk-reward payoffs.

Pitfall 3: The player roles, game board placement, team goal selection were customisable before the gameplay. Discussions around planning and resource allocation also concerned the abilities of different roles and combination of tokens required to solve a social issue. Authors postulate that this may have amounted to increased engagement motivation.

6 Conclusion

We have outlined the characteristics of the Aadarsh Gaon tabletop game and participants' responses during three phases of play testing. The design of the game and the impact of the game design on the four measures of interest were also discussed. The experiments releveled both strengths and weaknesses of the concept, the interaction techniques, and the elements of game design, as well as ideas and issues for future game research.

One of the main limitations of the study was the lack of quantitative measures to present the insights from the case study. Thematic coding of semi structured interviews could have also helped in classifying the results into actional recommendations. Questions on specific game mechanics were also not included in this study. More testing and design iterations are required to determine which game board components are the most suitable for the goals of the study. Further research on design elements or rule modifications is required to encouraged specificity in planning and resource allocation, along with long-term strategy. Finally, our experiments have shown promise in tabletop games that are designed for specific objectives, including as a tool for civic engagement. We plan to conduct further experiments and systematic evaluations in order to develop the next generation of the game.

References

1. Abt, C.: Serious Games. University Press of America, Lanham (1987)
2. Salen, K., Zimmerman, E.: Rules of Play. MIT Press, Cambridge (2004)

3. Dörner, R., Göbel, S., Effelsberg, W., Wiemeyer, J. (eds.): Serious Games. Springer, Heidelberg (2016). https://doi.org/10.1007/978-3-319-40612-1
4. Andersen, T.L., Kristensen, S., Nielsen, B.W., Grønbæk, K.: Designing an augmented reality board game with children. In: Proceeding of the 2004 Conference on Interaction Design and Children Building a Community - IDC 2004 (2004)
5. Sen, A.: Human rights and capabilities. J. Hum. Dev. 6(2), 151–166 (2005)
6. Rayan, D. (ed.): Empowerment and Poverty Reduction. The World Bank, June 2002
7. Amritanadamayi, M.: Mata Amritanandamayi Speech at United Nations 2015 - English Translated (2019)
8. Michael, D., Chen, S.: Serious Games: Games that Educate, Train, and Inform. Course Technology, Mason (2011)
9. Laamarti, F., Eid, M., El Saddik, A.: An overview of serious games. Int. J. Comput. Games Technol. 2014, 1–15 (2014)
10. Girard, C., Ecalle, J., Magnan, A.: Serious games as new educational tools: how effective are they? A meta-analysis of recent studies. J. Comput. Assist. Learn. 29(3), 207–219 (2012)
11. Connolly, T.M., Boyle, E.A., MacArthur, E., Hainey, T., Boyle, J.M.: A systematic literature review of empirical evidence on computer games and serious games. Comput. Educ. 59(2), 661–686 (2012)
12. Backlund, P., Hendrix, M.: Educational games - are they worth the effort? A literature survey of the effectiveness of serious games. In: 2013 5th International Conference on Games and Virtual Worlds for Serious Applications (VS-GAMES) (2013)
13. Wouters, P., van Nimwegen, C., van Oostendorp, H., van der Spek, E.D.: A metaanalysis of the cognitive and motivational effects of serious games. J. Educ. Psychol. 105(2), 249–265 (2013)
14. Giessen, H.W.: Serious games effects: an overview. Procedia - Soc. Behav. Sci. 174, 2240–2244 (2015)
15. Wouters, P., Van der Spek, E.D., Van Oostendorp, H.: Current practices in serious game research. In: Games-Based Learning Advancements for Multi-Sensory Human Computer Interfaces, pp. 232–250. IGI Global (2009)
16. Gordon, E., Baldwin-Philippi, J., Balestra, M.: Why we engage: how theories of human behavior contribute to our understanding of civic engagement in a digital era. SSRN Electron. J. (2013)
17. Lenhart, J.: Teens, Video Games, and Civics: Teens' Gaming Experiences Are Diverse and Include Significant Social Interaction and Civic Engagement. Eric.ed.gov. https://eric.ed.gov/?id=ED525058. Accessed 20 May 2018
18. Wu, J.S., Lee, J.J.: Climate change games as tools for education and engagement. Nat. Clim. Change 5(5), 413–418 (2015)
19. Poplin, A.: Playful public participation in urban planning: a case study for online serious games. Comput. Environ. Urban Syst. 36(3), 195–206 (2012)
20. Devisch, O., Poplin, A., Sofronie, S.: The gamification of civic participation: two experiments in improving the skills of citizens to reflect collectively on spatial issues. J. Urban Technol. 23(2), 81–102 (2016)
21. Gordon, E., Schirra, S.: S.: Playing with empathy. In: Proceedings of the 5th International Conference on Communities and Technologies - C&T 2011 (2011)
22. Hassan, L.: Governments should play games. Simul. Gaming 48(2), 249–267 (2016)
23. Harviainen, J.T., Hassan, L.: Governmental service gamification. Int. J. Innov. Digit. Econ. 10(3), 1–12 (2019)
24. Parker, B., Kozel, V.: Understanding poverty and vulnerability in India's Uttar Pradesh and Bihar: a Q-squared approach. World Dev. 35(2), 296–311 (2007)

25. Sheshadri, S., Coley, C., Jagadeesh, S., Kongeseri, S., Devanathan, S., Bhavani, R.R.: Community centric vocational education: a strategy for implementation of computerized TVET delivery in rural india. In: International Conference on Emerging Trends In TVET: Vision 2025 (2015)

26. Eyben, R., Kabeer, N., Cornwall, A.: Conceptualising empowerment and the implications for pro-poor growth: a paper for the DAC Poverty Network (2008)

27. Mason, A.D., King, E.M.: Engendering development through gender equality in rights, resources, and voice (English). A World Bank policy research report. World Bank, Washington DC (2001)

28. Mansuri, G., Rao, V.: Localizing Development. The World Bank (2012)

29. John, A., Gopalakrishnan, R., Javed, R.: Reflections on use of participatory methods in the capacity building program for tribal community health volunteers. Indian J. Community Health **27**(2), 290–294 (2015)

30. Kongeseri, S., Sheshadri, S., Coley, C., Muir, A., Bhavani, R.R.: Games for community development and problem solving: a multi-site case study. Adv. Sci. Lett. **24**(4), 2358–2361 (2018)

31. Zagal, J.P., Rick, J., Hsi, I.: Collaborative games: lessons learned from board games. Simul. Gaming **37**(1), 24–40 (2006)

Supporting the Game Construction Process: Development of Artefacts in the Context of a Toolkit to Game Design

Pedro Beça, Mónica Aresta$^{(\boxtimes)}$, Rita Santos, Ana Isabel Veloso, Gonçalo Gomes, and Mariana Pereira

DigiMedia, Departamento de Comunicação e Arte, Universidade de Aveiro, Campus Universitário de Santiago, 3810-193 Aveiro, Portugal
{pedrobeca, m.aresta, rita.santos, aiv, goncalo, marianagomespereira}@ua.pt

Abstract. The Gamers4Nature project aims to deliver a set of strategies to empower and encourage youngsters (upper-secondary and undergraduate students) to actively participate in games creation while raising knowledge about environmental preservation and biodiversity conservation. To accomplish these goals, a Toolkit to Game Design is being created, containing a set of resources and tools aiming to help in the creation of mobile digital games, namely a Game Construction Cards Set. This paper presents the creation process of the project's general identity and its concept adaptation to the Game Construction Cards Set, which required a deep understanding of the target audience and the development of a strategy to engage the participants in its activities. A general identity was defined, where a specific "language" to reach this audience was designed and a brand to support it was created. This "language" was applied in all graphic materials developed since day one, namely to the Game Construction Cards Set – focus of this paper. The validation of the prototypes was made through focus groups, using an iterative design approach. The focus groups participants' inputs were integrated in the design and helped with the graphic elements' evolution, allowing the project to maintain a coherent strategy in all its representations that exceeds its graphic language and a deeper identification with the developed artefacts.

Keywords: Toolkit to Game Design · Gamers4Nature · Dynamic brand · Graphic identity · Iterative design

1 Introduction

When designing a brand for a younger audience, it not only is important to have a well-thought brand (symbols, typography, colours…) but also to give a new experience of connection to the user. Brand communities, specialized in the consumer, diverge from traditional communities due to their commercial character, and its members shared interest in and enthusiasm for a brand. These are communities that contain common markers: consciousness of kind, shared ritual and moral responsibility [1].

© Springer Nature Switzerland AG 2019
N. Zagalo et al. (Eds.): VJ 2019, CCIS 1164, pp. 99–110, 2019.
https://doi.org/10.1007/978-3-030-37983-4_8

Aiming to be a place of comfort first and foremost [2], a brand community is one of the tools used in relationship marketing to, as the name implies, create and maintain long relationships with consumers [3]. Research in the marketing and branding consider consumer loyalty as one of the core indicators of success of marketing and branding strategy pointing out that brand is a cluster of emotional values [4] and emphasizing that brand values should be seen from the perspective of consumers [5].

In this scenario, the Gamers4Nature project intents to design and implement strategies able to encourage the active participation of youngsters in mobile game creation while raising knowledge about biodiversity conservation and environmental preservation.

To achieve this goal, a Toolkit to Game Design is being developed featuring a set of resources and tools designed to help in the creation of mobile digital games, namely a Game Construction Cards Set (GCCS) and educational resources on environmental preservation.

This paper presents the creation process of the general identity and its' concept adaptation to the GCCS. It is structured in five sections as follows: Gamers4Nature: Defining the Project's Identity, where concerns and decisions about the brand's identity are described; Game Construction Cards Set, where the process of creating and validating the cards is presented; Next Stage: The Educational Resources Card Set, where it is shown how the brand's identity is applied to other resources; and finally, the Conclusions.

2 Gamers4Nature: Defining the Project's Identity

The Gamers4Nature project aims to design and implement strategies able to encourage the active participation of young public (upper-secondary and undergraduate students) in mobile game creation, as a way to promote knowledge about environmental conservation and behaviour change towards nature. To answer to the project's brand identity briefing, it was extremely important to analyse the target audience and its expected behaviour while dealing with technologies within the near future. Several ideas emerged when designing this identity:

- the sense of community - game communities are extremely important and popular, and therefore the brand should evoke it;
- the brand's personality, as the brand should be dynamic and personal to the audience;
- the brand's ability to trigger user engagement.

During the creative process that supported the Gamers4Nature's brand, the following concepts were taken into consideration; *Brand Love* - the level of emotional and impassioned affection that a pleased consumer has with a particular brand [6]; *Brand Loyalty* - defined as the repeated support for a brand over the time [7]; *Word of Mouth* (WOM) - talking about a product and/or service between people apart from advertisement [8]; and *Brand Advocacy* - promotion or defense of an organization/product/brand by one consumer to another. This last concept, as it is seen as less informal and more protective, differs from WOM.

With the desire and intention to create a community in mind, it was essential to look at the brand identity and think about what type of approach would be more effective. During the review of the state-of-the art done through this project, the concept of Dynamic Identities emerged. Dynamic Identities, or living brands [9], are considered to be (in its basic sense) brands with energy able to transmit and reveal change, movement, and flexibility, reflected in their dynamism. A Dynamic Brand is considered to be an evolution, the next step of a Visual Identity, and can be extremely appealing for the openness, interactivity and broad innovation. One other important aspect of Dynamic Brands is the significance it has as a marketing strategy and branding [10].

The logo and brand were designed with all these ideas in mind. For the typography in Gamers4Nature, it was important to find a neutral font with all characters and symbols (e.g. "ç", "~") since the approach was to present a logo whose letters would change regularly, as is seen in coding (Fig. 1). It was chosen Heebo font as the logo font, and some characters were adapted.

G4N*
GAMERS4NATURE*
GAMERS4NATURE
GAMERS4NAT00R3
GAM3R$4NATURE(

Fig. 1. The project's logo.

This approach – to develop a logo able to be transformed by users – reflects the nowadays participatory culture [11] by allowing the involvement of users in the identity process, as they are able to "build their own brand", by combining letters, numbers, and signs that reconfigure the Gamers4Nature lettering.

The personal appropriation of the brand is a key element in brand community building, and it contains common markers: consciousness of kind, shared ritual and moral responsibility [1].

3 Game Construction Cards Set

3.1 Conceptual Framework

To frame the conceptual framework of this project, an exploratory literature review on the concept of games was conducted. Game emerges from the relation between the output of the game design development and the user's experience while playing the game. Amongst other perspectives, games are introduced as structures evolving around its formal system, the relation between the player and the game and the relation between the game and the rest of the world [12]; a relation between the player's experience and the interaction with the games' rules [13]; and as a formal systems made of formal and dramatic elements, system that engage players in a regulated conflict [14]. Being one of the project's goals to assist young students (upper-secondary and undergraduate) in the creation of mobile digital games, Fullerton's [14] approach to game design was considered as being the most suitable, as it includes an extensive description of nineteen game elements (e.g. rules, goals, character, story) and the connection between them. It was expected that taking this approach into the development of artefacts able to transmit information about the game elements (the GCCS) would ease the game creation process and engage users in the creation of games.

The Honeycomb Shape. As mentioned before, the brand's concept and the idea to create a brand able to be reused, redesigned and appropriated by its users should be present along the Gamers4Nature's project, namely in its artefacts and interfaces (both physical and digital). All resources would be included in the online platform but also able to be explored as a physical format – a physical artefact. This way, it would be possible to use the artefact in game design sessions (e.g. Game Jams), where participants would be able to interact with the physical objects and the information comprised in it.

There was, therefore, the need to question how to create a flow between these two supports. What would be the proper approach to both? How to transmit, in a physical artefact, the feeling of gaming and the non-linearity of gaming activities and give users the change to explore several paths and approaches while creating their own games?

As stated by Hale [15], a regular hexagonal grid (honeycombs) is the best way to divide a surface into regions of equal area with the least total perimeter. Hexagonal shapes are perfect for the aggregation of different elements or to simply branch out a map of the different ideas. Taking this into consideration, a set of hexagonal pieces and a honeycomb-based board were created, as a first way to validate and explore the project's conceptual framework.

3.2   Methodology

Iterative design is a process based in cycles of conceptualization, prototyping, testing and evaluation. It is an adaptive process in which designers and developers engage in cycles of defining an idea, developing a prototype that reflects that idea, test the prototype with a target-audience to see the idea in action, and then evaluate the results and make the necessary adjustments [16]. This approach, while leaving room for error, it also allows for the emergence of new viewpoints able to improve the original idea. The validation of the project's artefacts prototypes were made taking an iterative design approach, through interviews and focus groups made with experts and postgraduate students with expertise in game development. Focus groups are group interviews organized to promote the discussion about a specific subject. While guided by a moderator, these sessions allow for the discussion and interaction between participants and their perspectives, being adopted in the game design field as a way to evaluate and understand game play experiences [17, 18]. Focus groups were therefore considered to be the best approach to collect several participants' opinions about games, game design, game elements and the interaction between them.

3.3   Stage 1: Cards Set First's Artefacts

Honeycomb Board. The board given to evaluators to explore the cardboard pieces with the game elements name (19 pieces, one representing each game element) was designed with printed hexagonal shapes and had the A3 size. The hexagonal forms give the aspect of communities as it remembers the honeycombs and honeybees' communities. It was essential to develop and provide the board to instigate the user to make configurations with the cardboard pieces to connect them and so the Focus Group moderator didn't have to intervene so much. There were three elements present on the board: the honeycomb-like shape for the cardboard pieces; an area for participants to name the type of game they were thinking while exploring the cardboard pieces; and the project's description, with the base logo below (Fig. 2).

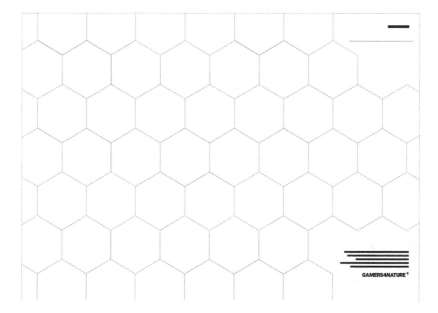

Fig. 2. The honeycomb board

Cardboard Pieces. The cardboard pieces were created with the same purpose of the board: to allow for an ease connection between elements. The hexagonal shape (3 cm side) seems to be the best approach for the group's aggregation of the cardboard pieces or organize a simple branch out a map with different ideas in each cardboard pieces. Six sets were printed, each one with a different colour – so it could be easier to separate or connect the sets, if needed. The used colours were a representation of the brand's Visual Identity, turning the validation cycle also into an exercise on how to communicate the brand (Fig. 3).

Fig. 3. The cardboard pieces.

Discussion: Three Game design researchers and one game developer were invited to use the cardboard pieces (Fig. 4) while talking about games and the game development process (during individual interviews), as well as nine postgraduate students (during two focus groups). Among the nine ICT (Information and Communication Technologies) postgraduate students, six had moderately high or high level of experience in game programming and development; six had some or average experience in constructing game stories and narratives; and five had some or average experience in game art and animation. One participant had no experience in game art and animation, and one had no experience in stories and narratives.

Fig. 4. Participant using the honeycomb board and cardboard pieces.

It was stated by all participants that both the board and the cardboard pieces were a valuable artefact in the exploration of game design concepts. It allowed for different ways to group the elements, to expand initial perspectives and to articulate different ideas. Nevertheless, it was clear that – in order to be used by a younger and less expert audience – the pieces would need to accommodate more information and therefore be redesigned. During the focus group's analysis process, it became evident that there was a need to develop a new way to introduce the element's information: although the hexagons and the honeycomb board had served its goals – to trigger the discussion and to explore the game elements concepts, namely the ones considered as "core-elements" – a larger (dimensions) artefact was needed, so they could accommodate more information about each game element and thus be used, during game creation sessions, by the project's target-audience (upper secondary and undergraduate students).

3.4   Stage 2: First Version of the Game Construction Cards Set

While the hexagonal cardboard pieces allowed for the exploration and discussion of each game element in the first stage, there was a need to develop a solution able to be used by the audience in game design sessions such as Game Jams. This new artefact should be manageable, able to be used by one or several users at the same time and contain the information addressing the different game elements and its importance to the game design process.

Considering the target audience, it became clear the need to add more information about each element. To do so, the size and format of the cards changed to a somewhat close standard size of $7,14 \times 10$ cm. The format of the card stayed with a hexagonal form as an evolutive element of the previous stage. With this format, the connective element between cards was lost, however it wasn't a key element of the cards at this point. The expansion of the cards gave us space to explain the game element's concepts that can be slightly difficult to understand by the target audience. Although this change implied that the honeycomb tray would have to be redesigned or just removed, this change opened doors for space to create a more playful design.

In the front part of the card, the only elements present were the logo, the number of the card (for easy identification of the cards), the concept name and a brief description. The back part had a small contextualization about the game element and a few examples of its presence in games were presented.

As in the previous stage, there were six sets of cards, each one with a different colour for the same exact reason, to easily separate or connect the sets. For the typography element, it was decided to continue with Heebo only for the text body. Instead of using the same font in the card's element, it was decided to experiment with more playful fonts to make the cards less monotonous and dull. After several readability tests, the font Agrandir Tight Heavy was selected. This font is a contemporary serifless type that claims to celebrate the beauty of being imperfect. Agrandir is especially interesting for the extremely unusual characters like the "ç" and "Q" that give the cards a youthful look. The first version of the GCCS is presented in Fig. 5.

Fig. 5. The game construction cards set (cycle 1)

Discussion: End-users (the target audience, upper secondary and undergraduate students) were invited to evaluate the new Game Construction Cards Set prototype. This process of validation was made through four focus groups: two with target-group A (upper secondary students) and two with target-group B (undergraduate students). Students of target-group A were upper secondary students attending an ICT (Information and Communication Technologies) course, 11 students divided in two groups, 10 male one female, aged between 15–17 (average: 16), with no previous experience in game creation activities. Students of target-group B were undergraduate students also attending an ICT course, eight students divided in two groups; six males, 2 females, aged between 19–25 (average: 21), four had previous experience with game creation activities.

Invited to analyse each card of the GCCS, they validated not only the information present in each card but also some design aspects: layout, text size and distribution, text's typography and the legibility of text over each colour. As the validation process focused on these aspects, and participants were not required to explore the relations between the game elements, the honeycomb tray was not introduced to participants.

The feedback about the size of the cards, size of the text and layout was positive, but participants mentioned that increasing the font size would help in the reading process. Moreover, the analysis of the participants' opinion also revealed that, while addressing the cards, participants adopted similar expressions (e.g. for the player card, they defined player as "the one who plays the game") - this suggested that, instead of using just the name of the element as the main focus of the card, the use of the sentences most used by participants would establish a natural connection between the game element's name and the card's content. In order to help the user's thought process, the sentences where presented as trigger expression/questions. This led to edits in the cards' layout, namely on its content, leading to a change in the front of the cards. This information was used for second cycle of the GCCS artefact development.

3.5   Stage 3: Redesigned Game Construction Cards Set

As in the previous stages, six sets of cards with different colours were developed. Each card addressed a game element, presenting in the front side the element's name, the trigger question and a brief description. In the back, the information was the same (with minor typo editions) showed in the previous cycle. As in this development cycle users would be challenged to create a game while using the cards, and in order to avoid any previous defined hierarchy or order, cards were no longer numbered (Fig. 6).

Fig. 6. The game construction cards set (cycle 2)

Discussion: End-users (the target audience, upper secondary and undergraduate students) were invited to evaluate the redesigned Game Construction Cards Set prototype. As in the previous cycle, this process of validation was made through focus groups: three with target-group A (upper secondary students) and seven with target-group B (undergraduate students).

Students of target-group A were the same students that participated in the previous development cycle (N = 10). Students of target-group B were undergraduate students attending an ICT course, 23 students divided in seven groups, 10 male and 13 female, aged between 18 and 25 years old (average: 21). Only three participants had never engaged in game creation activities.

All groups were challenged to create a game using the toolkit cards, which was achieved by the end of the sessions. Questioned about the cards and in what way they could use them during a game creation session, participants mentioned that the questions present in the front of the cards were a good trigger. Asked to talk about the cards' layout and information it comprised, they also mentioned the adequacy of its size, format, layout, font and text distribution.

4   Next Stage: The Educational Resources Card Set

With the first element of the Toolkit to Game Design – the GCCS – finished, requiring only minor adjustments (e.g. decisions about the material in which it will be printed), it was time to start working on another resource of the project, the educational resources to be used during the Game development sessions, focused on environmental preservation and biodiversity awareness. Following the "trigger question" approach taken in the second cycle of the GCCS, the topic approached in each card assumes the form of a question, along with and a small explanation of the concept (Fig. 7).

To tackle this content and to keep it in line with the GCCS, maintaining the brand's consistency, the card format needed to increase on its size: from 7,14 × 10 cm to 9,3 × 13 cm. As for the content for this card set, our first edition addresses micro plastics pollution problem. The graphic layout of the cards will not differ from the GCCS, but will have a new element: an illustration able to clarify and more easily address the concepts described in the texts. Illustrations will also be added to the back of the cards, along with a full explanation of the concept (Fig. 7).

The questions at the front of the cards will have the purpose of triggering the interest of the user. As the example below shows, the question "after all, what are micro plastics?" Allows the common to identify himself with other users with no expertise in the subject being discussed, and therefore be more comfortable in exploring it.

This card set is still in its prototyping phase, and therefore no tests have been made at the time.

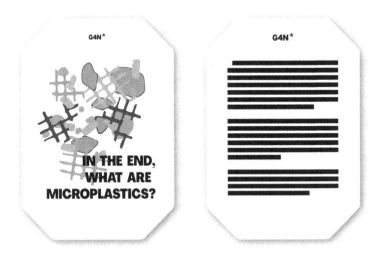

Fig. 7. Micro-plastics cards set

5   Conclusions

There are challenges when trying to communicate with younger audiences. However, there are design strategies that can help to guide and even change the perspective of a group. These strategies can begin with the visual identity of a product/service or how the brand presents itself to the world. Making a dynamic brand that does not rest on one fixed image and is personalized for the individual user was the project's solution. Also, by being flexible with the numbers of typographies that can be used, it acquired the freedom to play with layouts and find better solutions. The participants' inputs along the three stages helped with the graphic elements' evolution. It gave us the opportunity to find what type of physical form the Toolkit needed and how the contents could be shown. By using this methodology, the design process got less chaotic, simpler and quicker. For the next stage of the project, the Educational Resources Cards Set, it is intended to go through the same process as in the Game Construction Card Set . This process will make the Toolkit's evolution stronger and able to be used by students in the development of their own nature-related games.

Acknowledgments. This work is part of the Gamers4Nature project that has the financial support of FCT - Foundation for Science and Technology (Portugal)/ MCTES – Ministry of Science, Technology and Higher Education and FEDER under the PT2020 agreement.

References

1. Muniz, A.M., O'guinn, T.C.: Brand community. J. Consum. Res. **27**(4), 412–432 (2001)
2. Coelho, A., Bairrada, C., Peres, F.: Brand communities' relational outcomes, through brand love. J. Prod. Brand Manag. **28**, 154–165 (2019)
3. Habibi, R., Laroche, M., Richard, M.O.: Testing an extended model of consumer behavior in the context of social media-based brand communities. Comput. Hum. Behav. **62**, 292–302 (2016)
4. De Chernatony, L., McDonald, M.: Creating Powerful Brands in Consumer, Service and Industrial Markets. Butterworth Heinemann, London (2001)
5. Holbrook, M.: Consumer value: a framework for analysis and research. In: Introduction to Consumer Value, pp. 1–28. M.B. Holbrook, London (1999)
6. Carrol, B.A., Ahuvia, A.C.: Some antecedents and outcomes of brand love. Market Lett. **17**, 79 (2006)
7. Back, K.J.: The effects of image congruence on customers' brand loyalty in the upper middle-class hotel industry. J. Hospitality Tourism Res. **4**, 448–467 (2005)
8. Shirkhodaie, M., Rastgoo-Deylami, M.: Positive word of mouth marketing: explaining the roles of value congruity and brand love. J. Competitiveness **8**(1), 19–37 (2016)
9. van Nes, I., Identities, D.: How to Create a Living Brand. IS Publishers, Amsterdam (2012)
10. De Azevedo Kreutz, E.: Construindo Marcas Mutantes. Revista Latinoamericana de Comunicación **119**, 61–65 (2012)
11. Vasudevan, V., Kafai, Y.B.: Deborah fields, "the programmers' collective: fostering participatory culture by making music videos in a high school Scratch coding workshop". Iteractive Learn. Environ. **23**(5), 613–633 (2015)
12. Juul, J.: The game, the player, the world: looking for a heart of gameness. In: Level Up: Digital Games Research Conference Proceedings, pp. 30–45 (2003)

13. Hunicke, R., Leblanc, M., Zubec, R.: MDA: a formal approach to game design and game research. In: AAAI Workshop on Challenges in Game AI (2004)
14. Fullerton, T.: Game Design Workshop: A Playcentric Approach to Creating Innovative Games, 3rd ed. Taylor & Francis Group, Abingdon (2014)
15. Hales, T.C.: The honeycomb conjecture. Discrete Comput. Geom. **25**(1), 1–22 (2001)
16. Macklin, C., Sharp, J.M.: Games, Design and Play - A Detailed Approach to Iterative Game Design. Addison – Wesley (2016)
17. Eklund, L.: Focus group interviews as a way to evaluate and understand game play experiences. In: Lankoski, P., Björk, S. (eds.) Game Research Methods, pp. 133–148. TC Press, Pittsburgh (2015)
18. Poels, K., de Kort, Y., Ijsselsteijn, W.: It is always a lot of fun! Exploring dimensions of digital game experience using focus group methodology. In: Proceedings of the 2007 Conference on Future Play (Future Play 2007), NY, pp. 83–89 (2007)

eSports

The Portuguese eSports Ecosystem: An Exploratory Approach

Cátia Ferreira[(✉)]

CECC, Human Sciences Faculty, Universidade Católica Portuguesa,
Palma de Cima, 1649-023 Lisbon, Portugal
catia.ferreira@ucp.pt

Abstract. eSports are an emerging phenomena worldwide. I would like to argue that eSports are one of the activities that best illustrate the dynamics of network communication [1, 2]. What had appeared as a digital media phenomenon, shortly became a legacy media content. Media companies throughout the world are investing in broadcasting eSports competitions and establishing partnerships with individual content producers that are contributing to the emergence of a new professional activity - digital games streamers [3]. Additionally, eSports are asserting themselves both as a cultural and creative industry. They are part of a complex network of media, game producers, players, and individual digital content producers. Based on a qualitative methodology having document analysis as primary data collection method, this paper intends to discuss the growing relevance of eSports as a networked media phenomena and to present the particular case of Portugal. Data from an exploratory research will be presented aiming at maping the Portuguese eSports media ecosystem.

Keywords: eSports · Networked media · Portugal

1 Introduction

Digital games are one of the main cultural industries. According to the Global Games Market Report [4], the global games market generated $137.9 billion in 2018, 91% from which corresponding to digital games. There are more than 2 billion frequent players in the world [4], and what had appeared as an entertainment product in the 1970's soon became much more.

eSports are an emerging phenomena worldwide. The competitive play of digital games appeared as a local popular activity in the 1970's and 1980's, but rapidly conquered the players and fans all over the world. Nowadays eSports are already recognized as a sport, there are being created federations to support players and it is being discussed the possibility of integrating eSports as a demonstrative sport in 2024 Olympic Games.

I would like to argue that eSports are one of the activities that best illustrate the dynamics of network communication [1, 2]. What had appeared as a digital media phenomenon, shortly became a legacy media content. Media companies throughout the world are investing in broadcasting eSports competitions and establishing partnerships with individual content producers that are contributing to the emergence of a new

© Springer Nature Switzerland AG 2019
N. Zagalo et al. (Eds.): VJ 2019, CCIS 1164, pp. 113–122, 2019.
https://doi.org/10.1007/978-3-030-37983-4_9

professional activity – digital games streamers [3]. Additionally, eSports are asserting themselves both as a cultural and creative industry. They are part of a complex network of media, game producers, players, and individual digital content producers.

Based on a qualitative methodology, this paper intends to discuss the growing relevance of eSports as a networked media phenomena and to present the particular case of Portugal. Data from an exploratory research having document analysis as primary data collection method will be presented aiming to map the Portuguese eSports media ecosystem.

The paper is organized in three main sections. The first intending to characterize digital games ecosystem asserting its relevance as digital media; the second devoted to eSports and to understand it as a networked media and communication phenomenon; and the third and last will be focused on presenting the results of the exploratory empirical research.

2   The Digital Games Ecosystem

Digital games are among the most popular and widespread digital media. Since the 1970s, these media have evolved from a subculture phenomenon to a mainstream one, from pixelated graphic environments made available in arcade machines to a wide variety of high-resolution screens [5]. Since its beginning that the video games' industry was based on an ecology based of the 'well-functioning' of the system that articulated gamers, games and gaming platforms. In the first years games were made available essentially to be played in public spaces - arcade machines, but soon this entertainment product conquered also the private space through the development of a more portable gaming dedicated device, the console, first with Magnavox Odyssey and then with Atari Video Computer System (later renamed Atari 2600). The 1983 industry crash shook the balance of the system and resulted in a new positioning of players that from that moment on clearly demand high quality standards from the game developers. During the almost 50 years of the digital games industry, much has evolved even if the contemporary digital games ecosystem is made of the same basic elements: gamers, games and platforms; nevertheless, there is a growing complexity in each one of this elements.

From a binary initial classification of gamers and non-gamers, the beginning of the 2000's witnessed the renegotiation of what a gamer is with the assertion of web-based casual games and mobile games and the rise of a new general taxonomy that classified those who play in hardcore and casual gamers, distinguishing between regular and non-regular gamers, but also evincing the genres of games each tend to play. As games become more and more widespread worldwide and they turn into one of the main media industries, those who are engaged with digital games begin to take on roles that go beyond that of 'just' be players. Recognizing the complexification of gamers, Newzoo, a market research company specializing in games and eSports segments, proposed a new category the game enthusiasts [4], which comprises those who effectively play, but also those who are frequent viewers and those who own digital games and that aims at consolidating the change that has been occurring in the relationship that is established with games. Among each type of game enthusiasts there is a gradation of engagement: those who engage in playing range from non-players to lifestyle players, having casual and avid players as intermediate levels; those who engage in viewing, non-viewers, occasional, regular and devoted viewers; and those who own games, from non-buyers, to indifferent, dedicated or fanatic owners. And, according to Newzoo [4]: "[a]t the heart of these segments is the community that creates and shares gaming experiences". There are more than 2,5 billion game enthusiasts all over the world, 54% male and 46% female [6]. The great majority of them have between under 18 years old and 35 years old, being the average male player 33 years old and the female player 37 years old [4]. The typical digital game players is not the teenage boy or the 'computer nerd' living in his parents' basement anymore, but male and female educated adults that engage with different genres of games in different types of platforms.

Games are at the heart of this ecosystem. There are different genres of digital games, each offering a different play experience. Digital games classification has been highly discussed by game studies researchers and there are proposals to set the main genres of games [7, 8]. The classification system followed is the one proposed by Egenfeld-Nielsen, Smith, and Tosca [8], according to whom games may be classified taking into consideration four main genres: action, adventure, strategy and process-oriented. What sets the difference between each category is the criteria to be successful in the game: in action games the main criteria to be successful are hand/eye coordination and motor skills; in adventure games the central criteria to be successful are logic and deduction skills; in strategy ones, the criteria to be successful are management and strategy skills; and lastly, in process-oriented games, the criteria will be different according to the specificities of the game, ranging from role-playing to simulation games. Those games are characterized by not fitting in any of the other categories, which is becoming more and more common in contemporary titles, and by offering players the opportunity to explore virtual worlds. Action and process-oriented games are among the best-sellers [11], like *Call of Duty: Black Ops IV*, *Red Dead Redemption II* or *Minecraft*, and also among the most played, which include free-to play games like *League of Legends*.

The last element of the ecology of digital games concerns the devices used to play - the platforms. From the first arcade machines, enormous and only available in public spaces like coffee-shops and bars, game devices become smaller and portable, soon conquering the social space of the home - the living room. The continuous development of hardware shape the possibility for a forked path - dedicated and non-dedicated gaming platforms. Nowadays the games market is organized around five segments and four platforms: Console Games, Browser PC Games, Downloadable/Boxed PC Games, Mobile Games, and Tablet Games [4]. Being the Mobile segment the one that is growing fastest, having reached already 36% of the market share and being valued in $54.9 billion, according to Newzoo.

3 eSports as a Networked Media Phenomenon

eSports, or electronic sports, concern the competitive play of digital games, but, as it will be seen, nowadays it is much more than this, it is a network communication phenomenon.

The growing importance of eSports has been aligned with the development and structuration of eSports practice and spectatorship. According to Taylor [3], the history of eSports is organized in three different waves, each characterized by different dynamics, but reflecting the state of the art of the gaming industry. The first wave dates back to the 1970's and 1980's and to the emergence of arcade games and first domestic consoles – gamers competed within a shared physical space. The second, 1990's–2010, was shaped by the emergence of the internet, multiplayer networks and the configuration of eSports industry [9]. The third and last wave has started around 2010 and is being characterized by live-streaming, a practice that is leading eSports to become a "[…] media entertainment outlet as well." [3] Live-streaming is being explored to broadcast live-events as eSports tournaments, but also gaming and training sessions. Professional teams and players have embraced this practice to gain notoriety, to build their audiences and incomes. Notwithstanding, the relevance of live-streaming is also being extended into eSports' metaculture, being one of its main elements the 'stream communities' that are being settled [10].

eSports involve then two dimensions, on the one hand, practice centered on professional game playing and, on the other, spectatorship by the creative interactive audiences who consume but also produce media content. The eSports phenomenon add to the digital games ecosystem a new variable – the media and I would like to argue that it is one of the activities that best illustrate the dynamics of network communication [1, 2]:

"In the Informational Societies, where the network is the central organizational feature, a new communicational model has been taking shape. A communicational model characterized by the fusion of interpersonal communication and mass communication, connecting audiences, broadcasters, and publishers under a matrix networking media devices ranging from newspapers to videogames and giving newly mediated roles to their users" [2].

eSports network is organized around different elements and all have been crucial to its growing relevance as a media phenomenon: Game producers, Game Enthusiasts, Digital media, Legacy media, and Content producers (digital and legacy media). The competitive practice of digital games that characterized eSports in its early ages, despite remaining at its center, is not enough to conceptualize this phenomenon anymore. Live-streaming gave eSports a new visibility and what had appeared as a digital media phenomenon, has already become a legacy media content. Media companies throughout the world are investing in broadcasting eSports competitions and establishing partnerships with individual content producers that are contributing to the emergence of a new professional activity – digital game streamers. The eSports media network is being shaped around the articulation of digital and legacy media with the implementation of marketing and communication strategies that look forward to take advantage of this (media) phenomenon. Digital media are intrinsically connected to eSports, mainly digital games and online video broadcasting social media platforms. Legacy media worldwide are also investing in eSports, particularly TV broadcasters through live-events broadcasting, events coverage, and dedicated TV shows. Due to the presence of players, teams and streamers in different media outlets, these become appealing to brands that have been starting investing in the eSports network aiming at reaching communication and marketing strategic goals.

Live-streaming is really important within the contemporary eSports ecosystem. It has been explored to broadcast live-events as eSports tournaments and championships, but also gaming and training sessions. Professional teams and players have embraced this practice to gain notoriety, to build their audiences and incomes. Notwithstanding, gaming content streaming is not only devoted to professional players anymore. Gamers from all over the world may take advantage of video streaming platforms to share their experiences with a growing audience that look forward watching others play [3]. Online video broadcasting platforms as YouTube and Twitch have played an important role for eSports live-streaming. Twitch ended up assuming the main role and now it is considered to be a dedicated gaming streaming platform [12]. Twitch is a user-friendly platform both for streamers and viewers, being one of its main characteristics the articulation of live broadcasting (audio and video) with synchronous communication tools. The existence of chat channels that allow viewers to communicate with the broadcaster and with each other is considered to be one of its community fostering features [10].

Twitch offers users a wide range of content, among which eSports competitions broadcasting. Twitch has been setting partnerships with the main global professional gaming tournaments and championships, as well as with TV channels to extend the live-streaming of these events to a wider audience. Besides direct eSports streams, alternative content has been appearing in the platform, resulting both from Twitch policies as from streamers creativity. From 2012 to 2018 the time spent by Twitch viewers watching video content on the streaming platform have increased from 72 billion to a record of 560 billion minutes [13].

According to Statista, the most watched gaming content in the January 2019 was related with *Fortnite*, to which users devoted 27.3 million hours consuming content on an average of 20,400 channels [14]. In what concerns channels subscription, the most subscribed channel was Ninja [15], counting with over 13.2 million subscribers. The streamer that reached the higher amount of viewer hours was shroud, over 14.5 million, who is considered to be the fast growing Twitch streamer [16]. The streamer that achieved the highest peak of viewership in the last month was Squeezielive, with a record of viewer count of 388,941 [16]. Individual streamers are among the most popular. There are different types of streamers, that create different types of content and that may perform different roles that may be hybridized – gamers, entertainers and commentators [3]. At the heart of live streaming is interacting with the audience, which reinforces live streaming platforms as social media and a central element of gaming participatory cultures [10].

The assertion of eSports as a networked communication phenomenon is becoming evident as its financial and economic relevance increases and eSports become a significant player among the sponsorships market, along with traditional sports, teams and players [17]. eSports are becoming a business [18] and sponsorship has been a key element to understand it [19, 20], even though the eSports business model has been changing and adapting as this segment gains notoriety: "the business model moved from being purely sponsor-driven to being audience-focused" [18]. Which does not mean that sponsoring is losing relevance, but that its logics have been adapted to be more aligned with the trend of advertising avoidance, despite this trend not being so evident in this sector [20]. According to PwC [21] sponsorship and advertising are the most relevant revenue sources in terms of volume, representing one third of eSports economy, and it will continue to grow, the forecast is that it will grow almost 25% until 2022.

It is possible to identify two types of sponsors in eSports, the endemic and the non-endemic sponsors. The first have been accompanying eSports relevance growth almost since the beginning, while the latest are more recent, evincing the economic relevance of this media and sports phenomenon for brands [19, 20]. According to Nielsen [22], eSports are offering new opportunities for brands, since there are different ways to be part of this phenomenon: partnerships with game developers and with events operators, sponsoring of leagues, teams, gaming celebrities, and partnerships and sponsoring of streaming platforms and individual streamers. For branding and marketing communications purposes, these are important opportunities to deal with attention economy and to try to gain notoriety amid eSports highly engaged audiences [22]. In order to reach this goal classic sponsoring does not seem enough anymore, and more creative strategies are needed, strategies focusing on personalized and relevant content that would enrich audience's experience and engagement [18–23].

4 The Portuguese eSports Ecosystem

In order to map the Portuguese eSports ecosystem an exploratory qualitative research has been conducted, having document analysis as primary data collection technique. This exploratory research intends to be the first step of a more in-depth research focusing on eSports in Portugal and how a digital media phenomenon is reaching legacy media, asserting itself as a networked media phenomenon, but also to assess how eSports are being used as a marketing strategy.

The data that will be presented and discussed in this section correspond to the initial stage of the research, which is mainly centered on the role performed by the Portuguese Public Service Broadcasting organization (RTP - Radio and Television of Portugal) for the consolidation of eSports in Portugal. It was considered necessary to understand RTP's role in particular not only because it is a public service broadcaster which has an eSports project (RTP Arena), but mainly due to the articulation that has been done between digital and legacy media. The primary data sources were the RTP Accounts Reports from 2018, RTP Arena website and RTP Arena social media pages. These sources were completed with secondary ones, mainly news by Portuguese media outlets and Twitch statistic reports that allowed to identify other relevant elements of the Portuguese eSports ecosystem.

The main axis of this exploratory analysis was the role performed by the media, focusing on RTP and its combination of legacy and digital media. The variables were the media content produced for each channel (legacy and digital media) and the number of followers and views of the main social media platform of the RTP Arena project which is Twitch. Additionally, aiming at characterizing eSports as an ecosystem, it is considered important to identify and briefly present the main Portuguese professional players and teams, live-events and streamers. In order to identify the most prominent representatives, the key variables took into consideration were economic ones (prize moneys, sponsorships), and in the case of the streamers also the number of followers and views.

RTP is a key media player for the Portuguese eSports network. The Public Television and Radio Broadcaster, which has four national television open signal channels and four open signal radio stations, has been investing in eSports since the end of 2015 and this still is considered to be one of its emergent strategic investment areas [24]. In 2016, RTP has launched an online eSports platform devoted to the transmission and divulgation of national and international eSports championships – RTP Arena. Currently, RTP Arena is a media brand, being present in both legacy and digital media.

The presence of RTP Arena in legacy media is now restricted to a weekly TV show aired on RTP 3 - *RTP Arena Magazine*. The show counts with 128 episodes, and the latest 22 are made available in the digital RTP archive, RTP Play. In 2016 there was also a radio show, entitled *RTP Arena*, aired on Antena 3 radio station. In what concerns the digital media presence, the main element is the RTP Arena online platform, which is articulated with social media platforms. RTP has settle a partnership with Twitch, platform where it has three channels, and it is present in YouTube, Facebook, Twitter, and Instagram. The latest social media platforms are used to communicate and promote RTP Arena contents produced for the other media and eSports events and news. RTP Arena has been responsible for the coverage of different live events, among which Omen HP University Challenge Portugal, Lisboa Games Week, Comin Con Portugal, LPGO e TPGO, 4Gamers, and Allianz Cup. Since 2017, RTP Arena is the Twitch representative in Portugal. Resulting from the partnership, RTP Arena online transmissions are aired exclusively in its Twitch channels. Now there are three active RTP Arena channels (data of July, 2019): RTP Arena CS:GO, counting with 80,900 followers and 6,5 million views; RTP Arena, 27,200 followers and 747,900 views; and RTParena FIFA, 9,000 followers and 183,000 views. The three channels together count with over 108,100 followers and 7,4 million views.

There are some prominent professional players in Portugal, being the most well-known Ricardo "fox" Pacheco, who is specialized in *Counter-Strike: Global Offensive* (*CS: GO*). At the present moment he is part of the Giants club, which is sponsored by Vodafone and counts with over $80,000 in money prizes. "Fox" has been a professional eSports layer for more than 10 years and he is considered to be the best Portuguese player of *Counter-Strike*. Regarding the Portuguese teams, there are three major Portuguese clubs that represent several teams. K1ck is one of the oldest Portuguese teams being founded in 1998. More recently, it has become a club, K1ck eSports Club and a registered eSports brand counting already with over 800 awards. Giants is a club founded in 2008, which currently competes in 12 different games with 14 teams. And, For the Win eSports an eSports club created in 2011 and sponsored by Omen by HP.

Live-events are a crucial element in eSports media network. Championships and tournaments involving high value prizes appeal massive live audiences, both in physical and digital presence, from all over the world. In 2018 there were two major events that took place in Portugal, one international and the other national, and that were key to state the relevance of the Portuguese eSports sector. Blast Pro Series - Lisbon had its first edition in 2018 and it was truly successful. The event counted with over 20 thousand visitors, online views of the various tournaments exceeded

1.2 million; the streams of the *CS: GO* game surpassed more than 550 thousand unique viewers, and the final of this tournament was simultaneously assisted by 65 thousand spectators. This was the first time that an international tournament was staged in Portugal. Regarding national tournaments, the best known is the Moche XL eSports, which in its 2018 edition counted with also over 20 thousand visitors during the weekend. One of the main tournaments was the *CS: GO* competition with a final prize of $50,000; the remaining tournaments altogether awarded an equivalent amount, mainly *League of Legends* and FIFA ones. Meo XL eSports counted with the participation of some of the best national and international players.

The last element of the network is the figure of the streamer, professional streamers sponsored by different brands. Portugal is witnessing the emergence of the streamer, an appealing way to monetize the time spent playing. Among the most popular streamers are Zorlak, MoraisHD, ImpacktTV and Shikai (data of July 2019). Zorlak is specialized in *CS: GO*, counting with 273,700 followers and over 17,3 million views on Twitch. MoraisHD, a variety streamer, who counts with 137,200 followers and over 4,9 million views on Twitch. ImpaKtTV is a streamer specialized in the Battle Royale subgenre, who hosts the RTP3 TV show RTP Arena. He counts with 88,800 followers and over 3,7 million views on Twitch. The fourth streamer, Shikai is a memberEGN eSports team and considered the best Portuguese *Fortnite* player. Currently, he counts with 89,300 followers and over 3 million views on his Twitch channel.

Despite having being shaped since the late 1990's, the Portuguese eSports sector became more visible in the recent years, and live-streaming was key to that remediated visibility. More recently, the RTP investment in eSports contributed to present this phenomenon to a wider audience. RTP approach to eSports was key to configure this as a networked communication phenomenon, since it has contributed to the expansion of this phenomenon to legacy media, an open-signal TV channel and a radio station. Nevertheless, eSports in Portugal remain essentially a digital media-based network, which is aligned with the global trends and with the digital nature of this phenomenon.

The media coverage growth of eSports was primordial for the economic development of this sector. Portuguese players and teams have now more visibility, which is important for sponsoring opportunities and for consolidating the sector. The impact of this growth is also affecting the relevance of Portugal for staging live-events and capturing attention from international brands that are investing in eSports in other markets, like Samsung, Omen by HP, and Mercedes-Benz, for instance. And last, but not least, the consolidation of eSports is also contributing to the assertion of Portuguese live-streamers, which are also beginning to have the opportunity to monetize their content production activities.

5   Concluding Remarks

eSports are already recognized as a sport, there are being created federations all over the world and it is being discussed the possibility of integrating it as a demonstrative sport in Olympic Games. It involves both professional gamers and an interactive audience, the latter being able to experiment with different types of spectatorship, all having at its core an entertainment experience [25, 26].

As a network communication phenomenon, eSports are complex, representing the dynamics of the contemporary media ecosystem. It articulates digital and legacy media, as well as live-events, which involve the participation of professional gamers, audience, content streamers, and more and more brands. Brands are starting to take eSports really serious, since they allow them to target different audience segments and to explore different marketing and communication strategies. While eSports professional teams, players and tournaments start developing a relationship with brands and marketing in the second wave of eSports development [9, 20], mainly through sponsorships, this is a new phenomenon among non-professional gamers streamers, who are taking advantage of the relationship between live streaming and gaming culture to seek for a way to monetize their play time [3]. Nevertheless, its roots on digital media still are one of its most prominent dimensions, and Twitch plays a key role in eSports growing visibility.

Portugal despite being a small market has been quite an innovative and digital media early adopter one. eSports are one of the emerging phenomena that illustrates that. According to a news from the Portuguese newspaper *Público* [27], there are over 300 million eSports fans in Portugal. The Portuguese eSports sector has been developing at a slower pace than some international ones, like the Brazilian. Nevertheless, the investment that has been done by RTP through RTP Arena has been determinant for the sector's growth.

As a network media and communication phenomenon, eSports are fueling the emergence and consolidation of different cultural and creative industries, as it shapes the assertion of an engaged interactive audience. As its fan-base increases, as do the interest from brands to explore it as an alternative communication channel. eSports offer different opportunities to brands, sponsorship, for instance, has already been deeply explored. But there are strategies based on content that may be further explored. In order to make sense of this complex network further research is needed, particularly tackling regional contexts.

The Portuguese eSports segment still is asserting itself to be seen as more than a 'gamers' thing'. Recently it was formed the Portuguese Electronic Sports Federation and the Portuguese Football Federation created an eSports division devoted to football games tournaments, focusing specially on FIFA. 2019 is being an important year for eSports, as it saw the launch of a new prize, eSports Portugal Awards, which has it first edition in late March. The awards prize different categories from sport related ones, as best athlete and team, to events, entertainment, media and commercial ones. This prize reinforces the role of eSports amid the network of media and communication around which social experience takes shapes in contemporaneity, as it evinces the growing relevance of Portugal amid the international arena.

References

1. Cardoso, G.: Os Media na Sociedade em Rede. Fundação Calouste Gulbenkian, Lisbon (2005)
2. Cardoso, G.: From mass to networked communication: communicational models and the informational society. Int. J. Commun. **2**, 587–630 (2008)
3. Taylor, T.L.: Watch Me Play. Princeton University Press, Princeton (2018)

4. Newzoo: 2018 Global Games Market Report. Newzoo (2018)
5. Zagalo, N.: Videojogos em Portugal. FCA, Lisbon (2013)
6. Newzoo: Global Games Market Report: 2019. Newzoo (2019)
7. Wolf, M.J.P.: The Medium of the Video Game. Routledge, London (2002)
8. Egenfeldt-Nielsen, S., Smith, J., Tosca, S.: Understanding Video Games. Routledge, London (2008)
9. Taylor, T.L.: Raising the Stakes. MIT Press, Cambridge (2012)
10. Hamilton, W., Garretson, O., Kerne, A.: Streaming on twitch. In: CHI 2014. ACM (2014)
11. ESA - Entertainment Software Association: 2019 Essential Facts: About the Computer and Video Game Industry. ESA (2019)
12. Statista: Average Number of Concurrent Streamers. www.statista.com/statistics/761100/average-number-streamers-on-youtube-gaming-live-and-twitch. Accessed 15 July 2019
13. Statista: Number of minutes spent watching Twitch content worldwide 2012–1028. www.statista.com/statistics/819967/time-spent-watching-twitch/. Accessed 29 July 2019
14. Statista: Leading Gaming Content on Twitch. www.statista.com/statistics/507786/leading-game-content-twitch-by-number-hours-viewed/. Accessed 20 July 2019
15. Statista: Most Popular Twitch Channels. www.statista.com/statistics/486914/most-popular-twitch-channels-ranked-by-followers. Accessed 20 July 2019
16. TwitchMetrics: The Most Popular Twitch Streamers. www.twitchmetrics.net. Access 20 July 2019
17. Korpimies, S.: Sponsorships in eSports. In: Hiltscher, J., Scholz, T.M. (eds.) eSports Yearbook 2017/18, pp. 58–73. Books on Demand GmbH, Norderstedt (2019)
18. Scholz, T.M.: eSports is Business. Palgrave Macmillan, Cham (2019)
19. Freitas, B.D.A., Contreras-Espinosa, R.S., Correia, P.A.P.: The benefits and risks of sponsoring eSports: brief literature review. In: Hiltscher, J., Scholz, T.M. (eds.) eSports Yearbook 2017/18, pp. 49–57. Books on Demand GmbH, Norderstedt (2019)
20. Ströh, J.: The eSports Market and eSports Sponsoring. Tectum Verlag, Marburg (2017)
21. PwC: Sports Industry: Lost in Transition. PwC's Sport Survey 2018. PwC, Zurich (2018)
22. Nielsen: eSports Playbook For Brands 2019. Nielsen Company (2019)
23. Hallmann, K., Giel, T.: eSports – competitive sports or recreational activity? Sport Manag. Rev. **21**(1), 14–20 (2017)
24. RTP: Relatório e Contas 2017. RTP, Lisbon (2017)
25. Cheung, G., Huang, J.: Starcraft from the stands. In: Conference on Human Factors in Computing Systems, pp. 763–772 (2011)
26. Edge, N.: Evolution of the gaming experience. Elon J. Undergraduate Res. Commun. **4**(2), 33–39 (2013)
27. Gomes, N.R.: eSports: a indústria com 300 milhões de fãs está a criar empregos em Portugal. In: Público. www.publico.pt/2019/01/15/p3/noticia/esports-a-industria-com-300-milhoes-de-fas-esta-a-criar-empregos-em-portugal-1857553/amp. Accessed 29 July 2019

Game Design Decisions and Communication Theories Applied to eSports: A Literature Review

Gabriel G. Canavarro[1(✉)] [iD], João B. F. Sequeiros[1,2] [iD], and Farley Fernandes[1,2,3]

[1] Universidade da Beira Interior, Covilhã, Portugal
ggcanavarro@gmail.com
[2] Instituto de Telecomunicações, Covilhã, Portugal
jbfs@ubi.pt, farleymillano@gmail.com
[3] UNIDCOM/Universidade da Beira Interior, Covilhã, Portugal

Abstract. This paper aims to help Game Designers and video game researchers have a better understanding about what are the key motives for the success of eSports broadcasts and why people are more and more into spectating professional video game players perform. As there are few published works regarding the motivations of a eSports spectator, we decided to execute a review on the studies regarding players' favorites game design decisions, and communication studies about the different interests of a spectator so we could extract similarities of those relevant topics. A first data pool of 320 resources material were gathered at the beginning of the research, and ended with 16 investigations published after 2007. We stated how communication and game design studies complement each other when it concerns delivering a better entertainment experience for the eSports spectators.

Keywords: eSports · Game design · Game Streaming · Game ranking · Uses and Gratifications

1 Introduction

Watching someone else play a video game is something that people do since the creation of the digital games media, for a significant variety of reasons: because you were waiting for your brother to lose the game, so it is your turn to play, or you would want to learn a trick with a more skilled friend in that specific game, or even because you just enjoy to watch someone play more than you do like to actually play it. More and more people are watching others play games as the time progresses, specially electronic sports (eSports) games [1]. This systematic review examines academic researches about eSports and the most appealing reasons for the spectators. The 2018 "The Game Awards" featured five of the most relevant eSports games of that year: Dota 2 (the game with the biggest prize pool for competitors of all times, reaching $178,065,705.17 US Dollars at the time this review is being written [2]), Counter Strike: Global Offensive (the game with most tournaments events of 2018, 376 events

N. Zagalo et al. (Eds.): VJ 2019, CCIS 1164, pp. 123–135, 2019.
https://doi.org/10.1007/978-3-030-37983-4_10

[3]), League of Legends (most popular core PC Game from january 2017 to may of 2019, the date of this research is being written [4], the World championship finals of 2018 reached 99,6 million unique viewers during the broadcast with a concurrent viewer peak of million [5]), Overwatch (the only not-free-to-play game on this list, has more than 40 million players [6]) and Fortnite (Epic Games announced that it will grant a total prize pool of 100 million US Dollars for all eSport events of 2019 [7]).

According to Lee and Schoenstedt [8], this kind of international scale game events are appealing for global companies like Microsoft and Samsung, because sponsoring the event, teams and players means that your brand will be advertised constantly during the broadcast. They also state that online games have become a venue of common promotion, turning into a growing opportunity for sponsorships for a passionate audience.

Besides those big spectatorship numbers, online eSports games are considerably new if compared to offline digital games, and little is published about what makes them appealing to be watched. We will be focusing our research towards the Design decisions made by such computer games and recent communication academic works that can explain this phenomenon.

This investigation alone is part of a bigger research which is a Master Degree program final thesis and will be used as a main reference source for its literature review. The Thesis will be about CS: GO and game design reasons that makes it appealing to be watched. It is planned to be published on March 2020.

The remainder of the paper is structured as follows: Sect. 2 introduces our main Research Question, Sect. 3 gives a brief description of eSports and differentiates it from a regular digital game, Sect. 4 describes the methodology used in our study, Sect. 5 discuss the results found and in Sect. 6 we talk about our conclusions and future research.

2 Research Question

The main objective of this research was to collect and categorize recent work themed around the eSports, to understand how is it possible to categorize entertainment watching motives, and therefore conclude the individual reasons of success of eSports games as a leisure activity. For this work, our general research question (RQ) is stated as:

R.Q.: Based on the spectator point of view, what have been the main studied reasons that can justify eSports success?

To give a more objective answer, we branched the RQ into two specific research questions:

R.Q.1: Why are people becoming more attracted to digital game competitions?
R.Q.2: What Game Design decisions are responsible for an eSports game to become famous?

We started by reading Game Design and eSports papers, trying to restrict to this area of study exclusively, but the topic of "Uses and Gratifications" was largely quoted among the materials, so we decided to expand the borders of our interest in order to reach the communication area, and understand how it can help us answer the research question we created to guide our search.

3 eSports Characteristics: The Defining Attributes

In 2016, Jenny [9] gave eSports a very condensed and objective definition: "organized video game competitions". They state that competition is the main aspect of the eSports industry. As the time goes, the modality becomes better known to the world and Segal [10] creates an interesting link between eSports and conventional sports: "[...] they (eSports) have superstars, playoffs, fans, uniforms, comebacks, and upsets". But eSports differs from traditional sports like football, basketball and swimming, because it is made after connecting multiple platforms [9].

"Unlike football or cricket, esports is not rooted in any region or culture, so it has a more global appeal" [11]. And now that online gaming has become a solid established ground for teams, professional players, and streamers, "the notion of eSports has expanded to include not only competition through network games but also cultural and industrial activities related to network games", Jin [12].

While reading Bányai et al. [13], we found a definition that draws a line separating what differentiates a casual gamer from a eSports player: "An eSports player is a professional gamer who plays for competition, rather than for fun and/or relaxation, and define gaming as their job. Casual gamers play for fun and recreation, and to entertain themselves". We believe that there is space to debate if an eSports player must be mandatorily a professional who works as a gamer, but there are definitely differences between a casual and eSports player, especially when it comes to the competition factor. While investigating how live-streaming is changing video gaming community, Smith et al. [14] affirmed that eSports culture started during the arcade games era thanks to players competing in order to have their names featured inside the hi-score board found in some of the game machines. It is fairly common for an eSports game to have different roles for a player to choose and to follow as a play-style. For example, in DOTA 2 we have the following definitions: Carry, Support and Ganker. These execution representations are attached to the characters based on their stats, special abilities and items used inside the game. "selection and characterization of roles is based on a comparison of online guides" as stated by Eggert et al. [15].

Not only characters can be divided into groups, but the maps are also divided into areas for an easier virtual geographical perception of both players and spectators. Each team (in DOTA 2, teams are named Radiant and Dire, respectively) has a base and the rest of the map is divided into five major areas: Top lane, Middle Lane, Bottom Lane, Dire Jungle and Radiant Jungle [15].

4 Methods

For better understanding the need of this Literature review, we have also searched for past eSports and Game Design Literature Systematic Reviews to know what topics concerning similar fields of study have already been covered and published in English. After investigating Google Scholar database for Literature Reviews covering related topics (8 papers), we thought that a more in depth research would be needed about what makes eSports so appealing to both online viewers and also for the spectator watching inside the arena.

After reading such literature reviews ([13, 16–22]), relevant references that concerned related topics (20 papers), we went to Google Scholar for a first glimpse and started collecting data with a pertinent amount of citations (73 papers). Then, after this initial data harvest, now already with plenty related works and an overview about what has already been published and what is trending, we started our search in specific digital libraries, looking for papers concerning eSports from either a Game Design or Communication perspective.

In early April 2019, the following keywords were used to consult bibliographical databases for research material: "eSports", "Game Design Ranking", "Game Streaming" & "Uses and Gratifications game". The data were gathered from the following online library databases: Eric (37 papers), PubMed (72 papers) and ASSIA (146 results). Besides that, all the references presented on the chosen papers were considered and some of them were also used as study material (12 papers). We searched for Journal Articles, conference papers and technical reports. We have decided to search only for publications made in english language. The main objective is to be very selective and compile papers with fields of study related to our Research Question in the most objective way. The results section shows what was included, with a small description of the key factors. After the first research, we had 360 results. These sample went through our filtering criteria with 5 more phases: First we checked for works published after 2007, second we discarded the duplicates. After that, we read the title of all results for an inspection eliminating what we considered irrelevant. The remainers had both their abstract and conclusion read for a higher degree analysis, and then we fully read what we judged applicable, ending up with a sample of 16 of what we conclude are the most compatible with our Research Question. Those papers can be seen in Table 1, followed respectively by their year of publication, the sample size of whatever kind of samples used, if it helps us answer the Research Questions.1 and Research Questions.2 (presented here in our paper) and, finally, what were their own Research Questions and Outcomes.

Table 1. Overview of the analyzed works.

Reference	Year	Sample size	R. Q.1	R. Q.2	Paper research question & outcomes
[23]	2011	251	✓	✓	**R.Q.:** "This paper aims to explore the factors affecting consumers' loyalty toward online games based on the uses and gratifications theory and the flow theory." **Outcomes:** "The results focusing on popular massively multiplayer online role-playing games reveal that players' sense of

(*continued*)

Table 1. (*continued*)

Reference	Year	Sample size	R. Q.1	R. Q.2	Paper research question & outcomes
					control, perceived entertainment, and challenge affect their loyalty toward an online game. Conversely, sociality and interactivity produce negligible effects on loyalty"
[24]	2010	1242	✓	✓	**R.Q.:** "At what age level does video game playing time peak? RQ2: What motivations are stronger at different age levels? RQ3: What genre preferences are stronger at different age levels?" **Outcomes:** "Age differences yield a non-linear relationship with game playing time. [...] games may be especially potent learning tools if they are challenging yet doable. Further, if challenge is a motive for 5th graders, then this may be a group for whom virtual learning will be particularly attractive"
[25]	2010	337	✓	✓	**R.Q.:** "What conditions are associated with a players' proactive stickiness to a specific online game once they have encountered it?" **Outcomes:** "The model presented in this study provides a broad conceptual framework with a strong theoretical platform that helps enhance our understanding of the antecedents of online game proactive stickiness formation"
[14]	2013		✓	✗	**R.Q.:** "video game spectating different communities grow: what are the incentives of all stakeholders and the technologies involved" **Outcomes:** "Through our exploratory analysis of livestreaming communities, particularly 'Let's Play', we have found that there is malleability between the roles of the active and passive in users' experiences"
[26]	2014		✓	✗	**R.Q.:** "We investigate how the popular new medium of live video streaming, i.e., live streaming, fosters participation and community. Live-streaming combines high-fidelity computer graphics and video with low-fidelity text-based communication channels to create a unique social medium"

(*continued*)

Table 1. (*continued*)

Reference	Year	Sample size	R. Q.1	R. Q.2	Paper research question & outcomes
					Outcomes: "The assemblage of hot and cold media enable streams to provide and open place for people to go socialize. […] Streaming on Twitch establishes a new paradigm for online communities in a range of emerging contexts"
[27]	2011	127	✓	✓	**R.Q.:** "Who are the spectators and why do they spectate? RQ2 How do different stakeholders affect the spectator experience? RQ3 What makes spectating a game enjoyable?" **Outcomes:** "In this paper we have defined the video game spectator: a person whose intentions range from watching the game casually to being a fan at competitive gaming tournaments"
[28]	2007	3000	✗	✓	**R.Q.:** "how motivations of play relate to age, gender, usage patterns and in-game behaviors" **Outcomes:** "Different people choose to play games for very different reasons, and thus, the same video game may have very different meanings or consequences for different players"
[29]	2012	360	✓	✓	**R.Q.:** "More specifically, we choose the player as unit of analysis and ask: Which competitive and hedonic need gratifications drive continuous eSports use?" **Outcomes:** "We reveal that both competitive (competition and challenge) and hedonic need gratifications (escapism) drive continuous eSports use"
[30]	2015		✓	✓	**R.Q.:** "Our goal is to test whether country differences exist in eSports" **Outcomes:** "This study provides evidence of country differences in eSports"
[31]	2013	18	✗	✓	**R.Q.:** "Officially organized, spectator driven eSport tournaments occur within the notoriously transgressive and ruthless game EVE Online. In these tournaments spying, bribing and throwing matches is commonplace. […] We argue that this is problematic, against the 'spirit' of EVE Online and a misreading of the effect of transgressive acts on the success and enjoyment of the emerging eSport"

(*continued*)

Table 1. (*continued*)

Reference	Year	Sample size	R. Q.1	R. Q.2	Paper research question & outcomes
					Outcomes: "As EVE Online develops its eSport, this unbounded attitude towards player conduct should be retained in order to preserve this appeal"
[8]	2011	51	✓	✓	**R.Q.:** "whether eSports consumption stands alone as a distinct market or whether it is similar or compliments traditional sports consumption" **Outcomes:** "Correlation between eSports consumption and the seven traditional sports behavior (non288 eSports) involvements (i.e., game attendance, game participation, sports viewership, sports readership, sports listenership, Internet usage specific to sports, and purchase of team merchandise) indicated the similarities and differences that exist between the very different forms of sport consumptive behaviors
[9]	2016		✓	✗	**R.Q.:** "What elevates a game to the level of a sport?" **Outcomes:** "It appears that eSports include play and competition, are organized by rules, require skill, and have a broad following. However, eSports currently lacks great physicality and institutionalization"
[17]	2012		✓	✓	**R.Q.:** "The current study aims to advance our understanding by reporting a systematic review of recent literature addressing engagement in computer games" **Outcomes:** "The range of games and game platforms available is continually expanding and we are just beginning to understand the motivational appeal of different kinds of games"
[16]	2018		✗	✓	**R.Q.:** "This article aims to perform a literature review of the available research that focuses strictly on MOBA (multiplayer online battle arena) games" **Outcomes:** "MOBA games provide a research opportunity due to their large player base and accessibility of their APIs. Improving APIs or providing relevant datasets could be of help for future research"

(*continued*)

Table 1. (*continued*)

Reference	Year	Sample size	R. Q.1	R. Q.2	Paper research question & outcomes
[32]	2009	23	✓	✓	**R.Q.:** "This work seeks to understand young adults' motives for online gaming and extends previous research concerning social interaction in virtual contexts" **Outcomes:** "Therefore, playing FPS games can be interpreted as a way of connecting to people, connecting as "brothers in blood"
[33]	2007	34	✓	✓	**R.Q.:** "What makes playing Counter-Strike such an engaging and meaningful activity to the participants?" **Outcomes:** "In this paper we have moved between the three circuits of interactivity while discussing cognitive, technological, economical and cultural dimensions of Counter-strike gameplay"

5 Results

R.Q.1: Why Are People Becoming more Attracted to Digital Game Competitions?
During our research we faced a considerable variety of theories which aimed to justify the success of eSports among passive spectators, and after reading about twenty papers about Game Design we chose the "Uses and gratifications" [34] applied to digital games to be our main guide to answer this question. As stated by the author: "Early in the history of communications research, an approach was developed(Uses and Gratifications) to study the gratifications that attract and hold audiences to the kinds of media and the types of content that satisfy their social and psychological needs" [34].

After the interviews, Wu et al. [25] found that an undergraduate student plays an online game for different purposes like social interaction, to kill time, to earn benefits or even just for fun. After that, they go deep into the particular reason of "social interactions" (like making friends, sharing experiences and achieving collaborative missions), concluding that it is one of the major factors that drives players into participating in online games [25].

"The TwitchTV platform allows viewers to live chat while players are broadcasting, discussing what is happening with other viewers as well as conversing with the broadcaster directly.". Smith et al. [14] discuss that the themes of the conversations between the viewers and the caster during the broadcast depends on the community: sometimes it is a strategy and tactical debate, sometimes they are suggestions, and even comical discussions.

Inside streaming platforms, eSports is the most popular community when it comes to the three largest ones, ahead of the Let's Play and the Speedrunning communities [14]. But there is not a recipe for an ideal formation for broadcasting or commentating during professional games [33].

While studying the motives of playing among male and female children and teenagers, Greenberg et al. [24] concluded that "the two primary gratifications for both sexes are competition and challenge". And when it comes to category of video game genre (physical, traditional and imagination games), they show that boys and girls have different preferences, physical games (e.g., action, sports, racing) is the most popular among males in every single one of the four age groups (5th grade, 8th grade, 11th grade and college), and traditional games are the ladies favorite (e.g., classic board games, puzzles), beating male preferences for traditional games in four age groups as well [24].

When it comes to game themes, some art direction decisions combined with marketing decisions implicate on the fascination of the online game players, like: central myths, composed stories, legends and fantasy [23].

R.Q.2: What Game Design Decisions are Responsible for an eSports Game to Become Famous?

Considering how recent eSports online competitions are, there are just a few relevant studies regarding Game Design decisions (focused on the spectator) academic analysis, and they are spread talking about very different particular games or genres. Despite the fact that we are not focusing on any specific genre of online game, we have noticed that most of the papers which choose a defined game title to focus their research, usually decides to go after the two most popular MOBAs (Massive Online Battle Arenas): League of Legends (LoL) and DOTA 2.

Due to this spreadness of information and rarity of researches concerning both eSports games watchability, and also the communication methods and theories at the same time, we decided to choose papers (presented on Table 1) which talk about not only spectating eSports, but also the ones that concerns studies about the appealing of games regarding the gender and age of the users. Offline game design decisions or not competitive online games were also considered, as they are still relevant to the topic and could have the theory directly applied to the "spectating online competitive games" field of study as well.

Weiss and Schiele [29] discuss how competition, challenge and scapism affect eSports use in a positive way, confirming that "individuals expect eSports to provide opportunities for power obtaining". They highlight that when it comes to eSports, scapism is not about a social experience of shifting into digital avatars, looking forward to be a different virtual 'other', it is about "gathering the capabilities of highly skilled avatars while immersing into the competitive virtual world in order to gain competitive advantage, which is an instrument that leads to power in the virtual" [29].

Mora-Cantallops & Sicilia present an interesting insight about eSports throughout their literature review about MOBAs, they say that it is fascinating how strangers are allocated in a temporary squad to perform together to fulfill a relatively intricate common objective in a small period of time (most of the time in less than a hour) [16].

Case Studies

Cheung and Huang [27] spotted relevant topics concerning the game spectator experience, identifying and dividing the viewers into nine personas (The Bystander, Curious, Inspired, Pupil, Unsatisfied, Entertained, Assistant, Commentator and Crowd), and explained and exemplified how information asymmetry works during a Starcraft game broadcast.

Carter and Gibbs [31] brought a new perspective to this discussion when they research about EVE Online, a game in which "spying, bribing and throwing matches is commonplace". All of this makes EVE Online tournaments and metagame unique and entertaining for their community.

6 Conclusion and Future Research

The study collected data published over the past ten years, from a few topics related to eSports, and revealed how complex it is to measure success on this specific area of digital entertainment. Game Design theory and Communication Science theory work together in order to gather and bind the audience and consequently attract millionaires numbers to the events live-streaming spectators counters.

This Literature Review had the objective to give an initial insight about the current status for streaming and broadcast of eSports games in relation to its audience, and to present how the research was conducted.

We started our research focusing on Game Design and eSports area of study, but we decided that it was inevitable to approach the Uses and Gratifications as well, judging by the fact that it was a theory frequently referenced among such works.

Besides that, while Bányai et al. [13] argues that "further comparison and evaluation of sports and eSports is needed, developing the similarities and the differences between such activities." We noticed that there are more areas of study inside eSports domain that could be subject of study to be focused instead. ESports, communication and psychology are fairly related and still need plenty of investigation before we define what is responsible for such viewership accomplishment. More psychological approach would be worth studying in order to recognize, for example the relationship between Mihaly Csikszentmihalyi's Flow theory [35] and what the spectator feels during an eSports game presentation.

Toxicity is another meaningful topic inside eSports discussion that could work some more research. Turkay and Adinolf [36] discuss about toxic behaviour inside the eSports games and pro-players communities, and after studying the different approaches of game companies, "We believe that one of the strategies that game companies may try to build/support is modeling good behavior from pro-players. Social learning theory posits that people are likely to learn from their environment through the process of observational learning", and they also consider the importance of developing through workshops aimed to students, so they recognize and deal with toxicity during the online gaming experience.

Another important thing to mention is that mobile eSports games scene is growing (Arena of Valor is a game focused on the mobile players, with more than 20 events with a prize pool larger than $10.000 US Dollars and already had one with $1.000.000

US Dollar prize pool in a single event [37]) and is an area which could use more studies about the behaviour of the spectators, players and strategies. Also, there are also games with millions of downloads that does not have a eSports scene yet, like Pokemon GO (reached the number of 1 billions downloads [38]).

Acknowledgements. The authors would like to thank FCT - Fundação para a Ciência e Tecnologia, for the support given for the realization of this work, under research grant SFRH/BD/133838/2017.

References

1. Global eSports awareness 2019—Statistic. https://www.statista.com/statistics/545573/number-of-people-aware-of-esports-worldwide/
2. Dota 2 Prize Pools & Top Players - Esports Profile :: Esports Earnings. https://www.esportsearnings.com/games/231-dota-2
3. Events for Counter-Strike: Global Offensive - Esports Events :: Esports Earnings. https://www.esportsearnings.com/games/245-counter-strike-global-offensive/events
4. Most Popular Core PC Games—Global—Newzoo. https://newzoo.com/insights/rankings/top-20-core-pc-games/
5. Goslin, A.: The 2018 League of Legends World Finals had nearly 100 million viewers. https://www.riftherald.com/2018/12/11/18136237/riot-2018-league-of-legends-world-finals-viewers-prize-pool
6. Moore, B.: Overwatch has more than 40 million players (2018). https://www.pcgamer.com/overwatch-has-more-than-40-million-players/
7. Fortnite goes big on esports for 2019 with $100 million prize pool. http://social.techcrunch.com/2019/02/22/fortnite-goes-big-on-esports-for-2019-with-100-million-prize-pool/
8. Lee, D.: Comparison of eSports and traditional sports consumption motives. ICHPER-SD J. Res. **6**(2), 39–44 (2011)
9. Jenny, S.E., Manning, R.D., Keiper, M.C., Olrich, T.W.: Virtual(ly) athletes: where esports fit within the definition of "sport". Quest **69**, 1–18 (2017). https://doi.org/10.1080/00336297.2016.1144517
10. Segal, D.: Behind League of Legends, E-Sports's Main Attraction (2018). https://www.nytimes.com/2014/10/12/technology/riot-games-league-of-legends-main-attraction-esports.html
11. With Viewership and Revenue Booming, Esports Set to Compete with Traditional Sports. https://onlinebusiness.syr.edu/blog/esports-to-compete-with-traditional-sports/
12. Jin, D.Y.: Korea's Online Gaming Empire. MIT Press, Cambridge (2010)
13. Bányai, F., Griffiths, M.D., Király, O., Demetrovics, Z.: The psychology of eSports: a systematic literature review. J. Gambl. Stud. **35**, 351–365 (2019). https://doi.org/10.1007/s10899-018-9763-1
14. Smith, T., Obrist, M., Wright, P.: Live-streaming changes the (video) game. In: Proceedings of the 11th European Conference on Interactive TV and Video - EuroITV 2013, p. 131. ACM Press, Como (2013). https://doi.org/10.1145/2465958.2465971
15. Eggert, C., Herrlich, M., Smeddinck, J., Malaka, R.: Classification of player roles in the team-based multi-player game dota 2. In: Chorianopoulos, K., Divitini, M., Baalsrud Hauge, J., Jaccheri, L., Malaka, R. (eds.) Entertainment Computing - ICEC 2015, vol. 9353, pp. 112–125. Springer, Cham (2015). https://doi.org/10.1007/978-3-319-24589-8_9

16. Mora-Cantallops, M., Sicilia, M.-Á.: MOBA games: a literature review. Entertain. Comput. **26**, 128–138 (2018). https://doi.org/10.1016/j.entcom.2018.02.005

17. Boyle, E.A., Connolly, T.M., Hainey, T., Boyle, J.M.: Engagement in digital entertainment games: a systematic review. Comput. Hum. Behav. **28**, 771–780 (2012). https://doi.org/10.1016/j.chb.2011.11.020

18. Forsyth, S.R., Malone, R.E.: Smoking in video games: a systematic review. Nicotine Tob. Res. **18**, 1390–1398 (2016). https://doi.org/10.1093/ntr/ntv160

19. Boyle, E.A., et al.: An update to the systematic literature review of empirical evidence of the impacts and outcomes of computer games and serious games. Comput. Educ. **94**, 178–192 (2016). https://doi.org/10.1016/j.compedu.2015.11.003

20. Moreno-Ger, P., Burgos, D., Martínez-Ortiz, I., Sierra, J.L., Fernández-Manjón, B.: Educational game design for online education. Comput. Hum. Behav. **24**, 2530–2540 (2008). https://doi.org/10.1016/j.chb.2008.03.012

21. Sauvé, L., Renaud, L., Kaufman, D., Marquis, J.-S.: Distinguishing between games and simulations: a systematic review. J. Educ. Technol. Soc. **10**(3), 247–256 (2007)

22. Educational Technology & Society 15. https://www.researchgate.net/publication/270273830_Gamification_in_Education_A_Systematic_Mapping_Study

23. Huang, L., Hsieh, Y.: Predicting online game loyalty based on need gratification and experiential motives. Internet Res. **21**, 581–598 (2011). https://doi.org/10.1108/10662241111176380

24. Greenberg, B.S., Sherry, J., Lachlan, K., Lucas, K., Holmstrom, A.: Orientations to video games among gender and age groups. Simul. Gaming **41**, 238–259 (2010). https://doi.org/10.1177/1046878108319930

25. Wu, J.-H., Wang, S.-C., Tsai, H.-H.: Falling in love with online games: the uses and gratifications perspective. Comput. Hum. Behav. **26**, 1862–1871 (2010). https://doi.org/10.1016/j.chb.2010.07.033

26. Hamilton, W.A., Garretson, O., Kerne, A.: Streaming on twitch: fostering participatory communities of play within live mixed media. In: Proceedings of the 32nd Annual ACM Conference on Human Factors in Computing Systems - CHI 2014, pp. 1315–1324. ACM Press, Toronto (2014). https://doi.org/10.1145/2556288.2557048

27. Cheung, G., Huang, J.: Starcraft from the stands: understanding the game spectator. In: Proceedings of the 2011 Annual Conference on Human Factors in Computing Systems - CHI 2011, p. 763. ACM Press, Vancouver (2011). https://doi.org/10.1145/1978942.1979053

28. Yee, N.: Motivations of play in online games, **13**. https://pdfs.semanticscholar.org/a7a9/6b512e077088096927df2438ffa639f4a515.pdf

29. Weiss, T., Schiele, S.: Virtual worlds in competitive contexts: analyzing eSports consumer needs. Electron. Mark. **23**, 307–316 (2013). https://doi.org/10.1007/s12525-013-0127-5

30. Parshakov, P., Zavertiaeva, M.: Success in eSports: does country matter? SSRN Electron. J. (2015). https://doi.org/10.2139/ssrn.2662343

31. Carter, M., Gibbs, M.: eSports in EVE online: skullduggery, fair play and acceptability in an unbounded competition, **8**. http://marcuscarter.com/wp-content/uploads/2013/03/eSports-in-EVE-Online-referenced.pdf

32. Frostling-Henningsson, M.: First-person shooter games as a way of connecting to people: "brothers in blood". Cyberpsychol. Behav. **12**, 557–562 (2009). https://doi.org/10.1089/cpb.2008.0345

33. Rambusch, J., Jakobsson, P., Pargman, D.: Exploring e-sports: a case study of gameplay in counter-strike, **8**. https://www.researchgate.net/publication/237523631_Exploring_E-sports_A_Case_Study_of_Gameplay_in_Counter-strike

34. Ruggiero, T.E.: Uses and gratifications theory in the 21st century. Mass Commun. Soc. **3**, 3–37 (2000). https://doi.org/10.1207/S15327825MCS0301_02

35. (PDF) Flow: The Psychology of Optimal Experience. https://www.researchgate.net/publication/224927532_Flow_The_Psychology_of_Optimal_Experience
36. Adinolf, S., Turkay, S.: Toxic behaviors in esports games: player perceptions and coping strategies. In: Proceedings of the 2018 Annual Symposium on Computer-Human Interaction in Play Companion Extended Abstracts - CHI PLAY 2018, Extended Abstracts, pp. 365–372. ACM Press, Melbourne (2018). https://doi.org/10.1145/3270316.3271545
37. Largest Prize Pools For Arena of Valor - Esports Events : Esports Earnings. https://www.esportsearnings.com/games/529-arena-of-valor/largest-tournaments
38. Pokémon Go spurred an amazing era that continues with Sword and Shield - The Verge. https://www.theverge.com/2019/2/28/18243332/pokemon-go-sword-shield-franchise-history-niantic-nintendo-switch

How Society's Negative View of Videogames Can Discourage Brands from Sponsoring eSports

Bruno Duarte Abreu Freitas[1](✉) ⓘ,
Ruth Sofia Contreras-Espinosa[1] ⓘ,
and Pedro Álvaro Pereira Correia[2] ⓘ

[1] University of Vic - Central University of Catalonia, Vic, Spain
bruno22duarte@gmail.com
[2] University of Madeira, Funchal, Portugal

Abstract. The purpose of this research was to identify the main motives that contribute to society's negative view of videogames and that present a risk to the eSports sponsors' image. To achieve this, an exploratory, qualitative, and integrative literature review was conducted. According to the theoretical data, there are four main reasons why society has a negative perception of videogames. It is commonly believed that: (1) gaming is an unproductive activity, (2) violent videogames incite aggressive behaviors, (3) videogames lead to gaming-addiction, and (4) eSports lead to eSports-related gambling addiction. However, while the literature presents convincing evidence that gaming can create addiction and that eSports can promote gambling addiction, there is no conclusive evidence to assume that violent videogames lead to aggressiveness and there is evidence showing that playing videogames can be a productive activity. Nevertheless, these four beliefs are a threat to the eSports sponsors' image and may lead them to cancel their existing sponsorships or lead other brands to not want to sponsor eSports to prevent being associated with these negative notions. This research will help expand the minor literature on eSports sponsorships and advance the knowledge of why some eSports sponsorships are terminated and why some brands may be reluctant to sponsor eSports.

Keywords: eSports · Sponsorships · Market analysis · Marketing · Branding

1 Introduction

Electronic sports, commonly referred to as *eSports*, can be described as organized videogame competitions [1] where professional gamers, usually referred to as *pro-gamers*, compete [2] for the chance to win prizes, money, and prestige [3]. There are various levels of professionalism, including amateur [4], high-level amateur, and professional [5]. Still, while amateur tournaments are mostly held through the internet, with gamers competing from their own homes [6], important and high-level competitions are held in large arenas full of enthusiastic fans and broadcasted over the internet [7]. It should be noted that eSports are a collective term just like water sports. That is, they are composed by a multitude of different videogames and genres [1].

© Springer Nature Switzerland AG 2019
N. Zagalo et al. (Eds.): VJ 2019, CCIS 1164, pp. 136–149, 2019.
https://doi.org/10.1007/978-3-030-37983-4_11

In 2018, the eSports fan-base consisted of roughly 395 million people [8] and was experiencing an average annual growth of 13.5% [9]. This subsection of the videogame industry has evolved quite quickly and has now reached a worldwide scale [3], filling out entire football stadiums [10] and featuring its own developed ecosystem [11]. South Korea has even already established competitive gaming as an official sport and multiple western countries are also in the process of giving it the same type of recognition [12]. The reason why eSports have only now reached this level of popularity is due to the fact that the evolution of the information and communication technologies has only recently reached a state where the necessary technological and sociological conditions have been met to live stream and proliferate these events over an online and worldwide audience [13].

The development and professionalization of eSports have made it similar to regular sports [14]. Its market is very complex, being composed of multiple elements and entities [2], including the tournaments and leagues, the fan-base, media channels [1], event producers, gaming genres, game developers and publishers, etc. [2]. But the most important element for the survival of eSports is the sponsors [1, 3, 10, 15–17]. While the past small scale eSports events could be funded just by the event organizers and fans, the current scale that eSports has reached means that it needs sponsors to be sustainable [10]. There are different figures, for example, Shabir [2] states that sponsors are responsible for 60% of eSports revenue, SuperData [18] estimates 70%, Lokhman et al. [15] mentions 74%, Ströh [1] affirms that it is approximately 75%, and ONTIER [19] indicates that it is a maximum of 80%. Although there is still no agreement on what the real percentage is, what is agreed upon is that, unlike regular sports, which can also earn significant revenues from player sales, TV rights, private investors, etc. [20], eSports, in their current scale, receive most of their revenue from sponsors. Hence, they cannot survive without them [1–3, 10, 11, 15–26].

However, despite eSports' worldwide popularity [1, 2, 10, 27], gaming is still negatively perceived by some [28, 29]. This negative public perception is so infamous that it has created a cultural barrier [28]. Unlike regular sports, people have not accepted videogames. They even consider it to be a negative activity. It is not unusual to see videogames being accused of inciting aggressive behaviors and of leading to addiction [30]. Furthermore, videogames and eSports are still seen as belonging to a nerd culture [20]. Gaming has such a negative connotation that some employers would favor someone who simply did voluntary work at a random sports club over someone who is a former administrator of a renowned eSports institution [31]. Unfortunately, it does not seem like this mentality will change anytime soon [32]. This negative stigma is a challenge for the eSports industry because the negative image that society and the media give to videogames may spread and, in turn, negatively affect, not only eSports' image, but also the image of eSports sponsors [1]. Due to how vital sponsors are for eSports and the danger of these negative views leading brands to cancel their eSports sponsorships, the following literature review will seek to identify what are the main motives that are creating these negative perceptions. The review will also include some data that challenges these negative views. In short, the objective is to identify what are the main reasons that create the gaming stigma so that future studies may try to find ways to shield eSports from this threat.

2 Methodology

This research was structured as a review article. An exploratory and qualitative methodology was employed to gather, analyze, and synthesize the most pertinent literature of the study topic. Since there are very few data on the novel topic of eSports sponsorships and on what aspects may discourage brands from sponsoring eSports (which greatly limited this review of the literature), an integrative literature review method was employed. As it is common in integrative literature reviews, the contemporary literature was scrutinized with the intent of generating new knowledge and frameworks on what are the main motives that lead society to negatively view videogames. The scant nature of eSports sponsorships-related research meant that a light filter had to be used when deciding which literature to include or exclude. Nonetheless, only academic works, published books, and relevant statics websites were used as sources for this review. The statistics websites included in this review were limited to those that have performed various eSports-related market analyses. Statistic websites that have only conducted a small number of eSports analyses were not included. Data from general gaming and eSports-related websites were not included in this review in order to keep the literature at an acceptable level of quality and reliability. The only exception was an article from PCMAG.com, by Jeffrey L. Wilson, who provided a very interesting and unique insight on the physical deterioration issues of pro-players. Since the eSports market is constantly changing and evolving, preference was given to the latest literature, especially data published not before 2015, as old data may present outdated or obsolete information. Hence, older literature was kept to a minimum, only being included if it contained either issues that were still prevalent nowadays or if it presented very convincing arguments or interesting data. In total, 62 literary references were used in this literature review, with 51 of them being published not before 2015 and only 11 being published between 2013 and 2006. The main keywords that were used to search for the relevant literature were: "eSports", "sponsorship", "videogame", "videogame industry", "negative effect", "problem", "danger", "disorder", and "marketing". In other words, literature related to the negative aspects that society associates videogames with and how eSports sponsors may be negatively affected by them were extensively searched. The major databases that were used to locate relevant literature were: Scopus, Emerald Insight, Google Scholar, Google Books, Web of Science, Science Direct, Taylor and Francis Online, and Sage Publishing. In these databases, it was possible to find pertinent data on multiple journal articles, conference proceedings, and books. Relevant data was also found on the following statistics websites: Newzoo, Statista, and SuperData.

3 Literature Review

Throughout the literature review, it was possible to identify several aspects that contribute to society's negative views over videogames. However, after scrutinizing and synthesizing these data, it became apparent that the vast majority of these elements fell into one of four main categories, which will now be covered in detail.

3.1   Unproductive Activity

Numerous individuals believe that the act of playing videogames is a waste of time [28, 30, 33] and energy [30]. In essence, according to them, videogames are damaging people's productivity, creativity, literacy [27], lowering school grades, and promoting obesity and sedentary behaviors [33]. Entering into further detail, critics believe that the act of playing a videogame does not require any sort of work or strategic planning. Everything that the players must do is simply kill everything they see and nothing is learned from it. It is also believed that videogames completely eliminate reading habits. For critics, while the act of reading a book promotes literacy and writing, the act of playing videogames does not promote any of that. However, this is an ignorant notion as there is a wide variety of videogames, like *Final Fantasy* and *The Legend of Zelda*, which include vast amounts of text in the form of narratives that gamers must read. People also argue that gaming damages creativity as it is believed that videogames do not provide the necessary tools to promote imagination. Hence, gaming is seen as a trivial activity where individuals do not gain any sort of abilities [27]. But this is another uninformed criticism as several videogames, including *Minecraft*, place a heavy emphasis and highly promote creativity [34]. Moreover, since gaming is accused of turning otherwise productive members of society into mindless sheep who look at screens for excessive periods of time, it is common to hear people saying that gamers are unproductive individuals who should be making better use of their time. However, several of these negative notions are either wrong or have little to no scientific evidence [27]. In fact, several books and articles about the benefits and importance of videogames have been published [35–41]. For instance, research has shown that videogames promote teamwork, teach people to adhere to rules, improve technological and motor skills [1], help in education [35–37, 39, 40], and enhance the ability to conduct multimodal operations. This last one refers to the skill of simultaneously and quickly interpreting haptic, auditory, and visual data and responding in a fast and effective manner [27]. Similarly, another study concluded that pro-players present above-average problem-solving skills, pattern recognition, short-term memory, and visual-spatial abilities [42].

Because people believe that a gamer's life is centered on his videogames instead of his job [31], there is also the stereotype that gamers are overweight nerds living in their parents' basements. It is believed that, since gaming is an activity where people's attention is detached from reality [28], it promotes antisocialism [27, 29] and social isolation [30]. However, this belief ignores the fact that a considerable number of videogames are not solo experiences [27]. Furthermore, roughly 56% of gamers regularly play multiplayer videogames [43]. Still, there is also the notion that gamers would rather communicate only through the internet instead of in person [2]. But data also shows that gamers enjoy playing personally with their friends [43]. Hence, gaming also promotes social behaviors [42].

Although, at present, there is not as much incorrect gaming information being distributed, the social stigma that haunts the gaming industry is still very present [21]. Sadly, it will be very difficult to change society's notion of the solitary, geek, and obsessed gamer and turn it into an image of a technologically-skillful and healthy human [44]. This constant negative mental image that society has over gaming is a barrier that repels many potential eSports promoters [20].

3.2 Virtual Violence

Another very prevalent stereotype is that videogames promote violent behaviors [2, 27], drug use, and theft [2]. Since gamers are regularly perceived as antisocial individuals who prefer to play videogames than to be with others, there are some who believe that these are dangerous, unbalanced, and obsessive people. Thus, whenever an act of violence, like school shootings, are committed by someone from a young demographic, it is often believed that such acts were promoted by exposure to videogames [27]. In this sense, it is important to note that the media can greatly influence the acceptance of eSports. For instance, the topic of whether videogames promote violent behaviors began being spread by several media when school shootings started turning into a recurrent problem. Here, the media indicated that videogames, especially first-person shooters, were partially to blame. An example of this happened in 2002 when an article of a very popular German newspaper, called the *Frankfurter Allgemeine Zeitung*, stated that several games, including *Counter-Strike*, were training students to become school shooters. This led the German authorities to conduct some investigations, but the game was not banned. Nevertheless, there is always the risk that a popular eSports videogame may be banned due to its graphic violence, which may negatively affect the brands that were sponsoring it or were connected to that game [1].

The violent contents of various videogames have led several people to infer that they are a negative influence on the younger demographics. There are numerous eSports videogames, like *Counter-Strike*, *Halo*, and *Call of Duty*, which also present graphic and realistic depictions of violence and have the potential to create negative word of mouth about their contents [2]. The media has nicknamed these as *Killer Games* and some people believe that they lead to the loss of empathy or train gamers for the army [45]. For several times now, videogames have been blamed for real-world acts of violence and this trend will continue to persist, particularly now that a massive demographic of young people is starting to watch or participate in eSports [2].

Despite the belief that violent videogames lead to aggressive behaviors, there is, in fact, little to no evidence that supports these accusations [46]. Most studies have presented inconclusive data [47]. The unfortunate truth is that the majority of accusations over how videogames incite violent behaviors are partially based on ignorance. For instance, the *Huffington Post* once accused videogames of being more dangerous than guns. Nevertheless, all it takes is a quick online search about how gaming affects children to find a surprising number of effects like aggressiveness, insensitivity towards violence, etc. [32]. This problem has already started negatively affecting eSports. For instance, the violent content of several eSports videogames has decreased the International Olympic Committee's interest of including eSports in the 2024 Olympics. According to them, in order to be included as an Olympic sport, eSports must follow the Olympic values of non-violence and peace. But this will exclude some of the most popular eSports videogames (e.g. *Counter-Strike*, *Dota 2*, and *League of Legends*). This raised the concern of the eSports community as it would mean that the eSports' debut at the Olympics would not feature their favorite games and would have low viewership levels [2].

As can be seen, the media's negative portrayal of videogames can be a threat to the eSports market. This negative publicity means that eSports are always under the risk of losing partnerships. All it may take is the media blaming videogames for another school shooting for brands to end their eSports sponsorships to prevent any kind of damages to their image. This has already happened once when a shooting in Munich took the lives of 10 individuals and led to a heavy discussion on the effects of violent videogames. This led the ProSiebenSat.1 Media SE to suddenly call off their eSports TV show. Hence, considering that the most popular videogames and genres contain violent content, it becomes immediately apparent that the negative media portrayals of violent videogames are a threat to competitive gaming. If the media generalizes this to the eSports industry it may affect the entire competitive gaming market [1].

3.3   Gaming Addiction

Several people state that videogames are addicting [2, 33] and the truth is that research has presented convincing evidence to conclude that too much exposure to gaming can lead to addiction [2]. However, if someone wishes to become a pro-player, they must play them for as long as possible in order to have a chance of entering the professional eSports tournaments. This can lead to a very exhausting lifestyle [48], with people playing videogames for roughly 10 [2, 49, 50] to 16 h per day [20]. There are even gaming houses that serve as training camps where pro-players continuously hone their gaming skills. There are not any kinds of parties in these houses. The pro-players are aware that they are making a living out of eSports and they know that their careers are at stake. So they must practice as much as possible. In essence, eSports are just like regular sports. People must heavily commit to training if they wish to have a chance of entering, and staying, on the professional scene [49].

However, this perseverance has led to some incidents. For instance, in 2014 a 22-year-old was sent to the hospital with a collapsed lung and, since he was a pro-player, he still kept practicing his gaming skills 5 h per day at the hospital [48]. But there have been more severe cases. For example, an 18-year-old regular gamer was once found unconscious at an internet café due to continuously playing a videogame for 40 h. Unfortunately, despite being transported to the hospital, he still passed away. This latter incident proves without a doubt that gaming addiction is indeed a real and dangerous issue [51].

Excessive gaming can negatively affect the human body in several ways, including the brain [2]. Evidence has shown that, when young people stare at screens or play videogames for long periods of time, their neurological brain system can be damaged in a similar fashion to what happens to those who consume too much cocaine. Furthermore, excessive gaming has been connected to disorders like depression, anxiety, and psychosis, also referred to as the *Tetris Effect* [52]. The Tetris Effect is caused by excessive exposition to pattern-based activities. The name Tetris is used due to its pattern-based gameplay and because it was one of the very first videogames to cause addiction. This condition does not occur solely to those who play *Tetris*; it can affect anyone who plays a videogame for excessive periods of time. In the case of someone who played too much *Tetris*, a moderate case of Tetris Effect would manifest as a desire to perfectly group together ordinary real-life objects that they found. More severe cases could include seeing the tetrominoes themselves falling when not staring at the screen. Some people have even had their brain's ability to process information being severely damaged [53] or have even lost their grip on reality [51].

Regarding the pro-players, most of them must end their eSports careers in their mid-twenties [48]. This is because of the physical deterioration that this sport causes [54], like wrist or hand injuries due to the long gaming sessions [48] and the necessity of constant and fast button presses. For instance, the pro-player Aziz "Hax" Al-Yami has had his hand and wrists analyzed by surgeons 12 times and has undergone two operations. Sadly, it is common for pro-players to suffer from these issues, with some having to quit their careers even earlier than expected. To help fight these physical problems, Dr. Levi Harrison has appeared at several eSports tournaments to instruct both pro-players and the community on how to keep gaming safe and healthy [55].

Although gaming addiction is a real thing [51], in the case of eSports, the general public must learn to distinguish between the people who play to make a living (i.e. pro-players) from the people who play because they are really addicted to videogames [56]. Both professional athletes and pro-players train for around 10 h per day [2]. Despite this, it must be recognized that gaming addiction is a real problem that should not be ignored [51]. The increasing success of eSports has led more people to become addicted to videogames. This has raised several concerns about the pro-players' health and social life. Hence, several countries like China, Japan, South Korean, and the USA are now acknowledging that gaming addiction is a real health problem. Because of this, the media and the general public have become very cautious about how the eSports market is evolving since its major demographic is quite young and vulnerable to addiction [57].

3.4 Gambling Addiction

Another type of addiction that eSports can create is gambling addiction. The ease of skin gambling (i.e. betting in-game items) has the potential to persuade several individuals to experiment with gambling and even lead to addiction [58]. Interestingly, research has shown that, although gaming addiction does not promote eSports-related gambling, the more someone watches eSports, the more likely they are of engaging in eSports-related gambling and of developing a gambling addiction. This means that, when someone develops an eSports-related gambling addiction, it is very likely that it was due to high eSports consumption [59].

A different study has also suggested that eSports do not create new gamblers; they simply attract existing ones. In a study, most eSports gamblers indicated that they had gambled in other areas before betting on eSports. Hence, most eSports-related gambling addicts may have been individuals who were already addicted to gambling in other areas and eSports were not responsible for creating the gambling addiction. This data is in line with another research which concluded that most people addicted to online gambling had already shown signs of gambling addiction before trying online gambling [60]. Furthermore, several authors have stated that more research on eSports gambling addiction is necessary [58] because at the moment there is no reliable data about this issue [10].

Evidence has also shown that eSports gamblers are more engaged than other bettors. For instance, an eSports gambler will bet on more different kinds of eSports-related bets than a regular sports bettor [60] and will also place more bets [60, 61]. It is common for regular gamblers to bet one time per week, but eSports bettors usually gamble every day [61]. eSports gamblers are more likely to become addicted because most of them belong to a young demographic. Moreover, eSports have a lot of offshore and illegal gambling websites, which facilitates the chances of becoming addicted [60, 61].

It is also important to note that, although the eSports gambling market was only officially established in 2010 [10], it has already become more valuable than the entire eSports industry itself [61]. Just in 2014, more than one million eSports bets were placed on the Pinnacle website [62]. According to this website's director, eSports gambling has overtaken both golf and rugby, and are now their seventh most popular gambling area. The director also affirmed that eSports wagering is growing so fast that it will not take long for it to surpass hockey and that, in the long run, it may even surpass football and tennis [10]. Estimates show that, in 2016, there were roughly 6.5 million people [61] betting roughly $8 billion on eSports [2] and it is expected that by 2020 there will be 19 million individuals [10] wagering approximately $23 billion [2, 10].

eSports betting has become so popular that various of the world's largest gambling companies are now allowing people to wager on eSports [2]. However, this popularity may end up damaging eSports itself as research has already proven that eSports promote gambling and can create betting addiction [59]. This issue becomes even more problematic when we bear in mind that most eSports fans belong to a young demographic and thus are even more susceptible to developing addiction problems [60].

4 Conclusions

Being the most vital revenue source of competitive gaming, it is vital to make sure that eSports provide sponsors with a welcoming environment. However, there are some aspects that might discourage or prevent brands from sponsoring this market and may even lead existing brands to end their sponsorships. One of these is the still present negative perception that society has over videogames and the eSports industry. Through this literature review it was possible to identify four main aspects that seem to be promoting these negative views: (1) the belief that gaming is an unproductive activity, (2) the belief that violent videogames lead to aggressive behaviors, (3) the belief that gaming leads to addiction, and (4) the belief that eSports lead to gambling addiction. While the literature does not present conclusive evidence that videogames are unproductive or lead to violent behaviors (in fact there is evidence against these assumptions), the literature does show convincing evidence that videogames can lead to gaming addiction and that eSports may lead to gambling addiction.

Some people believe that playing videogames is a waste of time. But that would also mean that anyone who plays chess, for example, is also wasting their time, which is not a present stereotype. None of these activities contribute to one's physical health and there are very low chances of being able to enter the professional scenes or of making a living out of them. Still, none of these activities seem to be a waste of time. Both chess and videogames are good at training one's strategic thinking abilities for example and the varied nature of videogames means that they can provide even more benefits than simply playing chess. Videogames promote creativity, literacy, techno-logical and motor skills, teamwork, etc. This negative view of unproductivity could be easily minimized if the media placed a higher importance on showing the positive effects of videogames rather than solely focusing on the sensationalist attention-grabbing stories of unproven negative aspects of videogames. If the mass media called society's attention to how several studies have proven that gaming is a productive and positive activity, and listed several of its benefits, society would be much more inclined to understand that gaming is not unproductive. Unfortunately, dramatic stories are what catch the public's attention, so several media prefer to emphasize isolated issues related to how gaming has ruined someone's life. To make matters even worse, they tend to assume that those isolated issues are generalizable and fail to analyze the scientific studies which present a large spectrum of concrete evidence on how gaming is not an unproductive activity. The eSports sponsors themselves could also help here by showing the general public (e.g. through the mass media) how videogames are not unproductive since there are now several individuals making a living out of playing videogames in eSports or by being a gaming personality on appropriate social media like YouTube or Twitch.

Regarding the aspect of virtual violence, it is undeniable that several videogames contain explicit and very graphic content. However, this is not different from the movie industry. Just like with videogames, several films feature guns and people killing each other, and several of these movies are not rated for mature audiences only. Further-more, just like with films, videogames indicate in their covers the recommended age for the consumption of each one. Hence, and again, just like with movies, parents must make sure that they do not buy their children videogames that are not appropriate for their age. The same applies to videogame stores which, just like with alcohol or cigarettes, should not sell videogames that are not appropriate to the buyer's age. Whenever a child has access to videogames that are not appropriate for their age, the individual that gave them access to that videogame should take responsibility instead of passing the blame to the mature content of the game. The media also can be of tremendous help here. If the mass media made the public comprehend that the virtual violence of videogames is not different from the violence that is present on TV or in cinemas, society would better understand that videogames do not incite violence more than any other form of basic entertainment like movies. Furthermore, while a child needs their parents' money to gain access to a violent videogame, they can easily turn on the TV and gain immediate access to a panoply of violent content. Likewise, and as stated by Hilvoorde [32], attention should be called to why a game with virtual guns is negatively viewed by society but the selling of toy guns (some of them very realistic) for children is not. Both cases will lead children to immerse themselves in an imaginary or virtual world where they are using guns to kill each other. If the media brought these aspects to the attention of the general public, then there is a chance that the negative notions of virtual violence would be mitigated. Similarly, whenever school shootings occur, research should be conducted to analyze if the motive was centered on video-games or if it was related to any other issue (e.g. social or mental problems). Finally, eSports sponsors should call the general public's attention to how eSports are in fact less violent than several sports. Unlike boxing or football, eSports are not a contact sport. No pro-player walks out of a tournament covered in blood or with a broken arm. Likewise, unlike racing, the pro-player is never under the threat to risking his life by taking a sharp turn.

As recognized, the literature presents very compelling arguments and evidence that gaming addiction is a serious issue that must be dealt with. While pro-players have a reason to play videogames for long periods (i.e. that is what they do for a living), regular gamers do not and should not view gaming as a lifestyle. eSports sponsors and the media must educate the general public that, while pro-players have to spend up to 16 h per day playing videogames to improve their gaming skills, the general gamer should not play for so long. Pro-players are only allowed to engage in such long playing sessions because their careers and income are at stake. The general gamer should only threat gaming as the hobby it is. Just like with football, professionals spend the majority of their time training while the fans only treat it as a hobby. The demanding lifestyle of both football and eSports means that professionals must retire at a young age. This gruesome way of life is something that the general individual must avoid. Anyone who does nothing but play videogames for all day, every day, and cannot stop playing, has a high chance of being addicted and should seek medical help. In this sense, the appearance of medical professionals at eSports events, as indicated by Wilson [55], may prove to be a great way to help educate the general gamer on how to avoid gaming addiction and keep gaming as a healthy hobby. It should be in the best interests of eSports sponsors to implement these tactics as this will help shield their brands from negative views regarding gaming addiction.

Lastly, the literature also showed that eSports gambling addiction is a real problem and that appropriate measures must be implemented. Although most people addicted to gambling showed to already have gambling problems before starting to wager on eSports, the fact still remains that eSports are promoting gambling addiction. To mitigate this issue, both eSports sponsors and the media should educate parents to monitor their children's spending and make sure that they are not engaging in any form of eSports-related gambling (or gambling in general). As for adults, the media must educate people to be able to identify gambling problems in themselves and in others and to seek the appropriate medical help whenever these issues are detected. Furthermore, it would also be appropriate to sensitize eSports fans about the dangers of gambling through short presentations during the breaks between eSports matches (these same presentations could also be used to show the dangers, and how to avoid, gaming addiction).

Since the people who grew with videogames now comprise a very significant portion of the adult population, it is expected that these negative notions will diminish in the future. But the fact still remains that these are contemporary problems and present a risk both to the general gaming industry and to the eSports sponsors.

In short, even though there is evidence contradicting some of the negative beliefs about gaming, the truth is that all of these beliefs will not disappear in the short-term and that they have the potential to negatively affect the eSports sponsors' images. Thus, there is the ever-present risk of brands suddenly wanting to cancel their existing sponsorships or of brands that are not sponsoring wanting to avoid this market. Hence, the most important things to do would be to first mitigate the gaming problems that research has proven to exist (i.e. gaming addiction and eSports-related gambling addiction). Secondly, and as stated by Newman [27], although the logic that backs several of the accusations towards gaming is greatly flawed, this stigma is so voracious and persistent that corrective actions must be implemented to chance society's negative view. In this sense, it would be wise to follow the advice provided by AEVI [21] and try to alter the way the media views and approaches videogames so that a more realistic and positive image of gaming can be spread throughout society.

References

1. Ströh, J.H.A.: The eSports Market and eSports Sponsoring. Tectum Verlag, Marburg (2017)
2. Shabir, N.: Esports: The Complete Guide 17/18: A Guide for Gamers, Teams, Organisations and Other Entities in, or Looking to Get Into the Space. Independently Published, Wroclaw (2017)
3. Mooney, C.: Inside the E-Sports Industry. Norwood House Press, North Mankato (2018)
4. Hamari, J., Sjöblom, M.: What is eSports and why do people watch it? Internet Res. **27**(2), 211–232 (2017). https://doi.org/10.1108/IntR-04-2016-0085
5. SuperData. Esports Courtside: Playmakers of 2017, December 2017. http://strivesponsorship.com/wp-content/uploads/2017/12/SuperData-2017-Esports-Market-Brief.pdf. Accessed 6 Apr 2018
6. Stein, V., Scholz, T.M.: Sky is the limit – esports as entrepreneurial innovator for media management. In: Jesus, S.N.d., Pinto, P. (eds.) Proceedings of the International Congress on Interdisciplinarity in Social and Human Sciences, pp. 622–631. University of Algarve, Faro. CIEO – Research Centre for Spatial and Organizational Dynamics (2016). http://hdl.handle.net/10400.1/9888
7. Gifford, C.: Gaming Record Breakers. Carlton Books Limited, London (2017)
8. Statista. eSports audience size worldwide from 2012 to 2020, by type of viewers (in millions), February 2019. https://www.statista.com/statistics/490480/global-esports-audience-size-viewer-type/. Accessed 3 Mar 2019
9. Newzoo: Free 2018 Global Esports Market Report, 21 February 2018. http://resources.newzoo.com/2018-global-esports-market-report-light. Accessed 13 Apr 2018
10. Winnan, C.D.: An entrepreneur's guide to the exploding world of esports: understanding the commercial significance of counter-strike, league of legends and DotA 2. Kindle eBook: The Borderland Press
11. CGC Europe: Marketing Channel eSports – How to get the attention of young adults? (2015). http://docplayer.net/12867287-Marketing-channel-esports-how-to-get-the-attention-of-young-adults.html. Accessed 19 Jan 2018
12. Hiltscher, J., Scholz, T.M.: Preface. In: Hiltscher, J., Scholz, T.M. (eds.) eSports Yearbook 2015/16, pp. 7–8. Books on Demand GmbH, Norderstedt (2017). http://www.esportsyearbook.com/eyb201516.pdf
13. Carter, M., Gibbs, M.: eSports in EVE online: skullduggery, fair play and acceptability in an unbounded competition. In: Yannakakis, G.N., Aarseth, E., Jørgensen, K., Lester, J.C. (eds.) Proceedings of the 8th International Conference on the Foundations of Digital Games, pp. 47–54. Society for the Advancement of the Science of Digital Games, Chania (2013)

14. Lopez-Gonzalez, H., Griffiths, M.D.: Understanding the convergence of markets in online sports betting. Int. Rev. Sociol. Sport, 1–24 (2016). https://doi.org/10.1177/101269021668 0602

15. Lokhman, N., Karashchuk, O., Kornilova, O.: Analysis of eSports as a commercial activity. Probl. Perspect. Manag. **16**(1), 207–213 (2018). https://doi.org/10.21511/ppm.16(1).2018.20

16. Callus, P., Potter, C.: Michezo video: Nairobi's gamers and the developers who are promoting local content. Crit. Afr. Stud. **9**(3), 302–326 (2017). https://doi.org/10.1080/21681392.2017.1371620

17. Holden, J.T., Kaburakis, A., Rodenberg, R.: The future is now: Esports policy considerations and potential litigation. J. Leg. Aspects Sport **27**(1), 46–78 (2017). https://doi.org/10.1123/jlas.2016-0018

18. SuperData: 2017 Year in Review: Digital Games and Interactive Media (2018). https://www.superdataresearch.com/market-data/market-brief-year-in-review/. Accessed 7 Apr 2018

19. ONTIER: Guía legal sobre e-Sports: Presente y futuro de la regulación de los esports en España (2018). https://es.ontier.net/ia/guialegalesports-2018web.pdf

20. Taylor, T.L.: Raising the Stakes: E-Sports and the Professionalization of Computer Gaming. The MIT Press, Cambridge (2012)

21. AEVI. Libro blanco de los esports en España (2018). http://www.aevi.org.es/web/wp-content/uploads/2018/05/ES_libroblanco_online.pdf

22. Nichols, M.: Endemics vs Non-Endemics: eSports expanding its sponsorship horizons. European Sponsorship Association (2017). http://sponsorship.org/wp-content/uploads/2017/08/Sportcals-Endemics-vs-Non-Endemics-eSports-expanding-its-sponsorship-horizons.pdf

23. Seo, Y.: Electronic sports: a new marketing landscape of the experience economy. J. Mark. Manag. **29**(13–14), 1542–1560 (2013). https://doi.org/10.1080/0267257X.2013.822906

24. Simon, J.P.: User generated content – users, community of users and firms: toward new sources of co-innovation? info **18**(6), 4–25 (2016). https://doi.org/10.1108/info-04-2016-0015

25. SuperData: eSports: The market brief 2015, May 2015. https://pt.scribd.com/document/269675603/ESports-Market-Brief-2015-SuperData-Research. Accessed 7 Apr 2018

26. SuperData: European eSports Conference Brief, February 2017. http://strivesponsorship.com/wp-content/uploads/2017/04/Superdata-2017-esports-market-brief.pdf. Accessed 6 Apr 2018

27. Newman, J.: Playing with Videogames. Routledge, Abingdon (2008)

28. Li, R.: Good Luck Have Fun: The Rise of eSports. Skyhorse Publishing, New York (2016)

29. Brookey, R.A., Oates, T.P. (eds.): Playing to Win. Indiana University Press, Bloomington (2015)

30. Peša, A.R., Čičin-Šain, D., Blažević, T.: New business model in the growing e-sports industry. Poslovna izvrsnost: znanstveni časopis za promicanje kulture kvalitete i poslovne izvrsnosti **11**(2), 121–131 (2017). https://doi.org/10.22598/pi-be/2017.11.2.121

31. Scholz, T.: eSports in the working world. In: Christophers, J., Scholz, T. (eds.) eSports Yearbook 2009, pp. 57–58. Books on Demand GmbH, Norderstedt (2010). http://esportsyearbook.com/eyb2009_ebook.pdf

32. van Hilvoorde, I.: Sport and play in a digital world. Sport Ethics Philos. **10**(1), 1–4 (2016). https://doi.org/10.1080/17511321.2016.1171252

33. Tavinor, G.: The Art of Videogames. Wiley, Malden (2009)

34. Hill, V.: Digital citizenship through game design in Minecraft. New Libr. World **116**(7/8), 369–382 (2015). https://doi.org/10.1108/NLW-09-2014-0112

35. Beavis, C., Dezuanni, M., O'Mara, J. (eds.): Serious Play: Literacy, Learning and Digital Games. Routledge, New York (2017)

36. Becker, K.: Choosing and Using Digital Games in the Classroom: A Practical Guide. Springer, Heidelberg (2017). https://doi.org/10.1007/978-3-319-12223-6
37. Brown, H.J.: Videogames and Education. M.E. Sharpe, Armonk (2008)
38. Hergenrader, T.: The place of videogames in the digital humanities. Horizon **24**(1), 29–33 (2016). https://doi.org/10.1108/OTH-08-2015-0050
39. Shaffer, D.W.: How Computer Games Help Children Learn. Palgrave Macmillan, New York (2006)
40. Wankel, C., Blessinger, P. (eds.): Increasing Student Engagement and Retention Using Immersive Interfaces: Virtual Worlds, Gaming, and Simulation (Vol. 6C). Emerald Group Publishing Limited, Bingley (2012)
41. Scolari, C.A., Contreras-Espinosa, R.S.: How do teens learn to play video games? Informal learning strategies and video game literacy. J. Inf. Lit. **13**(1), 45–61 (2019). https://doi.org/10.11645/13.1.2358
42. Griffiths, M.: The psychosocial impact of professional gambling, professional video gaming & eSports. Casino Gaming Int. **28**, 59–63 (2017). http://irep.ntu.ac.uk/id/eprint/30079
43. ESA. 2018 Essential Facts About the Computer and Video Game Industry (2018). http://www.theesa.com/wp-content/uploads/2018/05/EF2018_FINAL.pdf
44. Liboriussen, B., Martin, P.: Special issue: games and gaming in China. Games Cult. **11**(3), 227–232 (2016). https://doi.org/10.1177/1555412015615296
45. Scholz, C.: Gamers as a safety hazard. In: Christophers, J., Scholz, T. (eds.) eSports Yearbook 2009, pp. 51–52. Books on Demand GmbH, Norderstedt (2010). http://esportsyearbook.com/eyb2009_ebook.pdf
46. Crawford, G., Gosling, V.K.: More than a game: sports-themed video games and player narratives. Sociol. Sport J. **26**(1), 50–66 (2009). https://doi.org/10.1123/ssj.26.1.50
47. Franke, T.: The perception of eSports - mainstream culture, real sport and marketisation. In: Hiltscher, J., Scholz, T.M. (eds.) eSports Yearbook 2013/14, pp. 111–144. Books on Demand GmbH, Norderstedt (2015). http://esportsyearbook.com/eyb201314.pdf
48. Stivers, C.: The first competitive video gaming anti-doping policy and its deficiencies under European Union law. San Diego Int. Law J. **18**(2), 263–294 (2017). http://digital.sandiego.edu/ilj/vol18/iss2/4/
49. Parkin, S.: Death by Video Game: Tales of Obsession from the Virtual Frontline. Serpent's Tail, London (2015)
50. Szablewicz, M.: A realm of mere representation? "Live" e-sports spectacles and the crafting of china's digital gaming image. Games Cult. **11**(3), 256–274 (2016). https://doi.org/10.1177/1555412015595298
51. Şentuna, B., Kanbur, D.: What kind of an activity is a virtual game? A postmodern approach in relation to concept of phantasm by Deleuze and the philosophy of Huizinga. Sport Ethics Philos. **10**(1), 42–50 (2016). https://doi.org/10.1080/17511321.2016.1177581
52. Holden, J.T., Kaburakis, A., Rodenberg, R.M.: Esports: Children, stimulants and video-gaming-induced inactivity. J. Paediatr. Child Health (2018). https://doi.org/10.1111/jpc.13897
53. Ackerman, D.: The Tetris effect: The Game that Hypnotized the World. PublicAffairs, New York (2016)
54. Zolides, A.: Lipstick bullets: labour and gender in professional gamer self-branding. Persona Stud. **1**(2), 42–53 (2015). https://doi.org/10.21153/ps2015vol1no2art467
55. Wilson, J.L.: How I Learned to Stop Hating and Love Esports, 5 June 2017. https://www.pcmag.com/article/354028/how-i-learned-to-stop-hating-and-love-esports. Accessed 10 June 2018

56. Nielsen, R.K.L., Karhulahti, V.: The problematic coexistence of "internet gaming disorder" and esports. In: Deterding, S., Canossa, A., Harteveld, C., Zhu, J., Sicart, M., (eds.) Proceedings of the 12th International Conference on the Foundations of Digital Games, pp. 1–4. ACM, New York (2017). https://doi.org/10.1145/3102071.3106359, https://dl.acm.org/citation.cfm?id=3106359&dl=ACM&coll=DL

57. Lu, Z.: From E-Heroin to E-Sports: the development of competitive gaming in China. Int. J. Hist. Sport **33**(18), 2186–2206 (2017). https://doi.org/10.1080/09523367.2017.1358167

58. Teichert, T., Gainsbury, S.M., Mühlbach, C.: Positioning of online gambling and gaming products from a consumer perspective: a blurring of perceived boundaries. Comput. Hum. Behav. **75**, 757–765 (2017). https://doi.org/10.1016/j.chb.2017.06.025

59. Macey, J., Hamari, J.: Investigating relationships between video gaming, spectating esports, and gambling. Comput. Hum. Behav. **80**, 344–353 (2018). https://doi.org/10.1016/j.chb.2017.11.027

60. Gainsbury, S.M., Abarbanel, B., Blaszczynski, A.: Intensity and gambling harms: exploring breadth of gambling involvement among esports bettors. Gaming Law Rev. **21**(8), 610–615 (2017). https://doi.org/10.1089/glr2.2017.21812

61. Gainsbury, S.M., Abarbanel, B., Blaszczynski, A.: Game on: comparison of demographic profiles, consumption behaviors, and gambling site selection criteria of esports and sports bettors. Gaming Law Rev. **21**(8), 575–587 (2017). https://doi.org/10.1089/glr2.2017.21813

62. Schneider, S.: eSport betting: the intersection of gaming and gambling. Gaming Law Rev. Econ. **19**(6), 419–420 (2015). https://doi.org/10.1089/glre.2015.1963

Group Dynamics in Esports: Delving into the Semi-professional League of Legends Amazonian Scenario

Tarcízio Macedo[1](✉) and Thiago Falcão[2]

[1] Federal University of Rio Grande do Sul (UFRGS), Porto Alegre, Brazil
tarcizio.macedo@bol.com.br
[2] Federal University of Paraíba (UFPB), João Pessoa, Brazil
thfalcao@gmail.com

Abstract. This article discusses the processes of construction of cohesion and group membership in a semiprofessional team of esports in the city of Belém, capital of the state of Pará, in the Brazilian Amazonian territory. This effort discusses what characterizes the progression and union of a particular team in a local competitive scenario in which ephemeral teams predominate. Based on an eleven-month ethnography with a set of players engaged in professional competitive practice, and through observations from field research, we compiled a set of 12 essential characteristics displayed by the team. Also, this study points to the development of an ethos of professionalism in a peripheral context, indicating the existence of an Amazonian esports scenario – in the northern region of Brazil, with emphasis in Belém, Pará. The results indicate the maintenance of a social fabric composed of a variety of other elements that constitute an ethos of group camaraderie that plays a central role in the competitive dynamics that underlie the team as a group.

Keywords: Esports · Professional gaming · Group dynamics

1 Introduction

In recent years, the discussion about the phenomenon of electronic sports (Esports)[1] has gained prominence in Brazil. It indeed grew from an academic standpoint, with many researchers [2–5] turning to face questions of competition and spectatorship, but the subject has also been approached from different angles, oriented towards questions

---

[1] "E-Sport" or "esport," commonly used abbreviations for "electronic sport," "organized competitive digital gaming" or "professional gaming", has become a recurring and predominant term in the global community of competitive and formalized digital games, although its origin is uncertain [1]. For more details on the debate on the concept of esports, see Tarcízio Macedo and Thiago Falcão [2].

This study was financed in part by the Coordenação de Aperfeiçoamento de Pessoal de Nível Superior – Brazil (CAPES) – Finance Code 001.

© Springer Nature Switzerland AG 2019
N. Zagalo et al. (Eds.): VJ 2019, CCIS 1164, pp. 150–165, 2019.
https://doi.org/10.1007/978-3-030-37983-4_12

of news production and spectacular consumption [5, 6]. This last situation suggests a specific treatment by the media and implies in the recognition and promotion of the practice, certifying the creation of teams and institutions dedicated to the activity at the national level, such as several professional teams and entities such as the Brazilian Confederation of Electronic Sports (CBDEL)[2], created in 2015 and recognized by the Ministry of Citizenship (Special Secretariat of Sport) as the Brazilian esport administration entity in 2019, and the Brazilian Association of eSports Clubs (ABCDE)[3], founded in 2016.

This research addresses a topic that is both relevant and challenging given its recent trend and relative scarcity of references compared to other more saturated themes in the field of digital games research. We seek to understand the processes for forming group cohesion in a team of semiprofessional players of the Multiplayer Online Battle Arena (MOBA) *League of Legends* (*LoL*), based on the scenario of a competitive community of the Brazilian Amazon, located in the city of Belém, capital of the state of Pará.

This paper undertakes a discussion about the process of formation and maintenance of the social fabric among players who engage in pro gaming, in the specific context of a city in the Brazilian Amazon. To answer this research question, we build on the local competitive community of *League of Legends* in Belém, Pará. From an ethnographic study of a team of semi-pro players engaged in professional gaming – *Infinite Five e-Sports* (also called *Infive* or *IN5* by its members)[4] –, we seek to comprehend how group dynamics among members manifest in this particular competitive context.

The prospect, then, is to understand esport practices based on the social experience of a given local competitive team, exploring the relationship between social and instrumental or functional. This study focuses on comprehension how group dynamics form among team players in this particular regional context, how the social fabric is created and developed at the core of this group. The discussion presented is situated at the notion of communication and the phenomenon of communicative practices as social experiences, as something that translates, and thus must be implicitly associated, from the ideas of sociality/sociability to a human form that places subjects in interaction, in relationships with each other, from several common reasons [7–9].

2 Methodological Procedures

The competitive gaming industry is marked by constant dynamics and instability [1, 10]. Pro gaming communities are often closed and difficult to approach [1, 11]. In regional and local scenarios arranged in what could be considered a periphery of esports – away from the major political and economic centers with a high concentration of inputs to the professionalization of video games –, sponsorship for teams and

---

[2] Available online at: https://cbdel.com.br/ (accessed 26 July 2019).

[3] Available online at: https://abcdesports.com.br/ (accessed 26 July 2019).

[4] Created on June 2017 in the city of Belém, Pará, it is made up of two line-ups in two distinct MOBAs, *League of Legends* and *Defense of the Ancients 2*. However, our focus above all is on the LoL team, which currently consists of eleven members, including full players, reserves, a manager and a coach.

individual players are difficult to find. Player turnover is high and even the presence of promotional activities by game developers is infrequent, if not nonexistent. These conditions make the esports landscape in regions like the Amazon a mobile target for researchers.

Given that the process of involvement and rapprochement in the elite esports scenario is challenging to consolidate, we chose to perform ethnographic research in a longitudinal study conducted with a group of competitive players over eleven months, from June 2017 to May 2018. Considering questions of anonymity, the data collected in this ethnography utilizes only the screen names of the players aiming to preserve the identities of the participants that are, then, referred to in the following Table 1.

Table 1. Current *Infinite Five e-Sports LoL* line-up configuration in 2018.

Name	Age	Gender	Role	Status
Sniper Holmes	21	Male	AD Carry (ADC)	Full
Choke7	21	Female	Support	Full
Veceid	18	Male	Top laner	Full
Darkanon	18	Male	Jungler	Full
Hidaka Sana	18	Male	Mid laner	Full
Hyouka	22	Male	Top laner	Reserve
Reeva	19	Male	Support	Reserve
Hitman	20	Male	ADC	Reserve
Ham	18	Male	Manager, captain and ADC	Manager and ADC reserve
XPeKeh	19	Male	Mid laner	Reserve
KaiserXD	26	Male	Coach	In testing phase (February 2018)

Thomas Apperley and Darshana Jayemane [13, p. 8] argue that the use of ethnographic approaches or methods "provide game studies with a way of connecting objects to practices, and understanding those practices in relation to the lives and experiences of the people who enact them". Thus, Apperley and Jayemane [13] argue that ethnography is a valuable approach to Game Studies, allowing to recognize the complex contexts in which the game develops. Furthermore, it provides an advantageous strategy for comprehension the different forms of play in a particular game, not only in terms of structural algorithm execution, but also in cultural, affective, and situated responses.

An extensive work of ethnographic studies of digital games prompts the discernment that "the play of digital games is integrated into the mundane practices of everyday life" [13, p. 10]. In short, the authors argue that ethnography provides the resources for an in-depth analysis of how people play digital games. Besides, an ethnographic methodological approach calls for a treatment of digital games that highlights the many practices that take place in and around the game [13]. Following these guidelines, we base the mechanism adopted in this empirical investigation on a methodological procedure divided into four steps: (i) the approach with the field, from a movement by the local community to access to a specific team – which goes back to June 2016 to June 2017; (ii) living with the team over eleven months and capturing data through the use of some specific instruments; (iii) the analysis of the collected data and, finally, (iv) the construction of conclusions from the obtained results. We introduce these approaches by weaving a mixed ethnographic account – personal and academic.

Firstly, the collection process took place during the eleven months, daily for instant messaging applications, and following the team's schedule and activity routine. We gathered the data through the use of the following instruments: (i) a field notebook (physical and another online, regularly crossed) for annotation of impressions both in the face-to-face activities, as well as via the internet; (ii) a professional camera used in specific face-to-face actions to record video and image on-site moments that could be reviewed and analyzed in the future; (iii) a smartphone was activated for both annotations and recording of audios for interviews and in-person activities; (iv) in online activities, whether meetings via Discord or from competing in competitive events, we utilized the software Camtasia 9 for screen and audio capture; (v) and finally, to access team instant messaging application materials, such as WhatsApp, we make frequent copies of the data (backups) so that we can review them later.

On the computer, we systematized the collected data by creating folders that attempted to perform classification based on the type of activity performed and its date. Then, after observing and recording these data, we performed a *découpage* of the collected material (audio and video material).

In the case of a micro-sociological ethnographic approach, the process of analyzing these data took place daily, from the moment when a degree of field saturation was reached, observed by the incidence of specific frequently evoked categories, such as camaraderie, communication, group cohesion, organization, socialization, instrumental/functional, and therefore, these were chosen to compose the analysis. Naturally, this step recursively uses ethnographic methods of description, trying to cross, on the one hand, information from data and subjects and, on the other hand, the attribution of sense and meaning to the analysis through interpretative comments.

3 Comprehending Group Membership

In the specific case of *LoL* local competitive community, as the subjects frequently report in this research, there is a dynamic that indicates a much more numerous grouping process than group development, as defined by Zimerman [12]. Hidaka Sana, for example, although not the only one, when speaking about *Infive*'s differential of never having disbanded[5] as something that contrasts with this constant dynamic of the teams in the local scenario in Belém, commented that signals about this question: "[…]

---

[5] The use of this term refers to the end of a team. Disbanding is mainly seen as a problem for younger players in the scenario. Darkanon, for example, argued that this act hinders competitive progression precisely because of the need to get used to new players, different gameplays and gameplay, among other things.

there are people here in Belém who are good, but they, like… they take a few days or months before the championships, make a random team, practice with the focus on playing that championship, then disband, with no interest in the competition, only to win the prize". (sic)

The competitive situation of the local community serves as an example for a particular "seriality" of renowned players who momentarily team up to create a team with the sole goal of playing one specific championship: players who share the same interest (winning, especially, and win the prize), but they hardly have an adequate link to each other until a particular incident[6] is able to modify the whole group configuration – so weak the ties that made that aggregation possible.

This argument illustrates a frequent discourse, both for the subjects and equally visible during our observation in the community, about typical disband behavior to many teams in the local community. Relations like this are not uncommon in this competitive scenario: to this day, many teams show ephemerality. What can be inferred from this scenario is that the lack of camaraderie, coordination, and synergy (or rapport) with the collective (the team, therefore) can also inhibit player performance and is equally responsible for the breakdown of teams in the local community.

Why is it that a strategic game like *LoL*, typically designed by instrumental and competitive dominance, is also endowed with elements of a social game? The first point is that messaging, gift-giving to other players, and the ability to play within groups (in specific competitive queues) allow it to imply meaning through context. These dynamics point to how players perform socially meaningful actions while engaging in a competitive collective, in the frame of the MOBA.

A second point refers to a problem Juul [14] discusses, about the social meaning and social goals in multiplayer games, in which mechanics[7] allow the player to perform actions in which each choice must take into account. If a shared understanding of goals is part of how you play multiplayer games, how would that influence the way you play? For Juul [14], these three considerations are visible in any multiplayer game, which allows an approximation to the context of this research. Because competitive multiplayer games, such as *League of Legends*, are nonetheless played in social environments, social considerations can also become part of the deliberations of a player and even a competitively engaged team or organization. Thus, for each choice in a game, there are three distinct frames that a player must weigh and perform against each other [14].

A considerable number of players and teams that are marked by disbanding in the local Belém community – i.e., the end of a competitive team – have a stereotypical

---

[6] Progression may be jeopardized because of the lack of coordination in a team or because of any other player's essential needs. As Taylor [1] argues, a player aspiring professionalism still possesses an activity somewhere between subculture and occupation.

[7] The term "mechanics" refers to a logic that governs games, i.e., their rules. A variety of *LoL* activities are subscribed to internal MOBA mechanics, implemented in their system through rules. From this perspective, interactions between players and the system proceed according to a determined mechanic: a series of rules that are necessarily taken into account even if they gradually disappear as a player becomes familiar with them [15]. In *LoL*, moreover, having "mechanics" is knowing how to play a character accurately/expertise.

hardcore[8] attitude towards the game, one that goes as follows: excellent performance in the game is more relevant than friendship. However, the affirmation by the members of *Infive*, as will be seen recurrently in the following pages, of the intimate social ties (relationships of sociability subscribed in camaraderie, companionship, friendship, fraternity, among others) as something of increasing relevance would not encourage casual attitude on the part of the team, as Juul [14] argues, regarding a similar *World of Warcraft* experience – in which friendship and fun would be more important than player performance during the game. Of course, this is not equivalent to the context subscribed to here.

Indeed, the clash of these perceptions is known to result in the termination of both parties and relationships. Juul [14] argues that any multiplayer game takes on meaning through the social relations that develop between players. However, in certain games like *LoL*, especially for players who engage in (semi)professional (esports) competitive practices, a considerable part of their actions take place outside the computer itself, in environments where players study, debate and build different modes of play as it encourages interaction in the player's space.

From this perspective, multiplayer games take on meaning from where and with whom you play, as a particular game, played with the same set of rules, can mean different things to different people [16]. As Juul [14] stresses, multiplayer games are marked by an ambiguity responsible for carrying, *pari passu*, both a notion of noble competition and a wide range of social consequences, of undetermined and variable meanings depending on where and with whom one plays. In this sense, "in multiplayer games, every action has many meanings" [14, p. 128].

4   "A Team, a Common Dream"[9]: The Development of Group Cohesion

Disserting about the processes of forming a certain group cohesion within *Infive* is essential, as addressing this issue leads us to the heart of an understanding of team configuration as a group. Zimerman [12] provides a point of insight that can guide the journey toward comprehension this relationship: the shift from the condition of a grouping to a group consists of an imminent transformation from "common interests" to "communal interests". Underlying this subtle difference is an essential aspect for the apprehension the group dynamics within the team. In the process of building this cohesion, there is no denying the relevance of the result of a personal skill (being an expert player to the game), a technical action with an end [15], nor can one neglect a social aspect and its inherent identity/identification.

---

[8] In contrast to casual players, hardcore players usually take the game "seriously," "usually making it an important part of their life" [15, p. 210].

[9] The quoted phrase that gives the title of this section is a reference to a document named "*A Team, A Common Dream: Professionalism in e-Sports*", created by Ham, the team captain and manager, to seek sponsorship from local businesses in Belém. Over time, this phrase signals a common aspect that guides the collective: the dream of being professional.

How to explain and what characterizes, then, the progression and union of a team in a local competitive scenario in which teams dismount predominate? How and from what does the group support itself? What makes *Infive* such a peculiar case in this scenario? The speeches of the subjects reveal a more assiduous grouping dynamics in the local community than the composition of groups, but also provide clues to the understanding of what would be the constituent vector of *Infive*. Through observations and experiences from field research, we ordered a set of 12 essential characteristics filled in by the team[10], based on an adaptation of Zimerman's [12] ideas to the context of professional gaming.

(1) **A first point concerns the idea that a group is not constituted merely as a sum of subjects**. Instead, it builds itself as a new entity, endowed with specific and proper laws and mechanisms for coordination and management [9, 12].

(2) **A second element is the understanding that a familiar task and goal provides orientation to the members of *Infive***. In a conversation between Ham and Reeva with some well-known players in the community, during a process of recruiting new players for the team in January 2018, Ham clarified the common interest that guides them: "what we have been sharing since joining the team is that, at least me and all the people I called, we have a lot of dreams of being up there one day, like, thinking out loud" (sic).

Once, when we were having a conversation on a random day, we asked Darkanon why he would be responsible for making him believe in *Infive*'s current stability in this community with such ephemeral teams. The response of the team's shot-caller indicated three aspects worth mentioning: "First, friendship, the goal we have and the things we achieve. Like, we won the championship, made money, gained visibility, will earn more now, it's a dream, ok?". (sic)

The connection Darkanon is making here, which harks back directly to this idea of a "dream" in common mentioned by Ham and many other subjects, points to three essential elements for team cohesion: firstly, it manifests friendship, therefore, a sense of camaraderie and companionship that sparks in the team – bonds of affective order. A second aspect concerns the existence of a common goal, objective and task and, finally, a third element relates to a competitive progression in the scenario from the achievement of results. In other words, a certain sense of accomplishment that comes from personal and group expertise.

(3) **A third relevant aspect concerns the size of the group**. According to Zimerman [12], this should not exceed a specific limit that could jeopardize the indispensable stability and preservation of communication, be it visual, auditory, and conceptual. There is a quantitative determination of social groups that cannot be lost sight of as it influences their organization, meaning that there are a variety of forms of

---

[10] Although it is possible to classify specific teams according to some general categories, listing elements that make up a process for the formation of collective group cohesion, such structuring is only evoked here to help locate the poles. We cannot forget that each social group, at any given moment, is in a *sui generis* and transient situation in the face of technologies, and can therefore only be situated on a complex *continuum*.

coexistence, unification, and mutual action between individuals, which usually cater to many associated subjects [8].

For Simmel [8], in the mere number of associated individuals, there remains an influence capable of telling about the forms of social life, the combinations, and interactions between the subjects. His argument revolves around the idea that after reaching a particular size, a group needs to establish forms and organs that will promote and maintain it – which, most likely, might not be necessary for a smaller group. Undoubtedly, a small team like *Infive* possesses a set of qualities, including specific types of interaction among its members (such as the camaraderie argued here), which may disappear if the group grows [8].

Simmel [8] considers this characteristic a quantitative group determination, which denotes a dual function: in a negative aspect, certain developments can only happen with the size number of members below or above a given amount of elements. In some championships, for example, a *LoL* team needs at least five full members, one coach, and one or two reserves. In a positive sense, developments occur on the group because of mere quantitative modifications – the definition of starting players and reserves, for example – but even such increments do not come automatically, as they also depend on features other than numerical [8]. In this particular example, the skill and competence within the game, or the personal skill of a player in a given role are strong contenders [15].

(4) Then comes **a fourth element that characterizes the team: the institution of the fulfillment of certain activities performed by its members**, including participation in various activities of the team, whether in training, game analysis, championships, etc. In this sense, **in addition to the need for clearly defined objectives, the group needs to take into account the preservation of a commitment to the collective**, including the space (the place and days of analysis meetings, training sessions, competitive events, among others), time (the times, the duration of the review meetings, the training sessions, etc.), and the combination of a number of rules, rules and other variables that normalize and delimit the proposed group activity. During an informal joining interview by Ham and Reeva with Hitman and XPeKeh, for example, Ham questioned both their plan for the game and whether they would be willing to commit to the team.

Here, even before approaching the description of the criteria required for a player claiming a place in the team, you can see one of the layers that pertain to joining the collective: to be part of *Infive*, one of the main requirements is the length of time on the team, which aligns with a common functional goal that a player has for the game.

(5) **A fifth characteristic of the team, as a group, is its understanding that a given unit will behave as the totality, and vice versa.** An analogy that helps perceive this aspect is the relationship between the separate pieces of a puzzle and the puzzle itself, as constructed by its parts. As we questioned Darkanon about a constant update and learning process in *LoL*, his speech evoked a rarefied perception of many championship-watching players: a certain tendency to credit a team's victory to the performance of a particular player (and, consequently, of

their individual ability) – in the case of *Infive*, usually the team's mid-laner, Hidaka Sana.

This kind of assumption, for him, comes from a statistical observation used to measure player performance, the KDAs[11] mentioned earlier (kills, deaths, and assistances). Through it, many players and spectators are led to believe that the one who got the most kills would be the best of the team. "Like, in a championship everyone only gave value to those who did a lot of damage. People look at KDA: 'Ah, this one killed more, this one is the best of the team'. Not that [Hidaka Sana] isn't, like, very good, he's very good, only he's not the best because our team doesn't have a better one, got it? We play together, there's no reason to say, 'oh, this one is the best', he may be the best mechanically, but, like, he's never the best on the team, got it? Guys don't see, just see, like, KDA. It is not just a figure, it is the whole composition of the team". (sic)

Darkanon's argument reinforces that the team's success depends directly on its ability to define and maintain coherent group identity and establish shared social incentives among members as recognition rather than individual incentives for participation [17]. Zimerman [12], in particular, posits the existence of a recognition link in group dynamics, through which it is perceptible how vitally each group member needs to be recognized by other members of the group as someone who belongs to the collective.

(6) This configuration leads to **the sixth aspect of *Infive*: even if the group is considered a new entity, provided with a group identity of its own, the specific characters of each member persist separately**. This issue comprehends individual playstyles as something related to the player identity that in turn mediates the interaction of the members in a team, as well as the attained group synergy. In a conversation via Discord with Hidaka Sana, as we approached the subject, Veceid suddenly arrived and presented his opinion on this issue. Then, a dialogue took place about what would be the "style of play", in the perception of each one, and how much this feature approaches the personality of each player:

Hidaka Sana: "Yeah, like, how the guy knows how to play, and how the guy likes playing the most depends on the guy, the personality. The guy can play more passively, the guy plays more actively, can play more... [...] C. [Veceid] likes to keep exchanging in the lane [route] all the time, he likes to be very aggressive, he keeps hitting the dude all the time". (sic)

Veceid: "Exchange, which he says, is damage exchange [...]. There are more than two playstyles, I think, it's not just offensive and defensive, like, V. [Hidaka Sana] changes his playing style a lot when he plays with different champions. Like, when he plays Galio he is more in his lane, he only comes out of his lane when he is level 6, but when he plays Aurelion Sol is not in the lane, he is just roaming, understand? Of course you will be better in a game style, my best style is to be aggressive [...]". (sic)

---

[11] The KDA index is a statistic that best defines competition performance by calculating three variables (kills, deaths, and assists – KDA). According to Ham, this statistic is simple: it is a sum of the number of kills and assists divided by the number of deaths.

This argument demonstrates that this common aspect is also, to a certain degree, the difference. Simmel [9] already argued, in the context of the action of the individual's relations, that for a group, being different from others is much more relevant than the similarity between its members. This differentiation encourages and largely determines the activity of individuals. "We need to observe the differences of others if we want to use them and take the proper place between them" [9, p. 46].

Darkanon, while not the only one, has shown how much he has given up his desire to play a favorite style of play for the group. In addition, he underlined how much this "one-on-one" mentality [15, p. 279] reigns in ranked matches in the solo queue[12]:

Mortensen [18] presents a way to comprehension this dilemma. Notwithstanding what Darkanon wants to play in a more aggressive champion style (his specialty), he knows that for the team's strategy composition, what will benefit his team is choosing a more defensive and utilitarian style of play. If you decide to follow your wishes, you risk losing the game and compromising the team's strategy. Perhaps he is found guilty and suffers some sanctions for this attitude, or even expelled from the team. "As part of a unit, pleasure is no longer just a matter of what you want; it has larger ramifications than the solitary options you make yourself" [18, p. 148).

The cases of Veceid and Darkanon adapting their styles to the changes imposed by the system demonstrate how players' actions are not necessarily a result of a player's desire for choice, but the conditions where the collective is more important than the wishes of the individual.

(7) **A seventh characteristic** that is also immanent in the understanding of the team **is the existence of some form of affective interaction among its members**, which usually manifests itself in the most diverse ways and through its particular communication network. In any strategy of communication, there is the possibility of creation of a group from any common element 7, as is the case of the dream of being a professional player in *Infive* members. These elements, among many others, in turn, provide a meeting point, a reference, an identifying link through which team players commune and from which they also strengthen the creation, maintenance, and participation in a common outcome. In this case, the relationship factor between the team members is also of the emotional order.

Thus, within the group, how the bonds (of knowledge, recognition, anger, happiness, and other forms of expression) manifest among themselves is increasingly valued. This example will be presented later in item 9.

(8) **In the group environment, and therefore of professional teams, there must always be a hierarchical distribution of positions and roles, of different modalities, according to criteria used by the group itself**. In *Infive*, each player assumes a place in the game domain, as shown in Table 1[13].

---

[12] Solo Queue (commonly referred to by the community as the abbreviation SoloQ) is an English term that refers to a specific queue in which a player enters matches without a known guest, that is, alone.

[13] Although observing this hierarchical dynamic is relevant in understanding the organization and coordination of the collective, due to the limits of this research, we will not fall within the scope of this analytical layer.

(9) **A ninth point concerns communication**. It constitutes one of the elements of particular relevance in the dynamics of the group – both within and outside the game – and therefore deserves an accurate analysis. Taylor and Jakobsson [19] argue that joining a group is to accept to automatically integrate a communication network, such as a chat channel dedicated specifically to group members, since they act as a micro-social network level and short term sometimes. These channels are used for general conversation, although they are also predominantly used for what they call "strategic interaction" [19, p. 82].

For most players, constant conversation through the activation of a communication network (numerous chat channels) is not only necessary to build coordination in the face of the diverse challenges posed by the competitive landscape (e.g. creating strategies and tactics, organizing comps[14], sharing information, marking leisure activities, among countless others), but it is the very basis from which subjects form and maintain, in part, both community and cultural norms of the team, as they build daily an atmosphere of brotherhood, relationships of solidarity, companionship, sociability, trust, and friendship. In short, they constitute everything that can be summed up by the word camaraderie – all the elements included by this term.

Conversation, as the overall generic medium for the most diverse situations subjects experience in common [8, 9], sometimes oscillates as a relevant sociability element in the context of maintaining camaraderie, sometimes as an indispensable element for coordination and team organization. The specific function of a chat, although formally designated as a simple mechanism for gaining practical experience, is capable of acquiring diverse uses and becoming a social space in which subjects not only weave gameplay, but also conduct socialization processes loaded with offline elements [19].

According to the Simmelian perspective [8, 9], this conversation consists of compelling content through which players communicate and understand the seriousness of the game. In the first case, the conversation has a naturalistic sense, which transforms it into mere chatter. In the second, it achieves its appropriate ends through content that becomes relevant as an art of conversation based on its laws [8, 9]. Although the content of a purely formal conversation [8, 9] is necessarily attractive, engaging, and even relevant, it should not become its purpose – there must, therefore, be no objective end.

In this respect, communication can be, as Maffesoli [7] argues, an act in itself as in conversations without great reasons in daily life: talking by talking, to pass the time, to be together, as mockery and playfulness, to divide a feeling, like emotion, a little moment, a little nothing of every day, whose act expresses the desire to be with the other, the desire for interaction and exchange, participation, sharing and the construction of a social bond, a be in common. Communicate by simply communicating.

Although the conversation had no operational and practical value for the players, it nonetheless served as a link, subject matter, social bond, and reason to be with the other. These moments of sharing, although they may be perceived as useless by some, consists of a fundamental element for the maintenance of the group substrate. They

---

[14] Term used to refer to team compositions.

reinforce a group of affinities, thus establishing a spiritual community rooted in the common form.

Infive, therefore, in this mentioned communication network, is not only made up of joint activities concerning the MOBA, but is also overwhelmingly marked by an incessant conversation about the game and themes far beyond. In this scope, the players of the team range from discussions about *LoL* mechanics, creation of *comps* and analysis of training and competitive events that participated, to the debate about their personal life, going through themes such as sex, university, politics, culture, and several other games, just to name a few from an extensive list.

Thus, comments about the individual or shared adventures of the players, especially the regular members engaged in the collective, become a core activity in these communicative environments, reinforcing at the same time the team's sense of group belonging and camaraderie[15]. Interaction with teammates becomes a vital and daily means for the collective's accomplishment. Of course, some team members are frequent out-of-game partners, though all are in the game, cultivating and sharing a reputation, status, and an ongoing story. *Infive* is an index that social relationships established in an esport team surpass the game environment.

In this context, the communication network also acts as a discriminatory device for the level of competitive progression in local professional gaming, for both a social purpose (the creation and maintenance of camaraderie ties) and an instrumental one (at building levels). During different episodes of conversations with the subjects, it is possible to identify different times when they explain this use of communication channels. Hidaka Sana and Darkanon, for example, provide explanations about the team's use of WhatsApp that illustrate well what we have argued so far about this dual understanding of this communication network as an environment for social, affective articulation (item 7) and team strategy.

[Hidaka Sana]: "We use [WhatsApp] for a lot of things, but I think most of the things we do is play there, we talk about our daily life, we talk about some things there. I really like to put my games there [...], [this] gives a reinforced friendship". [Darkanon]: "WhatsApp is about the team. Like, the team we only talk about things from the team, but, like, there are only friends there, usually, we say things, like, group, understand? 'Oh, I don't know what, man, let's get together to go tomorrow and stuff, I don't know what, talk about each other's lives and stuff, like, joking' [...]. WhatsApp isn't just for fun, because not everyone is always online in the game. Ever wondered if everyone would communicate only when they were online? It would be impossible, you know". (sic)

There is, therefore, a high amount of play and mockery within the group, as noted by Taylor and Jakobsson [19] in the context of *EverQuest*. According to them, the concept of "good group" is associated with how well members can perform tasks, and how enjoyable or fun it is to participate in interaction within it. In turn, this is a clear insight into the dynamics of *Infive*.

---

[15] Such conversations, however, also extend to face-to-face spaces, through social events created by the team.

Communication, therefore, becomes a link that usually flows from a team communication network in its multiple communication channels mentioned above. In turn, the absence of communication hardly makes pro gaming possible and directly impacts competitive progression. It is, therefore, both necessary for the development of a more functional (team coordination and organization) and social (camaraderie) aspect. However, although it thrives in these channels, it is also evidenced by a communication made in person.

(10) **A tenth element concerns the fact that a group self organizes as a gallery of mirrors in which each member can reflect others** [12]. As Simmel [9] argues, individuals exert effects on others and also suffer consequences on their part. In *Infive*, there is usually a specific and typical phenomenon, which is a characteristic present in several groups: resonance. As its name already precedes, it consists in the fact that communication brought by one of the team members will resonate with another, which in turn can directly impact the team's game, goals, and sense of unity.

It follows, for example, the importance assigned to communication to prevent a particular outcome in the game, to avoid the destabilization of relations. At *Infive*, the leading player recognized for effecting this type of communication is Hidaka Sana, according to reports by Ham, Darkanon, and Veceid. As we asked Hidaka Sana what other roles he would play in the game, his answer pointed to being a "safe haven" for in-game team members. "Within the game, I, besides being a mid laner, also serve to try to soften things. I'm, like, a safe haven, because I think V. [Darkanon] and me are the quietest on the team, and the least tilt as well. For example, I might be 0/10 [KDA's first two scores, so kills and kills, respectively], but I'm 0/10 playing the same as I'd be if I was 10/0: I'll be calm and confident just the same". (sic)

(11) **Another relevant feature in group dynamics concerns the emergence of an "active game of identifications"** [12, p. 30]. The importance of this debate looms as identifications constitute a formative element of a certain sense of professional identity.

The team then creates certain common elements that link them all, which offer a meeting point, aspects of identification and reference, objects through which the actors belong to this group share "a particular empathy with the community environment" [20, p. 14]. Among the items that mark group identification and cohesion, we can mention the team's own visual identity, the shirt (see Fig. 1) and the page on the social networking site Facebook[16], the *IN5* tag (a contraction of the word *Infive* since *LoL* tags have a limit to characters) that precedes the nickname[17] of the players in MOBA – at least the holders – and the most varied channels of communication of the team.

---

[16] Available online at: https://www.facebook.com/InFiveEsports/.

[17] The names of the players in the game environment.

Fig. 1. Infinite *Five e-Sports* shirt templates.

Regarding the pages on the social networking site Facebook of some esport teams in the competitive local *League of Legends* community in Belém, Darkanon mentioned the existence of a specific professional line that they are trying to cross. In his opinion, "there is growth, right? First shirt, then photos, then other things" (sic), so the page, along with the team uniform (see Fig. 1), would be responsible for indicating a more exceptional professionalism of a given team.

Although the team's official shirt is something materializing from a restructuring process and the construction of inputs for its professionalization since 2017 Darkanon has argued about its importance for the constitution of a professional identity at *Infive*.

Each of these elements also produces identification of each individual with the group, whereby players can operate a recognition of themselves from something external, whether in one object or another. In the end, what matters is recognizing oneself in another, from another [20]; or, as Simmel [9, p. 24] argues, the "common sharing of objects in the process of human sociation". A final aspect of collective identification (and affiliation) concerns the use of a team tag, permanently added to the player's nickname. In the case of the subjects here, the *IN5* tag precedes the names of each of the team players. For team members, this is a way of demonstrating group membership, a form of assuming the identity of the team, even if it is not mandatory to adopt the tag. The use of it offers stability and confidence of a player to a particular team, according to Ham.

(12) Finally, as Zimerman [12, p. 28] argues, "**in every group, two contradictory forces coexist permanently at play: one tending to its cohesion, and the other to its disintegration.**" At present, groups are more or less transiently organized, sharing values, even small ones that clash, attract, and repel each other all the time [20]. Of course, many factors are responsible for one or other of these forces overlapping at any given time [17, 20]. This dynamic is a constant clash of forces: on the one hand cohesive and on the other disruptive – in which communication, camaraderie, organization and coordination are defining components within a competitive team engaged in esport.

5   Final Considerations

Hidaka Sana once mentioned a particularity that *Infive* would have in relation to the other teams in the local community: "we never disbanded, so I think, at least, it's something that we have good differential, only our team and *Estafetas* [*Voadoras e-Sport*, another famous local team] that doesn't disband" (sic). If in the local scenario abounds a practice of disband between the teams, that is a tendency for the disintegration of the teams, surely *Infive* contrasts with this local pattern by having a certain cohesion, from the 12 elements described above, which meets with the community itself.

At the heart of this issue, there remains a bond of friendship and companionship, a relationship of sociability, friendship, trust, in short, elements that constitute the *ethos* of group camaraderie. Although this study discusses a specific team, we believe it provides insights that track some ways in which local amateur or semiprofessional teams committed to pro gaming practice stick together to achieve more significant leaps in the face of challenges towards professionalization in a particular local scenario absent from (significant) investments, sponsorships and away from the major centers in which esport is encouraged. Moreover, this research indicates, from a situated approach, how intrinsic a social aspect is for players moving towards professionalization in local competitive communities.

So, this study sought to argue and document to the development of an *ethos* of professionalism in a peripheral community, indicating the existence of an Amazonian esports scenario – in the North region of the Brazil, with emphasis on the city of Bélem, Pará. Thus, thinking about esports, according to T. Taylor [1, p. 33], helps to analyze "[…] the transition many groups face as they struggle to convert their leisure time and playful passions into serious play, where the stakes are high, reputations built, and money gained (and lost)". Furthermore, it means that the career path from amateur/semipro to professional is severely dependent on an active process of socialization in a given competitive local community – and all its variety of actors and forces.

This research, therefore, argued in favor of an approach that favors a social perspective within the competitive instrumental game, although it does not disregard the functional element that the agonistic experience instills in pro gaming itself. A valid argument for understanding the dynamics set out in competitive games can be summed up in one sentence: being a successful pro-player, especially in peripheral scenarios like Belém, not only depends on mastery of game mechanics, but also on rules of the social game inherent in this agonistic environment in which it plays and the local community in which it finds itself.

The argument leans toward conceiving that at a competitive level, *LoL* demands an interactional substratum either both in its social and instrumental sense. *Infive* players, therefore, need to be actively involved in the game – their objects and continually learning about their set of rules to do their best – as well as in a social game with other team members and the local setting, whose purpose is the pursuit of successful experiences.

References

1. Taylor, T.: Raising the Stakes: E-Sports and the Professionalization of Computer Gaming. MIT Press, Cambridge (2012)
2. Macedo, T., Falcão, T.: E-Sports, herdeiros de uma tradição. Intexto **45**(2), 246–267 (2019)
3. Seula, R., Amaro, M., Fragoso, S.: Play to win, profit & entertain: a study of double performance as athlete and streamer. In: DiGRA 18' – Digital Games Research Association Conference 2018, pp. 1–15. DiGRA, Turim (2018)
4. Montardo, S., Fragoso, S., Amaro, M., Paz, S.: Consumo digital como performance sociotécnica: Análise dos usos da plataforma de streaming de games Twitch. Comunicação, Mídia e Consumo **14**(40), 46–69 (2017)
5. Macedo, T.: Dos teclados às arenas: o consumo do *e-Sport* como espetáculo. In: Amaral Filho, O., Alves, R. (org.) Espetáculos Culturais na Amazônia, pp. 175–200. Editora CRV, Curitiba (2018)
6. Américo, M.: O jornalismo esportivo transmídia no ecossistema dos esportes eletrônicos (*E-Sports*). Estudos em Jornalismo e Mídia **11**(2), 316–327 (2014)
7. Maffesoli, M.: A comunicação em fim (teoria pós-moderna da comunicação). Revista Famecos **10**(20), 13–20 (2003)
8. Simmel, G.: Georg Simmel: sociologia. Ática, São Paulo (1983)
9. Simmel, G.: Questões fundamentais da sociologia. Zahar, Rio de Janeiro (2006)
10. Taylor, N.: Professional gaming. In: Mansell, R., Ang, P. (eds.) The International Encyclopedia of Digital Communication and Society, pp. 987–990. Wiley Blackwell, London (2015)
11. Taylor, N.: Play to the camera: video ethnography, spectatorship, and e-sports. Convergence **22**(2), 115–130 (2016)
12. Zimerman, D.: Fundamentos teóricos. In: Zimerman, D., Osorio, L. (org.) Como trabalhamos com grupos, pp. 23–31. Artes Médias, Porto Alegre (1997)
13. Apperley, T., Jayemane, D.: Game studies' material turn. Westminister Pap. Commun. Cult. **9**(1), 5–25 (2012)
14. Juul, J.: A Casual Revolution: Reinventing Video Games and Their Players. MIT Press, Cambridge (2010)
15. Falcão, T.: Não-humanos em jogo. Agência e Prescrição em World of Warcraft. Ph.D. dissertation, Programa de Pós-Graduação em Comunicação e Cultura Contemporâneas. Universidade Federal da Bahia, Salvador (2014)
16. Garfield, R.: Metagames. In: Dietz, J. (ed.) Horsemen of the Apocalypse: Essays on Roleplaying, pp. 14–21. Jolly Rogers Games, Charleston (2000)
17. Chen, M.: Communication, coordination, and camaraderie in World of Warcraft. Games Cult. **4**(1), 47–73 (2009)
18. Mortensen, T.: O Jogo enquanto Vida Moralmente Correta. Hedonismo Utilitário, a Ética do Jogo? Revista Fronteiras: estudos midiáticos **20**(20), 142–149 (2011)
19. Taylor, T., Jakobsson, M.: The Sopranos meets EverQuest: social networking in massively multiplayer online games. In: DAC 2003 – Digital Arts and Culture (DAC) 2003 Streaming Wor(l)ds Conference Proceedings, pp. 81–90. DAC, Melbourne (2003)
20. Maffesoli, M.: No fundo das aparências. Vozes, Petrópolis (2010)

Uses and Methodologies

Broad Environmental Change Blindness in Virtual Environments and Video Games

Daryl Marples[1]([✉]) [iD], Pelham Carter[2] [iD], Duke Gledhill[1] [iD],
and Simon Goodson[1] [iD]

[1] University of Huddersfield, Huddersfield, West Yorkshire HD1 3DH, UK
d.marples@hud.ac.uk
[2] Birmingham City University, Birmingham B4 7BD, UK

Abstract. For almost 120 years, it has been demonstrated in literature that humans are susceptible to many different types of change blindness; essentially if a change in a visual scene is not sudden or obvious, it fails to be detected. Research utilising video game environments provides the opportunity for the study of change blindness during dynamic and interactive tasks. This study examined participant perception of gradual broad changes to both colour and textural information across surfaces and objects in a video game mimicking that of a First-Person adventure or point and click game/genre escape room task. 119 participants were asked to solve a room escape puzzle, results demonstrated that perception of gradual textural changes to an environment across a range of decreasing durations (90 s, 45 s, 22.5 s & 11.25 s) were detected only by a very small proportion of participants (4.20%). There was no significant effect of the variation in time on detection rates.

Keywords: Attention · Change blindness · Virtual · Escape room · Change detection

1 Introduction

When a magician makes a coin 'disappear' a technique of misdirection is used to infer the transfer of the coin and holding that attention allows for the discreet, [1, 2] similarly film makers take advantage of the phenomenon that minor differences in a scene between cuts are generally not perceived by the viewer. This is despite millions of neurons attending to the scene and ready and waiting to react should they detect change [3].

In the 1980's psychologists became interested in these phenomena [4, 5] and over the intervening decades, a variety of types of change blindness [6] have been identified these include, blinks or eye motion [7], flashed blank images [8], or gradual subtle changes over time [4, 9].

It has been demonstrated that the limitations of working memory have direct correlations to the perception of colours relating to objects [10]. It has further been demonstrated that specific non-colour details pertaining to an image are recalled in more depth if that image is presented in monochrome thus reducing the memory load of storing colour data [11]. In relation to this, in attention tests with multiple differing coloured objects, where one is covered, few participants correctly identified the correct

© Springer Nature Switzerland AG 2019
N. Zagalo et al. (Eds.): VJ 2019, CCIS 1164, pp. 169–178, 2019.
https://doi.org/10.1007/978-3-030-37983-4_13

colour of the hidden object [12]. The reasons behind this are related to selective awareness governed by two visual input pathways [13], a 'selective' pathway that governs object recognition and is responsible for recognition of one or a very small number of objects at a time and a 'non-selective pathway' which is responsible for forming a broader impression of a scene, this system may give a broad understanding that there are objects in a scene, but not what those objects actually are, nor individual characteristics such as colour.

From a neurological perspective, the fact that these interweaving systems appear to operate in a semi-autonomous manner can be related to the fact that it has been demonstrated that storage and processing of different types of sensory data are handled independently within the structure of the brain, [14, 15]. The specific subcomponent of working memory connected to the retention of visual information is Visual Short-Term Memory (VSTM) [16]. However, for an element of a scene to be recorded in VSTM, it first must be attended to [17] in so much that a conscious representation of the object and it's component states are committed to memory. Given the limitations of working memory and that approximately 4 objects and their components states including colour information can simultaneously be recalled [18, 19]. In a complex environment with shifting focus, it is inevitable that much of the scene will not be recalled in detail. However, the perception of an object is related to the features of the object and its relationship to the contents of the VSTM and task goals [20]. Coherence theory [21] as a view of perception infers that in fact, the visual perception relies very little on actual memory and persistence after the withdrawing of attention as a scene can be sampled repeatedly and re-referenced at any given moment by the refocusing of attention [22]. Essentially the environment serves as "external memory". This external memory and its associated lack of processing is also referred to as distributed cognition [23], specifically where the cognitive work is offloaded to the environment. Essentially having the environment work to store and in some cases manipulate information, returning to collect only that data that later becomes pertinent.

Although many experiments have demonstrated that gradual change blindness can result in the non-detection of colour changes in otherwise static images, [24, 25] it has not been demonstrated what the results of changing broad environmental elements covering most of the visual field in a virtual environment would be. No known prior study has analysed the effect of colour, textural and object change across the visual field in a dynamic environment taking into account early and late changes to said properties [25]. No known prior study has analysed the impact that varying the duration of this change has either in such a dynamic environment and when duration has been investigated in static or smaller scenes [9] the time of change had been kept short under the assumption of an early attentive period. Inclusion of a range of durations allowed for the investigation of the potential role of later selection or distributed cognition [23] within dynamic, high cognitive load, environments and settings.

It was predicted that as gradual change is not consistently perceived therefore introducing such changes to all major materials in a virtual environment would not be noticed by the participants if distracted by a task requiring the utilisation of working memory.

The following hypotheses were considered:

1. There would be no significant effect of the time of change on the overall detection rate.
2. There would be no significant difference in the recollection of pre and post-state textural information.

2 Method

2.1 Participants

119 participants; 102 male, 17 female, age range 17 and 54 (m = 22.28, SD = 6.36) all reporting having normal vision or corrected to normal vision. All participants had normal colour vision; those reporting a type of colour blindness were excluded from the test. Participants were recruited primarily from students and staff in the department of computing and engineering, they were not paid for their participation and did not receive course credits.

2.2 Design

A mixed design was employed with the time of the environmental changes (duration) acting as the between-subjects variable (11.25 s, 22.5 s, 45 s, 90 s). The details recalled at pre-change or post-change accurately served as the within-subjects variable. Participants were randomly assigned to one of the four duration conditions, and all participants were assessed on how many pre and post-change textural and object properties could be accurately recalled. This allowed for the impact of duration of change to be assessed, as well as any preferences for early (pre-change) or late (post-change) attention to environmental changes.

2.3 Materials and Apparatus

In order to test the hypotheses a virtual environment with a distraction task was created, this took the form of an 'escape the room' game created in Unreal Development Kit (UDK); consisting of a bedsit living space 12 m^2 with en-suite bathroom 4 m^2, a variety of objects such as computers, drawers and other objects could be interacted with and manipulated to solve a series of interrelated problems and eventually escape the room.

The puzzle aspect of the environment acted as the distraction from the simultaneous broad changes being made to the textures of most of the surfaces and objects in the room (see Table 1 and Fig. 1). Thirteen textures were altered ranging from major elements that filled most of the visual space to smaller objects such as books. The changes were not limited to hue shifts, but also included contrast changes and pattern changes. Example changes are shown in with specific examples from the living room and bedroom shown in Figs. 2 and 3 respectively. These textural changes were insti-gated at the moment the player entered the room and participants were engaged in the

Table 1. List of colour and textural changes made over time.

Object	Initial texture	Post change texture
Living-space walls	Cream with 1 dark stripe	Pink with 2 dark stripes
Flooring	Light Beech laminate	Dark Oak laminate
Sofa	Red	Brown
Bed/Duvet	Purple with dark throw	Pink with dark throw
Curtains	Red Un-patterned	Orange with flower print
Bathroom walls	Cream	Pink
Alice in Wonderland book	Blue with cat	Purple with just a smile
War of the Worlds book	Red	Green
The Time Machine book	Pink/Purple	Blue/Orange
A Princess of Mars book	Yellow	Orange
Heart of Darkness book	Red	Purple
Picture frame	Green	Blue
Picture of cliffs	A sea and cliff Scene	A Gorilla's face is added

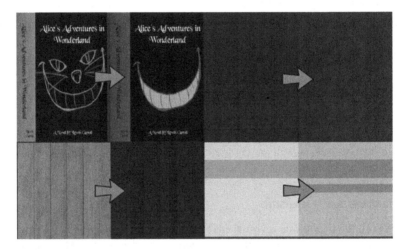

Fig. 1. Examples of variants of textural change, colour, contrast, pattern and image.

game for a total of 5 min. The changes described took place in the initial segment of that time and were static for the remaining time.

Following prior change blindness experiments [6, 26], an image of a gorilla was included in the scene; this was embedded into a prominent picture and gradually appeared at the same rate as the other changes.

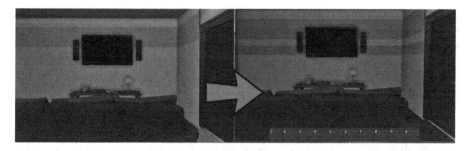

Fig. 2. The transition of textures in the living room area.

Fig. 3. The transition of textures in the bedroom area.

2.4 Procedure

The participants received instructions to solve the puzzle in the allocated time and no information about the nature of the test was provided to them. On-screen instructions explained basic interaction to the participants, after which they were immediately immersed in a virtual environment of a small single room apartment. The room contained several interactive objects to be examined, allowing the discovery of clues to progress the game. For instance, the computer on the desktop required a user name and password. Clues to this were contained on a post-it note on the desk and the password was the name of the artist in the painting. Further puzzles involved finding batteries to fit into a remote control unit in order that the TV could be switched on.

During their exploration of the environment, thirteen colour and/or pattern changes occurred to textures within the scene with the game remaining playable for a total of 5 min.

After 5 min of gameplay, the programme automatically ended the session and the participants were asked to immediately complete a post-test questionnaire. As participants were told that the experiment focused on gameplay, the questions began with queries relating to game design issues and slowly introduced specific questions about overall perception. The questions were designed so as not to lead the participant to provide a predetermined answer. The questions in order were;

- Briefly describe the main focus of the game
- What game genre does it belong to?

- Did you notice anything unusual or peculiar whilst playing?
- Did you notice anything change in the game?
- Please list any changes you think you noticed. Or simply type 'NONE' - following multiple-choice questions about the colours of particular objects, the final questions asked were:
  - Did you spot the gorilla?
  - If you answered YES to spotting the gorilla, where was it?

As the participants were naive to the aims of the experiment a general non-leading question about unusual events was asked first, followed by a more direct question regarding whether any change was noticed.

3 Results

52.5% of participants claimed to have noticed a change, yet only 4.2% actually identified a manipulated gradual change, this being a total of 5 participants out of 120 (see Table 2). All other noticed changes were unrelated changes triggered by participant action (such as saying a door opened or items could be picked up and moved). Despite the questionnaire allowing for multiple entries in colour selection when asked to describe individual objects, none of the participants chose more than one colour option.

Table 2. The changes detected in each of the time variants

Duration of texture changes	Number of participants	Number reporting change detection	Percentage
90 s	31	1	3.23%
45 s	27	2	7.40%
22.5 s	30	1	3.33%
11.25 s	31	1	3.23%
Total	119	5	4.20%

Table 3. Percentage identifications of gradual change item properties

Change item	Identified pre-change colour	Identified post-change colour	Incorrect identification	Did not know
Curtains	38.8	3.3	34.7	22.3
WotW book	9.1	15.7	21.5	53.3
Bedroom walls	6.6	25.8	44.2	23.3
Bathroom walls	6.6	6.6	61.7	25
Bed duvet	20.8	28.3	30.8	20
Mean total	16.38	15.94	38.94	28.78

When asked if they had noticed a gorilla in the room 11.6% claimed to have done so, though only 9.9% were able to accurately state where they had seen the gorilla (in the painting). It is important to note this question only determined whether they had seen the gorilla at some point during their experience, not whether they noticed it had gradually appeared. When detailing the changes they had noticed, only 1 participant stated they had seen the gorilla appear.

Specific questions were asked about the items' gradual changes that were core to the virtual experience (items close to focal points and tasks/goals) or covered a large area of the visual field (walls). As can be seen from Table 3, and consistent with prior studies, a large proportion of participants could not identify the colour or texture property of the gradual change items. In terms of which colour or texture properties reported there was little difference between the pre-change property (16.38%) and post-change property (15.94%).

This can be further seen when considering the total number of pre-change (M = .8, SD = .78) and post-change (M = .75, SD = .83) properties recalled.

When broken down by condition (11.25, 22.5, 45 and 90 s), the number of participants reporting something unusual related to the gradual change, correctly identifying a change, or accurately noticing the gorilla, there is no significant difference between groups.

Table 4. Total Percentage identifications of gradual change item properties by condition

Condition	Identified pre-change properties	Identified post-change properties
11.25 s	18.14	15.64
22.5 s	12.01	17.34
45 s	20.72	16.28
90 s	15.48	14.86

When considering the overall difference in pre and post-change identification across three of the four conditions the pre-change property is identified slightly more than the post-change, though the differences appear small, shown in Table 4. This is further supported by the mean number of pre and post-change properties identified as per Table 5.

Table 5. Mean total identification of pre and post-change properties by condition

Condition	Mean pre-change (SD)	Mean post-change (SD)
11.25 s	.87 (.87)	.68 (1.02)
22.5 s	.56 (.67)	.86 (.81)
45 s	1.03 (.85)	.77 (.64)
90 s	.77 (.64)	.67 (.79)

A mixed 4×2 ANOVA with duration serving as the between-subjects factor (11.25, 22.5, 45 and 90 s), and change property identification (pre-change, post-change) serving as the within-subjects factor showed no significant main effect condition ($F(3, 116) = .723$, $p = .54$), or change property identification ($F(1, 116) = .315$, $P = .576$). No significant interaction effect ($F(3, 116) = 1.31$, $p = .275$) was found.

4   Discussion

The aims of this research were to investigate whether gradual environmental changes are perceived and whether the duration of any changes affect perception rates.

It has been previously demonstrated that either colour changes [9] or small changes to a broader scene result in significant non-detection of those changes [27]. However, the results of this research have suggested that when combined with a distraction task, even the broadest of changes; in this case fundamentally altering the textures of an entire environment were not detected. The results show that overall; fewer than 5% of participants perceived any of these changes and many of the larger changes made were not detected by any participants. Given the limitations of Visual Short-Term Memory [28], it is unsurprising that the participants provided incorrect responses when asked to identify specific colours of objects. In addition, only 9.9% of participants correctly identified the location of the gorilla (Illustrated in Fig. 4) in the scene when it was clearly in a prominent and incongruous position and in an item required to solve a portion of the puzzle indicates that, as previously reported [20], participants only commit to memory elements that they perceive to be beneficial to the goals.

Fig. 4. Pre and post-change versions of the painting in which the face of a gorilla appears.

As previously demonstrated [9], small areas of static images can be changed over time and these changes are perceived approximately 30% of the time. It is clear that combined with a distraction task, and in a virtual representation of a scene, this detection of change when applied to the entire field of view falls away by approximately 90%.

Memory for specific scene details correlates with current theories of memory; the results indicated that in many cases as the actual colour or texture of elements perceived to be background objects and not perceived as salient, no specific memory was encoded of the colour of those objects [20]. This explains the lack of significant difference in the amount of pre and post-change information accurately recalled by participants. This in turn further supports the notion that some of the cognitive load in these situations is distributed to the environment under the assumption that the environment is stable and consistent in its properties [23].

Within a video games context, the results of these experiments reflect a commonly utilised method of removing temporary visual information from a scene. In many instances, detail information is added to a scene in the form of bullet holes, blood splatter or footprints in the snow. These elements commonly disappear over time to reduce processing and memory overhead and unless the player is attending to them directly will disappear without the player noticing.

While changes that include the removal of extraneous information will not be noticed and therefore will not break the flow of a game title. This research has demonstrated that broad changes can be gradually made to an environment without the player noticing these differences. From a design perspective, this understanding allows for the morphing of an entire environment. This feature may relate to narrative or define a specific sense of drama, mood, or mental state. It opens new areas for visual storytelling that have not yet been fully explored. Further research to could seek to identify if these results are replicated in virtual reality.

References

1. Downs, T.N.: Modern Coin Manipulation, pp. 1–105 (1900)
2. Martinez-Conde, S., Macknik, S.L.: Magic and the brain. Sci. Am. **299**(6), 72–79 (2008)
3. Dennett, D.: Consciousness Explained. Little, Brown and Co., Boston (1991)
4. Neisser, U., Becklen, R.: Selective looking: attending to visually specified events. Cogn. Psychol. **7**(4), 480–494 (1975)
5. Becklen, R., Cervone, D.: Selective looking and the noticing of unexpected events. Mem. Cogn. **11**(6), 601–608 (1983)
6. Simons, D.J., Chabris, C.F.: Gorillas in our midst: sustained inattentional blindness for dynamic events. Perception **28**(9), 1059–1074 (1999)
7. Grimes, J.: On the failure to detect changes in scenes across saccades. Proc. R. Soc., 89–110 (1996)
8. Blackmore, S.J., Brelstaff, G., Nelson, K., Trościanko, T.: Is the richness of our visual world an illusion? Transsaccadic memory for complex scenes. Perception **24**(9), 1075–1081 (1995)
9. Simons, D.J., Franconeri, S.L., Reimer, R.L.: Change blindness in the absence of a visual disruption. Perception **29**(10), 1143–1154 (2000)
10. Garden, S., Cornoldi, C., Logie, R.H.: Visuo-spatial working memory in navigation. Appl. Cogn. Psychol. **16**(1), 35–50 (2002)

11. Nijboer, T.C.W., Kanai, R., de Haan, E.H.F., van der Smagt, M.J.: Recognising the forest, but not the trees: an effect of colour on scene perception and recognition. Conscious. Cogn. **17**(3), 741–752 (2008)

12. Pilling, M., Gellatly, A.: Visual awareness of objects and their colour. Atten. Percept. Psychophys. **73**(7), 2026–2043 (2011)

13. Wolfe, J.M., Reinecke, A., Brawn, P.: Why don't we see changes? The role of attentional bottlenecks and limited visual memory. Vis. Cogn. **14**(4–8), 749–780 (2006)

14. Baddeley, A., Logie, R., Bressi, S., Della Sala, S., Spinnler, H.: Dementia and working memory. Q. J. Exp. Psychol. Sect. A **38**(4), 603–618 (1986)

15. Pessoa, L., Ungerleider, L.G.: Neural Correlates of Change Detection and Change Blindness in a Working Memory Task. Cereb Cortex **14**(5), 511–520 (2004)

16. Phillips, W.A., Baddeley, A.D.: Reaction time and short-term visual memory*. Psychon. Sci. **22**(2), 73–74 (1971)

17. Lamme, V.A.F.: Why visual attention and awareness are different. Trends Cogn. Sci. **7**(1), 12–18 (2003)

18. Hollingworth, A., Williams, C.C., Henderson, J.M.: To see and remember: visually specific information is retained in memory from previously attended objects in natural scenes. Psychon. Bull. Rev. **8**(4), 761–768 (2001)

19. Luck, S.J., Vogel, E.K.: The capacity of visual working memory for features and conjunctions. Nature **390**(6657), 279–284 (1997)

20. Hollingworth, A., Matsukura, M., Luck, S.J.: Visual working memory modulates rapid eye movements to simple onset targets. Psychol. Sci. **24**(5), 790–796 (2013)

21. Rensink, R.A.: The dynamic representation of scenes. Vis. Cogn. **7**(1–3), 17–42 (2000)

22. Ballard, D.H., Hayhoe, M.M., Pook, P.K., Rao, R.P.N.: Deictic codes for the embodiment of cognition. Behav. Brain Sci. **20**(4), 723–767 (1997)

23. Wilson, M.: Six views of embodied cognition. Psychon. Bull. Rev. **9**(4), 625–636 (2002)

24. Arrington, J.G., Levin, D.T., Varakin, D.A.: Color onsets and offsets, and luminance changes can cause change blindness. Perception **35**(12), 1665–1678 (2006)

25. Most, S.B., Simons, D.J., Scholl, B.J., Chabris, C.F.: Sustained inattentional blindness: dynamic events. Psyche (Stuttg) **6**(14), 1059–1074 (2000)

26. Drew, T., Võ, M.L.H., Wolfe, J.M.: The invisible gorilla strikes again: sustained inattentional blindness in expert observers. Psychol. Sci. **24**(9), 1848–1853 (2013)

27. Franconeri, S.L., Hollingworth, A., Simons, D.J.: Do new objects capture attention? Psychol. Sci. **16**(4), 275–281 (2005)

28. Baddeley, A.D., Hitch, G.: Working Memory. Psychol. Learn. Motiv. **8**, 47–89 (1974)

Virtual Reality Arcades: A Study on Usage Habits with Emphasis on Digital Gaming

Tuomas Kari[1,2(✉)]

[1] Institute for Advanced Management Systems Research, 20100 Turku, Finland
[2] Faculty of Information Technology, University of Jyvaskyla,
40014 Jyvaskyla, Finland
tuomas.t.kari@jyu.fi

Abstract. Virtual reality (VR) and VR gaming have seen substantial advancement during the recent years both in terms of technological development and the number of users. A notable rise has also occurred in the number of VR arcades. Despite the growing academic interest towards VR and VR gaming, there is still a dearth of understanding on the usage aspects of VR gaming and VR arcades. To address this gap, this study explored the habits of using VR arcades with emphasis on digital gaming. Specific focus was set on investigating differences between gender, age, and physical activity background. The study was exploratory in nature and based on a quantitative analysis of data collected from 126 respondents in Finland. The findings of this study bring new knowledge to this emerging subject, and thus, extend our understanding on the habits of using VR arcades and VR games. The study shows that digital gaming is clearly the most popular form of entertainment in VR arcades. Also, for the vast majority, the main purpose to visit VR arcades is gaming for fun, and it is more popular to visit VR arcades together with others than alone. The findings also demonstrate how VR gaming can be a new frontier for exergaming. Gender, age, and physical activity background differences are discussed. As a practical contribution, the findings are used to present implications for VR gaming and VR arcade stakeholders.

Keywords: Virtual reality · VR · VR arcade · Digital gaming · Exergaming · Entertainment · Usage habits

1 Introduction

During the recent decades, advancement in information technology has had a substantial impact on a number of fields, and digital gaming and entertainment are no exceptions. The emergence of novel sensors and other technological solutions has facilitated the design and development of digital games and other entertainment concepts. Such concepts have become increasingly multifaceted, not only from a technical perspective but also in respect to the wide variety of interaction possibilities available to the users.

A type of digital gaming and entertainment medium that has particularly benefited from the recent technological development is virtual reality (VR). VR can be defined in

© Springer Nature Switzerland AG 2019
N. Zagalo et al. (Eds.): VJ 2019, CCIS 1164, pp. 179–194, 2019.
https://doi.org/10.1007/978-3-030-37983-4_14

different ways and depending on the definition, include different kinds of solutions [1]. These VR solutions are generally designed in order to produce realistic virtual environments and to immerse the user by utilizing image, sound, haptic, and other sensations. The common goal is to simulate the user's physical presence in a virtual environment. Contemporary VR solutions most commonly use VR headsets that are equipped with different features and connected to different technologies. For a well-covering overview of VR history, definitions, and technologies, see [1]. In this study, the focus regarding VR is in such VR technologies that include a VR headset, but as pointed out by [1], a headset is not the only way to carry out a VR experience. However, such focus is most suitable for the purpose of this study as the emphasis is on digital gaming in VR arcades, where such technologies are the ones most commonly used.

Different types of VR arcades have been emerging around the globe during the past years and their popularity seems to be on a constant rise [2, 3]. In Finland, where this study was conducted, the number of VR arcades has been on a constant rise during the past few years. The types of VR experiences that different VR arcades provide vary a lot. Some are more focused on gaming whereas some are more focused on providing other forms of entertainment, such as audiovisual stories through VR or VR walks in the nature without any particular (game) goals. Most VR arcades seem to offer a variety of both games and other forms of entertainment, although the proportion of these varies between different VR arcades.

Academic interest towards investigating VR and VR gaming has increased steadily over the years, as the technology has become more accessible to different user groups. However, what has so far been quite limitedly studied is VR gaming – especially in the context of VR arcades. As the VR technology evolves, it affords new kinds of experiences and new ways of playing. Thus, there is a prevalent need to study the usage aspects of such VR solutions, for example, regarding the users, user behaviors, and issues such as why and how people actually use these solutions and play these games. Even though the amount of studies focusing on the usage aspects of VR has increased recently, there is still a dearth of understanding on the usage of VR games and VR arcades. The understanding of these issues is essential especially for the designers, developers, and marketers of VR games and entertainment in terms of providing users of different demographic backgrounds such VR gaming and entertainment solutions that they really want to use. Thus, subsequently advancing the diffusion and adoption of VR technologies. In addition, considering the exergaming [4, 5] character of VR gaming (especially in VR arcades), VR gaming can also be considered as a potential way to fight the problems of sedentary lifestyle, which are becoming increasingly widespread in the society. Indeed, popular VR exergames such as Soundboxing [6] and Beat Saber [7] have received a lot of praise for their ability to provide physical activity [e.g., 8].

This study addresses the aforementioned research gap concerning the users and usage habits of VR arcades and VR gaming. More precisely, this study takes an exploratory approach to investigate the habits of using VR arcades with emphasis on digital gaming, and focuses particularly on the differences between gender, age, and physical activity background. The main research questions that the study aims to answer are:

1. What are the typical habits of using VR arcades and digital games in VR arcades?
2. What kinds of gender, age, and physical activity background differences exist in the habits of using VR arcades and digital games in VR arcades?

In order to answer these questions, a quantitative study was conducted by collecting and analyzing data on the users' demographics, physical activity background, and the habits of using VR arcades. In this study, physical activity background refers to categories including aspects of physical activity level and the main purpose of conducting physical activity. This study followed an exploratory approach, meaning that the habits of using VR arcades were examined at a descriptive level without utilizing any prior theoretical framework. The study brings new knowledge to this interesting subject, and thus, extends our understanding on digital gaming and entertainment use in VR arcades. As a practical contribution, the findings are used to present implications for VR gaming and VR arcade stakeholders.

2 Background

As this study is exploratory in nature, any *a priori* hypotheses on how gender, age, and physical activity background are expected to be associated with the habits of using VR arcades (e.g., linear – non-linear or positive – negative) are not proposed. However, these kinds of relationships are expected to exist based on the findings of prior research on the differences in gaming related factors between genders, age groups, and physical activity backgrounds [9–19]. For example, [18] found that gender differentiates the perceived level of hedonic and utilitarian value of digital games: Most notably, males value greatly more games that are masculine and females give higher value to such game subcategories as professions, real-life simulation, and educative games. [16] found that there are differences between age groups in types of games played, social setting of playing, the used technologies, and the perceived importance of certain game features such as artwork, storyline, rewards, fantasy themes, and competitive multi-playing. [13] found differences between people with different physical activity backgrounds regarding the exertion level of playing exergames: the more physically active group the person belonged to, the more likely he or she was to mainly play at a light exertion level.

Furthermore, the innovation diffusion theory [20] states that, among other factors, socioeconomic characteristics (e.g., age and gender) and personality variables (e.g., physical activity background) influence the adoption and use of an innovation. This study focuses particularly on the habits of using VR arcades with emphasis on digital gaming. Habit, in this study, refers to the different ways people use VR arcades (e.g., forms of entertainment, purpose, social setting, and physical exertion). Similar conceptualization of habit has been previously used, for example, by [21] and [22].

2.1 Virtual Reality Arcades

VR arcades can be categorized based on the technology they use and provide. For one, there are VR arcades that provide VR headsets (often tethered, as standalone headsets were still relatively uncommon early 2019) with their controllers, such as the HTC VIVE or the Oculus RIFT. These are typically used by utilizing six-degrees-of-freedom motion tracking so that the user can move around in a space of approximately 15 square meters. Another typical type of VR arcades are the ones that provide, in addition to the headsets, different kinds of VR motion platforms, such as the Virtuix Omni. These motion platforms, also sometimes called VR treadmills, typically allow for omnidirectional walking and running on the platform. This enables the user to move within the virtual world environment by actually using their legs. Third typical type of VR arcades are those that offer free-roam VR experiences, for example, the Zero Latency VR arcades. Free-roam VR uses either standalone headsets or headsets connected to backpacks (with computers in them) that the users carry with them while playing. Free-roam VR frees the users from cables and other stationary equipment and allows them to move freely in a designated area that is usually set or build into a warehouse or similar large space, where the users have a rather large area to roam around.

Aforementioned typical VR arcade solutions offer novel opportunities for digital gaming and other forms of entertainment, and the available solutions present a wide mix of games and entertainment. Research has shown that VR games can provide heightened experiences, a higher degree of flow, a richer engagement with passive game elements, and a deeper immersion [23]. They also often provide some level of physical exertion to the users, bringing VR games close to the concept of exergaming [4, 5]. Exergaming can be characterized as a form of digital gaming that requires physical effort from the player in order to play the game and which determines the outcome of the game [4]. Due to this exergaming character of VR gaming, the physical activity background is also investigated.

VR also has its limitations and the developers are dealing with a number of issues to be solved. These issues are mostly not directly related to VR arcades but VR in general. For example, using VR can cause cybersickness (i.e., nausea, disorientation or similar symptoms) to some people. Also, as wearing a VR headset typically prevents seeing the physical world, the user can accidentally hit or run into walls, furniture, or other people. From a more technical perspective, [24] found that issues such as bugs, quality of graphics, and too complex controls can lead to negative user experiences.

Whereas previous research on the use of VR arcades is almost non-existent, various studies have been conducted on VR in general. Studies' perspectives range from more technology focused approaches to more user-centric approaches. As an example of a technology focused approach, [e.g., 25] have studied redirected walking, that is, steering algorithms that continuously redirect the user in order to make the virtual environment larger than the available physical space. As an example of a more user-centric approach, [e.g., 23] have studied player experiences of VR gaming.

3   Methodology

The data for this study were collected in two ways. First, an online survey was administered among Finnish consumers. Second, the author spent two separate days in a virtual reality arcade and collected data with survey forms. Online survey was selected for the main data collection method because of its effectiveness in gathering quantitative data for the purpose of this study. The online survey was created by using the LimeSurvey 3.15.8 software. Before the survey was launched, the questionnaire was pre-tested qualitatively with four game and information systems researchers to ensure that the questions effectively captured the topic under investigation. Based on the discussions and feedback, some minor modifications were made. The final survey questionnaire was online for two months during November 2018 – January 2019. During this period, the online survey was promoted by handing out invitation leaflets in three different VR arcades (all offered both games and other forms of entertainment) and by posting a survey link to a few Finnish discussion forums focusing on VR and/or digital gaming. To increase the response rate, the respondents who completed the online survey could choose to take part in a raffle of four gift cards to a collaborating VR arcade. The two data collection days in VR arcade took place during and after the online survey. Whereas the online survey also collected data for a purpose of another study, the forms only consisted the questions relevant for this study. The surveys were targeted for people who had at least some experience with VR arcades and could thus give responses based on actual usage.

The studied habits were selected based on previous literature [11–13]. Similarly, the questionnaire sections used in this study were adapted from previous literature [11–13] and focused specifically on the respondents' demographics, physical activity background, and habits of using VR arcades. The questions in the habit section are presented in Appendix A (translated from Finnish to English).

The descriptive questions about the habits of using VR arcades were all closed-ended multiple choice questions and investigated: (a) the main form of entertainment used in VR arcades (games, other entertainment, both), (b) the main purpose of visiting VR arcades (fun, utility, both), (c) the main social setting of visiting VR arcades (alone, together with others but single play/use, together with others and multiplay/use), (d) the main physical exertion level of playing (light, moderate, vigorous), (e) the main physical exertion level of using other forms of entertainment (light, moderate, vigorous), and (f) the perceived effects of using VR arcades on physical fitness (negative, no effects, positive). To avoid forced responses, the respondents also had the option "cannot say" with these questions.

The descriptive questions on the demographics and physical activity background were closed-ended multiple-choice questions. The question concerning the physical activity background was based on the 2009–2010 Finnish National Sport Survey [26] and included the following answer options (ordered from the highest physical activity level to the lowest physical activity level): competitive athlete, recreational sportsman, physically active for fitness, physically active for health, active in commuting and non-exercise, occasionally active, and sedentary. The respondents were asked to state which type of physically active person they see themselves to be by selecting between these seven categories. Each category was presented with a description. The categories are explained in more detail in Appendix B (translated from Finnish to English).

The data was analyzed with the IBM SPSS Statistics 24 software. The statistical significance and the strength of the dependencies between the responses and gender, age, and physical activity background were analyzed through contingency tables (crosstabs), the Pearson's χ^2 tests of independence, and the Cramér's V coefficients. The respondents who could not state their physical activity background as well as those who answered "cannot say" to the habit questions were excluded from the respective analysis. In some cases, the common condition "No more than 20% of the expected counts are less than 5 and all individual expected counts are 1 or greater" for the validity of χ^2 test [27, p. 734] was not met. Hence, following the widely used guidelines by [28] and [29], the results of the Pearson's χ^2 tests of independence were advanced by using (Monte Carlo) exact tests. Monte Carlo [30] test was based on 10 000 sampled tables and a 99% confidence level. This procedure is considered reliable and independent of the dimension, distribution, allocation, and the balance of the analyzed data [30]. The level of significance was set to 0.05. These methods enabled to examine both the linear and the non-linear dependencies, which suited well the study's exploratory nature.

4   Results

The surveys yielded a total of 130 responses (76 from the online survey and 54 from the survey forms), out of which 126 were valid and included in the analysis. As the survey was promoted for those who had experience of using VR arcades, almost all respondents had such experience. There was one respondent who stated to have visited VR arcades zero times yet still answered the survey. This respondent was removed from the analysis together with three others who showed content non-responsivity by responding similarly to all questions [31]. Descriptive statistics concerning gender, age, and physical activity background of the analysis sample are presented in Table 1.

Table 1. Descriptive statistics of the sample.

	Sample (N = 126)	
	n	%
Gender		
Male	74	58.7
Female	52	41.3
Other	0	0.0
Age		
–19 years	9	7.1
20–29 years	40	31.7
30–39 years	46	36.5
40– years	31	24.6
Physical Activity Background		
Competitive athlete	5	4.0
Recreational sportsman	11	8.8
Physically active for fitness	38	30.4
Physically active for health	30	24.0
Active in commuting and non-exercise	23	18.4
Occasionally active	18	14.4
Sedentary	0	0.0
N/A	1	–

In terms of gender, out of the 126 respondents, 58.7% identified themselves as males and 41.3% as females. According to the 2018 Finnish Player Barometer [14], digital gaming (80.1% vs. 72.0%) as well as gaming with VR platforms (8.8% vs. 4.0%) is more popular among males than females in Finland. The mean age of the respondents was 32 years (SD = 9.3 years, Median = 32.0), which is not far from the mean age of digital game players in Finland (38.2 years) [14]. Regarding the physical activity background, the distribution was reasonably close to that of Finnish National Exercise Survey [26]. Overall, the sample can be seen as representative. Out of all the respondents, only 14 (11.1%) owned virtual reality devices themselves. This indicates that for the most, VR arcades are the most accessible option to consuming VR games and entertainment. In line with this, the 2018 Finnish Player Barometer reported that only 6.7% of Finns have ever tried playing with VR platforms and the amount of active (at least once a month) VR players is 1% [14].

4.1   Habits of Using Virtual Reality Arcades

The responses to the six descriptive questions about the habits of using VR arcades are summarized in Table 2. The responses suggest the following: In terms of the form of entertainment used in VR arcades, most respondents (64.3%) mainly played games, whereas 8.7% mainly used other forms of entertainment, and 27% mainly used both games and other forms of entertainment when visiting VR arcades.

Regarding the purpose of using VR arcades, for the vast majority (91.3%), the main purpose to visit VR arcades was fun. For 3.2% the main purpose was utility related (e.g., exercise or other utility), and for 5.6% the main purpose was both fun and utility combined.

In terms of social setting, it was much more popular to visit VR arcades together with others than alone. 14.4% mainly visited alone, whereas 85.6% mainly visited with others. Out of those who mainly visited with others, 54.2% also mainly played or used the VR in a multiplayer/multiuser mode, whereas 45.8% still mainly played or used the VR alone.

Regarding the exertion level in VR arcades, playing is clearly conducted with more physical intensity than other forms of entertainment. Of the respondents, 58.3% played with mainly moderate and 5% with mainly vigorous exertion level, whereas other forms of entertainment were mainly consumed with light (79%) exertion level. Concerning the effects to physical fitness, most users perceived the use of VR arcades to not have had significant effects.

Table 2. The habits of using virtual reality arcades among the respondents.

	Sample (N = 126)	
	n	%
Form of entertainment		
Games	81	64.3
Other entertainment	11	8.7
Both	34	27.0
N/A	0	–
Purpose of using		
Fun	115	91.3
Utility	4	3.2
Both fun and utility	7	5.6
N/A	0	–
Social setting		
Alone	18	14.4
Together with others – single play/use	49	39.2
Together with other – multiplay/use	58	46.4
N/A	1	–
Exertion level of playing		
Light	44	36.7
Moderate	70	58.3
Vigorous	6	5.0
N/A	6	–
Exertion level of other entertainment		
Light	79	79.0
Moderate	21	21.0
Vigorous	0	0.0
N/A	26	–
Effects to physical fitness		
Negative	1	0.9
No significant effect	101	93.5
Positive	6	5.6
N/A	18	–

4.2   Gender

Table 3 summarizes the results of the Pearson's χ^2 tests of independence that were used to examine the statistical significance and strength of the dependencies between gender and the responses.

Table 3. Gender dependencies.

	n	χ^2	df	p	p (Monte Carlo)	V
Form of entertainment	126	11.342	2	**0.003**	**0.003**	0.300
Purpose of using	126	0.602	2	0.740	0.795	0.069
Social setting	125	13.919	2	**0.001**	**0.001**	0.334
Exertion level of playing	120	2.897	2	0.235	0.238	0.155
Exertion level of entertainment	100	0.669	1	0.414	0.467	0.082
Effects to physical fitness	108	1.951	2	0.377	0.514	0.134

The habits in which there was a statistically significant dependency with gender were form of entertainment ($\chi^2(2) = 11.342$, p = 0.003, V = 0.300) and social setting ($\chi^2(2) = 13.919$, p = 0.001, V = 0.334).

When visiting VR arcades, males mainly played games more compared to females, whereas females mainly used also other forms of entertainment more compared to males. Of the 74 male (m) respondents and 52 female (f) respondents, 74.3% (m) and 50% (f) stated to be mainly playing games in VR arcades, 23% (m) and 32.7% (f) stated to be mainly using both games and other forms of entertainment, and 2.7% (m) and 17.3% (f) stated to be mainly using other forms of entertainment.

Males visited VR arcades alone more compared to females. Interestingly, while females visited VR arcades more together with others, males visiting together with others more often also played games or used entertainment together with others, whereas females more often played games or used entertainment alone even when visiting together with others. Of the 74 male and 51 female respondents, 17.6% (m) and 9.8% (f) stated to be mainly visiting VR arcades alone, 25.7% (m) and 58.8% (f) stated to be mainly visiting VR arcades together with others but playing games or using entertainment alone, whereas 56.8% (m) and 31.4% (f) stated to be mainly visiting VR arcades together with others and also playing games or using entertainment with others.

4.3   Age

Table 4 summarizes the results of the Pearson's χ^2 tests of independence that were used to examine the statistical significance and strength of the dependencies between age and the responses.

Table 4. Age dependencies.

	n	χ^2	df	p	p (Monte Carlo)	V
Form of entertainment	126	20.373	6	**0.002**	**0.003**	0.284
Purpose of using	126	4.116	6	0.661	0.681	0.128
Social setting	125	25.826	6	**<0.001**	**<0.001**	0.321
Exertion level of playing	120	4.380	6	0.625	0.629	0.135
Exertion level of entertainment	100	4.620	3	0.202	0.208	0.215
Effects to physical fitness	108	17.159	6	**0.009**	**0.014**	0.282

The habits in which there was a statistically significant dependency with age were form of entertainment ($\chi^2(6) = 20.373$, p = 0.003, V = 0.284), social setting ($\chi^2(6) = 25.862$, p < 0.001, V = 0.321), and effects to physical fitness ($\chi^2(6) = 17.159$, p = 0.014, V = 0.282).

In all investigated age groups, people mainly played games when visiting VR arcades. However, it was more common the younger the age group was. In contrast, using mainly other forms of entertainment when visiting VR arcades was more common the older the age group was.

People in the age group 30–39 visited VR arcades alone more than the people in the two younger and the oldest age groups when compared. Interestingly, when visiting VR arcades together with others, people in the youngest and the oldest age group still mainly played games or used entertainment alone, whereas people in the age groups 20–29 and 30–39 also mainly played games or used entertainment together with others.

Regarding the effects to physical fitness, the most common perception in all age groups was that using VR arcades had not affected their physical fitness significantly. However, the perception of improved physical fitness due to using VR arcades was clearly higher in the youngest age group (33%) compared to the other age groups (2.8%, 5.1%, and 5.6%).

4.4 Physical Activity Background

Table 5 summarizes the results of the Pearson's χ^2 tests of independence that were used to examine the statistical significance and strength of the dependencies between physical activity background and the responses.

Table 5. Physical activity background dependencies.

	n	χ^2	df	p	p (Monte Carlo)	V
Form of entertainment	125	13.564	10	0.194	0.190	0.233
Purpose of using	125	12.868	10	0.231	0.212	0.227
Social setting	124	10.763	10	0.376	0.382	0.208
Exertion level of playing	119	4.298	10	0.933	0.948	0.134
Exertion level of other entertainment	100	15.124	5	**0.010**	**0.012**	0.389
Effects to physical fitness	107	9.918	10	0.448	0.381	0.215

The only habit in which there was a statistically significant dependency with physical activity background was *exertion level of other entertainment* ($\chi^2(5) = 15.124$, p = 0.012, V = 0.389).

Using other forms of entertainment was most commonly conducted with light exertion level in all physical activity groups except recreational sportsman, in which the use was divided equally between light and moderate exertion levels. Overall, it can be said that the physical activity background had a very small influence on the habits of using VR arcades.

5 Discussion and Conclusions

This study explored the habits of using VR arcades with emphasis on digital gaming. Specific focus was set on investigating differences between gender, age, and physical activity background. The main purpose of the study was to find out (1) What are the typical habits of using VR arcades and digital games in VR arcades? and (2) What kinds of gender, age, and physical activity background differences exist in the habits of using VR arcades and digital games in VR arcades?. The study followed an exploratory and quantitative approach.

The main findings concerning the habits of using VR arcades show that digital gaming is clearly the most popular form of entertainment in VR arcades. Further, for the vast majority, the main purpose to visit VR arcades is fun, and purely utility related purposes are quite uncommon. This does not mean that the users would not perceive also utilitarian benefits from using VR arcades, but tells that the main purpose for using is fun. From a practical standpoint, this implies that VR arcades should develop and market their offering by using fun and amusement as a spearhead. Further, VR game designers who design VR games for physical activity or other utilitarian purposes, should also pay close attention to the fun aspect of the games.

In terms of the social setting, it is much more popular to visit VR arcades together with others than alone. Interestingly though, almost half of the respondents who visited VR arcades together with others used the games and entertainment alone. This suggest that VR gaming in VR arcades, or VR games in general, perhaps do not support multiplaying at a sufficient level. Thus, designers of VR games could provide more opportunities for gaming that is specifically designed to support good multiplayer experiences, for example by designing games that can be played by two or more players simultaneously each player wearing their own headset. VR arcades should also contemplate whether their offering has suitable multiplayer games and implement more such games into use. VR arcades should also market the available multiplayer opportunities more.

The findings also show that gaming compared to other forms of entertainment in VR arcades is conducted with a much more physically intensive level. Also, as over half of the respondents reported to be mainly playing with moderate exertion level, it shows that VR gaming can provide adequate intensity for physical activity as advised in the global physical activity recommendations [32]. Thus, it can potentially have positive health outcomes in that sense. Even though most of the respondent did not perceive notable changes in their physical fitness, the potential of VR gaming is still notable and worth to consider when planning physical activity promotion campaigns. This also demonstrates that VR gaming can be a new frontier for exergaming and suggest that users would welcome games that offer physical exertion. From a practical standpoint, this gives a signal to the designers of VR games to include physical movements and exertion in the games.

Regarding gender differences, the findings show that while gaming is the most popular form of entertainment in VR arcades for both represented genders, when compared, males mainly play games more, whereas females mainly use more also other forms of entertainment. This suggests that females might be more open to VR experiences that do not involve gaming actions per se. From a practical perspective, this implies that designers of VR games could perhaps provide more such (non-gaming) VR entertainment that would potentially attract the female audience specifically. This finding could also be utilized in marketing, for example, females might be a more potential target group for VR marketing messages that illustrate how one can "just relax" in VR. Furthermore, VR arcades should make sure that they provide both gaming and other VR entertainment options.

Regarding age differences, the most notable finding was that although people mainly play games when visiting VR arcades in all investigated age groups, it is more common the younger the age group is. In contrast, using mainly other forms of entertainment when visiting VR arcades is more common the older the age group is. For practitioners, this suggest that age is a factor that should be taken into account when designing content and interactions for VR experiences as well as when marketing VR gaming and experiences to different age groups, in particular, when the target group is of certain age.

Regarding the relationships between physical activity background and habits of using VR arcades, the findings show that there are not many differences in usage habits between people with different physical activity backgrounds. But when examining the distribution of physical activity backgrounds among the respondents, it shows that most were in the "medium" categories *active for health* and *active for fitness*, whereas those in the most and the least active categories comprised a much smaller proportion. However, this also follows and could be due to the distribution of Finnish people's physical activity backgrounds [26]. Nevertheless, it might be that when communicating specifically about the physical activity side of VR gaming, those with medium physical activity levels are perhaps the most potential target group. Further, if targeting the more active and the more inactive people, special focus and strategies need to be considered in order to be successful. For example, marketing messages could be specifically tailored for those who are very active and for those who are rather inactive.

To conclude, the main contribution of the study is the new knowledge and understanding on digital gaming and entertainment use in VR arcades, and on the differences between different user groups. As a practical contribution, the designers, developers, and marketing people of VR gaming and VR arcades can use the findings and the presented implications in designing and developing more captivating VR games and VR arcade experiences, which would be better accepted by the users and would gain more success in the market, thus advancing their acceptance and diffusion.

6 Limitations and Future Research

This study has three notable limitations. First, the operationalization of some of the surveyed concepts (e.g., the purpose, social setting, exertion level, and perceived effects of playing) was done in a relatively simplistic manner, as they were measured with single-item measures. These measures also focused on subjective perceived measures rather than on objective measures of the concepts. Hence, future research could benefit from measuring the concepts with multiple questions, thus also allowing to evaluate the reliability and validity of the measures. Future studies could also examine the relationships between the concepts, which was not done in this study. Second, the data grouping used in this study is only one way to examine the gathered data. Future studies could use other criteria for the data grouping, for example, based on other demographics, and thus, provide additional insights on the role of relevant background factors for digital gaming and entertainment use in VR arcades. Third, as the study was conducted in Finland and the survey administered in Finnish, it limits the generalizability of the findings. The results might differ in some other gaming cultures, which is something for future studies to investigate. In addition, scholars can draw from this study in designing their studies. They could also benefit from using alternative data collection methods, such as qualitative interviews, and from using other data analysis methods.

Appendix A. Usage Habits in VR Arcades Questions

1. **When you visit virtual reality arcades, do you mainly use games or other forms of entertainment?**

   - Games
   - Other forms of entertainment
   - Both equally
   - Cannot say

2. **Do you visit virtual reality arcades mainly for fun or for utility?**

   - For fun
   - For exercise utility
   - For other utility
   - Both for fun and utility
   - Cannot say

(In the analysis, the options 'For exercise utility' and 'For other utility' were combined)

3. **Do you visit VR arcades mainly alone or together with other people?**

   - Alone
   - Together with other people but we use games and other entertainment alone
   - Together with other people and we use games and other entertainment together (multiplayer games and similar)
   - Cannot say

4. **At what physical exertion level do you mainly play games in VR arcades?**

   - Light (no sweating or accelerated breathing)
   - Moderate (some sweating and accelerated breathing)
   - Vigorous (strong sweating and accelerated breathing)
   - Cannot say

5. **At what physical exertion level do you mainly use other forms of entertainment in VR arcades?**

- Light (no sweating or accelerated breathing)
- Moderate (some sweating and accelerated breathing)
- Vigorous (strong sweating and accelerated breathing)
- Cannot say

6. **How do you perceive that the use of VR arcades has affected your physical fitness?**

- Significantly positively
- Somewhat positively
- No significant effect
- Somewhat negatively
- Significantly negatively
- Cannot say

(In the analysis, the two 'Negatively' answers and the two 'Positively' answers were combined as one 'Negatively' and one 'Positively' answers).

Appendix B. Physical Activity Background Question

1. **In which of the following physical activity categories you see yourself to best belong to (choose one):**

- Competitive athlete (participates in physical activity mainly to gain success in competitions)
- Recreational sportsman (participates in physical activity mainly to improve and develop fitness)
- Active for fitness (participates in physical activity mainly to maintain fitness)
- Active for health (participates in physical activity mainly to maintain health)
- Active in non-exercise (aims to maintain some sort of physical activity in daily life)
- Occasionally active (does not pay much attention to physical activity in daily life)
- Sedentary (aims to avoid all kinds of physical activity in daily life)
- In none of the above/Cannot say

References

1. Sherman, W.R., Craig, A.B.: Understanding Virtual Reality: Interface, Application, and Design. Morgan Kaufmann, Cambridge (2018)
2. Forbes: VR Wave Breaking Outside The Home. https://www.forbes.com/sites/charliefink/2018/05/28/vr-wave-breaking-outside-the-home/#67259296770e. Accessed 06 July 2019

3. Venturebeat: VR arcades are playing a leading role in the consumer market. https://venturebeat.com/2018/07/05/vr-arcades-are-playing-a-leading-role-in-the-consumer-market. Accessed 06 July 2019
4. Kari, T., Makkonen, M.: Explaining the usage intentions of exergames. In: Proceedings of the 35th International Conference on Information Systems, pp. 1–18. Association for Information Systems (AIS), Auckland, New Zealand (2014)
5. Mueller, F., Khot, R.A., Gerling, K., Mandryk, R.: Exertion games. Found. Trends® Hum.–Comput. Interact. **10**(1), 1–86 (2016)
6. Maxint LLC: Soundboxing. https://www.soundboxing.co. Accessed 11 July 2019
7. Beat Games, Beat Saber. https://beatsaber.com. Accessed 11 July 2019
8. VR Fitness Insider: Job Stauffer's Story About Losing 60 pounds and Reclaiming His Health with VR. https://www.vrfitnessinsider.com/job-stauffers-story-losing-60-pounds-reclaiming-health-vr. Accessed 11 July 2019
9. Bonanno, P., Kommers, P.A.: Gender differences and styles in the use of digital games. Educ. Psychol. **25**(1), 13–41 (2005)
10. Hoeft, F., Watson, C.L., Kesler, S.R., Bettinger, K.E., Reiss, A.L.: Gender differences in the mesocorticolimbic system during computer game-play. J. Psychiatr. Res. **42**(4), 253–258 (2008)
11. Kari, T., Makkonen, M., Moilanen, P., Frank, L.: The habits of playing and the reasons for not playing exergames: gender differences in Finland. In: Proceeding of the 25th Bled eConference, pp. 512–526. University of Maribor, Bled (2012)
12. Kari, T., Makkonen, M., Moilanen, P., Frank, L.: The habits of playing and the reasons for not playing exergames: age differences in Finland. Int. J. WWW/Internet **11**(1), 30–42 (2013)
13. Kari, T.: Explaining the adoption and habits of playing exergames: the role of physical activity background and digital gaming frequency. In: Proceedings of the 21st Americas Conference on Information Systems, pp. 1–13. Association for Information Systems (AIS), Fajardo, Puerto Rico (2015)
14. Kinnunen, J., Lilja, P., Mäyrä, F.: Finnish player barometer 2018 [Pelaajabarometri 2018], (Report). University of Tampere, Tampere, Finland (2018)
15. Liu, C.C.: Understanding player behavior in online games: the role of gender. Technol. Forecast. Soc. Change **111**, 265–274 (2016)
16. Salmon, J.P., Dolan, S.M., Drake, R.S., Wilson, G.C., Klein, R.M., Eskes, G.A.: A survey of video game preferences in adults: building better games for older adults. Entertain. Comput. **21**, 45–64 (2017)
17. Schwarz, A., et al.: Which game narratives do adolescents of different gameplay and sociodemographic backgrounds prefer? A mixed-methods analysis. Games Health J. **8**(3), 1–10 (2018)
18. Storgards, J.H., Sokura, B.: The role of gender in the hedonic and utilitarian value of digital games. In: Proceedings of the 15th Americas Conference on Information Systems, pp. 1–9. Association for Information Systems (AIS), San Francisco, CA (2009)
19. Wilhelm, C.: Gender role orientation and gaming behavior revisited: examining mediated and moderated effects. Inf. Commun. Soc. **21**(2), 224–240 (2018)
20. Rogers, E.M.: Diffusion of innovations, 5th edn. Free Press, New York (2003)
21. Böhler, E., Schüz, J.: Cellular telephone use among primary school children in Germany. Eur. J. Epidemiol. **19**(11), 1043–1050 (2004)
22. Komulainen, J., Takatalo, J., Lehtonen, M., Nyman, G.: Psychologically structured approach to user experience in games. In: Proceedings of the 5th Nordic Conference on Human-Computer Interaction: Building Bridges, pp. 487–490. ACM, Lund (2008)

23. Tan, C.T., Leong, T.W., Shen, S., Dubravs, C., Si, C.: Exploring gameplay experiences on the oculus rift. In: Proceedings of the 2015 Annual Symposium on Computer-Human Interaction in Play, pp. 253–263. ACM, London (2015)
24. Farič, N., et al.: What players of virtual reality exercise games want: thematic analysis of web-based reviews. J. Med. Internet Res. 21(9), e13833 (2019)
25. Thomas, J., Rosenberg, E.S.: A general reactive algorithm for redirected walking using artificial potential functions. In: Proceedings of the 2019 IEEE Conference on Virtual Reality and 3D User Interfaces, pp. 56–62. IEEE, Osaka (2019)
26. Finnish Sports Federation.: National Exercise Survey 2009–2010 [Kansallinen Liikuntatutkimus 2009–2010]. Finnish Sports Federation, Helsinki, Finland (2011)
27. Yates, D., Moore, D., McCabe, G.: The Practice of Statistics, 1st edn. W.H. Freeman, New York (1999)
28. Cochran, W.G.: Some methods of strengthening the common chi-square tests. Biometrics 10, 417–451 (1954)
29. Agresti, A.: Categorical Data Analysis. Wiley, New York (2002)
30. Mehta, C.R., Patel, N.R.: IBM SPSS Exact Tests. IBM Corporation, Cambridge (2012)
31. Meade, A.W., Craig, S.B.: Identifying careless responses in survey data. Psychol. Methods 17(3), 437–456 (2012)
32. World Health Organization: Global recommendations on physical activity for health. World Health Organization, Geneva, Switzerland (2010)

Jizo: A Gamified Digital App for Senior Cyclo-Tourism in the miOne Community

Cláudia Pedro Ortet$^{(\boxtimes)}$ ⓘ, Liliana Vale Costa ⓘ,
and Ana Isabel Veloso ⓘ

DigiMedia, Department of Communication and Art, University of Aveiro,
Aveiro, Portugal
{claudiaortet,lilianavale,aiv}@ua.pt

Abstract. The continued growth of the aging population has led to a greater interest in the subject of gerontechnology. In the case of the digital game industry, senior citizens are becoming better consumers, so the role of games to their wellbeing are becoming more important in order to meet their needs and preferences. Still, there is a general lack of information and products that address cyclo-tourism, and, so far, almost non attention was given to the way gamification can motivate senior citizens to this matter. The aim of this research is to understand how gamification interventions can motivate senior citizens to adhere to cyclo-tourism. This paper reports on the results obtained from the literature and related work, as well as the involvement of two different groups of senior citizens aged 55 or over (7 focus group participants from a Portuguese University of Third Age, and 31 cyclists' interviewees from 8 countries), using a Development Research method. Based on the insights from the literature, interviews with cyclists and focus groups with senior citizens, the researcher and the focus group participants were able to co-design a cyclo-tourism app entitled Jizo. Findings indicate that certain gamification techniques and elements can trigger senior citizens' motivations towards cyclo-tourism, being essential integrative parts of an app in this context. The game elements that were highlighted were: social relationships, progression, challenges, competition, feedback and rewards. These were divided into pre-, in loco and post-cyclo-tourism experience. These data support the view on gamification capability to motivate sustainable cyclo-tourism.

Keywords: Senior citizens · Gamification · Motivation · Cyclo-tourism · Co-design · Jizo

1 Introduction

Today's sedentarism is often associated to the age group of senior citizens, given the increase in the risk of mortality [1], the growth of an aging population and the prevalence of mobility and health impairments. In the light of this problem, several studies (*e.g.* [2, 3]) have shown a renewed attention in merging physical exercise with digital games, while engaging senior citizen's communities with digital platforms. Indeed, physical exercise and the use of Information and Communication Technologies are suggested to have a great potential to overcome this problem.

© Springer Nature Switzerland AG 2019
N. Zagalo et al. (Eds.): VJ 2019, CCIS 1164, pp. 195–207, 2019.
https://doi.org/10.1007/978-3-030-37983-4_15

Physical exercise can improve health-related quality of life and individual satisfaction, as well as physical and psychological well-being, and when doing it regularly, it can delay functional deteriorations and prevent chronic diseases [4–6].

Regarding the senior citizens' use of digital platforms, the overdependence in ICT and the subsequent challenges of an increasingly aging society should be considered given that this fact is often correlated to the personal human aging process, lack of access to digital platforms and knowledge of interface conventions [7]. A cognitive challenge may arise when learning how to use computers and/or the Internet, since that is considered to be a new skill. Additionally, technological activities tend to be difficult in terms of cognitive functions (*e.g.* speed of information processing, selective memory and memory). Therefore, it is possible to stimulate senior citizens' autonomy, cognitive abilities and engagement in interpersonal relations and productive activity by encouraging them to use computers and the Internet to perform everyday tasks [8].

For the development of the tourism market and products, it is important to identify new demographic challenges and the transformation in the structure of society. Senior tourists have a greater consumption power in terms of leisure and tourism products, in comparison to younger tourists, generally because they have higher income, in comparison to other age groups [9].

So, in order to combine physical exercise to tourism, cyclo-tourism seem to be adequate, since it is an unexplored sector with a great sustainability potential in rural areas [10]. Although cycling has been regarded as a physical exercise connected with the health and fitness sector, its application in mobility, transports and tourism sector have also an important role [11].

The aim of this study is twofold: (a) describe the process of involving a group of adult learners aged 55 and over from a Portuguese University of Third Age in the design process of the cyclo-tourism app; and (b) design a prototype of a cyclo-tourism app that demonstrates the way gamification can motivate senior citizens to cyclo-tourism.

The paper is structured as follows: Sect. 2 describes related work on cycling exergames and gamified applications to cycling and tourism, as well as gamification applied to the cyclo-tourism contexts. Section 3 covers the participatory design process, data collection, analysis procedures and ethical issues. Section 4 presents the prototype of the cyclo-tourism app 'Jizo'. Section 5 is relative to the evaluation process and its discussion.

2 Background and Related Work

Considering the potential benefits to senior citizens from playing games, it is important to understand the game elements and strategies that can motivate them to adhere to the game-playing activity. Beyond individual's extrinsic motivations (*e.g.* rewards and resources), intrinsic motivations (*e.g.* respect and status) play an important role in changes in behavior and characterize the concept of gamification [12–14]. Gamification can be defined as the use of elements and techniques of game design in the context of non-game environment, attempting to motivate the user to perform an ordinary activity [15]. The main idea is to take the base of digital games and to implement it in situations of the real world (*e.g.* entertainment industry, health, education, tourism), frequently with the intention of motivating specific behaviours within non-game scenarios [16].

The following sections have three examples each of gamification in tourism, cycling exergames and gamification in cycling. These examples were selected because of their suitability, relevance and popularity.

2.1 Gamification in Tourism

Gamification is becoming a major tendency in tourism and the leading motivations to play a tourism game are: (i) obtain suitable information about a destination in pre-, during and post-experience; (ii) and be able to interact with others [17]. For that, combining both physical and digital spaces is imperative in order to merge virtual and reality in the users' mindset, marketing an imaginary world of fantasy and fun (*i.e.* mixed-reality games). The following is an account of some game that address the tourism context.

2.1.1 REXplorer
This game was designed especially for tourists of Regensburg in Germany, with the purpose of informing them about the city history in a playfully experience [18]. This mobile digital game offers user meetings with spirits of historical figures that are associated with important buildings in a town setting. To awake and communicate with the spirits characters, the user waves the mobile phone through the air, imitating the mechanism of casting a spell. According to the authors of this game, one of the features that people often appreciate and distinguishes from others is the freedom of pathway, choices and pace [18].

2.1.2 Eye Shakespeare
Eye Shakespeare, developed by Stratford upon Avon city, hometown of Shakespeare, is a gamified mobile app that use Augmented Reality (AR) to introduce a 3D virtual Shakespeare character to tourists, who announces his birthplace, guides them during their visit and enables them to take a photo together with his virtual figure. Instead of traditional tour guides, this virtual character who tells Shakespeare stories is a different and entertaining way of exploring the places and history settings. It provides a fun and interactive touristic experience by using some game elements (*e.g.* reward and story-telling) [19].

These (*i.e.* REXplorer and Eye Shakespeare) are good examples of digital games applied to tourism, where they succeed to inform users about the history and culture of the city or a relevant character in a playful manner.

2.2 Cycling Exergames

Despite the cognitive benefits of physical exercise in later life, only a small portion of senior citizens do it at the recommended levels (at least 30 min a day) and that fact rushed to the proliferation of studies (*e.g.* [20, 21]) that observe the use of exergaming technologies (*e.g.* Microsoft Kinect, Nintendo Wii) to motivate senior citizens to do physical exercise with the combination of digital game features and fitness activities.

2.2.1 Join-in Exerbiking

A considerable number of senior citizens share happy memories about riding a bicycle outdoors at a younger age but do not have the opportunity to ride it again. This may be due to functional limitations related to the aging process, augmented road traffic or access to convenient motorized transportation. In Join-in Exerbiking [22], users participate in multi-player online rides where they can even virtually ride their bike outdoors (*e.g.* in a park or by the seawall), while using an elliptical bicycle with a tablet mounted on the handlebar. When cycling, they also see a route map, textual information and other users' photos.

2.2.2 Pedal Tanks

Pedal Tanks was created with a customized controller for the purpose of physical exercise [23]. A significant benefit of this platform is that the workout itself is a direct contribution to the digital game, since the RPM sensors enable to use the bicycle speed as an input to the game, and the handlebars buttons allow easy effort while using the bicycle because it provides enough buttons for a varied set of actions [23].

2.2.3 Pedal Kart

The Pedal Kart's goal was to design and create an exergame in order to provide the weekly recommended physical exercise with an elliptical bicycle, while being pleasant enough to motivate people to exercise more and more often [24]. The design principles of connecting real movements directly to in-game movements and guaranteeing a variety of movement intensities, they contributed to ensure that users perform a good level of workout. Basically, the use of Pedal Tanks motivated the users to do repetitive physical exercise movements in comparison with the users who did not use the exergame [24].

In these cycling exergames (*i.e.* Exerbiking, Pedal Tanks and Pedal Kart), exergaming is suggested to foster short-term and mid-term enjoyment and engagement and integrate physical exercises in the individuals' daily life.

2.3 Gamification in Cycling

By searching on Google Play and Apple Store using the terms "cycling", "tourism" and "cyclo-tourism" between July 2018 and May 2019, a significant number of apps that can track and register rides were identified. Most of them were very similar and were excluded to avoid repetition, others were paid and were not relevant for this study, since most cycling users tend to prefer non-payed apps. Therefore, only three apps were chosen taking into consideration its popularity, classification, functionalities and relevance to the theme: Cyclers, Strava and Zwift. To this study, the popularity and classification criteria was based on the number of downloads and comments in the Google Play and App Store; the functionalities were related to the gamification elements; and the relevance was related with the theme (*i.e.* Cyclo-tourism, subjacent Cycling and Gamification).

2.3.1 Cyclers

Cyclers: Navigation & Community for Cyclists, previously known by UrbanCyclers, stand out for a gamification strategy, with special relevance to social features in cycling. It enables the user to discover cycling routes, adding combinations with public transport and bicycle sharing. It notifies the user about the dangers, closures and restrictions along the route, providing short-term weather prediction and voice guidance navigation. Cyclers can also track and save users' rides, as well as monitor their personal statistics. This app enables the user to find the most popular route by reading crowdsourced heatmaps and to rate routes they have cycled, helping cities to plan a better cycling infrastructure. In order to maintain the user motivated to continue to use the app and, more importantly, to use the bicycle, the app offers prizes and badges for each cycling achievements, and the option of sharing and following friends.

2.3.2 Strava

Strava enables users to track and upload the end-user's ride activities using GPS data, either from the app on a smartphone or via a third-party GPS bicycle computer (*e.g.* Garmin, TomTom, Fitbit) [25]. It is known as an "athlete's social media", since it allows millions of cyclists to connect with each other by sharing their ride activities and photos, commenting on each other's rides and give 'kudos'. Groups can also create clubs to organize activities or to build communities. Currently, Strava can be used to log a wide range of riding data including GPS tracked routes displayed on a map, speed, distance, power output and heart rate. The segments mark road sections that can be created by Strava users and record a chart with the time every Strava user has been there before. This is considered to be an addicted tool because it incites the athlete to pursuit for KOMs or QOMs (*i.e.* King of the Mountain and Queen of the Mountain), creating an engagement in the use of the digital platform for physical activity [25]. Strava users can sign up for various motivational tasks (*e.g.* distance, challenge, climbing goal), since it can meet their intrinsic and extrinsic motivations (*e.g.* personal realization and rewards). Progress is tracked after each riding activity is registered and a badge is awarded when a challenge is completed.

2.3.3 Zwift

Although Zwift seems to be an exergame because of the bicycle use while looking to a monitor with Virtual Reality (VR), their creators reported that it is a software where they are gamifying cities and routes to motivate people to train indoors [26].

This software consists on: (a) riding virtual roads where users can explore routes inspired by real world cycling routes (*e.g.* Tour de France, La Vuelta and Giro d'Italia); (b) discover the virtual world of Zwift named Watopia by climbing mountains and sprinting down famous stretches of road or even riding inside a bubbling volcano; (c) structured workouts with the elite World Tour coaches with custom-made programs to each user's fitness level, being possible to train alone or to join in a scheduled group workout; (d) social group rides with users from around the world; and (e) challenges and events where the user can select many events with different levels (*i.e.* from social easy rides to intense races with real prizes), in which friendly competition can maintain people motivated to finish a route and giving the best of themselves [27].

3   Method

The qualitative approach is contextual and occurs in a natural setting. Whether following a rigorous procedure, it can even be used to corroborate theoretical propositions from the literature review; and be applied to a number of contexts where little is known about a phenomenon, offering new perspectives of analysis [28]. By using the Development Research Method, problem-solving is divided into six phases: (1) Analyse the problematic and assess previous studies; (2) Elaborate a model during the conception process; (3) Develop strategies for different achievements; (4) Evaluate the possibilities of realization; (5) Propose a prototype; and (6) Implement it [29].

This study was done within the scope of the Master's dissertation in Multimedia Communication, supported by the SEDUCE 2.0 project POCI-01-0145-FEDER-031696 (SEDUCE 2.0 - Senior Citizen Use of Communication and Information in miOne community). Table 1 shows the scheduled activities carried out in this project that this paper covers.

Table 1. Scheduled activities that were carried out in the Development Research

Steps	Dates	Activities	Method	Data collection
1-Analysis and Evaluation of the Situation	July 2018 to April 2019	Literature review App analysis	Literature Review	Literature Review
2-Concept and Design of the Prototype	April 2019 to May 2019	Conception: Involve a group of senior citizens at the University of Third Age in the co-design process; Interview a group of cyclists aged 55 and over from Portugal and other countries Development: Design of a digital app prototype	AXE approach Participatory Action Research Focus Groups Interviews	Participant Observation Field Notes Co-Design Group Discussion Interview Guide
3-Implementation and Evaluation	May 2019 to June 2019	Test of the prototype	AXE approach User eXperience	Participant Observation Field Notes

3.1   Semi-structured Interviews

Interviews are a method used in PAR, which enable the participants to report their perceived context [30], offering the researcher a broader perspective on the participants' ideas and thoughts, and show the story behind the individuals' experience.

The general interview guide approach safeguards that the same topics are discussed and, therefore, the same information is collected from each interviewee. This provides not only focus, but also some freedom and adaptability in getting the information from the participant, while pursuing in-depth information around the topic [31].

3.2   Co-design Techniques in Development Research Method

Based on cyclists' inputs from the interviews and literature review, a set of applied theories and practices that involve the end-user in activities that inform, test and drive the development of digital products and services were used in a focus group, encouraging them to be co-designers [32]. This develops a shared sense of ownership of the project perceived by both the researcher and participants, since all contribute to it.

As part of the co-design technique used, PICTIVE engaged senior citizens in the design process, once it enabled non-technological people to contribute with ideas to the development process [33]. PICTIVE is a paper mock-up technique that embodies graphical user interfaces in paper or plastic, enabling users to have a sense of what the prototype will look like and how it will behave, avoiding the need for specialized knowledge [33].

Scenario Building was another technique that was used, since it can help the researcher to be familiar with the interfaces and the applications of artefacts in Human activity [34]. Scenarios can be concrete and flexible, supporting the designers' work with the mutability of design conditions and addressing the challenge of technical design. They can promote work-oriented communication among researchers and participants, facilitating design activities and encouraging different opinions and points of view, inevitably contributing to the design process, and meeting the users' needs and concerns in different contexts [34].

Combined with the techniques mentioned before, Collage was also used. Collage is a technique that has been used over 1000 years ago, best-known from its usage by famous artists (*e.g.* Picasso, Braque). It is often characterized by the use of pieces of materials and gluing them into a flat surface to represent a phenomenon [35] and produce new ideas. Collage can also be considered as a collecting technique, since different items can be gathered and grouped according to a certain pattern [36].

3.3   The Participants

The sample used in this study was purposively selected and, therefore, data cannot be extrapolated to other contexts.

In terms of the interviewees, they were invited via Facebook and Strava cycling groups. The criteria used for the participants selection were: (a) being a cyclist; (b) being aged 55 years or older; and (c) voluntary participation. The sample consisted in 31 participants, 54,8% females (n = 17) and 45,2% males (n = 14). Regarding the cyclists' nationalities, 42% were from UK (n = 13), 26% from US (n = 8), 13% from Portugal (n = 4), 7% from Denmark (n = 2), 3% from Netherlands (n = 1), 3% from Canada (n = 1), 3% from Italy (n = 1) and 3% from France (n = 1).

In relation to the focus group sessions, the criteria for selecting the participants of the University of Third Age were: (a) being aged 55 years old or older; (b) know how to read and write; (c) know how to ride a bike; (d) voluntary participation; and (e) interest in learning Informatics. The sample consisted in 7 participants, 71,4% males (n = 5) and 28,6% females (n = 2), aged between 57 and 80 years old.

3.4   Data Collection and Analysing Procedures

Data was collected from April 2019 to June 2019 and focus group participants had a 2-hour session per week. In ensuring internal validity, the following strategies were used: triangulation of multiple sources of data collected (*i.e.* field notes, questionnaires and document analysis) and repeated observations at the research site.

After collecting the data, the participants' perspectives gathered from the focus group and interviews were divided into words, phrases or sentences using open coding. Then, their compilation in different categories was followed according to its context and number of occurrences. Data collection and analysis was performed using the NVivo 12 Plus software.

3.5   Ethical Issues

This study is part of the SEDUCE 2.0 research project and it safeguards: (a) The informed consent of the participants aged 55 and over; (b) voluntary participation; (c) involvement of the research team in the process; and (d) that the risks of participating in the study do not outweigh the risks associated with the participants' daily lives.

4   Jizo App

4.1   Gamification Elements

In order to design the gamified digital app Jizo, the participants' inputs and some guidelines suggested in the literature were taken into consideration. When surveyed about the gamification elements that were important for an app to have, the participants have proposed the following elements for including in the Jizo app: (a) Progression: The end-user can monitor their rides when using the Jizo app; (b) Social Relationships: The social relationships are explored by adding friends, inviting them to a ride, and commenting and liking their rides; (c) Challenges: A set of goals are suggested for the end-user to achieve; (d) Competition: Rankings/Leaderboards encourage the end-users to be better than other users; (e) Feedback: The app provides feedback by commenting the user rides and progress; (f) Rewards: The end-users are awarded with badges (virtual or real) for accomplishing an achievement; and (g) Win States: Users' victory or loss conditions are determined in each challenge.

While progression can increase intrinsic motivation, the other elements are known for increasing extrinsic motivation.

When applying these gamified elements to senior cyclo-tourism, a set of endorsements were suggested to each experience stage:

- Pre-experience: route recommendations, weather forecast, information about cycling equipment and bicycle rental shops;
- In loco: route directions, performance monitoring, points achievements and rewards; and
- Post-experience: motivational quotes and feedback, unlock resources, badges earnings, rankings and leaderboards.

4.2   Prototyping

Based on the literature review on game design, the problems found in cycling apps, the co-design sessions and the input from cyclists, a prototype of a cyclo-tourism app was proposed. The prototyping process was divided into three phases: (i) sketching; (ii) first version; and (iii) final version.

Sketching seemed to be the best way to shorten the development process while maintaining some quality standards. In early phases of the design process, problem finding, analysis and conceptual design were some of the activities that were undertaken. Subsequently, the chances of amending errors were the highest and the use of low-expenditure sketches and material models during the design process were crucial [37]. Since self-made sketches can support the limited Human memory capacity and mental processing for a complete problem analysis by developing useful ideas and concepts [38], the feedback given when sketching should be as valuable as the reduction of complexity, which is a prerequisite to defining solutions [39].

Basically, rectangles were drawn to reproduce a smartphone screen and other rectangles, circles and text were added to it, in order to illustrate different scenarios. After having a considerable number of screens, it was important to link them to form sequences, until a satisfactory boarding screens were reached to represent all the app functionalities. By using Adobe XD and Adobe Illustrator for a more cohesive and aesthetically appealing look, colors, icons, fonts and other visual aspects were added to create a homogeneous interface (Fig. 1).

Fig. 1. Screenshots of the Jizo app

4.2.1   Typography

The predominant font used in the prototype is Gibson, which is sans serif, simple and easy to read because of the simpler lines. Open Sans, also a sans serif font, is used in some titles, in order to create some visual hierarchy.

4.2.2   Colour

Following motivational and psychological theories, orange was the predominant color chosen for this prototype. Orange is associated to an optimistic, enriching and revitalizing matter, keeping people inspired to look at the brighter side of life, being the color of encouragement and vivacity. When using orange in business, it suggests adventure, journeys, energy, flamboyance and fun, stimulating social communication and self-confidence [40], consequently, being appropriated to use in travel and sports business, which are main fields covered in this prototype.

4.2.3   Logo

Jizo is a Japanese and Buddhist divinity that vowed to protect travelers in their physical and spiritual journey, being easy to pronounce, but also for being short and meaningful. The logo was designed in Adobe Illustrator and the typographic representation of the word Jizo used a gradient in orange. In addition, such elements as a cyclist with a youngster on a digital device landed on the planet Earth represents the cyclo-tourism in an intergenerational context.

5   Evaluation and Discussion

To ease the navigation and show all the app features, a script was used so that the participants would access and perform the same activities throughout the session. In the end of prototype testing, the participants identified the app strengths, weaknesses, opportunities and threats (*i.e.* SWOT analysis).

The Jizo strengths highlighted by the participants were the following: (i) introductory tutorial; (ii) the functionality to invite friends for a ride and tracking their location; (iii) explore local and touristic routes, and points of interest (POIs); (iv) take photos without leaving the app; (v) all cycling information available; (vi) originality; (vii) accessibility; and (viii) layout and design. The main weaknesses were: (i) icons identification; (ii) lettering size; and (iii) few monitoring statistics available. Relative to the opportunities, these were: (i) the ability to be used worldwide; (ii) extension for other activities; (iii) be an official cyclo-tourism app; (iv) connect people from all over the world; and (v) motivate to cyclo-tourism. The Jizo threats were: (i) other apps on the market; and (ii) the fact of not being well promoted and divulgated.

The main conclusions drawn from the evaluation of the app prototyped by cyclists and senior citizens from a University of Third Age are that the implemented prototype can motivate senior citizens to cyclo-tourism. However, it presents usability aspects that need to be improved in order to meet the app requirements, therefore, second iteration will be needed to redesign some of the functionalities.

6   Conclusions and Further Work

According to initial expectations, this research found that senior citizens involved in cyclo-tourism tend to use a smartphone and cycling apps. The participants also stated that gamification elements are important and can motivate them to the activity. The main gamification elements that motivates senior citizens towards cyclo-tourism are the competition and challenges, with constant feedback about their progression, in order to receive rewards and share the information with their groups and friends. Therefore, the findings have important implications for developing a gamified app targeted to senior citizens aged 55 and over and identify the intrinsic and extrinsic motivations to cyclo-tourism.

One of the major differentiator aspects of Jizo, when in comparison with other similar apps, is the option of inviting a friend, allowing to track the user location and, therefore, facilitating the meeting of users. Other important aspect is the fact that this app was designed by and to senior citizens, being more suitable to this target audience. While other apps can shortly serve senior citizens in this use, they fail to keep them engaged to the activity. Therefore, Jizo aims to revolutionize in this field, since, according to the tests, it can increase intrinsic and extrinsic motivation, maintaining the user interested in the continuity of the cyclo-tourism activity.

A number of limitations of this research study should be considered. Firstly, as mentioned before, Gamification and Senior Cyclo-tourism is an unexplored topic, being this research innovative and not a replication or adaptation from other similar studies. Secondly, a convenience sample was used, so attempts to generalize beyond these respondents are not warranted and results should be interpreted with caution. Considering that this study has an international dimension, getting a random sample of each country would be interesting but unfeasible in a short period. For that, the research would need to be extended in time. Thirdly, there may be some members' bias in the results obtained, owning to the fact that the focus group participants were from the same institute. However, the researcher ensured that all participants expressed their individual and collective opinions and experiences with, for example, the use of cards.

Regarding future work, further research needs to be carried out in motivation and the psychologic field in order to deepen the understanding in gamification and motivation, while observing if the communication skills can affect anxiety and have an impact on behavior change and frequency of cyclo-tourism. A game narrative could be a more interactive and efficient way to motivate senior citizens and different generations. During prototype design and development, mechanisms of Artificial Intelligence (AI) and Augmented Reality could also be considered in order to associate virtual avatars to a set of points of interest and local history or tourism. The possibility of exergaming Jizo would be an asset to this study and probably, also, a significant contribution to people who are unable to ride outside due to fears and/or physical limitations.

Acknowledgments. The study reported in this publication was supported by Fundação para a Ciência e Tecnologia (FCT) and ESF under Community Support Framework III – the project SEDUCE 2.0 nr. POCI-01-0145-FEDER-031696. The authors wish to thank the participants from the University of Third Age of Gafanha da Nazaré and the cyclists' interviewees.

References

1. Rezende, L.F.M.D., Rey-López, J.P., Matsudo, V.K.R., Luiz, O.D.C.: Sedentary behavior and health outcomes among older adults: a systematic review. BMC Public Health **14**, 333 (2014)
2. Groot, G.C.L.D., Fagerström, L.: Older adults motivating factors and barriers to exercise to prevent falls. Scand. J. Occup. Ther. **18**, 153–160 (2010)
3. Derboven, J., Gils, M.V., Grooff, D.D.: Designing for collaboration: a study in intergenerational social game design. Univ. Access Inf. Soc. **11**, 57–65 (2011)
4. Mandolesi, L., et al.: Effects of physical exercise on cognitive functioning and wellbeing: biological and psychological benefits. Front. Psychol. **9**, 509 (2018)
5. Mazo, G.Z., Mota, J., Gonçalves, L.H., Matos, M.G., Carvalho, J.: Actividade física e qualidade de vida de mulheres idosas da cidade de Florianópolis, Brasil. Revista Portuguesa de Ciências do Desporto. **2008**, 414–423 (2008)
6. Rikli, R.E., Jones, C.J.: Senior Fitness Test Manual. Human Kinetics, Champaign (2013)
7. Pasqualotti, A., Pasqualotti, P.R., Zanin, J.: Ambientes de interação, mediação e comunicação: análise dos critérios de usabilidade e acessibilidade no atendimento às expectativas da pessoa idosa. Centro Universitário Feevale, Novo Hamburgo – RS Brasil (2007)
8. Zheng, R., Hill, R.D., Gardner, M.K.: Engaging Older Adults with Modern Technology: Internet Use and Information Access Needs. Information Science Reference, Hershey (2013)
9. Aln, E., Dominguez, T., Los, N.: New opportunities for the tourism market: senior tourism and accessible tourism. In: Visions for Global Tourism Industry - Creating and Sustaining Competitive Strategies (2012)
10. Gazzola, P., Pavione, E., Grechi, D., Ossola, P.: Cycle tourism as a driver for the sustainable development of little-known or remote territories: the experience of the Apennine regions of Northern Italy. Sustainability **10**, 1863 (2018)
11. Cox, P.: Strategies promoting cycle tourism in Belgium: practices and implications. Tour. Plan. Dev. **9**, 25–39 (2012)
12. Maslow, A.H., Frager, R.: Motivation and personality. Pearson Education, New Delhi (1987)
13. Vianna, Y., Vianna, M., Medina, B., Tanaka, S.: Gamification, INC. – Como reinventar empresas a partir de jogos (1ªed) MJV Press, Brasil (2013)
14. Werbach, K., Hunter, D.: For the Win: How Game Thinking Can Revolutionize Your Business. Wharton Digital Press, Philadelphia (2012)
15. Deterding, S., Dixon, D., Khaled, R., Nacke, L.: From game design elements to gamefulness. In: Proceedings of the 15th International Academic MindTrek Conference on Envisioning Future Media Environments - MindTrek 11 (2011)
16. Sailer, M., Hense, J.U., Mayr, S.K., Mandl, H.: How gamification motivates: an experimental study of the effects of specific game design elements on psychological need satisfaction. Comput. Hum. Behav. **69**, 371–380 (2017)
17. Xu, F., Tian, F., Buhalis, D., Weber, J.: Marketing tourism via electronic games: understanding the motivation of tourist players. In: 2013 5th International Conference on Games and Virtual Worlds for Serious Applications (VS-GAMES) (2013)
18. Ballagas, R., Kuntze, A., Walz, S.P.: Gaming tourism: lessons from evaluating REXplorer, a pervasive game for tourists. In: Indulska, J., Patterson, D.J., Rodden, T., Ott, M. (eds.) Pervasive 2008. LNCS, vol. 5013, pp. 244–261. Springer, Heidelberg (2008). https://doi.org/10.1007/978-3-540-79576-6_15

19. Xu, F., Buhalis, D.: Serious games and the gamification in tourism. Tour. Manag. **2017**(60), 244–256 (2017)
20. Smith, S.T., Schoene, D.: The use of exercise-based videogames for training and rehabilitation of physical function in older adults: current practice and guidelines for future research. Aging Health **8**, 243–252 (2012)
21. Barnett, L.M., Bangay, S., Mckenzie, S., Ridgers, N.D.: Active gaming as a mechanism to promote physical activity and fundamental movement skill in children. Front. Public Health. **1**, 74 (2013)
22. Join-in Project.: Introduction to exergames designed in Join-in – Exerbiking, AntiqueHunt, Walking game (2014)
23. Hagen, K., Chorianopoulos, K., Wang, A.I., Jaccheri, L., Weie, S.: Gameplay as exercise. In: Proceedings of the 2016 CHI Conference Extended Abstracts on Human Factors in Computing Systems – CHI EA 16, pp. 1872–1878 (2016)
24. Skjæran, M., Wang, A.I.: Pedal Kart – the creation and evaluation of a cardiovascular exercise bike game. Norwegian University of Science Technology (2018)
25. Strava: Everything you need to know about the world's leading cycling app (2018). https://www.cyclingweekly.com/tag/strava
26. Bailey, M.: Zwift: The story behind the indoor cycling phenomenon (2017). https://www.telegraph.co.uk/health-fitness/body/zwift-story-behindindoor-cycling-phenomenon/
27. Zwift: What do I need to start Riding in Zwift? (2018). https://support.zwift.com/en_us/what-do-i-need-to-start-riding-in-zwift-B18y0kZB7
28. Sutton, J., Austin, Z.: Qualitative research: data collection, analysis and management. Can. J. Hosp. Pharm. **68**(3), 226–231 (2015)
29. Maren, J.V.: Méthodes de recherche pour l'education. De Boeck Université, Belgique (1996). http://classiques.uqac.ca/contemporains/Van_der_Maren_jeanmarie/methodes_recherche_education/methodes.html
30. Stringer, E.T.: Action Research, 2nd edn. Sage, Thousand Oaks (1999)
31. Watson, T.W.: Guidelines for Conducting Interviews. PsycEXTRA Dataset (1997)
32. Muller, M., Druin, A.: Participatory design; the third space in HCI. In: Human-Computer Interaction Handbook: Fundamentals, Evolving Technologies and Emerging Applications. Human Factors and Ergonomics, pp. 1051–1068 (2003)
33. Schuler, D., Namioka, A.: Participatory Design: Principles and Practices. CRC, Boca Raton (1993)
34. Carroll, J.M.: Five reasons for scenario-based design. Interact. Comput. **13**, 43–60 (2000)
35. Butler-Kisber, L., Poldma, T.: The power of visual approaches in qualitative inquiry: the use of collage making and concept mapping in experiential research. J. Res. Pract. **6**(2) (2010). Article M18
36. Cardinal, R., Elsner, J.: The Cultures of Collecting. Reaktion Books, London (1994)
37. Römer, A., Pache, M., Weißhahn, G., Lindemann, U., Hacker, W.: Effort-saving product representations in design—results of a questionnaire survey. Des. Stud. **22**, 473–491 (2001)
38. Rubin, M.A., Rowe, P.G.: Design thinking. J. Arch. Educ. (1984-) **43**(3), 45 (1990)
39. Schütze, M., Sachse, P., Römer, A.: Support value of sketching in the design process. Res. Eng. Design **14**, 89–97 (2003)
40. Scott-Kemis, J.: The Color Orange (2009). https://www.empower-yourself-with-color-psychology.com/color-orange.html

Gamification for Graphic Education:
A Case Study on Innovative Methodology

Jackeline Lima Farbiarz[1](✉) ⓘ, Alexandre Farbiarz[2](✉) ⓘ,
Guilherme Xavier[1] ⓘ, and Cynthia Macedo Dias[1] ⓘ

[1] Pontifícia Universidade Católica do Rio de Janeiro, Rio de Janeiro, Brazil
{jackeline,guix}@puc-rio.br, cymadi@gmail.com
[2] Universidade Federal Fluminense, Niterói, Brazil
alexandre.farbiarz@gmail.com

Abstract. This paper presents a case study on the *Commercium & Cognitionis* project, which aligns technology and playfulness, implementing the use of smartphones and gamification as pedagogical tools that value didactic content and interaction. Aiming at students of the *Visual and Graphic Languages* discipline of a Journalism course in Brazil, the proposal is aligned with the insertion of urban youth into a highly imagetic and technological contemporary culture. The study reflects research which demonstrates journalism students' lack of interest in visual communication contents and the dynamics of a game that combines competition and collaboration in the search for knowledge to solve the proposed challenges. Adopting active pedagogical methods which exploit skills and abilities in the game allowed the combination of systemic and procedural evaluation in the discipline, as well as the evaluation of knowledge construction. To reach the play goal, it was necessary for the student-player to pursue the didactic objectives, as the evaluation of the experience indicates that dedication to the game positively influenced the academic dedication, also stimulating access and meaningful learning on the programmatic contents and guaranteeing autonomy and independence in the educational process.

Keywords: Education · Innovation · Technology · Gamification

1 Introduction

Journalism students enter the course with expectations of graduating as professionals in the area, focused mainly on news production for print, digital, audiovisual or sound. Besides other options demanded by the journalism market, in the curriculum of the Journalism course at Fluminense Federal University (UFF), students have at their disposal seven different emphasis areas, focusing on professional practice. The graphic area disciplines with an emphasis on Editorial Design were established by a view that "In recent years, Communication studies have evolved towards understanding language and media theory, not only as a field of action but as a place of knowledge" [1].

However, in continuous research carried out since 1994 and reported for the first time in 2001 [2], about 2,100 students attending graphic subjects from UFF's Social Communication and Journalism courses made clear that there is a growing focus on

© Springer Nature Switzerland AG 2019
N. Zagalo et al. (Eds.): VJ 2019, CCIS 1164, pp. 208–219, 2019.
https://doi.org/10.1007/978-3-030-37983-4_16

future positions in the journalism market and a decreasing focus on visual communication. These results indicate that graphic language content, despite its importance in the formation of future journalism professionals, does not belong in the students' priority interests. As a result, innovative strategies focusing on motivation and engagement should be adopted in disciplines related to this area.

Taking these issues as premises, the *Commercium & Cognitionis* (CetC) project seeks to associate technology and teaching practice playfully, developing tools that value didactic content and interaction and help meaningful learning. Given the clear insertion of urban contemporary youth in a highly imaginative and technological culture [3], the first pedagogical strategy evaluated was the insertion of digital information and communication technologies, such as smartphones. The second was the association of the discipline pedagogical project with a gamification process, which consists of incorporating game elements in other situations, unrelated to games, to maximize engagement and motivation behaviors among participants [4].

2 Literature Review and Related Statistic Research

This project is based on our experiences as teachers, a literature review including the areas of Education, Design, Game Studies and Cyber culture and related statistic research, such as ICT Kids [5], which indicates that in 2015, 82% of the Brazilian population between 9 and 17 years old used the Internet and 97% of these by cellphones and smartphones. The Brazilian Institute of Geography and Statistics census [6] shows that there was a 320% increase in absolute values between 2005 and 2015 in the Brazilian Population's World Wide Web access. Research by Torres, Teixeira and França [7], with low-income young people between 15 and 19 years old in Brazil revealed that more than 70% of them claim to study in schools with computers, but there was little use of the equipment, as well as a frequent ban on cellphones and other mobile devices.

As Lévy [8] states, "the emergence of cyberspace follows, translates, and favors a general evolution of civilization". Education, then, must be part of that evolution. In this context, appropriating mobile devices as a privileged interface for content access assumes that

> The current scenario brings a unique situation: the proclaimed extinction of material supports and its replacement by non-supports that had, in fact, been changing by a variety of technologies that simultaneously promote abrupt distinctions and homogenizations, either in texts and readers[1] [9].

Gamification was another strategy chosen in the *Commercium & Cognitionis* (CetC) project because of its configurative approach to game's elements, generally, in non-game situations [4]. One of the most characteristic gamification principles is the tripod *points, badges,* and *leaderboards* (PBL). According to Werbach and Hunter [10], points are a way for the player to track their progress; badges are symbolic indications of tasks fully or

---

[1] "A atualidade apresenta uma situação singular: a apregoada extinção de um suporte material e a sua substituição por um não-suporte que revelou-se, na realidade, a substituição por uma variedade de suportes tecnológicos que promovem simultaneamente abruptas distinções e homogeneizações nos textos e nos leitores".

to be performed; and leaderboards are the comparative way in which players rank their positions in comparison to others, being a fine resource for generating feedback.

These features, so characteristic among a variety of games, resemble the system of grades, distinctions, and classifications in educational tests and exams. The difference lies in what Hunicke, LeBlanc and Zubek [11] characterize in games, structurally, by the acronym MDA: *mechanics*, *dynamics* and *aesthetics*. Therefore, while gamification establishes mechanics that determine the cause and consequence rules among players' interactions, the interest in the process lies in the dynamics produced and, in greater depth, in the aesthetics experienced.

We can say that gamification involves planning interactions to optimize results, influencing interactors' positive actions and attitudes through game resources, without defining absolute win and defeat conditions. Such experiences include matching metrics that monitor the "game" outcome process and skill development. By promoting such processes in groups, intrinsic motivation can be stimulated from socialization and relatedness [12], in which gamification approaches the connectivism of Siemens and Stephen Downes [13]. In addition, according to Bíró [14], gamification, when lining flexible itineraries to meet different learning styles, approaches concepts related to constructivism.

The report produced for the World Government Summit by Oxford Analytica [15] and the literary review by Surendeleg, Murwa, Yun and Kim [16], among other studies, have focused on the subtleties of gamification when applied in educational processes. Mechanics, dynamics, and aesthetics in games are diverse, as much diverse are the possibilities for effects to be produced by their use in instructional contexts. In this sense, we do not seek to adhere to generalizations – either of efficacy nor uselessness of gamification as a one-fits-all solution – but to present an experience of applying certain concepts in an undergraduate course.

3   The *Commercium & Cognitionis* Project

3.1   The Preceding Route

In their first year, students of the Fluminense Federal University (UFF) Journalism course, in Brazil, have a mandatory 60-h *Visual and Graphic Languages* course. It had been taught by the same teacher for about fifteen years when, in 2017, he retired. One of the authors of this article, a professor of the institution in the same emphasis area, was invited to take up the discipline. The teachers had different backgrounds and views on the content and the pedagogical approach, which led to the reformulation of the course syllabus.

Since 2006, the new teacher and other authors of this article have been developing another project integrating games and education: a first-person multiplayer 3D game that would function as a discipline of the same course, but in the online format. *Project Gutenberg*, the work in progress, consisted of a virtual environment simulating a medieval German monastery, where Gutenberg would have developed his printing press [17]. In this environment, students could interact with each other and with contents from interactive objects like codices and scrolls, and doing so, access texts, images, videos, and perform a series of evaluation activities (Fig. 1).

Fig. 1. Reading table and bookcase with codices and scrolls in the living room space.

Unfortunately, given high development costs, it was not possible to fully produce the game, even with almost 90% of the expected content already done. The game narrative was about graphic production processes with emphasis on typography and relief printing processes and would become the first module of the optional 60 h course called *Printed Graphic Production*.

Given the need to take the required discipline and develop strategies and solutions to the problems identified, it was initially decided to take advantage of the developed topics and contents for the online game and update them (Table 1) until they meet the new course objective: to impart initial knowledge about basic elements of graphic-visual systems.

Table 1. Changes in the syllabus topics and respective semesters.

2017.2	2018.2	2019.2
1. Paper	1. Supports	1. Media and Supports
2. Inks	2. Colors and Inks	2. Colors and Inks
3. Woodcut	3. Fonts	3. Editorial Production and Finishing
4. Fonts and Movable Type	4. Layout	4. Layout
5. Editorial Production and Finishing	5. Editorial Production	5. Editorial Production
6. Typographic Printing	6. Graphics Systems	6. Graphics Systems
7. Printing Offices	7. Printing Offices	7. Finishing
8. Graphics Systems	8. Finishing	8. Digital Broadcast
9. Technology Impacts	9. Technology Impacts	9. Technology Impacts

Table 1 indicates the transition from relief printing processes and specific printed media topics to broader *Visual and Graphic Language* topics, including digital media and systems. The change process took four semesters, due to the time needed to research, produce and edit the large number of new texts and videos necessary for the discipline's website.

3.2   The Ongoing Project

Making changes in the discipline was not aimed at promoting a reactive response to a didactic discourse, but rather, to empower students' skills and abilities through a system of rules and procedures geared to motivate them. Our goal was to evoke: (1) collaboration, interaction and partnership; (2) autonomy in the search for knowledge; (3) responsibility in the construction of the knowledge path; (4) flexibility to different styles of teaching and learning; and (5) diversity of expression forms.

The core game mechanic consists in accessing up to 560 different contents employing cards (Fig. 2), associated with a system of rules for scoring. Student-players receive two cards weekly, covering one of the program's nine topics, with printed QRCodes (Fig. 3) that allowed smartphone access to otherwise hidden contents (such as short texts, texts with images and videos) hosted on the course's website, made with WordPress blog structure (Fig. 4). Individual access to content intends to empower responsibility and autonomy in the search for information, as well as to accommodate different learning styles and rhythms.

Fig. 2. "Paper" theme card front.

Fig. 3. QRCode on the back of the card being scanned.

Fig. 4. Access to a video format content.

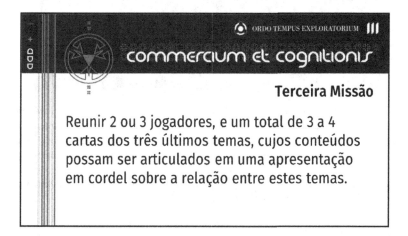

Fig. 5. Third game mission ('Gather 2 or 3 players, and a total of 3 to 4 cards from the last three themes, whose contents can be articulated in a cordel presentation on the relationship between these themes'.).

After receiving the cards, the student-players are informed of a "Mission" that they must fulfill for the following week, articulating among small groups the content accessed through the smartphone (Fig. 5). For each syllabus topic, different missions are proposed, which are equally valued as they include the presentation of a brief research results, either orally, through a video or a product, thus stimulating collaboration and diversity of expression forms (Fig. 6). Pedagogically, it is intended that the articulation between student-players and different contents with a common goal bring meaning to the accessed material. Besides, it stimulates the research and the construction of new knowledge beyond the game, in consonance with the autonomy, accountability, and flexibility objectives.

Missions represent a "challenge" that, in light of ludology, can be defined as an invitation to solve a problem imposed by the participatory system, with the student-player's competence and ability. Choosing which missions to perform in a group responds to the "flow" theory, essential in the gamified process [18], by dynamically balancing the activity's difficulty level with the student-player's skills.

Fig. 6. Oral and visual presentation of the cordel mission (Cordel literature also known in Brazil as a leaflet, popular verse literature, or simply cordel, is a popular literary genre often written in rhyming form, originated in oral accounts and later printed in booklets. Dating back to the 16th century, when the Renaissance popularized the printing of oral accounts, it remains a popular literary form in Brazil. The name stems from the way traditionally leaflets were displayed for sale, hanging from ropes, twine or string in Portugal. Some poems are illustrated with woodcuts, also used on the covers. https://en.wikipedia.org/wiki/Cordel_literature.).

In support of the game dynamics, the teacher deepens the contents each week, bringing audiovisual and/or material resources or promoting a practical workshop. These weekly activities seek to complement any gaps in the information collected by student-players within the game, as well as to exercise debate and transposition of knowledge from the theoretical to the practical dimension.

Another game dynamic was based on content cards, divided into five "suits", each associated with different content types and with a value between 1 and 5, initially unknown by student-players (Fig. 7). The content was quantified according to its categories and values, providing a larger number of single-paragraph texts and fewer videos with more elaborate and "interesting" material. Towards the end of the semester, rules governing these values are revealed and bonuses and discounts are set, according to the "suit" arrangements held by each student-player. To find out the "suits" values, each student-player also receives in the first encounter a card containing one of the 15 existing rules. In the quest to increase their "hand" value, and aided by the knowledge of the rules they can access, student-players are encouraged to exchange their cards. Through this dynamic, we sought to playfully promote dialogue and knowledge exchange, with the consequent expansion of the content scope available to each student.

Fig. 7. The five suits of platonic polyhedra cards.

To enhance the cards search and exchange between student-players, the game also demands them to record each card acquired or exchanged in an online logbook. Each record adds up points to their total score, converted into part of the course grade, which represents the search and contact with each card contents.

Regarding the course, the rules and procedures are intended to enable dialogical and, therefore, nonlinear inter-relationships between subjects based on a linear structure of gradual access of topics. In games, this "lifting" effect based on previous knowledge is known as *scaffolding* [10]: Just as a building relies on its scaffolding to be completed, games consider their players to continuously face challenges and overcome obstacles. By dealing with the content progressively, based on readings and missions' presentations, the teacher can monitor and mediate the work. Doing so, he deepens the content accessed by student-players as the gradual presentation of the game rules also proves to be productive for their understanding, working as a kind of "tutorial mode" that demonstrates what is necessary to know and pay attention to each step.

At the apex of knowledge construction, student-players gather in teams to produce a final assignment, supported by the contents of the cards, missions, classes and any other material, external to the discipline, which they access according to their interest. For the final assignment, students have to produce a printable or digital journalistic publication, given the discipline area (Fig. 8). Teams create editorial lines and develop articles with a direct or indirect focus on the topics discussed. Therefore, the missions also aim to gradually develop the skills and abilities necessary for student-players to accomplish this more complex task. In addition to the publication content, both graphic design and creativity are scored.

Fig. 8. Final assignment "Nona Arte" magazine.

Based on the gamification processes, all activities are rewarded by points, according to their importance concerning the discipline objectives. In addition to the score for registering cards exchanges in the logbook, the final grade includes the missions, the final score of the "hand" of cards and the final assignment: All those within a systemic and procedural assessment of student's development in the learning process. The game dynamics of ranking disclosure and related points obtained are used as a motivation and engagement strategy, as well as encouraging control over their development, both in the game and the course.

3.3   Complementary Adjustments and Strategies

Several project dynamics have been changed after each edition, seeking to enhance the development of competences, motivation, and engagement of student-players. The course syllabus changes (Table 1), in turn, led to the development of new strategies, which have been added to the ongoing project.

New workshops are being developed as a first strategy, in support of the syllabus topics. This was motivated by the curriculum update and the need to broaden the scope of the Typography topic inside the *Visual and Graphic Languages* program, after technological updating of graphic media and related processes, including digital ones. The workshops, still under development, update the thematic topics and seek to integrate the practice of design and digital printed visual-graphic production with videos that stimulate student-players in their final assignment accomplishment.

Nine mini-games are also being developed, as a second strategy for the playful exercise of the program topics. This is in line with the same principles of development of student-player autonomy competences in other languages and resources, closer to their semiotic domains. To achieve positive results in mini-games, the student-player must rely on the content provided in the cards. However, in the absence of these contents, he is expected to exercise both his collaborative competence - in articulation with colleagues - and autonomy - in the external search for information necessary to overcome the challenge proposed by each mini-game.

4   Considerations

At the end of each of the four semesters in which the project was applied, 109 student-players responded to an online survey hosted on Google Drive. This consisted of 5 open and 15 closed questions, about different experiment aspects. About the weekly missions, on average, 80% of the students stated these were necessary for learning, and 66% stated the missions stimulated their research skills. Most relevant, however, was that 80% agreed the missions encouraged the student-players' collaboration.

Collaboration, as it seems, was the most developed skill within the gamified experience, according to 87.7% of respondents, especially when pointing out that their participation in the game was more collaborative than competitive. One of the extensive answers demonstrates this: "No one was competing, the general interest was to get good results in the end and we realized the easiest way to do that was to collaborate with each other". Answers also indicates the proposed interactive format was successful as a way to value collaboration above competition between students. We also detected identities and sociability construction, especially in the accomplishment of weekly group missions [19].

It is also noteworthy that 73.33% of respondents agreed they had good performance in the discipline and 53.3% of them preferred the game to a traditional evaluation form, although only 46.7% of them said they enjoyed playing. However, the most relevant answer was that 66.7% of the students stated gamification contributed to better contents understanding, with participation in the discipline and autonomy development, ratifying the initial project objectives. Lastly, 83.33% of respondents believe the contents will be important in their academic and professional lives, even though they are at the beginning of their course. Once more, another extensive answer leaves us with this comprehension: "I think this more dynamic way of learning through missions has contributed to a better content fixation, which I believe would not happen with lectures".

Most of the printed and digital publications presented in the final course assignments demonstrated quality, both visually and content-wise. These results indicate the development of competences through the missions was central to the student-player's appropriation of the basic concepts of Graphic and Visual Language, especially considering they are newcomers to a Journalism course, with little or no skills in the matter.

Thus, the adoption of active and innovative pedagogical methods which explore competences and skills with game elements made possible to combine systemic and procedural assessment in the discipline, as well as in knowledge construction. The dynamics of the game combined competition and collaboration in the search for knowledge and solution for proposed challenges. Associating the didactic challenge (in the elaboration of the week-by-week presentations and final assignment) with the playful challenge (in the conquest of points to a personal score) balanced the gradual acquisition of discipline contents and the rules knowledge that structured the experience. In order to achieve the ludic objective, the student-player needed to pursue the didactic objective. Our evaluation of the project indicates that dedication to the gamified course positively influenced the academic engagement, stimulating access and meaningful learning about the contents, guaranteeing the student-player autonomy and independence in the educational process.

However, from the feedback obtained from the students, we find that, as for all active methodology, their lack of habit in active participation remains a challenge, shaped by school institution's standards that still remain today, both at Brazilian Basic Education and at University, as the evidence-based evaluative collaboration exemplified in one of the extensive replies: "While it was nice not having tests, it was tiring to almost every week be presenting something new and to do the final assignment at the same time as other disciplines' final tests and assignments".

We believe we have presented an alternative to traditional learning methods, which consider the multimodal media context in which students are inserted, opening the way for greater interaction between them and their teachers, which culminate in engagement and learning [20]. With such strategies, students are kept in a "flow" zone [18], while promoting the development of cognitive processes through stimuli so absent in traditional teaching methods but clearly recognized when games are nearby.

Acknowledgment. The LINC-Design laboratory (PUC-Rio), the Vice-Rectorate for Academic Affairs (VRAC /PUC-Rio), the research group educ@midias.com (UFF). This work was carried out with the support of the Higher Education Personnel Improvement Coordination - Brazil (CAPES) - Financing Code 001.

References

1. UFF: Universidade Federal Fluminense: Curso de Jornalismo - Projeto Pedagógico de Curso: Formulário n° 02 - Princípios Norteadores (Journalism Course - Course Pedagogical Project: Form 2 - Guiding Principles). Curso de Jornalismo, Niterói (2016)
2. Farbiarz, A.: Universidade-aluno: uma ponte em construção (Student-University: a bridge under construction). Dissertação (Mestrado em Educação e Linguagem), Faculdade de Educação. Universidade de São Paulo, São Paulo (2001)
3. Kellner, D.: A Cultura da Mídia – Estudos Culturais: identidade e política entre o moderno e o pós-moderno (Media Culture - Cultural Studies: Identity and Politics between the Modern and the Postmodern). EDUSC, São Paulo (2001)
4. Deterding, S., Khaled, R., Nacke, L.E., Dixon, D.: Gamification: toward a definition. In: CHI 2011 Conference on Human Factors in Computing Systems, pp. 6–9. ACM, Vancouver, Canada, (2011)

5. CETIC.BR: TIC Kids Online Brasil (2016). http://cetic.br/media/analises/tic_kids_online_brasil_2016_coletiva_de_imprensa.pdf. Accessed 03 Oct 2017

6. IBGE: Pesquisa Nacional por Amostra de Domicílios - PNAD (2017). https://www.ibge.gov.br/estatisticas-novoportal/sociais/populacao/9127-pesquisa-nacional-por-amostra-de-domicilios.html?edicao=9131&t=destaques. Accessed 15 Nov 2017

7. Torres, H.G., Teixeira, J.M., França, D.: O que os jovens de baixa renda pensam sobre a escola (What do low-income youth think about school). In: Série Estudos & Pesquisas Educacionais n 4, pp. 167–204. Centro Brasileiro de Análise e Planejamento/Fundação Victor Civita, São Paulo (2014)

8. Lévy, P.: Cibercultura (Cyberculture). Editora 34, Rio de Janeiro (2001)

9. Farbiarz, A., Farbiarz, J.L., Nojima, V.L.M.S.: Uma visão semiótica bakhtiniana relação universidade aluno em cursos de design (A Bakhtinian Semiotic View of University Student Relations in Design Courses), In: 1º Encontro de semiótica aplicada ao design. Núcleo de Design PUC-Rio, Rio de Janeiro (2003)

10. Werbach, K., Hunter, D.: For the Win: How Game Thinking Can Revolutionize Your Business. Wharton Digital Press, Pennsylvania (2012)

11. Hunicke, R., Leblanc, M., Zubek, R.: MDA: a formal approach to game design and game research. In: Challenges in Games AI Workshop, Nineteenth National Conference of Artificial Intelligence, pp. 1–5. AAAI Press, San Jose (2004)

12. Ryan, R.M., Deci, E.L.: Self-determination theory and the facilitation of intrinsic motivation, social development, and well-being. Am. Psychol. **55**(1), 68–78 (2000)

13. Siemens, G.: Connectivism: a learning theory for the digital age. Int. J. Instr. Technol. Distance Learn. **2**, 3–10 (2005). http://www.itdl.org/Journal/Jan_05/article01.htm. Accessed 10 Mar 2016

14. Bíró, G.I.: Didactics 2.0: a pedagogical analysis of gamification theory from a comparative perspective with a special view to the components of learning. Procedia – Soc. Behav. Sci. **141**, 148–151 (2014)

15. World Government Summit: Gamification and the Future of Education. Oxford Analytica Ltd., United Kingdom (2016) http://www.oxan.com. Accessed 15 Aug 2017

16. Surendeleg, G., Murwa, V., Yun, H.-K., Kim, Y.S.: The role of gamification in education – a literature review. Contemp. Eng. Sci. **7**(29), 1609–1616 (2014)

17. Farbiarz, A., Xavier, G., Farbiarz, J.L.: Novas tecnologias no ensino de graduação em Comunicação (New Technologies in Undergraduate Communication Education). ECCOM - Educação, Cultura e Comunicação, vol. 10, pp. 245–255 (2019). http://fatea.br/seer3/index.php/ECCOM/article/view/966/964. Accessed 29 June 2019

18. Csikszentmihalyi, M.: Flow: the Psychology of Optimal Experience. Harper Perennial Modern Classics Edition, New York (1990)

19. Moita, F.: Game on: jogos eletrônicos na escola e na vida da geração @ (Game on: Electronic games at school and in the life of the generation @). Editora Alínea, Campinas, SP (2007)

20. Kapp, K.M.: The Gamification of Learning and Instruction: Game-Based Methods and Strategies for Training and Education. Pfeiffer, New York (2012)

Game Criticism

Personalized Game Reviews

Miguel Ribeiro[(✉)] and Carlos Martinho

INESC-ID and Instituto Superior Técnico, University of Lisbon, Lisbon, Portugal
{miguelmeloribeiro,carlos.martinho}@tecnico.pt

Abstract. One way of subjective evaluation of games is through game reviews. These are critical analyses, aiming to give information about the quality of the games. While the experience of playing a game is inherently personal and different for each player, current approaches to the evaluation of this experience do not take into account the individual characteristics of each player. We firmly believe game review scores should take into account the personality of the player. To verify this, we created a game review score system, using multiple machine learning algorithms, that computes multiple review scores for different personalities which allow us to provide a more holistic perspective of this value, based on multiple and distinct player profiles. Our results support that the approach is statistically and significantly better than using the weighted average score provided by *metacritic.com*, currently one of the most popular websites that aggregate video game reviews, among other media products.

Keywords: Review system · Player model · Machine learning · Digital game

1 Introduction

1.1 Motivation

We believe that the game review industry is an important way to disseminate new games and help players selecting the games to buy [5]. Nowadays there are hundreds of digital game review websites all over the world [5]. However, we noticed that none of them takes into account the individual traits of each person. With this work, we present an innovative system to give personalized game reviews according to each player's personality.

1.2 Problem

Even though recommending games is a well known activity in the game industry, people base their recommendations on their own subjective opinion. To a certain point, these are unreliable reviews unless you have previously seen and agreed with a fair amount of previous reviews from the same reviewer. As a result, a review score can lack meaning for the specific player reading it, as different players will enjoy different games. How can we make review scores more personalized?

© Springer Nature Switzerland AG 2019
N. Zagalo et al. (Eds.): VJ 2019, CCIS 1164, pp. 223–237, 2019.
https://doi.org/10.1007/978-3-030-37983-4_17

1.3 Hypothesis

Defining a player profiling model for both the player and the game, and using machine learning to train our review system based on such profiles, will enable us to provide game reviews scores more suitable for each individual user of the review system.

2 Related Work

2.1 Game Reviews

A review, also called critical analysis, is the study of a particular sector in relation to its pre-established requirements, aiming to give objective information on the same based subjective and personal appreciation. Game Reviews are one kind of review. The purpose of the reviewers is usually to help with the decision making about how to spend money, time, or other resources. Moreover, the aim of game reviews is to help users by leading them to games that make them happy [10]. A well-written game review can attract new players [5].

Nowadays there are hundreds of game review companies, websites or magazines and most of them work with similar methods[1]. We found they only vary in the type of score used in the reviews to evaluate a certain game, usually within a numerical range (e.g. 0 to 10, 0 to 100, 1 to 5), like/dislike ratios, and others similar scales. Such reviews rarely consider the particular preferences of the person evaluating the game. There are several well known cases of online game review websites such as GameSpot[2] and Imagine Games Network[3] (IGN) that work as entertainment websites that do reviews by themselves. On the other hand, GameRankings[4] and Metacritic[5] use a wider approach because they do not do reviews, they work as aggregators from other known websites and magazines that do reviews. GameRankings uses the average of each game review they receive[6], while Metacritic additionally weights individual scores based on the reliability of the sources (these weights are not disclosed to the general public). Both websites normalize the values by converting each review score to a scale from 0 to 100 and then they apply their formula to obtain the final score[7]. Another way of doing game reviews, more popular in Youtube channels as Angry Centaur Gaming[8] and UnfairReviews[9] is to rate the game as a "buy/wait for sale/never touch" (or similar recommendation scale), avoiding using a review score altogether. Finally, digital game distribution platforms such as Good Old

---

[1] http://www.metacritic.com/faq.
[2] https://www.gamespot.com.
[3] https://ign.com.
[4] https://www.gamerankings.com.
[5] http://metacritic.com.
[6] https://www.gamerankings.com/help.html.
[7] http://www.metacritic.com/about-metascores.
[8] https://www.youtube.com/user/AngryCentaurGaming.
[9] https://www.youtube.com/user/UnfairReviews.

Games[10] (GOG) and Steam[11] only use user reviews instead of professional ones. Steam categorizes games based on a like/dislike ratio and GOG uses a 5-point scale. Digital mobile game distribution platforms, such as the App Store[12] and Google Play[13] additionally have an editorial selection of recommended games. Regardless of not all distribution platform provides with user reviews at this time, this is the current trend.

2.2 Player Models

Players tend to have preferences on game genres [7]. Their interests are commonly influenced by the type of player they are and are derived from their personality traits [8]. Although there are diverse ways to model players, in this work we explored four player models that we consider relevant to our work: Bartle Player Types, Quantic Foundry's Gamer Motivation Profile, Demographic Game Design (DGD) and BrainHex. The Bartle Player Types is a study by Richard Bartle that brought us one of the first and most consistent player models, classifying a player's actions in relation to his personality [12]. According to this study, by analyzing the interaction patterns, four different types of players were found [3]. These pattern types are Achievers, Killers, Explorers, and Socialisers, which are relevant to Massive Multiplayer Online games but not always to other game genres.

Quantic Foundry was founded in 2015 by Nick Yee and Nicolas Ducheneaut who came up with an empirical Gamer Motivation Profile (GMP), by gathering data over time from more than three hundred thousand English-speaking gamers from many geographic regions [16]. In this model, there are three high-level motivations, namely Extraversion, Conscientiousness, and Openness (named after the traits from the Five Factor Model [9]) but these can be divided into six middle-level motivations which are Action and Social, Mastery and Achievement, Immersion and Creativity. Then each one of these can be divided into two low-level motivations, based on factor analysis of how they cluster together.

The Demographic Game Design (DGD) model proposed by Chris Bateman is an adaptation of the Myers-Briggs typology to games and it is focused on market-oriented game design [2]. In this model, the players are organized into four categories, namely Conqueror, Manager, Wanderer, and Participant.

The fourth, and last, player model that we studied was the BrainHex model [11]. We claim the BrainHex model to be the more adequate to our work because it is independently measured, we had free access to its coding, was revised in 2008 and based on a study with 60,000 participants. This player model was the successor of the DGD and DGD2, and illustrates gameplay behaviour in terms of seven different archetypes in the human nervous system. These seven dimensions of the BrainHex[14] model are Achiever, Conqueror, Daredevil, Mastermind,

---

[10] https://www.gog.com.
[11] https://www.pcgamer.com.
[12] https://www.appstore.com.
[13] https://play.google.com.
[14] http://blog.brainhex.com.

Seeker, Socialiser and Survivor. The BrainHex model was the model we used in this research for player profiling.

2.3 Game Profiling

Game are generally classified into game genres, e.g. first-person shooters, role-playing games, real-time strategy, etc. This characterization is not without difficulty, and the definition of what constitutes a genre and what are the boundaries between genres has been a matter of debate [13].

In this research, rather than classifying a game based on the inherent challenges and skills required to overcome such challenges with the actions provided by the game [1,8], we classify games by how much they offer the opportunity to the player to experience each dimension of play specified by the BrainHex model, e.g. exploring, interacting with other players, etc. As such, we have developed a "BrainHex" questionnaire for games, that classify them across these dimensions. The full questionnaire can be found in [14].

2.4 Explored Machine Learning Algorithms

Because we wanted to compare our approach to websites that provide aggregate reviews for video games, we decided to use a numerical score for our reviews. Since our system works with numerical and continuous attributes, we only analyzed algorithms that performed within these conditions. In particular, and because we would be using a multidimensional player profiling model, BrainHex, that classifies players into distinct dimensions, we explored the K-Nearest-Neighbor, Linear Regression, M5Prime, and Multilayer Perceptron algorithms [15]. We used the software Waikato Environment for Knowledge Analysis (WEKA), which is a machine learning and data preprocessing workbench [4]. WEKA uses as input a single relational table named Attribute-Relation File Format (ARFF) [6].

3 Methods and Procedures

3.1 Approaches

In our work, we considered two approaches to give personalized review scores, as can be seen in Fig. 1. The first one, Review System (RS), takes into account each player's BrainHex model, and is applied individually for each game. The second approach, Generic Review System (GRS), receives as input the players' BrainHex model and the games' BrainHex model, and can be applied to any game by characterizing the game using the BrainHex model.

3.2 Methodology

We followed a 7-stage pipeline, composed by: *User Questionnaire, Game Filtering, Dataset Filtering and ARFF Preparation, Algorithm Filtering, Review System, Review System Validation* and *GRS and Metacritic Comparison*, as can be seen in Fig. 2. Each stage will be detailed in the next sections.

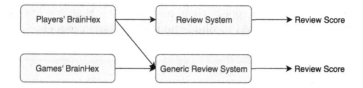

Fig. 1. Two approaches to give personalized review scores.

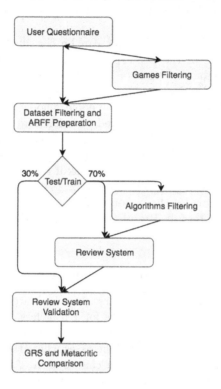

Fig. 2. Flow chart of the six stages of our methodology.

3.3   User Questionnaire

In order to get the BrainHex model of the players and their own evaluation on selected digital games as an integer value between 1 and 10, we created a survey on *Google Forms*. This questionnaire was anonymous and took around 10 min to fill, and was divided into three distinct sections. In the first part we collect the demographic data of the players. Secondly, we asked the players to give their own review score, an integer value between 1 and 10, to the selected digital games. Furthermore in this part of the survey, it had a section for users to add reviews for a maximum of 3 games that were not explicitly in the questionnaire. Lastly, the third section begun by giving a link to the BrainHex test where the players had to fill their survey and report their results. With that, we obtained their personal BrainHex model used to build the review system models.

3.4   Game Filtering

For this work, we chose a list of digital games from different genres, and for the most diverse kinds of systems. We decided to consider only recent games, with maximum of 4 years from their launch at the time of the study, in order to get game reviews from recent memories.

Our hypothesis is that digital games can be classified by how much they support the dimensions of the BrainHex model, in other words, we evaluate their content in terms of the behavior they promote and/or allow. To obtain the 'BrainHex model' of each selected game, we decided to reproduce the Brain-Hex's survey in *Google Forms*, and ask people who have already played the selected game to answer it. The developed questionnaire is composed by items similar to the original BrainHex questionnaire, in which we replaced the user desires by what the game offers in terms of gameplay. For example, while in the original BrainHex survey an item would ask if the participant enjoys to co-operate in-game with strangers, our 'BrainHex' game survey would ask if the game encourages or provides the opportunity for the players to play coopera-tively with strangers. The full 'BrainHex' game questionnaire can be found in [14].

3.5   Dataset Filtering and ARFF Preparation

Our data was filtered in three steps. First, we eliminated all instances of the users that had played the selected games for 1 h or less. In our opinion, 1 h is not enough time to get a consistent idea to evaluate them. This restriction to the dataset was applied in order to remove the cases where the user started to play the game and gave up without giving a chance to it. Afterwards, we divided the obtained data into 70% of the instances for training, and the other 30% for testing. This division was done, separately, for each digital game. Lastly, we imposed another restriction on our training dataset to identify and remove outlier instances, and improve the predictive performance of our review system. We consider outlier instances those reviews that got very different scores compared to the other reviews that had similar player types. This data constraint was applied only for the training set because we did not want to get previous knowledge of the testing datasets. Finally, we created the correspondent ARFF files for both, training and testing datasets.

3.6   Algorithm Filtering

At this stage of the pipeline, we explored and analyzed the four machine learning algorithms mentioned before. We observed that all four algorithms performed similarly and thus, we chose the Linear Regression algorithm because it has a more direct implementation. The idea of the Linear Regression algorithm is to express the class (in our case, the review score) as a linear combination of the attributes (in our case the dimensions of the player's BrainHex model), with predetermined weights. The aim is to come up with good values for the weights that make the model match the desired output. More details on the algorithms selected, their parameters, their performance and the overall selection process can be found in [14].

3.7   Review System

During this part of our methodology pipeline, we had the aim to preprocess, process and analyze the results of our training datasets, using WEKA, and with that create the respective review system models.

3.8   Review System Validation

In the sixth stage of our methodology pipeline, our goal was to evaluate each one of our developed review systems. To achieve that, we used the software WEKA. When we analyzed and validated the accuracy of our review system models, based on our training datasets, we used tenfold cross-validation and the MAE metric, one of the most commonly used measure metrics [15].

3.9   GRS and Metacritic Comparison

In the last step of our methodology pipeline, we had the aim to evaluate and compare the GRS and Metacritic models. To achieve that, we used the software IBM SPSS Statistics, version 25.

4   Results

4.1   Demographic Results

We obtained 300 answers to our questionnaire, for a dataset with a total of 1254 instances of game reviews.

We started our questionnaire by asking respondent gender, where we got 84.3% male respondents and 15.7% female respondents. Then, we asked their age, where we got 9.0% of the answers from people under 18 years old, 54.3% within the range from 18 to 23 years old, 23.3% from 24 to 29 years old, 10.3% from 30 to 39 years old and 3.0% above 39 years old. Afterwards, we asked how often they play digital games, in order to know how they would see themselves as players. Here we divided into not gamer if they answered that do not play digital games, casual gamer if the answer was they play occasionally when the opportunity presents itself, and hardcore gamer if they answered they make some time in their schedules to play digital games. The results in this question showed 56.0% of the users were classified as hardcore gamer, 41.7% as casual gamer, and 2.3% as not gamer.

4.2   Game Filtering Results

A list of the chosen digital games, with their correspondent BrainHex's dimension scores, can be seen in Table 1.

Table 1. The 12 selected digital games with their 7 BrainHex's archetypes scores. Meaning: Achiever (AC), Conqueror (CO), Daredevil (DA), Mastermind (MA), Seeker (SE), Socialiser (SO), Survivor (SU).

Digital game	AC	CO	DA	MA	SE	SO	SU
CoD Black Ops III	16	8	6	17	10	14	13
Clash Royale	8	12	6	6	−8	9	−8
Dark Souls III	14	19	2	14	18	9	7
FIFA 18	2	18	6	−2	−6	14	−8
Fortnite	−2	17	15	8	6	18	1
God of War 4	15	14	2	16	6	−10	4
Grand Theft Auto V	14	5	8	−2	14	10	5
Pokemon GO	19	12	−6	0	4	14	−8
Rocket League	2	14	11	3	−4	14	−1
The Elder Scrolls V	17	9	6	9	20	−10	−2
The Sims 4	14	0	−4	10	4	8	−4
The Witcher 3	16	15	−3	12	20	−10	0

The selected digital games were obtained through an iterative process where, with the open answers to the first 50 questionnaires, we noticed that the games *Clash Royale* and *Rocket League* were being reviewed frequently, so we decided to add them to the study. On the other hand, we observed that the digital games *Civilization VI*, *Gran Turismo Sport* and *Resident Evil VII* that firstly were in the study, were not considered anymore for this research because we got few reviews from the players, and we needed games with several reviews to build more stable and consistent review systems.

We developed a second user questionnaire in order to obtain the BrainHex model for each selected game and to understand the concordance of the players opinions about what the game has to offer. We analyzed the opinion deviation for each BrainHex dimension, by subtracting the lower value from the higher one and normalize it to $[0, 1]$ and express it as a percentage. We did this process game by game, and registered those overall opinion deviations. We analyzed the obtained values for all selected games, and obtained a percentage average of opinion deviations of 12.3%. After collecting all these opinions and analyzing their similarity, we had to decide which of those scores we would use in our model. First, we chose randomly the values for each archetype, from the opinions we already had. Then, for each dimension where the opinions differed by more than 15%, we tested all possible combinations using the Linear Regression algorithm in WEKA and validating it with tenfold cross-validation technique in the GRS model. We studied what values had the lowest MAEs and we selected them.

4.3 Review System Training Results

We developed and explored our review system models using the training dataset files in the software WEKA. The analyzed results for the Linear Regression Algorithm are presented below.

Linear Regression Algorithm Training Results

The outcome of the Linear Regression algorithm is an expression of a class as a linear combination of the attributes with their predetermined weights.

In order to analyze the changes of applying the restrictions to our training datasets, we used the tenfold cross-validation technique in three distinct dataset phases. The first phase was the dataset without restrictions, by this we mean all 877 training instances. The second phase includes all previous instances, except those which users answered that played the selected digital games for one hour or less, where it gave us a total of 843 instances. In the third, and last phase, we added a restriction to the dataset to exclude the identified outliers, which gave us a total of 809 instances. All these results can be observed in Table 2.

Table 2. GRS and the 12 selected digital games with their correspondent number of instances (NI) and overall mean-absolute error (MAE) divided into three phases, the first without restrictions to the dataset; the second without those instances of the games played for 1 h or less; and the third restriction without other identified outliers. Finally, the last column is the improvement percentage, of the overall (MAE) from the first to the third phase.

Digital game	NI	MAE	NI	MAE	NI	MAE	Improvement (%)
GRS	877	1.313	843	1.255	809	1.096	16.5
Call of Duty Black Ops III	42	1.311	41	1.231	40	1.112	15.2
Clash Royale	78	1.498	73	1.407	65	1.044	30.3
Dark Souls III	48	1.354	46	1.108	44	1.031	23.9
FIFA 18	63	1.404	62	1.436	60	1.343	4.3
Fortnite	99	1.856	88	1.712	84	1.393	24.9
God of War 4	47	1.140	46	1.150	45	0.863	24.3
Grand Theft Auto V	117	1.101	114	1.052	109	0.867	21.3
Pokemon GO	132	1.785	128	1.797	123	1.670	6.4
Rocket League	67	1.328	65	1.299	64	1.242	6.5
The Elder Scrolls V: Skyrim	78	1.113	77	1.114	76	1.023	8.1
The Sims 4	49	1.390	46	1.370	44	1.267	8.8
The Witcher 3: Wild Hunt	57	0.965	56	0.860	55	0.667	30.9

We could observe that, with few instances removed, the constraints imposed to the dataset improved the prediction performance of the system for the training dataset. The first constraint imposed to the system, improved the performance of nine out of thirteen review systems, which is considered to be positive. Besides, the second restriction was even more notable because it improved all review systems, and so, we consider them to be our final review systems for all selected games and for the GRS.

4.4   Generic Review System

In this section, we present the Generic Review System using linear regression. Equations 1 and 2 describe the composition and attribute weighting of the obtained linear regression model, where $Review$ is the predicted review score; w_i is the predetermined weight for dimensions i; k is the number of BrainHex model dimensions or archetypes; and a_i is the archetype value of dimension i $(a_0 = 1)$.

$$Review = \sum_{i=0}^{k} w_i \times a_i. \tag{1}$$

The linear regression model obtained for the GRS, was the following:

$$\begin{aligned}
Review = {} & 0.047 \times Achiever - 0.017 \times Conqueror \\
& + 0.014 \times Daredevil + 0.012 \times Mastermind \\
& - 0.020 \times Seeker + 0.019 \times Socialiser \\
& + 0.015 \times Survivor - 0.130 \times AchieverGAME \\
& + 0.000 \times ConquerorGAME - 0.115 \times DaredevilGAME \\
& - 0.092 \times MastermindGAME + 0.028 \times SeekerGAME \\
& - 0.095 \times SocialiserGAME + 0.145 \times SurvivorGAME \\
& + 10.493.
\end{aligned} \tag{2}$$

4.5   Review System Validation Results

During this stage of our methodology pipeline, we validated our developed review systems using the 30% correspondent testing dataset files. In the next subsection, we present and analyze all these results.

Linear Regression Algorithm Validation Results

In this phase, we analyzed and compared the MAE obtained from the training and testing datasets for the selected games and for the GRS. The validation results of the training datasets, after applying all restrictions explained before, with the testing datasets, can be seen in Table 3. It is possible to observe the selected digital games and the GRS, with the respective number of instances and MAEs.

Table 3. The Generic Review System (GRS) and the 12 selected digital games with their correspondent number of instances (NI) and mean-absolute errors (MAE), for Linear Regression algorithm.

Digital game	NI	Linear regression (MAE)
GRS	809	1.381
Call of Duty Black Ops III	40	1.688
Clash Royale	65	1.614
Dark Souls III	44	1.229
FIFA 18	60	1.143
Fortnite	84	2.030
God of War 4	45	0.720
Grand Theft Auto V	109	1.102
Pokemon GO	123	1.670
Rocket League	64	1.414
The Elder Scrolls V: Skyrim	76	1.253
The Sims 4	44	1.526
The Witcher 3: Wild Hunt	55	0.863

Table 4. The Wilcoxon test results with the Z and asymptotic significance (2-tailed) scores and their correspondent review comparisons between Participant-GRS, Participant-Metacritic, and GRS-Metacritic.

	Part-GRS	Part-Metacritic	GRS-Metacritic
Z	−0.956	−5.810	−9.351
Asymp. Sig. (2-tailed)	0.339	0.000	0.000

4.6 Comparing GRS to Metacritic Scores

Metacritic is one of the most worldwide known and active website that aggregates video game reviews at the time of this writing. To understand the significance of the review scores generated by GRS, we decided to compare it with the Metacritic score for the same game. To that end, we start by comparing the distributions of the participant reviews, the GRS reviews and the Metacritic reviews. Since the data does not pass a Normality test (Kolmogorov-Smirnov $p = 0.000$ for all distributions), we will follow a non-parametric approach.

A Friedman test ($\chi^2(2) = 57.242, p = 0.000$) shows there is a statistically significant difference between the three distributions. To better understand where these differences were, we used a Wilcoxon test to compare the different pairs of distributions. The results are presented in Table 4.

Table 5. The Wilcoxon signed ranks test with the Z and asymptotic significance (2-tailed) scores and their correspondent error comparisons between GRS and Metacritic.

	Metacritic Error - GRS Error
Z	-2.867
Asymp. Sig. (2-tailed)	0.004

Metacritic-GRS Error	NI	Mean Rank
Negative Ranks	160	187.83
Positive Ranks	220	192.44
Tie	0	
Total	380	

The obtained results support that the predictive review distribution of our GRS model are indistinct from the participants reviews ($Z = -90.956$, $p = 0.339$). Moreover, it supports that the Metacritic reviews are distinct from both the participants reviews ($Z = -5.810$, $p = 0.000$) and the GRS reviews ($Z = -9.351$, $p = 0.000$). The GRS reviews are thus similar to the participants reviews and significantly distinct from the Metacritic reviews, but not necessarily better.

To understand which model is better, we compared the distributions of GRS and Metacritic prediction errors. In other words, we compare the distribution of the absolute value of the difference between the GRS score prediction and the participant's review score to the distribution of the absolute value of the difference between the Metacritic score and the participant's review score. A Kolmogorov-Smirnov normality test suggests that both distributions do not follow a normal distributions ($p = 0.000$). As such, a non-parametric analysis will be performed.

The results of the Wilcoxon test between the two error distributions (GRS and Metacritic) are presented in Table 5. The Wilcoxon signed rank test supports that there is a significant difference between the two error distributions ($Z = -2.867$, $p = 0.004$). The GRS prediction is thus statistically significantly better (Mean Rank = 187.32) than using the Metacritic score as a predictor of the user review (Mean Rank = 192.44).

Fig. 3. The user Miguel has a predicted review score of 7.8 out of 10, and his six friends with their names, photos and predicted review scores in a circle, or the real review scores in a hexagon, and the highest and lowest BrainHex dimensions in a small green and red circles, accordingly [17]. (Color figure online)

5 Conclusions

Currently, game review scores do not take into account the individual preferences of their readers. This work is an exploratory study in the creation of personalized game reviews, and brings two main contributions to the field.

One the one hand, it explores how a player model such as BrainHex, that captures what is most important for the player in terms of the game experience, provides a good set of features to be explored by machine learning to provide with personalized game reviews. In particular, we showed how linear regression, when applied to a set of 1284 game reviews of 12 games from the whole spectrum of game genres, is able to outperform expert knowledge such as the weighted aggregated review score of Metacritic, which is one of the most popular game review websites at the time of this writing. By taking into account individual preferences, review scores are more accurately predicted by the system.

On the other hand, we explored how a player model, such as BrainHex, could be used to categorize games by the dimensions of play they offer to the player that interact with them, in contrast to the traditional characterization of games as belonging to a certain genre. This allows our Generic Review System to learn from information captured by reviews from other games that offer similar dimensions of play to the player. This also simplifies the maintenance of such a system: adding a new game consist of providing its BrainHex signature. The predicted review should be readily available.

We hope such personalized game reviews will benefit the users of the system by helping players to decide if they should spend their money and time on a specific game. Considering that the game market is each time more saturated with offers, we hope this will lead to less frustration and more confidence in their purchases.

5.1   Future Work and Application

In future research, we will replicate the methods used in our research with other player models or even personality models. Moreover, we think it would be an interesting addition to this work if future studies would take into account more personal information about the players such as gender, age, favorite game genres, and also their background.

Furthermore, we firmly believe our model could be offered through a web service containing a database of BrainHex model for a series of games. The users would enter their BrainHex profile and the web service would provide them with personalized game reviews. Additionally to their predicted game review score, the users would have access to the predicted and real review scores of their friends. Figure 3 shows a possible example. In this example, Miguel has a preview score of 7.8 out of 10 listed along the predicted (circle) and real (hexagon) review scores of his friends. The highest (green) and lowest (red) scores of the BrainHex model of each user is also highlighted. The values presented in Fig. 3 were obtained using our data (the names used are fictional).

Acknowledgments. This work was supported by national funds through Fundação para a Ciência e a Tecnologia (FCT) with reference UID/CEC/50021/2019. We would also like to thank Prof. Layla Hirsh Martínez from Pontificia Universidad Católica del Perú for her advice and support in this work.

References

1. Adams, E.: Fundamentals of Game Design, 3rd edn. Pearson Education, London (2014)

2. Bateman, C., Lowenhaupt, R., Nacke, L.: Player typology in theory and practice. In: DiGRA Conference (2011)

3. Bartle, R.: Hearts, clubs, diamonds, spades: players who suit MUDs. J. MUD Res. **1**, 19 (1996)

4. Bouckaert, R.R., et al.: WEKA - experiences with a Java open-source project. J. Mach. Learn. Res. **11**, 2533–2541 (2010)

5. Huang, J.: What can we recommend to game players?-Implementing a system of analyzing game reviews. University of Tampere, Tampere (2018)

6. Hall, M., Frank, E., Holmes, G., Pfahringer, B., Reutemann, P., Witten, I.H.: The WEKA data mining software: an update. ACM SIGKDD Explor. Newslett. **11**, 10–18 (2009)

7. Lazzaro, N.: Why we play games: four keys to more emotion without story. In: Game Developers Conference (2004)

8. Martinho, C., Santos, P., Prada, R.: Design e desenvolvimento de jogos. FCA (2014)

9. McCrae, R.R., John, O.P.: An introduction to the five-factor model and its applications. J. Pers. **60**, 175–215 (1992)

10. McNamara, A.: Up against the wall: game makers take on the press. In: Game Developer's Conference (2008)

11. Nacke, L.E., Bateman, C., Mandryk, R.L.: BrainHex a neurobiological gamer typology survey. Entertain. Comput. **5**, 55–62 (2014)

12. Quandt, T., Kröger, S.: Multiplayer: The Social Aspects of Digital Gaming. Routledge, Abingdon (2014)

13. Rabin, S.: Introduction to Game Development, 2nd edn. Nelson Education, Toronto (2010)

14. Ribeiro, M.: Personalized game reviews. M.Sc. thesis. Instituto Superior Técnico, supervised by C. Martinho (2019)

15. Witten, I.H., Frank, E., Hall, M.A., Pal, C.J.: Data Mining: Practical Machine Learning Tools and Techniques, 4th edn. Morgan Kaufmann, Burlington (2016)

16. Yee, N.: The gamer motivation profile what we learned from 250,000 gamers. In: Proceedings of the 2016 Annual Symposium on Computer-Human Interaction in Play, p. 2. ACM (2016)

17. VilaGames: FIFA 18 - PS4 n.d. https://www.vilagamesonline.com.br/produto/ps4/fifa-18-ps4-2

The Symbolic Labyrinth in the Mythogame: The Axes Minos-Daedalus and Theseus-Minotaur in the Contemporary Video Game

Antonio José Planells de la Maza[(⊠)]

Tecnocampus – Pompeu Fabra University, 08302 Mataró, Barcelona, Spain
aplanells@tecnocampus.cat

Abstract. This research is based on the mythical stories that develop the concept of the labyrinth, both as a physical structure and as a symbolic and psychological space, in its application to contemporary video games. Through the stories of Daedalus, Minos, Theseus, Ariadne and the Minotaur we analyse, on the one hand, the physical use of the labyrinth as a game structure and, on the other hand, the symbolic design of the mythems in the mythogame.

From the symbolic dimension we establish a double axis of analysis: the axis of the relationship between creation and power represented by Daedalus and Minos and, on the other hand, the relationship between the hero and the challenge exemplified in the case of Theseus and the Minotaur. Finally, we make a vindication of Ariadne's thread as a metaphor derived from the labyrinths without challenge and with a single path through the genre of walking simulators.

Keywords: Video games · Labyrinth · Maze

1 Introduction

From ancient Babylon to the present day, the labyrinth has become a mystery, a complex and hidden element that has had multiple readings according to the cultural context in which it emerges. Thus, from the symbolic perspective, it has been considered a simile or evocation of the religious underworld [1], the duality between life and death [2] or even, from the viewpoint of analytical psychology, the metaphor of the mother's body as the first territory to be explored by the child [3]. On the other hand, the labyrinth has also been seen as a tortuous route in which it is sometimes easy to lose one's way without a guide [4], deriving from this perspective all kinds of physical constructions (gardens, parks, palaces, temples or other architectural projects). In this sense, what impact has the labyrinth had on video games, both symbolically and physically?

In this research we analyse the impact of the concept of the labyrinth, both as a physical structure and in its mythical-symbolic manifestation, through two mythical stories that are very popular in Western culture: the construction of the labyrinth of Daedalus under the order of Minos and the struggle between Theseus and the Minotaur. From these texts we are interested in verifying to what extent the game is, on the one

© Springer Nature Switzerland AG 2019
N. Zagalo et al. (Eds.): VJ 2019, CCIS 1164, pp. 238–247, 2019.
https://doi.org/10.1007/978-3-030-37983-4_18

hand, a labyrinth with spaces of freedom in which its actors participate in the primi-genian cosmovision and, on the other hand, an expressive medium that actively par-ticipates in the cultural heritage of our societies, beyond the productive and capitalist discourses of its industrial side.

To this end, we will use Durand's mitocritic [5] and we will carry out a qualitative analysis of certain mythemes, that is, of the smallest mythically significant units. In this sense, the mythical units that define the structures of the imaginary (and that are necessary to analyse the videoludic labyrinth from the symbolic perspective) are the archetypes [6] of Minos, Daedalus, Theseus, the Minotaur and Ariadne. We will not directly apply the mythical text but we will analyze the video game as a story that is executed and, even more concretely, as a system in which playable actions [7] suppose the most expressive form of the interactive medium. Thus, video games as playable myths are not defined exclusively by their verbal or visual inheritance, but also (or mainly) by how they overlap the symbolic-mythical essence in the interaction with the player.

For all these reasons, we first explain the mythical stories, their evolution and the relationship between the archetypes. We then give a brief introduction to the concept of the labyrinth in video games as a physical space and then we analyse it from the symbolic perspective using the axes in pairs of the mythical archetypes.

2 The Mythical Stories of the Labyrinth

2.1 Minos and Daedalus

Apollodorus [8] tells that from the union of Princess Europe and Zeus (who, according to certain versions of the myth, would have kidnapped her by adopting the form of a bull) was born Minos, the great king of Crete predestined to control and subdue much of the Greek islands and the Peloponnese. Minos, at the zenith of his conquests, married Pasiphaë, and had several children including Androgeus and Ariadne.

But the mythical cycle demands the rise and fall of its protagonists, especially when they awaken the envy of the gods [4, 9, 10]. Thus, the anger of the god Poseidon at the fault of the king of Crete (the promised and failed sacrifice of a beautiful white bull) provoked his revenge: Pasiphaë would fall in love with the white bull and, with the help of Daedalus, the expert Athenian artisan who at that time was in the court of Knossos, the queen would consummate her sexual intercourse using a fake wooden cow into which she would enter, to confuse the bull. From this relationship would arise a monstrosity: the Minotaur (or Bull of Minos), named Asterion, a creature with the head and tail of a bull and the body of a man.

Family embarrassment fell upon Minos and, after visiting the Oracle, he forced Daedalus to design an intricate labyrinth in which to confine the monster forever. But this was not the king's only tragedy. Prince Androgeus, who had gone to participate in the pan-Athenean festivities, died in combat against the Marathon bull sent by Aegeus, king of Athens (although other versions consider that he was assassinated by young Athenians jealous of his success). Minos, in response, besieged the city and submitted it in exchange for a tribute: every nine years Athens had to send to Crete seven men and seven women to satiate the Minotaur.

2.2   Theseus and the Minotaur

Theseus, son of Aegean, became Athens' most popular hero and was quickly instrumentalised as part of the political propaganda of the Greek polis [10]. After multiple adventures of youth, culminating in the death of the Marathon Bull, Theseus was recognized by Aegeus as his son and, from this moment on, his future was tied to the destiny of his family and city. It had been 18 years since Minos imposed tribute on Athens and, on this occasion, Theseus volunteered to kill the Minotaur.

Once on the island of Crete, and according to his real origin, Minos invited Theseus to dinner, where he met Ariadne. The young woman fell in love with the Athenian prince and, after speaking with Daedalus (who gave her a sword and a long ball of thread), decided to help Theseus in exchange for marrying him and returning to Athens together. Theseus accepted.

At the entrance to the labyrinth, the young Athenian tied one end of the ball and went alone in search of the monster. After an arduous battle, Theseus emerged victorious and, after recovering the wool thread, he found his way out and was able to escape from the labyrinth.

The final part of the myth is tragic for those who supported Theseus. Ariadne was abandoned (according to the different versions, because of Theseus' laziness or because of Dionysus' intervention to marry her later) and Daedalus and his son, Icarus, were locked up in the labyrinth. Using wings made by the Athenian builder both rose above the labyrinth but with different results: Daedalus survived but Icarus got too close to the sun, lost the wax that attached the wings and fell forever into the depths of the sea.

3   Labyrinths, Mazes and Games

As we have seen in the previous section, the mythical stories around the labyrinth prefigure both a spatial and symbolic structure that easily takes us back to the ludic foundations of the contemporary video game. From a point of view of the essential myths of the original texts, Theseus (the hero or player) must end up with a threat (the Minotaur and, therefore, the power of Minos over Athens, or game challenge) through a structure full of dangers (the labyrinth of Daedalus or the game levels) with the help of his abilities and Ariadne (the special power of the game hero). But before carrying out the analysis from a symbolic perspective, it is essential to establish the idiomatic differences in relation to the concept of the labyrinth, as well as its particularities.

Unlike other languages, English distinguishes between the concepts of labyrinth and maze. The first and easiest difference appears in the unicursal design of the first and multicursal conception of the second [11, 12]. That is to say, while the unicursal labyrinth foresees a single path where walkers cannot get lost (the user can follow the route marked by the walls that will always eventually reach its destination), the multicursal maze is a more complex structure endowed with multiple branching paths and dead ends in which the intrepid explorer may be lost. Umberto Eco employs the concepts of univiary and mannerist labyrinth, respectively [4], and adds a third type called infinite network [4] or rhizome [4, 11]. In the latter case, the maze has neither inside nor outside and all its points are connected. Now, how do all these theoretical structures affect video games?

Espen Aarseth established already in 1997 the need to reinstate and analyze the double meaning of the word labyrinth (as unicursal and multicursal system) in the same theoretical framework close to the concept of ergodic text [11]. In this sense and going into greater detail, Clara Fernández Vara [12] analyzes this triad in its application to digital gaming. In the case of the unicursal labyrinth, Fernández Vara considers that it is an unproductive structure in videogames since the absence of challenge (the player can only go forward) implies an "on rails" experience, like a theme park ride. Nevertheless, this problem present in the digital game has been almost the hegemonic labyrinthic form in the analog game and, very especially, in the Game of the Goose [13]. In this type of games, the unicursal labyrinth constitutes the essence of the game and the movement, normally determined by an element of chance, allows the player to discover the different contents (symbolic, religious or mystical) of its different squares. This form of labyrinth, found in games from Mehen to Monopoly, was practically hegemonic in board games until the arrival of the so-called Eurogames [14].

On the other hand, the multicursal labyrinth has introduced interesting opportunities for video games, allowing from static mazes in classic games such as Pac-Man (1980) to more dynamic structures, both for their spatial configuration and for the opportunities offered by the different points of view [15]. In this sense, it is remarkable to see how the history of the non-analogue game found in pinball and its complex electromechanical designs a first approach to the multicursal maze [16]. In these first arcades, the physical maze involved entering the metal ball into a network of lights, colours and sounds with the aim of keeping the ball as long as possible within the maze. From this first multicursal experience, the video game has expanded its possibilities of design and creation until today, turning the multicursal maze into a specific genre [16].

The last type of labyrinth, the rhizomatic maze, is for Fernández Vara [12] the one that best expresses the encyclopaedic dimension attributed to video games by Murray [17] and, therefore, allows for greater challenges at the navigation level. Furthermore, this informative fragmentation can be promoted as a ludic challenge thanks to the new procedural proposals and, in general, with the constant search for modern video games to broaden their spatial horizons: from open world games to sandbox games.

Although these three labyrinth models allow us to catalogue the physical configuration of a large part of video games, little or nothing tells us about the symbolic dimension of their mythical origin. Therefore, in the following sections we will see how these physical spaces can interact in three axes relative to the myths previously seen, but from the symbolic: the relationship of creation and power expressed by the artisan Daedalus and the politician Minos, the relationship of hero and challenge created by Theseus and the Minotaur and, finally, the metaphor of Ariadne's thread as a modern vindication of the unicursal labyrinth.

4 Daedalus and Minos: Mazes of Creativity and Power

The maze is often considered an inextricable and impenetrable structure, but also a prodigy of human ingenuity. In this sense, artistic vision and architectural design made of its creator, Daedalus, a renowned craftsman and, in general, the symbolic father of builders [18]. Thus, while the Athenian creator symbolises technique and creativity in the creation of structures, Minos, the implacable Cretan king, symbolises the exercise of a tyrannical power that needs to hide its own miseries (in this case, family tragedies) in order to maintain the symbolic and political status of his position. Son of Zeus, and punished by the gods, Minos first confines the beast, turns him into a legend and then confines the builder and his son. In other words, Minos stands as a metaphor for implacable and proud power, but cowardly and fearful of his own miseries. He thus becomes a wall [19].

In this way, the axis between Daedalus and Minos represents the relationship between technique and creativity at the service of a specific type of power that instrumentalises it for very specific purposes. The idea of the player as the builder Daedalus has found multiple representations, especially in games in which the construction technique emerges as the main game mechanic. In this case, we refer to the entire tradition of games ranging from *SimCity* (Maxis, 1989) to *Minecraft* (Mojang, 2011) or *Super Mario Maker 2* (Nintendo, 2019). Similarly, Minos' exercise of despotic power has been reflected in the comic saga *Tropico* (PopTop Software, 2001–2019). In these games, the player plays the role of a Caribbean dictator who brings together the main defining notes of the Cretan tyrant: the opaque exercise of absolute power but which is, in turn, deeply fearful of the different social collectives that populate the island and may become a threat [20]. There is also a set of games that combine part of the literal construction of a maze with a despotic exercise of power to subject it to its control. In this case, titles such as *Dungeon Keeper* (Bullfrog Production, 1997) or *Dungeons* (Realmforge Studios, 2011) place the player in a curious position: he must build a physical maze (Daedalus) and, in turn, he must protect its heart (the shame of Minos) from intruders.

However, the title that has deepened the most in the Daedalus-Minos axis is not so much linked to the literal mechanics of construction and management of mazes as to the submission and acceptance that the creator has towards a given power. In this case, *Papers, Please* (Lucas Pope, 2013) simulates the daily life of a border crossing immigration officer in the fictional totalitarian state of Arstotzka in which the player must decide, through an ingenious puzzle system, who can enter and who cannot. The game establishes a private, partial and rigid moral system in which the user cannot negotiate its moral impact through decision making, partly because of imperfect and incomplete information, partly because of the labyrinthine design of alienation typical of totalitarian bureaucracies [21]. The symbolic and mental labyrinth developed by Pope's title entails a framework of constructive cooperation: the player (Daedalus) participates actively in the repressive action (Minos) accepting certain decisions as long as they favour his main strategy. An example can illustrate this: A woman is persecuted by her abusive husband. She does not have the papers to access Arstotzka. The player may decide to let the woman pass or not. A priori seems to be an easy decision (it is always better to let her in to prevent her from dying at the hands of the abuser). However, *Papers, Please* establishes a bureaucratic penalty system whereby any incursion into the territory of the State by a subject without valid papers implies a significant discount on the salary of the civil servant who has allowed it. At the moment when the family of the inspector has problems to acquire food, medicine or a dignified living conditions is when the dilemma emerges.

Papers, Please exposes a Daedalus who accepts Minos' orders, the established power, simply out of pragmatism. The absence of reflection on the acts gives way to obedience to orders, to a bureaucratization that does not imply evil but its banalization [22]. Far from being a monster, *Papers, Please* turn the player into a bureaucrat, into an entity that participates in the construction and maintenance of a psychological, social and political labyrinth that an authoritarian, cowardly and opaque power decided to raise.

5 Theseus and the Minotaur: Hero and Challenge

As stated above, Theseus personifies not only a hero but a nation. In his origin, Theseus incarnates the pre-Trojan hero who must pass multiple tests (usually against mytho-logical monsters) as he shows both the moralizing and civilizing spirit of Athens itself [23] and the highest ideals of humanity [2]. Thus, the victory of the hero of the polis against the Minotaur is inscribed in the growing power that Athens displayed towards its rivals and, most especially, against the Minoan civilization [24].

In later times, under the influence of Christianity, the relationship between Theseus and the Minotaur is based on the values of salvation and condemnation. Thus, according to Kerényi [1], the Minotaur, located in the center of the labyrinth, appears as the representative of hell, the demon. The path of the maze is a wrong way leading to perdition unless the new Theseus (Christ) brings salvation with him.

While Theseus undergoes small modifications (from a state hero with certain weaknesses and punished by the gods to the incarnation of the pure Christian hero) it will be the figure of the Minotaur that will show the greatest complexity. Born of a forbidden relationship, he will suffer a profound dehumanization. Thus, his name will change from Asterion to Minotaur, thus broadening its monstrous dimension and denying all possible humanity [23]. Imprisoned for life in the labyrinth, he will end up becoming its centre and the symbol of the threat to all those who go astray in unknown territory [19]. In contrast to Theseus, the Minotaur thus appears to be evil, irrational and sinful.

However, not all visions have been limited to this simplification. Far from being the other side of the coin of the heroic Theseus, the Minotaur can also be understood as a single and marginalized being, the scapegoat of a family shame that passively observes an adverse and continuous world that he fails to understand [2]. This was precisely the perspective taken by Jorge Luis Borges in his short story *The House of Asterion* (1947) in which a childish and innocent Asterion plays alone or with a double imaginary in his house, the Cretan labyrinth. Far from being a violent and bloodthirsty animal, Asterion is naive, reflective and awaits for a prophecy: to be liberated from his loneliness. In this short story, the Minotaur is the true hero, the one who suffers calvary and confinement.

His wait is his victory, while a Theseus stunned by the ease of his mission ("The Minotaur barely defended himself" he will say) will become the help Asterion needs to sublimate his end [2].

From a ludic perspective, the axis has also seen different degrees of depth depending on the ludofictional world [25] it wants to be traced. The most basic, that of the hero who must put an end to the evil unleashed by a beast, is also the most common, and is already present in the inheritance of the first role-playing games. In this sense it is also very interesting to see how video games have deepened some other visions, both of Theseus and of the Minotaur.

On the part of Theseus his journey into the maze is the most common. This is where the aforementioned role-playing and digital games are inscribed, with multiple examples such as the classic *Theseus and the Minotaur* (TSR, 1982; a game in which, curiously enough, the objective is to save a captive Ariadne and then escape from the maze), *Eye of Beholder* (Westwood Studios, 1991) or *Diablo III* (Blizzard Entertainment, 2012). On the other hand, when the hero has to flee from the maze, the symbolic level becomes stronger. The playable myth or mythogame, as a "bastard" language that interweaves the classical heritage with the possibilities of interaction with a player [7], has connected the heroes fleeing from the maze with contemporary cultural contexts. Thus, cybertextual heroes [26] (the protagonist and the player's interaction) are today a disturbed Theseus with an absence of epicity. That is to say, a Theseus that no longer embodies the high values of Humanity, but Humanity itself. Son of a troubled time [27], between economic, psychological and humanitarian crises, he tries to escape from complex mazes, without the help of Ariadne, and always subject to a directed freedom [28] more pronounced than ever. This is the case with games such as *Spec Ops: The Line* (Yager Development, 2012), a war maze where the heroic actions of a deranged Theseus are questioned, *The Stanley Parable* (Davey Wreden, 2013) where the story of the hero in relation to his autonomy is put in tension, *Bioshock* (2K, 2007), where the flight is marked by a voice of authority (Frank Fontaine as a particular Minos), *Portal* (Valve Corporation, 2007), where a cybernetic Minos plays with the protagonist or *This War of Mine* (11 bit studios, 2014), a disempowered Theseus that will have to escape the horrors of war only with the abilities of the civilian population.

On the other hand, the Minotaur has hardly played a leading role in video games. Although it is common to find evil heroes whose moral background hardly affects their heroic character (for example, in *God of War* (SCE Santa Mónica Studio, 2005–2018)) it is not easy to find, on the other hand, the incarnation of really evil beings. Some proposals such as *Overlord* (Triumph Studios, 2007) make it possible to control evil, but always with a touch of comedy and, in a way, quickly generating a position of heroism.

A game that has given a different impulse to the classic relationship between an unbroken hero and a perverse demon, and that has brought him closer to Borges' resemantization of the Asterion perspective, is *Undertale* (Toby Fox, 2015). In *Undertale* an ancient war between Humans and Monsters condemned the latter to live in the Underground Maze. Years later, the protagonist (called Frisk, but whose name does not appear in the whole game) falls into a deep cave and, from that moment on, our particular Theseus will have to interact with different monsters in order to leave this unique maze. What differentiates *Undertale* from other role-playing games is not so much the archetypal structure (hero, maze, and monsters as a threat to their exit) as the possibilities of interaction. The encounters with the monsters are solved with specific mini-puzzles for each one of them and, in general, they allow to follow a violent (combat) or peaceful route (dialoguing and listening to the problems of each creature of the Underground). In Fox's game, the voice of Asterion appears as an option and, for this reason, it is possible to humanize both the monsters and the protagonist. It is possible not to kill any of them and even gain their trust and friendship. In fact, the most conciliatory end is also that of the inversion of heroism: the understanding of others makes monsters and humans live together in a common world in which the maze can no longer exist.

6   The Return of the Unicursal Labyrinth: Ariadne's Thread

Until now we have seen how the video game, in its form of a multicursal maze, established a clear ludic structure, whether physical, symbolic or psychological. Now, what about the unicursal labyrinth?

As we saw previously, Fernández Vara considers that the unicursal labyrinth is not usually useful as a game structure. In this way, although a unicursal game can pose certain conflicts along the way (puzzles, obstacles or enemies, to give just a few examples) [11], in the end the structural experience "on rails" notably limits the demand for challenges [12]. Although this is still the case, it is also true that in recent times a new genre of games has emerged that has enjoyed great popularity and that exalts, precisely, the idea of the unicursal labyrinth: the so-called Walking Simulators.

Walking simulators have been defined, with considerable controversy, as games whose central mechanics are the immersive use of exploration and the application of the environmental storytelling [29]. They are unicursal labyrinths that prioritize the discovery of a story through walking and the interaction of different objects, thus approaching the Romantic tradition of walking as an aesthetic practice [29]. It is also important to highlight the relevance not only of the environmental storytelling but especially of what is known as indexical storytelling, that is to say, the generation of stories through traces, both on the part of the designer and on the player [30]. In the case of walking simulators, we are dealing with a storytelling produced by the designer that can be called "interpretation of remains", in other words, a story constituted by the traces left behind by other agents who have previously inhabited this space. In this way, the union of the game mechanics of walking and interacting with objects provokes the emergence of a story that, in the absence of immediate conflict, arises with its own rhythm and time, together with the interpretative process that the player must carry out.

Nowadays, one of the most popular walking simulators is *What Remains of Edith Finch* (Giant Sparrow, 2017). In this game the protagonist, Edith Finch, suffers a family curse in which all but one of the members of the same generation die. After the death of her mother, Edith returns to the family's home to learn, through small experiences, how each of them died. In this way, Giant Sparrow's game drives us through a labyrinth and accompanies us, like Ariadne's thread, in each stop we must make to understand, chronologically, the different family tragedies. In this sense, the thread of Minos' daughter has always been conceived as the mutual connection of the different phases of existence, in their simplest or most intricate forms, but always pointing out, as a vital knot or nucleus, a concrete cohesion [4]. This is precisely the meaning of Edith's experience: the absence of challenge and the dramatic support that, like Ariadne's thread, deals with the different phases of life but, above all, deals with its global meaning.

7 Conclusions

The relevance of the stories about the labyrinth lies neither in its narrative structure (which influences traditional role-playing and its digital transition as primitive game quests) nor physically (which impacts on the conformation of the genre of game mazes), nor even in the direct application of archetypes to the fictional world. Its true impact emerges when the video game, or rather, the mythogame, turns the entire symbolic heritage into playable actions, allowing the player to intervene more or less broadly in everything that happens in the fictional world, associating it in an integral way with its social, cultural and political context.

From the point of view of the multicursal maze, that is, the one that allows multiple paths and exposes the player to a system of challenges, the contemporary video game remains anchored in a strong dependence on the classic archetypes: the construction of the maze as a simple space in which the player, represented by a perfect hero, will end up defeating the forces of evil, incarnated in a set of enemies of different power. However, some titles have tried to go further, putting the themes in dialogue with their social context and translating the conclusions of this debate into meaningful and powerful playable actions. This is the case, for example, of *Papers, Please* as the framework of a bureaucratic Daedalus who, alienated in the face of pragmatism, actively supports the maze erected in honour of the authoritarianism of a modern Minos. Or that of *Undertale*, a role-playing game where the relationship between Theseus and the Minotaur is called into question in order to highlight other possible non-violent ludic possibilities and which manages to humanise both the merciless hero and the heartless monster.

Finally, Ariadne's thread, the classic metaphor of the union of the different vital phases in a linear and coherent route, takes on special relevance with the arrival of walking simulators, a type of game that emphasizes the exploration of space without the need for conflict or challenge: it is, therefore, a form of storytelling focused on the walk and interaction with objects applying techniques such as environmental storytelling and indexical storytelling. In this sense, games such as What Remains of Edith Finch claim the unicursal labyrinth as an aesthetic walk that experiments with the different life phases of a family trauma.

References

1. Kerényi, K.: En el laberinto. Siruela, Madrid (2006)
2. Ramírez, D.: Morador de laberinto: mito, símbolo y ontología en "La casa de Asterión", de Jorge Luis Borges. Ciencia Ergo Sum **18**(3), 225–232 (2011)

3. Grotstein, J.: Klein's archaic Oedipus complex and its possible relationship to the myth of the labyrinth: notes on the origin of courage. J. Anal. Psychol. **42**, 585–611 (1997)
4. Santargangeli, P.: El libro de los laberintos. Siruela, Madrid (2002)
5. Durand, G.: De la mitocrítica al mitoanálisis. Anthropos, Barcelona (1993)
6. Jung, C.: Arquetipos e inconsciente colectivos. Paidós, Barcelona (2009)
7. Garin Boronat, M.: Mitojuegos. Sobre el héroe y el mito en el imaginario Nintendo. Comunicación **7**(1), 94–15 (2009)
8. Apolodoro: Biblioteca. Gredos, Madrid (1991)
9. Elíade, M.: Aspects du mythe. Gallimard, Paris (1963)
10. García Gual, C.: Diccionario de mitos. Siglo XXI, Madrid (2003)
11. Aarseth, E.J.: Cybertext: Perspectives on Ergodic Literature. Johns Hopkins University Press, Baltimore (1997)
12. Fernández Vara, C.: Labyrinth and Maze. Video game navigation challenges. In: Space Time Play, pp. 74–77 (2007)
13. Martínez Vazquez de Prada, M.J.: El tablero de la Oca. Juego, figuración, símbolo. 451 Editores, Madrid (2008)
14. Woods, S.: Eurogames: The Design, Culture and Play of Modern European Board Games. McFarland, Jefferson (2012)
15. Planells de la Maza, A.J.: El cine primitivo y el nacimiento de los videojuegos. Usos sociales y analogías estéticas. Telos **88**, 46–57 (2011)
16. Mateu, F.: Analogías y divergencias de la simbología laberíntica entre cine y videojuegos. Quaderns **12**, 69–86 (2017)
17. Murray, J.H.: Hamlet on the Holodeck: The Future of Narrative in Cyberspace. The MIT Press, Cambridge (1997)
18. Reed Doob, P.: The Idea of the Labyrinth. From Classical Antiquity Through the Middle Ages. Cornell University Press, London (1990)
19. Buhigas Tallon, J.: Laberintos. Historia, mito, geometría. La esfera de los libros, Madrid (2013)
20. Planells de la Maza, A.J.: Mundos posibles, grupos de presión y opinión pública en el videojuego Tropico 4. Trípodos **37**, 63–77 (2015)
21. Sicart, M.: Papers, please. Ethics. In: Thomas Payne, M., Huntemann, Nina B. (eds.) How to Play Video Games, pp. 149–156. New York University Press, New York (2019)
22. Arendt, H.: Eichmann in Jerusalem. Viking Press, New York (1963)
23. Mills, S.: Theseus, Tragedy and the Athenian Empire. Claredon Press, Oxford (1997)
24. Cox, K.: Labyrinths: Navigating Daedalus' Legacy: the Role of Labyrinths in Selected Contemporary Fiction. The University of Hull, Hull (2005)
25. Planells de la Maza, A.J.: Possible Worlds in Video Games: From Classic Narrative to Meaningful Actions. Carnegie Mellon University ETC Press, Pittsburgh (2017)
26. Molina Ahumada, E.P.: Lo heroico en clave digital: mito, literatura y videojuego. Espéculo **54**, 80–92 (2015)
27. Pérez Latorre, O., Navarro Remesal, V., Planells de la Maza, A.J., Sánchez Serradilla, C.: Recessionary games. Video games and the social imaginary of the Great Recession (2009–2015). Convergence (2017). https://doi.org/10.1177/1354856517744489
28. Navarro Remesal, V.: Libertad dirigida. Una gramática del análisis y diseño de videojuegos. Shangri-la Ediciones, Valencia (2016)
29. Carbo-Mascarell, R.: Walking simulators: the digitization of an aesthetic practice. In: Proceedings of 1st International Joint Conference of DiGRA and FDG, vol. 13, no. 1. DiGRA, Dundee (2016)
30. Fernández Vara, C.: Game spaces speak volumes: indexical storytelling. In: Proceedings of DiGRA 2011 Conference: Think Design Play, vol. 6. DiGRA, Utrecht (2011)

Classifying Multiplayer Hybrid Games to Identify Diverse Player Participation

Ryan Javanshir[✉], Beth Carroll, and David Millard

University of Southampton, Southampton, UK
{rjlg15, e.carroll, dem}@soton.ac.uk

Abstract. Hybrid games are types of games that use multiple media channels, technologies or domains to expand the magic circle of play. However, there is little research on the classification of such games, and how different types affect player participation. We use a model to formalize the various structures of hybrid games, construct a classification scheme and use this as a platform for discussing how different types of hybrid games affect player participation. This paper provides a methodology whereby hybrid games can be classified, potentially fostering ideas for diverse hybrid games to be made. These classifications also enable assumptions to be made about how player participation varies depending on the channel structure of a hybrid game.

Keywords: Hybrid games · Game design · Transmedia · Player participation

1 Introduction

In *Homo Ludens*, Johan Huizinga coined the term "magic circle of play" [6], to describe the demarcation between reality and a game world. He elaborates: "All play moves and has its being within a play-ground marked off beforehand either materially or ideally, deliberately or as a matter of course" [6]. Although inside the magic circle is the content of the game and its play, the magic circle itself is constructed by the players. As Salen and Zimmerman explain "To play a game means entering into a magic circle, or perhaps creating one as a game begins ... The game simply begins when one or more players decide to play" [17].

As more technologies and media channels become available to us, there is greater opportunity to both expand the magic circle, and create Venn diagram magic circles where different levels of participation occur. One example is the popularization of virtual reality (VR) multiplayer games. Research into the design of games that utilise VR with other media channels for multiplayer have provided insight into how added immersion and perspectives afforded to by VR mixed with multi-channel multiplayer can promote diverse gameplay [5, 10, 12, 15]. Such games create not only new and interesting forms of gameplay, but also provide tools for team building, communication exercises, interview tools and learning [1, 2, 4, 16, 19].

Although such games offer fruitful ground for exploring how multi-channel games can be designed, VR is only one channel that can be utilised to reshape the magic circle of play [6]. Games that blend different methods of play and require players to use

© Springer Nature Switzerland AG 2019
N. Zagalo et al. (Eds.): VJ 2019, CCIS 1164, pp. 248–260, 2019.
https://doi.org/10.1007/978-3-030-37983-4_19

different channels are sometimes known as *hybrid games*. This broad term encompasses many different types of game, including blending table top games with livestreaming tools that invite the audience into the magic circle [11], augmenting gameplay using Sifteo Cubes [10], and including live motion captured facial expressions as a mechanic in the game [18].

We aim to use a model [7] to formalize the various structures a hybrid game can take, constructing a classification scheme. We then use this to discuss how various forms of participation can occur within each type, addressing the question to what extent does the channel structure of a hybrid game affect player participation?

2 Background

In this section, we explore the concept of a hybrid game, including its definition, and how they are identified. We then consider literature from the field of transmedia storytelling to provide ideas of varying player participation.

2.1 Hybrid Games

The research surrounding hybrid games includes confusion with the term itself. Much research concerns itself with augmented board games [14], with definitions being determined by the technology that is used. Magerkurth takes a technological approach in defining hybrid games, commenting: "in contrast to traditional computer entertainment, hybrid gaming applications define game elements from the physical and the social domains as integral parts of the gaming experience" [13]. Other approaches such as [9] seek to take a cognitive approach, where hybridity is understood as an experience of various domains blending together. They argue that a cognitive approach "enables the inclusion of hybrid games outside of technological compositions, where the hybridity is not a result of new technology" [9]. Thus, they see hybrid games as "blends of different conceptual domains related to games" [9], where the domains themselves are subjectively determined by the interpretation of those identifying the hybridity.

2.2 Player Participation

The inherent characteristics of unique domains and media channels in hybrid games offer not only opportunities for diverse gameplay, but also different levels of player participation. Drawing from transmedia storytelling discourse, we can appreciate that different media channels means different content for diverse audiences. In Convergence Culture, Henry Jenkins defines participatory culture as an environment that blurs the distinction between producer and audience, contrasting to the "older notions of passive media spectatorship" [8]. Applied similarly to hybrid games, audiences of streams are no longer passive consumers of gameplay. Players are not limited to watching their friends play when there are not enough controllers, because they too can become involved by downloading the instruction manual that is part of the hybrid game, and help complete the puzzle. Extending this, we can borrow the idea discussed by Christy Dena when she talks about Alternate Reality Games (ARG) [3]. In her work she quotes ARG designers 42 Entertainment: "tens of thousands of enthusiasts mobilized in public for pervasive missions, three-quarters of a million active participants working online to talk about and solve the immersive mystery, and nearly two-and-a-half million casual participants tracking the experience" [3], to illustrate how works can provide different content for various audience members looking for different types of experiences. Using the term tiers, she comments that various techniques "provide separate content to different audiences and in doing so facilitate a different experience of a work or world" [3]. Similarly, we can design hybrid games that use different media channels to facilitate different levels of participation and accommodate the skills and desires of various players.

3   Methodology

In [7], a model was developed that could capture the key elements of ARGs and transmedia stories. In this paper, we sought to modify this model and use it to formally represent different types of hybrid games. The model has proven to be a useful tool in representing stories that use multiple media channels, and so is justifiably utilised to represent games that use multiple media channels.

3.1   The Hybrid Game Model

The model is based around the concept of a channel; a subset of a media channel that is defined by its boundary. Channels communicate different information and require different skills to navigate. Players use channels to participate in the game, such as a VR headset, a PDF book, a mobile phone or a PC game. Using a more domain approach, we might include a subset or genre of a PDF a unique channel e.g. instruction manual vs. a novel. Channels can consist of instances that have either a passive or active characteristic. Instances denote the various ways in which a channel is consumed e.g. A person playing a VR games can stream their content, spawning two instances with the first being the active channel controlled by the player and the second being the passive content on a screen observed by an audience. Instances are associated with players, indicating what channels the players are using to participate in the game. We have opted to model five players, as this is sufficient for the purposes of this study.

Figure 1 shows an example hybrid game. This game uses multiple channels together to create a single magic circle of play. Player one is playing on a PC, player two is using a mobile and has access to the PDF, player three is on a console, player four is using VR and player five only has access to the PDF.

Example

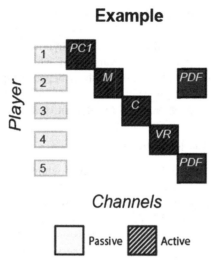

Fig. 1. An example hybrid game

3.2 Identifying Various Hybrid Games

We use examples in section four of different games that are currently available to play. We started our search for these games on the *Steam* platform, then followed the 'recommended titles' and 'more like this' links as well as discussions in community boards which lead us to other similar titles. We use these examples to illustrate our different categories of hybrid games, and not as an exhaustive list of hybrid games. We picked our examples based on popularity and how well the game illustrated the types identified in Sect. 4. Table 1 shows the games we use as illustrative examples. For practical reasons, it is impossible to systemically review all the affordances of each type in each genre of game. Consequently, we focus primarily on multiplayer hybrid games that have a large puzzle element.

Table 1. Example hybrid games

Title	Publisher	Publication date
Keep Talking and Nobody Explodes	Steel Crate Games	2015
Star Trek Bridge Crew	Ubisoft	2016
The Jackbox Party Pack 3	Jackbox Games	2016
Screencheat	Samurai Prank	2014

4   Classification of Hybrid Games

In this section, we identify eight different types of hybrid game, illustrate them using the model introduced in Sect. 3, give examples of what games use this type, and provide some discussion around the relationships between types and player participation. These types of hybrid game illustrate eight ways in which a game may be presented, giving different players access to different channels.

4.1   Type 1: One Segregated with Many

This type involves one player using a single channel whilst the rest of the players share another channel. In Fig. 2, player one is playing in VR whilst the other players are using a PDF, as seen in *Keep Talking*. Player one does not have access to the PDF and the other players cannot see the VR content. The PDF channel has been included as a single channel, but this does not mean that there is only one PDF being viewed, or one printed PDF. It means that these players have access to the same PDF information.

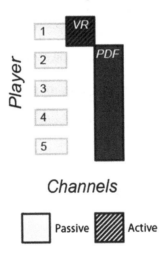

Fig. 2. Type 1 model

This type is effective in segregating player one from the rest of the group, potentially creating a sense of exclusion and panic in that player. This is readily seen in *Keep Talking*, where player one is subject to the most stress by having to push buttons and cut wires to stop a bomb from exploding, and being completely reliant on the other players, who are equipped with PDF manuals, for instructions on how to do this.

Participation varies, with high participation on the part of player one, and varied participation amongst the other players. In *Keep Talking* players often assign themselves to specific puzzles, which have different levels of difficulty, and require different levels of participation from saying a few words to having a long back and forth communication.

4.2 Type 2: One with Many

This type includes one player using a single channel and the other players using a separate channel. Where this type differs is that all players can see the content that player one sees. In Fig. 3, we see the same game as in Fig. 1, but the players who are using the PDF can see what is happening (denoted as '(0)') e.g. VR screen mirroring.

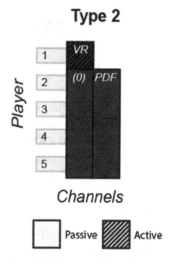

Fig. 3. Type 2 model

The ability for the whole group to see what is happening demystifies what player one is doing, potentially alleviating some of the stress that player one feels. This type almost becomes a group exercise where one player has been nominated to input what is required, but every player has equal opportunity for participation. Communication, although still important, is not as crucial as it is in type 1, where player one has to listen to what they have to do as well as communicate what they see and hear.

4.3 Type 3: Level Playing Field with Core

In this type, all players have access to one shared channel as well as access to their own unique channels. In Fig. 4, the players are watching content on the TV, and have access to their own mobile phones, as in *Jackbox*.

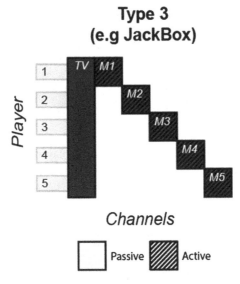

Fig. 4. Type 3 model

This type affords more of a level playing field than the previous types in terms of participation. In *Jackbox*, all players have a chance to contribute to what is seen on the screen in the *Quiplash* minigame. However, this participation can vary depending on the game itself. In the minigame *Fakin' It*, one player must maintain a lie while the other players attempt to find out who the liar is.

4.4   Type 4: Everyone Segregated

Type 4 includes potentially unique channels for each player. Unlike type three there is no shared channel, and the players can only view their own channel. Figure 5 shows a game where player one is consuming content in VR and the other players are playing the game on a screen (denoted as 'G'), as in *Star Trek*). In a sense, this type is comparable to most online games, where players have access to one channel, and cannot view what the other players are doing e.g. competitive first person shooters. However, this type has been included to illustrate the potential for different usage of various distinct channels in a single game, instead of all players using the same channel e.g. all using VR.

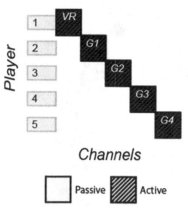

Fig. 5. Type 4 model

The affordances for participation are equal in that each person has access to only one channel, however the level of participation or difficulty is variable depending on what channel any particular player is using. In *Star Trek*, where the players must control their starship on the bridge, the different roles associated with the players require different skills that suit particular players. These roles may become more or less difficult depending on the channel that is used e.g. some roles are easier in VR, because you can look around more easily.

4.5 Type 5: One Segregated with Multiple Teams

This type is similar to type 1 in that one player is segregated from the rest of the group. The difference in this type is that the rest of the players are split up into two or more sub groups. In Fig. 6, one player is playing the game using VR, whilst the rest of the players split into two groups, playing the game using channels shared amongst members of that group. This could be for example, players two and three attempting to find player one in a game of hide and seek whilst players four and five attempt to conceal player one.

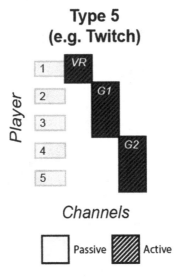

Fig. 6. Type 5 model

This effect in this type is analogous to a recent phenomenon that has emerged on streaming websites such as *Twitch*. Streamers often have a mass audience who interact with each other on the live chat that accompanies the stream. In such events, streamers may invite the audience to form into two groups, one favouring a particular decision the streamer will take in a game, and another favouring a different option. The group that makes the best case for their option ultimately decide what the streamer does. Although this example is rudimentary participation, it highlights how such a situation can form.

4.6 Type 6: Round Robin

This type can only be illustrated by using the idea of phases. In such a game, multiple phases to one play through must be present, with each player potentially getting a chance to use a different channel in each phase. Figure 7 shows five phases, with each player getting a chance to use the VR channel. In each phase, the players have access to only their channel until the next phase.

This type provides equal opportunity for participation amongst the players, with each player potentially having a go at all the channels. Although it may not be practical for the game to require players move from one channel to another e.g. having to take the VR headset off and moving to a PC etc., some channels provide swift and easy transfer such as books or mobile and tablet apps.

Type 6

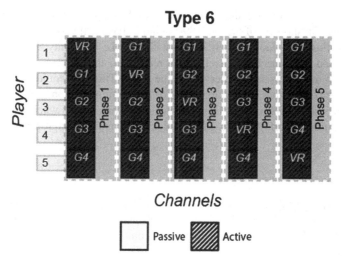

Fig. 7. Type 6 model

4.7   Type 7: Open Segregation

This type provides an environment where each player can only control their own channel, but can view everyone else's channel, as in *Screencheat*. Figure 8 shows players controlling the game in VR whilst at the same time being afforded the ability to see other players' channels (denoted as '(0)') e.g. as a minicam on the bottom right of the screen.

Type 7
(e.g. Screencheat)

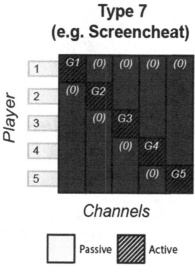

Fig. 8. Type 7 model

Much like the arguments and accusations of cheating that formed from old split screen first person shooters of the late 1990s, games that use this type with the intention that players must only look at their screen will provoke irritability. Instead, this type should be used as a mechanic itself. In *Screencheat*, the players must look at the perspective of other players in order to win the game. This type could also weaken the difficulty of puzzle games, disrupting some of the communication mechanics that are the main purpose of such games. However, team working games where more than one player is required to perform an in-game task could provide an appropriate fit with this type.

4.8   Type 8: Open Nomination

Much like type 2, this type includes separate channels that can be both seen and interacted with by all players. Figure 9 shows all players having access to the game as well as the PDF. In such a scenario, all players could have controllers or input devices linked to one game that all do the same actions. This could provide the emergence of unique player behaviour for each game played, e.g. the group assigns a button to each player, that has to be pressed in the right order and in quick succession to complete the mission.

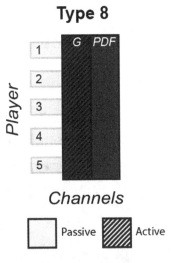

Fig. 9. Type 8 model

In other cases, this type can be utilised to augment a game, such as including a companion app or book with the game that must be referred to every so often in order to progress the game. In such cases, all players involved can enjoy all the channels available as play occurs.

5 Conclusion

In this paper, we have presented a modified model that can be used to formally represent different types of hybrid games. By doing so, we were able to make some assumptions about how player participation can vary based on the channel structure of a hybrid game.

We believe that by formalising the structures in this way, we are able to identify techniques that can be utilised by game designers in developing hybrid games. With ever increasing demands for entertaining experiences that cater for diverse audiences, there is sizable room for hybrid games to grow.

For our future work, we intent to explore how hybrid games can tell stories, and the effect these different types have on the narrative.

References

1. Bodanr, J.: Talk it Out; Promoting Verbal Communication Through Virtual Reality Games. Victoria University of Wellington, Wellington (2017)
2. Crawford, S.B., Monks, S.M., Wells, R.N.: Virtual reality as an interview technique in evaluation of emergency medicine applicants. AEM Educ. Train. **2**(4), 328–333 (2018)
3. Dena, C.: Emerging participatory culture practices: player-created tiers in alternate reality games. Convergence **14**(1), 41–57 (2008)
4. Hastings, C., Brunotte, J.: The 2016 PanSIG Journal, November 2017 (2018)
5. Hsu, M., Lin, Y.: Party animals: creating immersive gaming experience for physically co-present VR and Non-VR Players, pp. 222–225 (2017)
6. Huizinga, J.: Homo ludens: a study of the play-element in culture. Eur. Early Child. Educ. Res. J. **19**(2), 1–24 (2007)
7. Javanshir, R., Carroll, B., Millard, D.E.: A model for describing alternate reality games. In: Rouse, R., Koenitz, H., Haahr, M. (eds.) ICIDS 2018. LNCS, vol. 11318, pp. 250–258. Springer, Cham (2018). https://doi.org/10.1007/978-3-030-04028-4_25
8. Jenkins, H.: Convergence Culture. New York University Press, New York (2006)
9. Kankainen, V., Arjoranta, J., Nummenmaa, T.: Games as blends: understanding hybrid games previous research **16**(4) (2017)
10. Lee, G.A., Hart, J.D., Smith, R.T.: Demonstrating emotion sharing and augmentation in cooperative virtual reality games, October 2018
11. Lessel, P., Altmeyer, M.: Tabletop game meets live-streaming: empowering the audience
12. Liszio, S., Masuch, M.: Designing shared virtual reality gaming experiences in local multi-platform games. In: Wallner, G., Kriglstein, S., Hlavacs, H., Malaka, R., Lugmayr, A., Yang, H.-S. (eds.) ICEC 2016. LNCS, vol. 9926, pp. 235–240. Springer, Cham (2016). https://doi.org/10.1007/978-3-319-46100-7_23
13. Magerkurth, C.: Hybrid gaming environments: keeping the human in the loop within the Internet of Things. Univers. Access Inf. Soc. **11**(3), 273–283 (2012)
14. Mora, S., Fagerbekk, T., Monnier, M., Schroeder, E., Divitini, M.: Anyboard: a platform for hybrid board games. In: Wallner, G., Kriglstein, S., Hlavacs, H., Malaka, R., Lugmayr, A., Yang, H.-S. (eds.) ICEC 2016. LNCS, vol. 9926, pp. 161–172. Springer, Cham (2016). https://doi.org/10.1007/978-3-319-46100-7_14

15. Robles de Medina, S.: TALK ME THROUGH THIS! The design of a two player virtual reality communication-based game experience Keio university graduate school of media design Sergio Robles de Medina. Keio University (2016)
16. Sajjadi, P., Omar, E., Gutierrez, C., Trullemans, S., De Troyer, O.: Maze commander: a collaborative asynchronous game using the oculus rift & the sifteo cubes, May 2016 (2014)
17. Salen, K., Zimmerman, E.: Rules of Play: Game Design Fundamentals. MIT Press, Cambridge (2003)
18. Sekwao, G., Modolin, S.: Virtual Reality Games for Team Building Interventions. Jonkoping University, Jönköping (2018)
19. Van Wijk, L.: Keep talking and nobody explodes: a qualitative study on nonverbal communication factors identified in a group problem-solving task (2019)

E.T. Phone Home, or from Pit to Surface: Intersections Between Archaeology and Media Archaeology

Emmanoel Ferreira[✉]

Universidade Federal Fluminense, Niterói, Rio de Janeiro, Brazil
emmanoferreira@midia.uff.br

Abstract. This paper demonstrates the possibilities of intersection between archaeology – as a discipline, as a field – and media archaeology, taking as a case study the excavation of the Atari cartridges held in Alamogordo, New Mexico, USA, on April 2014. It also indicates how the conjunction of these two archaeologies can provide new (and alternative) historical narratives to "facts" crystallized by time and often accepted as unquestionable truths, opening possibilities for new understandings about cultural, social, and economic aspects concerning certain media phenomena.

Keywords: Archaeology · Media · Video games · Atari · E.T.

1 Introduction

April 26, 2014. One of the most significant urban legends in the history of video games was finally unveiled. After almost three days of intense and uninterrupted work, the team headed by the landfill specialist Joe Lewandowski and archaeologist Andrew Reinhard found the first of the 1,300 Atari 2600 cartridges buried more than thirty years earlier – in September 1983 – in the Otero-Greentree Regional Landfill located in the city of Alamogordo, New Mexico, USA.

The famous urban legend said that in 1983, Atari had buried all the unsold and returned cartridges of E.T. – The Extraterrestrial game, due to its sales failure. In the years and decades that followed, the title gained fame as the worst game developed for that platform – and perhaps the worst game in video games history – and as the game that was accountable for the famous video game crash of 1983. However, no one could say with certainty whether the story of the cartridges' burial was true or whether it was just another urban legend, among many others, of the history of video games, since the documentation about that burial, in particular, was scarce, scattered, and outdated. To the relief of many people, on that April 26th, the world was finally able to see with its own eyes the crumpled boxes of E.T. cartridges and other Atari 2600 games and

---

In order to differentiate, throughout the text, (i) archaeology as a discipline/field and (ii) other types of "archaeology" (media archaeology, game archaeology), the paper makes use of "archaeology" when referring to the first scenario (i), and "media archaeology", "archaeology of games", when referring to the second (ii).

© Springer Nature Switzerland AG 2019
N. Zagalo et al. (Eds.): VJ 2019, CCIS 1164, pp. 261–275, 2019.
https://doi.org/10.1007/978-3-030-37983-4_20

accessories being brought from the depths of the mythical Alamogordo sanitary landfill. In Reinhard's words: "After about four hours of additional digging on April 26, the Atari level was reached, and bucket-loaded after bucket-load of games were retrieved and then dumped for us to review. Rothaus [one of Reinhard's team members] found the first Atari game, an E.T. cartridge still in the box with its instruction manual and a coupon for the Raiders of the Lost Ark. I walked it up with film director Zak Penn to show the crowd of a few hundred gamers and residents, and then the team began to work in earnest, attempting to get through as much of the Atari deposit possible in the time we had" [1].

Contrary to urban legend, not only specimens from the E.T. game had been buried, but more than forty titles from the Atari 2600 and Atari 5200 platforms, "going against Atari's corporate claim that it had buried only returned or broken stock" [1], calling into question the theory, sustained for more than thirty years, that the E.T. title was the trigger for the 1983 video game crash (Fig. 1).

Fig. 1. Richard Rothaus and Andrew Reinhard at the site of the excavations; in the photo, an E.T. cartridge box. Source: Andrew Reinhard [1].

The overall goal of this article is to explore the possible relations, intersections and crossings between archaeology – as a discipline, as a field – and what is conventionally called media archaeology [2–5], which, in the words of Huhtamo and Parikka [3], "rummages textual, visual and auditory archives as well as collections of artifacts, emphasizing both the discursive and the material manifestations of culture." According to the authors: "On the basis of their discoveries, media archaeologists have begun to construct alternate histories of suppressed, neglected, and forgotten media that do not point teleologically to the present media-cultural condition as their 'perfection'. Dead ends, losers, and inventions that never made it into a material product have important stories to tell" [3].

From these relationships, it delves into unraveling discursive traces that somehow helped shaping the "official" history of particular cultural and media artifacts – in this case video games – in order to understand and undertake – in the ways opened by authors such as Huhtamo and Parikka – alternative versions of such histories, pointing to cultural, social, and economic potential that were somehow left aside or, paraphrasing Zielinski [5], left in the "deep time of the media".

2 Media Archaeology, Revisited

Over the last few years, one has witnessed a movement, in most varied contexts, towards an inevitable resumption of the historical past. Be it in fashion, in product design, and even in video games, terms such as *vintage* and *retro* seem to have gained unprecedented notoriety. This movement is far from being something solely related to ordinary, everyday affairs. Andreas Huyssen, in his seminal work "Present Pasts: Media, Politics, Amnesia" [6], had already pointed to a growing need to "musealize" the world, in a society in which the increasing information flow brought the imminent threat of forgetting to individuals. In Huyssen's words: "The turn toward memory is subliminally energized by the desire to anchor ourselves in a world characterized by an increasing instability of time and by the fracturing of lived space" [6].

According to Huyssen, this fear of forgetting points to an interesting paradox, because it is precisely in contemporary society that one finds more and more technologies for storing and safeguarding data, from the CDs by the end of the 20th century, to hard disks with trillions of bytes available at ever more affordable prices. *Pari passu* to an increasing supply of devices to maintain historical memory, one witness the fear of a total loss of this same memory.

It is precisely within a critique of forgetting particular "histories" that gains strength media archaeology. More than the desire to tell alternative stories, "media archaeologists" seek to bring to the surface – a metaphor directly connected to the field of archaeology – devices (material or even immaterial) relegated to burial by the "history written by the victors"; inventions that never arrived to see the light of day, but which had a fundamental importance, although not publicly attested, in the constitution of knowledges of a certain period, especially in the formulation and development of media objects that would see the light of day and become representatives of their species. In the words of Michael Goddard: "A media archaeological perspective, then, is necessarily non-linear and disputes the established distribution between winners and losers in teleological media narratives, be they inventors, technical inventions, media devices or assemblages" [2].

Imbibing, therefore, from a "media-archaeological" perspective – borrowing Goddard's words – is to search the depths of the historical vestiges of media, at specific times, trying to find traces of devices or media assemblages that have remained in oblivion – be it for economic, political or cultural reasons – but that contribute to a better and greater understanding of the dynamic forces that have moved and still move a particular sector of society. As already pointed out in other works [7, 8], about the history of video game consoles and specific computer platforms, the "history" of personal computers widely spread and publicized in magazines, books, documentaries and other media, sets aside a number of platforms that had significant importance in the countries where they were marketed, such as the MSX platform, launched in Japan in 1983. In some middle-east countries, such as Kuwait, and other eastern countries, such as the former USSR, the MSX platform was widely used in educational activities. For example, the MSX model distributed in the USSR – the Yamaha КУВТ[1] (YIS503II) – had networking capabilities and was thus used as a teaching and learning tool during classes. Remarkably, this occurred in the mid-1980s, using resources that even nowadays, i.e., more than thirty years afterward, are not available in every corner of the world.

Media archaeology, therefore, seeks to bridge the past and the present, unveiling technological and media assemblages that appear as pioneers, which, conversely, owe a grand deal to ventures and inventions from the past. It shows that the history of innovations can be connected to enterprises carried out in other times and places, and for this very reason – in a combination of political and economic forces – were left aside from the global scenario or, as it is common to say, from the "grand scheme of things."

Huhtamo and Parikka [3] point to some theorists as being in some way media archaeologists, even before the emergence of this term, like Walter Benjamin and Marshall McLuhan. Noteworthy, in this case, is Benjamin's immense (and unfinished) work on Parisian passages in the nineteenth century, in which the author rescues that type of urban architecture/topology to think about the cultural, social, and economic changes of the French capital at that time. In the words of Huhtamo and Parikka, "Benjamin is arguably the most prominent forerunner – beside Foucault – of media-archaeological modes of cultural analysis and is a major influence for cultural studies." [3]. About the work of McLuhan, the authors point out that perhaps his most significant contribution to media archaeology lies in its emphasis on temporal connections between different media instances, which has even influenced authors such as Bolter and Grusin [9] in their work on the notion of *remediation*.

According to Huhtamo and Parikka, various fields and theories have contributed to the formation of what is nowadays understood by media archaeology, among them cultural materialism, visual and media anthropology, and the notion of nonlinear temporality. Despite encompassing several theoretical and epistemological lines, the common denominator – the "driving force" – of media archaeology would lie in the criticism of the "canonized narratives of media culture". In the authors' words: "Much has been left by the roadside out of negligence or ideological bias. For media critic Geert Lovink, media archaeology is by nature a 'discipline' of reading against the grain, a 'hermeneutic reading of the new' against the grain of the past, rather than telling of histories of the technologies from the past to present" [3].

---

[1] The acronym КУВТ stands for Комплект У чебной В ычислительной Т ехники, which, translated from Russian, means "Computer Equipment Kit for Education." See Yamaha YIS503II. In: MSX Resource Center, https://www.msx.org/wiki/Yamaha_YIS–503IIR, last accessed 2019/06/30.

In fact, this interpretation has an extremely political bias for it seeks to "disturb" globalizing and "true" historical narratives by pointing, very appropriately, to possible causes and reasons why cultural manifestations resulting from interactions with tech-nological devices are not even quoted in the various (encyclopedic) media histories, in particular, for the scope of this work, of video games. Besides, the media archaeo-logical perspective allows unofficial undertakings – resulting from processes of appropriation, subversion, reinvention, such as modding, hacking, circuit bending, Maker and Do-It-Yourself (DIY) cultures – to be shared to an audience once alienated from such manifestations, as in the Brazilian pirate versions of music and football games for the PS2 platform, Rock Band Brazil (modified version of Guitar Hero, by Harmonix) and Bomba Patch (modified version of Winning Eleven 10, by Konami), as analyzed by Oliveira et al. [10].

3   Archaeology and Archaeogaming

As previously stated in this paper, the "media-archaeological" perspective seeks, among other things, to construct "new past and present" [4], based on epistemological keys that seek to build histories that flee from teleological perspectives. In this sense, media archaeology inherits much from the genealogical method of Michel Foucault. In Parikka's words, such a perspective "[...] reminds of Foucault's genealogical method of questioning simple origins and teleological and pre-determined ways of under-standing (media) cultural change" [4].

However, in some situations – such as the Atari cartridge burial in 1983, which has resulted in a very specific historical, cultural and economic interpretation concerning Atari in particular and the video game industry in general – it seems that another archaeology – the original – can bring exciting contributions to media archaeology, in the broad sense, and to the archaeology of games, in particular.

According to Reinhard [11], archaeology "is the study of the ancient and recent human past through material remains in pursuit of a broad and comprehensive understanding of human culture". In his work Archaeogaming: An Introduction to Archaeology in and of Video Games [11], Andrew Reinhard advocates that archae-ology can bring different contributions to the archaeology of/in games, which the author calls archaeogaming. According to Reinhard [11], archaeogaming can be sub-divided into five distinct fronts/categories, namely:

(1) Archaeogaming as the study of video games in their materiality. This approach seeks to understand social, cultural, and economic aspects through the analysis of the materialities of the video game media (and everything that surrounds it), such as packaging, manuals, cartridges, translations, versions, localizations, paratexts, technical aspects, resembling the media archaeology perspective.

(2) Archaeogaming as the study of archaeology within video games. This approach seeks to understand how the representation of archaeology (its activities, its methods, the people that develop it, etc.) occurs within video games. A notable example is the Tomb Raider series, whose main character, Lara Croft, is an archeologist.

(3) Archaeogaming as the application of archaeological methods in synthetic spaces. This approach seeks to perform archaeological activities (such as they would be in "real life") in virtual environments. In Reinhard's words, "Instead of studying the material culture (and intangible heritage) of cultures and civilizations that exist in 'meatspace,' we instead study those in the immaterial world." [11].

(4) Archaeogaming as the study of mirroring between game design and "real world." This approach seeks to understand the relationships between the choices made by game designers and the material ('real') world.

(5) Archaeogaming as the archaeology of immaterial aspects of video games. This approach seeks to recover game mechanics, codes, engines, etc., in short, constituent elements of video games, aiming at its maintenance as "immaterial culture," also approaching the media archaeology perspective. It is, for example, what Nick Montfort and Ian Bogost do in their work Racing the Beam [12] when the authors rescue the core mechanics of Combat – one of the first nine titles released for the Atari 2600 platform – to think about how particular mechanics found in modern-day games connect with mechanics found in Combat[2].

In this sense, archaeogaming as a whole would distance itself from media archaeology *per se*, since, according to Reinhard's categorization, it would not only be concerned with recovering traces (material or immaterial) of video games in order to present alternative histories (as previously explained in the topic on media archaeology), something that categories 1 and 5 above would more closely approximate. Furthermore, in addition to the aspects that bring it closer to the media-archaeological perspective, archaeogaming intends to approximate games with the field of archaeology, in its strictest sense, as can be deduced from categories 2 and 3 of Reinhard's division. Reinhard further asserts that games can provide ample space for archaeologists, whether as consultants in the historical reconstruction of virtual worlds, or in the application of archaeological methods in the recovery and preservation of digital artifacts, or even on a smaller scale as field archaeologists, in the recovery of material artifacts, as in the case of the excavation of the Alamogordo landfill. One of the goals of this article is to understand the importance of the field archaeologist in recovering, cataloging, and analyzing material artifacts related to video games, and how this action can bring new perspectives to media archaeology.

4   HSW: Yar's, Raiders, and E.T.

In 1981, engineer Howard Scott Warshaw (HSW) was hired by Atari as a game developer/programmer. His first work for the 2600 system, Yar's Revenge, an adaptation of the arcade game Star Castle, became a great success of criticism and sales, being until now considered one of the best games for the Atari 2600 platform [13].

---

[2] Beyond Combat, another eight titles were released alongside the Atari 2600 platform, in October 1977: Air-Sea Battle, Basic Math, Blackjack, Indy 500, Star Ship, Street Racer, Surround, Video Olympics. Available: https://gamicus.gamepedia.com/List_of_video_game_console_launch_games #Atari_2600/, last accessed 2019/06/30.

One of Yar's innovations for that time was to present an elaborate backstory to the game – not directly into in-game content, but from a *paratext* [14, 15]: a comic book that came along with the cartridge, titled Yar's Revenge: The Qotile Ultimatum! The book presented the events that occurred before the beginning of the game, providing the player with information about the game world. Besides, Yar's sported game mechanics that were not common among Atari 2600 games, like the ability to choose between two weapons (each for a specific goal) and sequenced objectives.

In terms of market reception, Yar's is among the 40 best-selling games for the Atari 2600, with approximately 800,000 copies sold worldwide[3] (Figs. 2 and 3).

Fig. 2. Yar's Revenge game box (left). Source: Amazon.com.

Fig. 3. Yar's Revenge: the Qotile Ultimatum! comic book cover (right). Source: Comic Book Realm.

In 1982, Atari began its partnership with the film industry, specifically with director Steven Spielberg, to develop games based on cinema blockbusters, starting what would be frequent practice decades later: the development of games based on huge cinema franchises. After the success of the first film dedicated to Indiana Jones – Raiders of the Lost Ark – released in 1981, directed by Spielberg and starring Harrison Ford – Atari decided it would be an opportunity to launch a game based on that movie. With the great success achieved by Yar's Revenge that same year, Warshaw was chosen to develop and program the game, which was released on November 1982 (Figs. 4 and 5).

---

[3] VGChartz, http://www.vgchartz.com/article/250871/the–best–selling–atari–2600–games–of–all–time/, last accessed 2019/06/30. In the Wikipedia entry "List of best–selling Atari 2600 video games", which considers various sources, Yar's appears at position 13, with approximately 1 million copies sold. See: https://en.wikipedia.org/wiki/List_of_best–selling_Atari_2600_video_games/, last accessed 2019/06/30.

Fig. 4. Raiders of the Lost Ark game box (left). Source: eBay.

Fig. 5. Poster of the eponymous film (right). Source: Limited Runs.

As well as Yar's, Raiders was a blockbuster, leveraging more than 500,000 copies sold worldwide, appearing among the sixty best–selling games for the Atari 2600[4]. For this game, Warshaw also decided to take an unconventional approach, trying to escape from the commonplace mechanics found on most of Atari games.

Continuing its venture of approaching the newly created video game industry and the almost century-old film industry, in July 1982 Atari closed the biggest deal ever made between the two industries at the time: to hold the production rights of the E.T. game, based upon the film released in June of that year (also directed by Spielberg, and an immediate success in theaters), Atari spent 22 million dollars in royalties paid to Universal Pictures, the film producer [16]. After the deal was closed, the game development began immediately, since the cartridge should be available to the public on that year's Christmas. Once again, among other reasons, due to the success of *Raiders*, Warshaw was chosen to develop the game. However, unlike Yar's and Raiders, Warshaw would have only five weeks to finish the game, a time window far distant from the average six-month that developers had in order to finish a title for the Atari 2600.

As in Yar's and Raiders, Warshaw decided to take an unorthodox way, avoiding the commonplace applied to most of the games of the time. In the words of the game designer: "Even though I only had five weeks, I still wanted to innovate" [17]. After the period of time that was entrusted to him, Warshaw personally presented the final version of the game to Spielberg, which, according to the game designer, immediately approved it [17] – one of the conditions imposed by Warshaw to develop E.T. was that

---

[4] According to the website VGChartz, the title obtained a total of approximately 500,000 and copies sold. However, there are other versions about this number, such as that of Warshaw himself, which point to the number of 1 million copies sold. See http://www.vgchartz.com/article/250871/the–best–selling–atari–2600–games–of–all–time/ and http://www.digitpress.com/library/interviews/interview_howard_scott_warshaw.html/, last accessed (both links) 2019/06/30.

Spielberg approved the final version of the game, before its release. Thus, in December 1982, the E.T. cartridge was released in the USA.

After the film's immense success in theaters, released six months earlier, consumers were eager to the game launch, so that they could interact with E.T. and Elliott on their TV screens. Soon after its launch, E.T. had a successful reception with the consumer public. The game reached the fourth place in the Top 15 Video Games list of the Jan. 8, 1983 issue of Billboard Magazine (i.e., only two weeks after the release of the game), second only to Pitfall, Donkey Kong and Frogger [18]. However, with the passage of days, weeks, and months, consumers began a strange movement of returning the cartridge to Atari dealers, many of them either pointing out that they did not understand how to play the game, or that the game was too complicated, or that it was merely a bad game. In the same issue of the Billboard magazine quoted above, the cover article "Video Game Firms Ready Formal Return Policies," signed by Earl Paige, stated: "Retailers of video games are expecting formal return programs to be adopted soon by certain software manufacturers. They anticipate the announcement of at least one such program at the Consumer Electronics Show (CES) in Las Vegas this week. The development [of such programs] is largely the result of intensifying competition among game makers. It's also been fueled by last month's stock market furor over disappointing Atari sales, in particular, the 'E.T.' cartridge (Billboard, Dec. 18)" [19][5].

Paradoxically, E.T. was one of the most commercially successful cartridges in the history of Atari 2600, with approximately 2 million units sold worldwide (out of the five million cartridges produced), thus ranking among the top-10 best-selling games in the company history[6]. However, of this amount, it is said that between 2.5 and 3.5 million were returned to Atari [20]. How, then, can we explain this supposed paradox? As widely disseminated until recently, would E.T. have been the main culprit in the fall and failure of Atari in particular and the video game industry in general in that year 1983, especially given the earlier hits of developer Howard Scott Warshaw?

5 Rewriting the History of a Legend

Until the recovery of the Atari cartridges in the Alamogordo landfill in April 2014, little was inquired about the real reasons for the 1983 game crash. The most apparent answers included stating that E.T. had mainly been to blame for the failure of the industry, along with a large number of low-quality titles being produced for that platform. This commonplace was publicized both in the press and in the academic literature. It takes only a few seconds for someone to access Google, search for the keywords "ET", "game" and "Atari" to obtain an avalanche of links that point – directly or indirectly – to the association between E.T. and the game crash of 1983, as seen in this stories: "How E.T. the Extra-Terrestrial Nearly Destroyed the Video Game Industry" [21]; "How hacking fixed the worst video game of all time" [13]; "Total

---

[5] The Billboard edition (December 18) quoted by Page can be accessed at the following link: https://books.google.com/books?id=jSQEAAAAMBAJ&lpg=PP1&hl=en&pg=PP1#v=onepage&q&f=false, last accessed 2019/06/30.

[6] VGChartz, http://www.vgchartz.com/platform/31/atari–2600/, last accessed 2019/06/30.

Failure: The World's Worst Video Game" [22]; "The Atari E.T. Video Game: Was it the Worst Video Game of All Time?" [23]. In the words of Cocilova [13]: "According to urban legend, a landfill somewhere in the small city of Alamogordo, New Mexico, bulges with millions of copies of the worst game ever made – a game that many observers blamed for the North American video-game sales crash of 1983. Atari bubble burst because of a little alien".

Brumfiel [22] says: "Within a year since the E.T.'s release, the entire video game industry collapsed." In his Everything 80s podcast, Max [23] points out: "The Atari E. T. video game has been considered one of the worst games of all time, if not the worst. It's also been associated with destroying Atari and almost bringing the video game industry to its knees."

Even a piece of the academic literature could not get away from this commonplace. Heather Chaplin, an author renowned for her work on the history of video games, is emphatic in stating: "In December 1982 Atari released a game based on Spielberg's E. T. that was so bad that Al Alcorn, who had already quit Atari, wanted to cry when saw it. Five million copies of E.T. sat in an Atari warehouse gathering dust before finally being dumped in a landfill [...]. By the end of the year, the video game industry was declared dead" [24].

To what extent, then, can the Alamogordo excavation contribute to a better understanding of the real reasons for the video game industry crash in 1983? If not altogether, at least as far as E.T.'s accountability for the crash of Atari and the video game industry is concerned, the traces unveiled by the April 2014 excavation in Alamogordo may point to new and alternative narratives about events that took place more than 30 years ago.

First, the Alamogordo excavation can correct quantitative and qualitative information on Atari's 1983 dump. Most of the pre-excavation claims pointed out that Atari had buried – if not wholly, at least mostly – unsold and/or returned cartridges of E.T. game [25]. Quantitatively, after the excavation, it is estimated that the number of games buried was 800,000 – and not millions, as legend has it [25]. Out of the recovered cartridges, E.T. accounted for only 10% of the total. For example, out of the total number of 802 cartridge boxes retrieved in the excavation, E.T. counted only for 49. On the other hand, Star Raiders counted for 66, Warlords for 91, Defenders for 101, and Centipede for 179 (Reinhard, *forthcoming*). Also, 53 Atari 2600 titles were cataloged by the archaeological team led by Andrew Reinhard and Richard Rothaus, including bestsellers like Asteroids, Missile Command and Space Invaders (Reinhard, *forthcoming*)[7]. In addition to the games, the excavation also recovered several other Atari items, such as consoles and accessories. This information alone allows the construction of new narratives about E.T., about Atari and finally about the video game crash of 1983. As pointed out by Manny Gerard, Warner/Atari executive at the time of the release of E.T., and by Nolan Bushnell, one of the founders of Atari: "The notion that E.T. caused the demise of Atari is simply stupid. It's just stupid" [26]. "Atari committed suicide. It was not homicide. And it wasn't the E.T. cartridge. It was a

---

[7] http://www.vgchartz.com/article/250871/the-best-selling-atari-2600-games-of-all-time/, last accessed 2019/09/30.

concomitant effect of a lot of missteps in technology, and deployment, and marketing [...]. The cause of the fall was Atari trying to sell yet another 10 million Atari 2600s into a market that was saturated" [27].

Secondly, it is essential to note that the Alamogordo excavation venture had, as one of its driving forces, the production of a documentary, Atari: Game Over [16]. Produced by the Canadian media agency Fuel Entertainment and directed by Zak Penn, a writer known for his work on various film blockbusters, as X-Men 3 (2006) and The Avengers (2012), Atari: Game Over was in considerable measure responsible for giving voice to the various actors who participated in both the excavation itself, as the archaeologists Andrew Reinhard and Richard Rothaus, and the history of video games in general and Atari and E.T. in particular, such as Nolan Bushnell and Howard Scott Warshaw. In addition to such figures connected to the history of Atari, the film has opened space for people connected to the entertainment and gaming industry – such as Ernest Cline, author of bestselling Player Number One, Mike Mika, game designer and video game collector, Seamus Blackley, co-creator of the Xbox platform, among others – to expose their critical analysis on E.T., as well as on the legacy – in this case, positive – left by Warshaw.

It is important to note that a significant part of the tales about E.T. being the worst game in history and being the culprit for the 1983 video game crash was accessed and disseminated via paratexts to the game itself, especially web forums and news pages. Being E.T. a transmedial work *per se*, it was expected that fans of the film would get information about the game through diverse media and, through word of mouth, inaccurate information would spread to the world. As Susana Tosca and Lisbeth Klastrup point out: "Another way to think about this transmedial world audience is to describe what they do as the creation of transmedial meta-texts, or 'paratext', as they are also called: that is, texts about texts, meant to guide, comment on, interpret, review, critique and explain the fictional text that they take their point of departure in." [14]. Thus, it was also via one paratext, in this case, the E.T. Game Over documentary, that other narratives about E.T. and the reasons for the crash could be shown. Also, from this point on, a bunch of web sites, in mentioning the documentary, would take another (less harsh) stance regarding the game. These "paratext induced" tales corroborates the importance of the archaeological work made in Alamogordo, in conjunction with media archaeology work – for instance, in retrieving "lost" print media of the early 1980 s about the E.T. game – if one intends to comprehend a media phenomenon in a broader sense.

In terms of game design, as well as Yar's and Raiders, E.T. brought a series of innovations for that time, such as its "3D" world in a cube format, which the player could explore contiguously. Game characters, such as the scientist or the FBI agent, had specific actions – respectively leading the little alien to the lab and stealing the pieces of the phone from the player – game mechanics that were not common to see in video games of that time. When running out of energy, the player (E.T.) could call for Elliott to come to him and reload his energy – an ordinary action in modern-day games, but a rare one in games of that time. Finally, E.T. had one of the most elaborate Easter Eggs of the Atari 2600: by gathering seven pieces of candy and handing them to Elliott, in addition to attaching all parts of his phone, the player should lead E.T. to one of the pits of the game, the one containing a flower, and touch on it. First, the flower would become a Yar (a reference to Warshaw's Yar's Revenge). After finishing the game and starting a new session, the player could repeat the same procedure. This time, the flower would turn into Indiana Jones (a reference to the game Raiders of the Lost Ark, also by Warshaw). Regarding its innovative features (for that time), E.T. could be considered a classic of video games. Victor Navarro-Remesal, discussing the concept of what makes a classic, mentions, regarding the fan's idea for the concept: "A classic is, for them [fans], old, innovative at its time and has achieved some degree of excellence in its design." [28].

Fan communities are one of the key actors responsible for the bounce-back status of E.T. as a classic. For instance, the site neocomputer.org, run by a fan of the game, mentions several innovations – in addition to the ones cited above – brought by E.T. Paradoxically, these innovations may point to possible reasons for the players' lack of understanding about E.T., contributing to the harsh criticism the game received when launched. As listed on the site, regarding E.T.:

- It was one of the first home video games with a title screen
- It featured an open-ended world with gameplay focused on exploration
- It was completely non-violent. You can't hurt the bad-guys, and they can't hurt you. There isn't even any competition!
- You could complete the game. There are also several goals that you need to complete to win the game
- There were multiple ways to complete goals. You can actually finish the game without falling in a single well
- The game not only had an ending, it also featured an animated cut-scene as a reward
- The game featured optional additional goals to complete (side quests)[8] (Fig. 6).

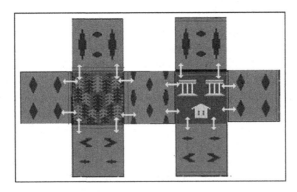

Fig. 6. Cube-like world of E.T., flattened. Source: PC World.

Besides Neocomputer.org, Duane Alan Hahn, another E.T. fan, runs the website Random Terrain, in which he discusses the top qualities of the game. Also, he provides additional material related to the game, as the game manual, tips, maps, as well as links

---

[8] http://www.neocomputer.org/projects/et/, last accessed 2019/7/7.

to other E.T. related websites. As Duane points out at the beginning of his page: "I didn't even know most people supposedly hated the game until I got Internet access in 1999. Since there was an abundance of anti-E.T. pages and articles out there, including ones that encouraged you to destroy E.T. cartridges, I thought it was about time that someone who liked the game spoke up."[9]. Seconding the importance of fans in the "fixing" of certain media history, Navarro-Remesal explains: "Fans may be less reliable as historians but, at the same time, they engage with and record aspects of the history of the medium that are usually left behind by official institutions." [28]. Mora-Cantallops and Bergillos [29], when discussing flopped games and systems, affirm: "At this point it is interesting to note how fan activity lead to second opportunities or recognition for many of these games and systems.".

Certainly, E.T. had its design problems, like any other game throughout game history. One of its flaws laid on its difficulty, due to the uncommon game mechanics it sported, requiring that players carefully read the manual; also, its dynamics hampered a more direct and fluid interaction, contrary to most of the games of the platform. According to Cocilova [13]: "Gameplay was inscrutable, and nothing that appeared on-screen made intuitive sense." Besides, technical problems related to poor accuracy in sprite collision caused E.T. to fall into the game pits even though its feet were out of the pit area, increasing players' irritability. This problem was even assumed by Warshaw, who said that he would have been able to correct it if he had a few more weeks to finish the game. In the 2000s, the site Neocomputer launched a project in order to try to correct some game bugs, including the mentioned sprite collision issue[10].

On the other hand, many people – after the release of Atari: Game Over – pointed out Warshaw's brilliance when developing E.T. Seamus Blackley, in an interview with director Zak Penn, states: "In context, given the time and the situation that Howard was to live in, to program that game, it really is an astonishing master work." [25]. Ernest Cline, in his turn, says: "He made an amazing fucking game that's a whole self-contained world in five weeks. That's even more impressive." [30]. Nolan Bushnell, one of Atari's "parents," tells Zak Penn: "He should be applauded for being able to have done anything in the time was allotted." [27]. The gaming media itself began to create new narratives for E.T. after the discovery of Alamogordo, as in the article entitled "Why E.T. was not the worst game in history," by Tracey Lien[11].

Another significant change brought about by the Alamogordo excavation regards the price of E.T. cartridges – if not for all, at least for those recovered from the landfill. After the cataloging of the recovered items, then owned by the city hall, part of the cartridges (not just E.T., but all the recovered items) was sent to museums, and another part sold on eBay auctions. According to Megan Geuss, E.T. got the highest prices at the auctions, reaching values around 1,500 USD for each cartridge[12]. As Reinhard [1] corroborates: "The games, artifacts by virtue of being non-natural creations of some

---

[9] https://www.randomterrain.com/atari-2600-memories-et.html/, last accessed 2019/09/30.

[10] http://www.neocomputer.org/projects/et/, last accessed 2019/7/7.

[11] https://www.polygon.com/2014/6/3/5775026/et–myth–worst–game–ever, last accessed 2019/06/30.

[12] https://arstechnica.com/gaming/2015/08/881–et–cartridges–buried–in–new–mexico–desert–sell–for–107930–15/, last accessed 2019/06/30.

cultural importance, became highly valued, almost ritual objects defining a generation of players, placing 1980s pop culture front and center".

6 Final Thoughts

This work sought to demonstrate the possibilities of intersection between archaeology and media archaeology, taking as a case study the excavation of the Atari cartridges held in Alamogordo in 2014. It also sought to demonstrate how the conjunction of those two archaeologies can provide new and alternative historical narratives to "facts" crystallized by time and accepted as often unquestionable truths.

Archaeology, in a broad sense, can work in parallel with – and aid – media archaeology, in bringing to surface technological material artifacts that were given by lost once and for all. As in traditional archaeology, when lost artifacts from a particular culture, in a particular time, are discovered and can, therefore, shine new lights on unknown or mistaken aspects of such culture, archaeology, when working in conjunction with media archaeology, can also uncover media histories that never saw the light of day or even fix erroneous histories that found their place in the sacred throne of books, articles, news and in popular culture.

In addition to complex excavations, such as the one of Alamogordo, others, such as the ones carried out by fans, geeks, hobbyists and makers in electronic dumps in various cities around the world or in almost-never-visited attics, basements and garages, may also work in conjunction with media archaeology, yielding similar results to that of Alamogordo, opening up possibilities for new understandings of particular media-related cultural, social and economic phenomena.

References

1. Reinhard, A.: Excavating Atari: where the media was the archaeology. J. Contemp. Archaeol. **2**(1), 86–93 (2015)
2. Goddard, M.: Arqueologia das mídias, "anarqueologia" e ecologia das mídias. In: Mello, J., Conter, M. (orgs.). (An)arqueologia das mídias. Appris, Curitiba (2017)
3. Huhtamo, E., Parikka, J.: Introduction. In: Media Archaeology: Approaches, Applications, and Implications. University of California Press, Berkeley (2011)
4. Parikka, J.: What is Media Archaeology?. Polity Press, Cambridge (2012)
5. Zielinski, S.: Deep Time of the Media. The MIT Press, Cambridge (2006)
6. Huyssen, A.: Present pasts: media, politics, amnesia. Public Cult. **12**(1), 21–38 (2000)
7. Ferreira, E.: A guerra dos clones: transgressão e criatividade na autora dos videogames no Brasil. Sessões do Imaginário, n. 38 (2017)
8. Ferreira, E.: Isto não é uma cópia: apropriações do global para o local na autora dos videogames no Brasil. In: Torres, A., Scucato, A., Chafin, A. (eds.). Os desafios do audiovisual. Study 513, Rio de Janeiro (2019)
9. Bolter, J., Grusin, R.: Remediation: Understanding New Media. The MIT Press, Cambridge (1999)

10. Oliveira, T., Ferreira, E., Carvalho, L., Boechat, A.: Tribute and resistance: participation and affective engagement in Brazilian fangame makers and modders' subcultures. GAME: Ital. J. Game Stud. **2**(3), 17–31 (2014)

11. Reinhard, A.: Archaeogaming. Berghahn, New York (2018)

12. Montfort, N., Bogost, I.: Racing the Beam: The Atari Video Computer System. The MIT Press, Cambridge (2009)

13. Cocilova, A.: How hacking fixed the worst video game of all time. In: PCWorld, 16 April 2013 (2013). https://www.pcworld.com/article/2032869/how-hacking-fixed-the-worst-video–game-of-all-time.html/. Accessed 30 June 2019

14. Tosca, S., Klastrup, L.: Transmedial Worlds in Everyday Life: Networked Reception, Social Media and Fictional Worlds. Routledge, New York and London (2019)

15. Gray, J.: Show Sold Separately. Promos, Spoilers, and Other Media Paratexts. New York University Press, New York (2010)

16. Penn, Z.: Atari: Game Over. Documentary, Color, 66 min. Fuel Entertainment, Ottawa (2014)

17. Warshaw, H.: Interview. In: Penn, Z. (ed.) Atari: Game Over. Fuel Entertainment, Ottawa (2014)

18. Top 15 Video Games. Billboard: The International Newsweekly of Music & Home Entertainment, 8 January (1983). https://books.google.com/books?id=PSQEAAAAMBAJ&lpg=PT2&hl=en&pg=PP1#v=onepage&q&f=false/. Accessed 30 June 2019

19. Paige, E.: Video game firms ready formal return policies. In: Billboard: The International Newsweekly of Music & Home Entertainment, 8 January (1983). https://books.google.com/books?id=PSQEAAAAMBAJ&lpg=PT2&hl=en&pg=PP1#v=onepage&q&f=false/. Accessed 30 June 2019

20. Mikkelson, D.: Buried Atari cartridges. In: Snopes, 26 April (2014). https://www.snopes.com/fact–check/five–million–et–pieces/. Accessed 30 June 2019

21. Morris, A.: How E.T. the extra-terrestrial nearly destroyed the video game industry. In: allBusiness. https://www.allbusiness.com/how–et–the–extra–terrestrial–nearly–destroyed–the–video–game–industry–5049–1.html. Accessed 30 June 2019

22. Brumfiel, G.: Total failure: the world's worst video game. In: NPR, 31 May (2017). https://www.npr.org/2017/05/31/530235165/total-failure-the-worlds-worst-video-game/. Accessed 30 June 2019

23. Max. The Atari E.T. video game: was it the worst video game of all time? In: Everything 80s Podcast, 23 December (2018). https://www.everything80spodcast.com/et-videogame/. Accessed 30 June 2019

24. Chaplin, H., Ruby, A.: Smartbomb: The Quest for Art, Entertainment, and Big Bucks in the Videogame Revolution. Algonquin Books, Chapel Hill (2006)

25. Blackley, S.: Interview. In: Penn, Z. (ed.) Atari: Game Over. Fuel Entertainment, Ottawa (2014)

26. Gerard, M.: Interview. In: Penn, Z. (ed.) Atari: Game Over. Fuel Entertainment, Ottawa (2014)

27. Bushnell, N.: Interview. In: Penn, Z. (ed.) Atari: Game Over. Fuel Entertainment, Ottawa (2014)

28. Navarro-Remesal, V.: Museums of failure: fans as curators of "Bad", unreleased, and "Flopped" videogames. In: Swalwell, M., Stuckey, H., Ndalianis, A. (eds.) Fans and Videogames: Histories, Fandom, Archives. Routledge, New York and London (2017)

29. Mora-Cantallops, M., Bergillos, I.: Fan preservation of 'flopped' games and systems: the case of the Virtual Boy in Spain. Catalan J. Commun. Cult. Stud. **10**(2), 213–229 (2018)

30. Cline, E.: Interview. In: Penn, Z. (ed.) Atari: Game Over. Fuel Entertainment, Ottawa (2014)

Author Index

Printed in the United States
By Bookmasters